THE UNIVERSITY OF
WINCHESTER

Martial Rose Library
Tel: 01962 827306

1 6 DEC 2011

2 6 JAN 2012

2 8 FEB 2012

- 5 APR 2013

To be returned on or before the day marked above, subject to recall.

In the Limelight and Under the Microscope

Forms and Functions of Female Celebrity

Edited by
SU HOLMES AND DIANE NEGRA

continuum

The Continuum International Publishing Group
80 Maiden Lane, New York, NY 10038
The Tower Building, 11 York Road, London SE1 7NX

www.continuumbooks.com

Library of Congress Cataloging-in-Publication Data
In the limelight and under the microscope : forms and functions of female celebrity/edited by Su Holmes and Diane Negra.
    p. cm.
  Includes bibliographical references and index.
  ISBN-13: 978-1-4411-5495-8 (hardcover : alk. paper)
  ISBN-10: 1-4411-5495-7 (hardcover : alk. paper)
  ISBN-13: 978-0-8264-3855-3 (pbk. : alk. paper)
  ISBN-10: 0-8264-3855-5 (pbk. : alk. paper) 1. Fame—Social aspects. 2. Celebrities in mass media. 3. Women in mass media. 4. Celebrities—Political activity. 5. Women in popular culture. I. Holmes, Su. II. Negra, Diane, 1966-
  BJ1470.5.I5 2011
  305.42–dc22   2010033019

ISBN: HB: 978-1-4411-5495-8
        PB: 978-0-8264-3855-3

Typeset by Pindar NZ, Auckland, New Zealand
Printed and bound in the United States of America

Contents

Acknowledgments

This book would not be possible without the fine efforts of our contributors who researched and wrote the articles gathered here under considerable pressures of time and work. We also thank Katie Gallof, our editor at Continuum, for her warm support of this project and consistent good guidance along the way. Kind acknowledgments to Karen Jackman and Tomasz Kozyra, Deborah Jermyn and Sean Redmond, and for their valuable contributions to the development of this volume, Ginette Vincendeau and Kylie Jarrett.

Contributors

Leslie Abramson is a Lecturer in Film Studies at Lake Forest College. Her work has been published in *American Cinema of the 1960s* (2008), *New Constellations: Movie Stars of the 1960s* (2010), and publications including *Literature/Film Quarterly*.

Kim Allen is a Research Fellow at the Institute for Policy Studies in Education (IPSE) at London Metropolitan University. She specializes in research on the impact of popular culture on young people's identities and future aspirations, particularly in relation to education and work. Kim's work in this area is underpinned by a critical analysis of the relationship between celebrity culture and contemporary regimes of personhood, and is particularly concerned with the ways in which representations of the self within celebrity culture are classed and gendered. She is also interested in young people's educational choices and aspirations for careers in the creative industries and her doctoral research examined the experiences and future aspirations of young women in performing arts education in the UK.

Ruth Barton is a Lecturer in Film Studies at Trinity College Dublin and author of a number of books on Irish cinema. She has written a biography of Hedy Lamarr for University of Kentucky Press.

Emma Bell is a Senior Lecturer in Film and Screen Studies at the University of Brighton. Her research interests include gender and popular culture, scientific and medical imaging, the ethics of representation (especially of persons with disabilities and with mental health diagnoses), artists' filmmaking, and critical theory. She works from an interdisciplinary approach, drawing on film and cultural studies, art history, philosophy, critical theory, and politics. Her previous publications include work on representations of mental distress, avant-garde cinema, critical theory, and Dogme 95. She is currently working on a monograph on popular culture and the dissemination of scientific knowledge.

Candice Haddad is a PhD student in the Department of Communication Studies at the University of Michigan, Ann Arbor. In 2009 she completed her master's degree in the Department of Radio-Television-Film, University of Texas at Austin. Her scholarly interests focus on the intersections of identity in media and popular culture within a global context. She is particularly interested in examining potential sites of subversion and activism in mainstream media from a critical race and feminist perspective.

Catherine Hindson is a Lecturer in Performance Studies at the University of Bristol. Her research on the histories of popular performance in the late nineteenth and early twentieth centuries explores the intersections between metropolitan culture, day-to-day life and the entertainment industries. She has published on celebrity performers including the dancers Loïe Fuller and Jane Avril, the chanteuse Yvette Guilbert, and the impressionist Cissie Loftus, and on skirt dancing, poster art and trickery, magic, and illusion. Her current research focuses on the role that the charity work undertaken by well-known Victorian and Edwardian actresses played in their celebrity identities.

Su Holmes is a Reader in Television Studies at the University of East Anglia. She is the author of *British TV and Film Culture in the 1950s* (Intellect, 2005), *Entertaining TV: The BBC and Popular Television Culture in the 1950s* (Manchester University Press, 2008), and *The Quiz Show* (Edinburgh University Press, 2008), and she is co-editor of *Understanding Reality TV* (Routledge, 2004), *Framing Celebrity* (Routledge, 2006) and *Stardom and Celebrity: A Reader* (Sage, 2007). She is also the co-editor of the Routledge journal *Celebrity Studies*.

Joselyn K. Leimbach is a PhD candidate in Gender Studies at Indiana University. She obtained her M.A in Women's Studies from San Diego State University where she researched the representations of African American lesbians in US mainstream film. Her interests include media representations of lesbians and configurations of marginalized identities.

Alice Leppert is a PhD candidate in the Department of Communication Studies at the University of Minnesota. She is writing her dissertation on the pedagogical dimensions of US family sitcoms of the 1980s. She also studies film and television history and women in celebrity culture.

Caitlin Yunuen Lewis is a PhD student in Film Studies at University College Dublin. Her dissertation examines Irish postfeminist culture and neoliberalism after the Celtic Tiger, and is generously funded by a scholarship from the Irish Research Council for the Humanities and Social Sciences.

April Miller is Assistant Professor and Director of Film Studies at the University of Northern Colorado. Her research focuses primarily on the intersections between literature, film, and socio-scientific concerns such as criminality and mental illness. She is currently completing a book manuscript entitled *Offending Women: Modernism, Crime, and Creative Production*, which investigates the female criminal and her often-overlapping sites of representation in modernist literature, journalism, and silent film.

Anne Morey is Associate Professor of English at Texas A&M University. Her book *Hollywood Outsiders: The Adaptation of the Film Industry, 1913–1934* (University of Minnesota Press, 2003) deals with Hollywood's critics and co-opters in the later silent and early sound periods. She has published in *Film History, Quarterly Review of Film and Video*, and *Tulsa Studies in Women's Literature*, among other venues. She is presently at work on a history of religious filmmaking in the United States from the late nineteenth century to the present, a project she is pursuing as Vaughn Fellow at the Robert Penn Warren Center for the Humanities at Vanderbilt University, 2010–2011.

Diane Negra is Professor of Film Studies and Screen Culture and Head of Film Studies at University College Dublin. She is the author, editor or co-editor of six books including *Off-White Hollywood: American Culture and Ethnic Female Stardom* (Routledge, 2001), *A Feminist Reader in Early Cinema* (Duke, 2002), *The Irish in Us: Irishness, Performativity and Popular Culture* (Duke, 2006), *Interrogating Postfeminism: Gender and the Politics of Popular Culture* (Duke, 2007), *What a Girl Wants?: Fantasizing the Reclamation of Self in Postfeminism* (Routledge, 2008), and *Old and New Media After Katrina* (Palgrave, 2010).

Abigail Salerno teaches film and literature in the English Department at Southern Connecticut State University. She is currently working on a book-length manuscript on blindness and cinematic melodrama.

Margaret Schwartz is Assistant Professor of Communication and Media Studies at Fordham University. She is particularly interested in exploring the human body as a mediated yet material object. Her work has appeared in *Genders* and *Framework*, and her translation of the seminal Argentine avant-garde novel *The Museum of Eterna's Novel* is available from Open Letter Books. She is working on a book about celebrity corpses.

Anna Watkins Fisher is a doctoral student in the Department of Modern Culture and Media at Brown University. She holds an MA in Performance Studies from New York University and a BA from Duke University. She works at the intersection of contemporary art and performance, media studies, and critical theory.

Julie Wilson is a Visiting Assistant Professor of Critical Media Studies at Allegheny College. She is currently completing her dissertation, "Bleeding Hearts: Humanitarian Stars and the Making of Global Citizens," which traces historical intersections of Western stardom and global liberalism. Her essay, "Star Testing: The Emerging Politics of Celebrity Gossip," was recently published in *The Velvet Light Trap*.

Introduction

In the Limelight and Under the Microscope
— The Forms and Functions of Female Celebrity

SU HOLMES AND DIANE NEGRA

A DISTINCT SET OF INTERESTS, CONCERNS AND CULTURAL STIMULI have led to the inception of this collection — in particular a desire to highlight and interrogate what seem to be stark differences in the contemporary treatment of male and female celebrities (differences which have tended not to be discussed in academic work). It was with this in mind that in 2008 we organized a conference entitled "Going Cheap? Female Celebrity in the Tabloid, Reality and Scandal Genres" — an event that emerged from our desire to explore a gendered dynamic of popular interest and pleasure in the misfortunes of female celebrities that seemed to be moving into the cultural foreground. At its most extreme, this dynamic took shape in a desire for narrative culmination as thanatotic imperative. When Heath Ledger died suddenly that year, A. O. Scott of *The New York Times* railed against the "rituals of media cannibalism," positing Ledger as "ensnared in a pathological gossip culture that chews up the private lives of celebrities."[1] But on the internet, shocked early responses to the star's death made sense of the loss (and thus Ledger's "value") by expressing surprise and anger that it was Ledger who had died, rather than one of the many headline-making *female* celebrities whose travails normally dominate coverage. "'Heath before Britney?' wrote one, alluding to pop star Britney Spears. 'Something is seriously wrong with the world.'"[2]

By summer 2008, such gender-based representational incongruities were explicit enough to attract media commentary in their own right. Although

---

1. A. O. Scott, "Prince of Intensity With a Lightness of Touch," *The New York Times*, January 24, 2008.
2. This comment was posted by meleaux on USAToday.com on January 28, 2008.

journalistic reflection on this disparity was hardly pervasive, Alex Wilson surveyed the comparative treatment of male and female celebrities when it came to events such as drunk-driving, suicide attempts, and episodes of mental illness. After interviewing a number of industry professionals, she asserted that:

> [M]onths of parallel incidents like these seem to demonstrate disparate standards of coverage. Men who fall from grace are treated with gravity and distance, while women in similar circumstances are objects of derision, titillation and black comedy.[3]

It seemed to us that such contrasts might not only catalyze reflection about the intensifying double standard underlying a postfeminist cover story about gender egalitarianism, they were also indicative of important "blind spots" in academic understandings of celebrity. In turn, such discourses foregrounded celebrity culture as an urgent focus for work in critical gender studies on myriad levels. For example, in the postfeminist representational environment that is now widely understood to characterize the current era, femininity is routinely conceptualized as torn between chaos and (over) control, serenity, and agitation. In this regard, female celebrity models for managing the (feminized) "work–life balance" are often positioned as only precariously and temporarily stabilized; we are invited to play a "waiting game" to see when their hard-won achievements will collapse under the simultaneous weight of relationships, family, and career. One reason why stories of professionally accomplished/personally troubled female celebrities circulate so actively is that when women struggle or fail, their actions are seen to constitute "proof" that for women the "work–life balance" is really an impossible one. It is useful to bear this in mind when assessing a media climate dominated by stories that work to consolidate a strong cultural consensus about "out of bounds" behavior for women and proffer the pleasures of identifying and judging it. At the same time, this assertion about the construction of female celebrity careers is in itself shot through with the judgments which structure the contemporary crisis of value surrounding celebrity: after all, the concept of work (as well as "merit" or "talent") is increasingly seen as being evacuated from contemporary explanations of fame — especially in its gendered (feminine) forms.

As the title of our conference above suggests, we began to research this field in a period of high discursive activity (across a range of media platforms) regarding the figure of the so-called female celebrity "trainwreck." Such representations did not merely circulate particular discourses on the boundaries and politics of "appropriate" versions of contemporary femininity; they

---

3. Alex Williams, "Boys Will Be Boys, Girls Will be Hounded by the Media," *The New York Times*, February 17, 2008.

also played a highly visible role in fuelling and sustaining oft-cited anxieties about the "declining" currency of modern celebrity. Indeed, a major strand of the coverage of physically, emotionally and/or financially "out of control" female celebrities is predicated on public fears that we don't know what talent is anymore and that the traditional expectation that fame is based on talent is dying out, giving rise to a set of "illegitimate" female celebrities who are famous for "nothing." As we considered this phenomenon further, it seemed especially important that it be fully historically contextualized — if condemnatory discourses around female celebrity had reached a point of particular intensity in the dawning days of the global financial meltdown, it seemed to us that there were significant antecedents to the contemporary "cheapening" of female celebrity that necessitated analysis.

Accordingly, this book represents an effort to gather together scholarship that assesses the complex and varied historical placement of the female celebrity. A consistent element across the essays in this collection is the question of the female celebrity's role in testing dominant social norms. April Miller's account here of a set of 1920s female celebrity criminals subject to stagy show trials very much works in this vein, as does Catherine Hindson's examination of the notoriety of nineteenth-century courtesan/celebrity mistress/actress Lillie Langtry. In addition, Emma Bell's essay examines how revelations of mental illness play a complex and key role in marking out culturally "acceptable" forms of femininity and female celebrity. According to Bell, apparent "bad girl" excesses are "increasingly being reframed as symptoms of 'mad-girl' mental distress." In each of these examinations, the authors underscore the frequent positioning of the female celebrity in scenarios of scandal that characteristically (though not inevitably) fortify conventional understandings of gender, age, class, sexuality, and race/ethnicity.[4]

The contributors to this book unearth a set of rich research results that in many cases re-position the celebrities under investigation. Such is the case, for instance, in Ruth Barton's account of mid-twentieth-century Hollywood femme fatale Hedy Lamarr, who Barton finds was a deeply intellectually curious and highly technically proficient woman whose insights brought about the innovations in radar technology that underpin the contemporary cellular phone. Likewise, Abigail Salerno calls attention to the political activism of Helen Keller, an activism that was in part staged and tested through struggles over how Keller would be portrayed in film.

Another structuring element of this book is our belief that too many accounts of stardom and celebrity history begin with the invention of cinema. We seek to emphasize the importance of the pre-cinematic period and thus this book delves into the nineteenth century through Hindson's study of

---

4. For a fuller discussion of scandal and Hollywood culture see Adrienne L. McLean and David A. Cook, *Headline Hollywood: A Century of Film Scandal* (New Brunswick, NJ: Rutgers University Press, 2001).

"Professional Beauty" Lillie Langtry. Operating under a public persona that in many ways prefigures the dynamics of contemporary female fame, Langtry maintained a career that was anticipatory of the dynamic of contemporary celebrity. Hindson reads Langtry's celebrity as a conduit for period anxieties about the role of women in the public life of the modern city.

This book is also concerned to emphasize in various ways the political character of female celebrity. Richard Dyer's work[5] has of course long encouraged us to think of star images as "political" — insofar as such images can be read in relation to the ideological discourses (and thus power relations) of their time. Focusing on a case study from the 1960s, the (rarely examined) image of film star and celebrity Mia Farrow, Leslie Abramson's contribution to this book examines Farrow in relation to industrial and cultural shifts in Hollywood cinema, and discourses (and anxieties) surrounding femininity in a period of rapid cultural and industrial change. But more specifically, and for anyone in doubt about the direct and indirect political functions of celebrity, we recommend a reading of Anna Watkins Fisher's essay in this volume in which she persuasively argues that vigorous public condemnation of Britney Spears in the "trainwreck" phase of her career served to divert criticism from a failing leader during the presidency of George W. Bush. Paradigms of female celebrity are being most conspicuously tested/revised at this writing by pop star Lady Gaga, whose political functions most often go without scrutiny but whose strikingly unbounded celebrity text raises key questions about subjectivity in digital culture, questions with a clear political resonance. Gaga, it might be argued, compensates for the terrors of radical isolation and fractured subjectivity through the staging of a set of fantasies of merger, mergers of sexuality and technology most notably, though she also at times invokes the mergers that accompany original maternal plenitude. Given to endlessly thanking her fans and asserting that without them she would be nothing, Lady Gaga consistently refers to them as "little monsters" in a discursive maneuver of juvenilization.

Two essays in particular here, those by Joselyn K. Leimbach and Candice Haddad, illuminate how female celebrity intersects with the politics of race and sexuality. Leimbach's article scrutinizes the precise discursive calibrations of cable TV figures Suze Orman and Rachel Maddow, who both seek to personify "out" lesbianism while maintaining strong ongoing commitments to the political and economic status quo. Framed in the context of a neoliberal "family values" that has positioned itself to incorporate rather than oppose affluent gay couples and families, Leimbach shows how the "homonormativity" of Orman and Maddow entails a careful and consistent de-politicization of lesbianism. In a slightly different fashion, Caitlin Yunuen Lewis' essay here considers how the strongly authorially marked cinematic

---

5. Richard Dyer, *Stars* (London: British Film Institute, 1979); and *Heavenly Bodies: Film Stars and Society* (Basingstoke: Macmillan, 1986).

output of director Sofia Coppola (as well as her placement in interviews, lifestyle publications and advertisements for high-end brands) stages a romanticization of whiteness as blankness.

All the essays in this book maintain a consistent, careful effort to precisely contextualize the dynamics of female celebrity within sociohistorical forma-tions. For example, it was not, we believe, an accident of historical timing that an intensely and negatively scrutinizing public gaze was trained so often on female celebrities in a practice that reached fever pitch in 2008. In a moment of flux that can now be pinpointed as the dawning of the global financial crisis, female celebrity was conceptualized as a kind of "asset bub-ble" subject to the misplaced investigative functions of a tabloidized press. As a means of repressing the unsustainable nature of speculative financial practices, the scapegoating of female celebrities for their violation of (largely minor) social taboos was indicative of a range of energetic efforts to hold at bay the dawning revelations of vast white-collar crime. In this way, the immin-ent collapse of the financial industries is interlinked with the positioning of female celebrity as itself an overvalued and depreciating asset.

As this collection goes to press, it remains very evidently the case that female celebrities maintain a disproportionate level of representation in a variety of media forms. (Even a succession of male celebrity adultery scandals in 2009–2010 were noteworthy for their ability to generate "insta-celebrity" for the women involved.) The intensified discourses of celebrity couplehood and family life associated with postfeminist culture remain firmly in place even under new recessionary cultural conditions while a proliferation of new media technologies is expanding instantaneous and "on-demand" access to celebrity culture. As Chelsea Bullock has argued, new media networks can be seen to be "changing the very ontology of celebrity."[6] Exemplary in this regard is Lady Gaga, whose phenomenal rise to fame in recent years has been underpinned by a canny deployment of new media including haptic technologies that promulgate fantasies of enhanced intimacy with fans. Future work in celebrity studies will need to attend closely to the ways in which new communication channels like Twitter feeds and interactive web-sites are re-writing the terms of celebrity/fan engagement, raising the stakes for omnimediated (and seemingly omnipresent) celebrity and adapting to a fully convergent media environment.[7]

This book is being published at a time when steeply pitched female fame trajectories are becoming increasingly common — not least in reality TV. While often invoked as the very epitome (and also instigator of) the

---

6. Bullock, Chelsea "*The Fame* of Lady Gaga: Affect, Assemblage, and 'Authentic Insincerity' in Contemporary Celebrity Transformation," unpublished essay.

7. For an early exploratory account of these issues see Liz Ellcessor, "People I Want to Know: Twitter, Celebrity and Social Connection," *FlowTV* 9(14), May 28, 2009. Ellcessor delin-eates a key question: "as media scholars, how can we approach online sociality in relation to prior histories of media use, stardom, and connections forged through popular culture?"

declining currency of fame, reality TV celebrity is often positioned as "feminine," whether in terms of its apparent evacuation of (masculine-defined and active) concepts such as "talent" or "work," its micro-obsession with the "private," or with respect to its most visible and successful beneficiaries. In line with this book's aim to forge a dialogue between past and present conditions of female celebrity, Alice Leppert and Julie Wilson's essay here on Lauren Conrad, star of the immensely popular reality series, *The Hills*, explores how the gendered articulation of reality TV celebrity allows television to capitalize on earlier forms of female stardom (such as those emerging from Hollywood cinema) previously inaccessible within US reality TV, thus opening up "new horizons for commodifying female stars and their fans." At the same time, and as explored by Kim Allen's study of how a group of 16- to 19-year-old girls negotiate discourses of celebrity in their everyday lives, we should be wary of making assumptions about the gendered *reception* of celebrity when so little empirical research in this field currently exists. Indeed, in examining how a group of girls in state-funded performing arts courses constructed their identities and "imagined futures as 'potential celebrities'," a number of assumptions about girls' "passive" and uncritical consumption of celebrity are problematized.

Nevertheless, if Leppert and Wilson's essay foregrounds a highly capitalist rhetoric, and the fact that those outside of the media "frame" finance the success of those "inside" it,[8] this may give us cause to question the often simplistic claims to "democratization" which circulate around reality TV fame — as peddled, for example, by the narratives which attended the rise of the global, overnight celebrity of *Britain's Got Talent* contestant Susan Boyle in 2009.[9] Positioned variously as evidence of the restoration of a democratized fame culture and a spectacle of transcendence in the face of the age- and gender-based codes structuring public life, the then 48-year-old's delivery of "I Dreamed a Dream" from *Les Miserables* (in a powerful, if contrived, re-staging of the authenticity of the "discovery scene") has been downloaded from YouTube over 94 million times. What Boyle's case does indisputably make clear is the intensity and rapidity of circulation now available to celebrity texts.

But the cultural fascination with Boyle's rapid rise to visibility can only be

---

8. Nick Couldry, *The Place of Media Power: Pilgrims and Witnesses of the Media Age* (London: Routledge, 2000).

9. For more on Boyle's celebrity see Su Holmes, "Dreaming a Dream: Susan Boyle and Celebrity Culture," and Diane Negra, "Picturing Family Values." These essays appear in *The Velvet Light Trap* 65 (Spring, 2010): 74–6 and 60–1 respectively. Of course, reality TV often couples its gendered address with problematic depictions of race and ethnicity, class, consumerism, and regional identities. For a discussion of how this operates in the mode of the makeover see Brenda R. Weber, *Makeover TV: Selfhood, Citizenship and Celebrity* (Durham: Duke University Press, 2009). For an assessment of the dynamics of race, ethnicity, and region in one reality TV series, see Jon Kraszewski, "Coming to a Beach Near You! Examinations of Ethnic and State Identity in *Jersey Shore*," *FlowTV* 11(8), February 19, 2010.

explained within a context that recognizes the sexist and ageist logics that structure female celebrity culture. Indeed, the compelling nature of her audition performance pivots on the concept of "surprise" as the judges react to the perceived disjuncture between her appearance (middle-aged, overweight, and not conventionally "attractive") and her talent.[10] The politics of aging and female celebrity/stardom are explored from a different perspective by Anne Morey's essay in this collection in her discussion of the female "grotesque" in Hollywood cinema. In view of the fact that the aging process rapidly depreciates the commercial value of the female star (in a strikingly different fashion from that of her male counterparts), Morey explores how the role of the "grotesque" may offer an important intervention in this regard: indeed, Morey argues that its association with the critically acclaimed actress may position the grotesque as a source of "professional and even personal power."

In our hyper-surveilled celebrity culture, markers of aging are relentlessly scrutinized and judged, with women variously castigated for the "sin" of "letting themselves go," or mocked for displaying highly visible, or unattractive cosmetic surgery procedures.[11] But while it is possible to argue that the body is *the* key terrain upon which discourses surrounding female celebrity are mapped, this is especially true with regard to contemporary crisis celebrity, in the guise of the female "trainwreck." In fact, as Margaret Schwartz argues in this collection in her analysis of the fad for "upskirt" paparazzi shots, it is possible to posit a link between the anatomical and the cultural here: both the female genitals and the concept of female celebrity are seen as representing a perceived "lack," "unearthing an unconscious connection between female celebrity and male pleasure, emptiness, and trashiness." The intense scrutinizing functions of a culture of checkbook journalism and paparazzism, as well as the circulating capacities of the internet, have furthered this emphasis on corporeal/sexual surveillance, enabling for instance, the sex tape to emerge as a new credential for female celebrityhood (Paris Hilton, Kim Kardashian).

Indeed, while such technological shifts have tended to facilitate the promotion of a set of high-profile, sexed-up "bad girls," other typological categories have also emerged or been re-energized. Postfeminist culture's embrace of marriage as the preeminent state of achieved femininity, and its re-certification of stereotypes like the "golddigger," have also helped to usher in a wave of celebrity "wives" whose dependent status (whether actual or imaginary) is grist for public condemnation — even as such women become style icons and revenue-generating figures sometimes far in excess of their partners. In recent years, the British tabloid press has coined the now widely

---

10. Holmes, "Dreaming a Dream: Susan Boyle and Celebrity Culture," 75.
11. Kirsty Fairclough, "Fame is a Losing Game: Gossip Blogging, Bitch Culture and Postfeminism," *Genders* 48 (2008).

used term "WAG" to designate a new category of high-profile, free-spending (and thus "freeloading") "Wives and Girlfriends" (frequently of soccer players on the England national team), the most celebrated/excoriated of whom have been Victoria Beckham, Coleen McLoughlin, and Cheryl Cole. Equally, the apparent *absence* of a partner can prompt judgments about women who seemingly flout the current codes of family values, exposing (and perhaps acting upon) the kinds of profit interests now so bound up with mass media portrayals of family life. When female celebrity life choices and personal circumstances do not fit (or no longer fit) within a "family values" script, one option is for them to be cast in the mode of another postfeminist archetype, the "sad singleton." Celebrities such as Renee Zellweger and Jennifer Aniston are thus treated with dismay or bemusement when they show up on the red carpet alone and/or "can't find a man." Most recently, in the wake of the high-profile breakup of her marriage, Sandra Bullock has sought to quell such typologization by deploying two tropes of female postfeminist value: the solicitous mother and the sexually enlightened "bi-curious" woman.[12]

The idea of not conforming to (or perhaps falling in between) social types, is surely dramatized by Britney Spears. No longer simply a sexualized, while simultaneously juvenilized, starlet, but not a "safe" maternal figure, Spears appears to pose a representational and ideological problem for a culture which valorizes the security of female typology. In fact, typifying the extent to which the experience of actually "being famous" is self-reflexively encoded into much contemporary celebrity coverage, Spears sought to respond to the discursive and representational climate surrounding her in her hit song, "Piece of Me." While "answering back" to the opprobrium waiting to be heaped on female celebrities in the current media landscape ("I'm Mrs. Lifestyles of the rich and famous/I'm Mrs. Oh my god that Britney's shameless/. . . Hopin' I'll resort to some havoc/And end up settlin' in court/Now are you sure you want a piece of me?"), the song also referenced the gendered difficulty involved in negotiating the work–life balance ("Guess I can't see the harm in workin' and being a mama/And with a kid on my arm I'm still an exceptional earner"). The song also foregrounds the gendered pressures of living under cultural — and thus corporeal — surveillance ("I'm Mrs. She's too big now she's too thin"), as well as what Spears positions as the seemingly absurd interest in the minutiae of her everyday existence ("I'm

---

12. In an astonishing sequence of revelations around a star whose persona had previously been exceptionally stable and scandal-free, in April 2010, Bullock won an Oscar and the next week saw the end of her marriage to television star and motorcycle afficianado Jesse James — who, it was disclosed, had committed serial adultery with a range of women, most notably a tattoo model with a penchant for Nazi iconography. A month later, Bullock revealed that she had secretly adopted an African-American child from New Orleans. In June, 2010, Bullock's first major public appearance after the scandal was at the MTV Music Awards where she shared an onstage kiss with Scarlett Johannson.

Mrs. 'Most likely to get on TV for stripping on the streets'/When getting' the groceries, no, for real . . ./Are you kiddin' me?").[13]

As these lyrics (to say nothing of the example of Bullock above) suggest, constructions of motherhood have become an increasingly visible framework through which female celebrity is refracted, judged, and policed, from notions of the "unfit mother" (which usually circle around so-called "white trash" celebrities in the US and UK, such as Britney Spears, Kerry Katona, and Katie Price), and discourses of motherhood as redemption ("taming" the previous "wild girl") (see Bell in this collection), to the aspirational image of the "yummy mummy" who can apparently "have it all."[14]

In examining this contemporary celebrity landscape and the discursive circulation of women within it, we have speculated on the politics of what we tentatively called the "new gendering of fame."[15] In using the word "new" here, however, we were mindful that claims of change and development in this area are complex and, as such, they should be up for contestation and debate. In addition, the more we thought about the contours of the history that preceded our period of interest, the more we were struck by the *paucity* of detailed attention to the gendered politics of fame itself. This in turn spoke to wider critical and methodological issues in approaching the history of celebrity. Despite the growth of historical scholarship on celebrity, there is still a tendency to position much of modern celebrity as inherently "new": the idea, or rather lament, that modern fame is intrinsically different from and "new" in relation to (apparently golden) "times past" has made a successful bid for legitimacy and acceptance, both in popular media discourse and in aspects of academic scholarship. Yet such assertions can often simplify and dehistoricize rather than illuminate, especially when there remains much historical research in celebrity studies still to be done. As we have

---

13. An earlier Spears song, the 2001 "I'm Not a Girl, Not Yet a Woman," also resonated autobiographically, attempting to take possession of the productive indeterminacy that was central to the star's persona. In this respect the song stands as an interesting parallel to "Piece of Me"'s protest against over-categorization.

14. See Diane Negra, *What a Girl Wants? Fantasizing the Reclamation of Self in Postfeminism* (London: Routledge, 2008) and Deborah Jermyn, "Still Something Else Besides a Mother? Negotiating Celebrity Motherhood in Sarah Jessica Parker's Star Story," *Social Semiotics* 18(2) (June, 2008): 163–76.

15. See the introduction to the special issue of *Genders Online* entitled "Going Cheap? Female Celebrity in the Reality, Tabloid and Scandal Genres." The work which we and others did in relation to this topic appeared in issue 48 (Fall 2008). Essays by Bell, Schwartz, and Leppert and Wilson, which first appeared there, are adapted and updated to varying degrees for their inclusion in this volume. The topic of contemporary schadenfreude has also been explored (without emphasis on gender) by Steve Cross and Jo Littler in "Celebrity and Schadenfrude: the Cultural Economy of Fame in Freefall," *Cultural Studies* 24(3) (May, 2010): 395–417. Cross and Littler contend that pleasure in celebrity misfortune functions as an oblique awareness of social inequality though one which is ultimately not in any way productive of social change. They note "the proliferation of celebrity discourse over the past two decades can be understood (although this is a point rarely made) in relation to a broader context of the rise of neoliberal capitalism and its savagely widening global disparities of wealth and power" (396).

noted above, it is a key concern of this book to map historical continuities in female celebrity representation in an effort to more precisely and accurately delineate "new" and "old" phenomena.

In speaking of the critical and methodological challenges that structure *all* historical research, John Corner has noted the "double dangers" of both an "over-distanced approach (the past as very much 'another country') and an undue proximity (the past as . . . simply 'today with oddities')."[16] Yet Corner also indicates how an "enriched sense of 'then' produces, in its differences and commonalities combined, a stronger and more imaginative sense of 'now'."[17] It is in this spirit that we wanted to explore some of the historical narratives which precede our sense of "now."

At the same time, stopping the "flow" of celebrity culture in order to interrogate its structures at any one time is a challenging task. Andrew Scahill et al. have recently commented that:

> "Celebrity" . . . is always a topic that promises immense irrelevancy and dangerous outmodishness in equal measure. It is a Sisyphean task to attempt to explain and understand it in any comprehensive way . . . Rather [we can only ever offer] . . . a flash insight into this crucial and mercurial subject.[18]

Given the apparently ephemeral, intangible, and transient nature of the phenomenon, the case study may have a particularly crucial role to play in exploring histories of celebrity. Thus, in asking such questions, *In the Limelight and Under the Microscope: Forms and Functions of Female Celebrity* seeks to open up an informed and productive dialogue about the historical traject-ories at work in the cultural dynamics of female celebrity, generating a rich set of articles whose case studies range from Lillie Langtry to Helen Keller, and from Sofia Coppola to Britney Spears. In this regard, the intention of this book is not to provide a metanarrative on how historical trajectories of fame are gendered (something which would in any case be unsuited to an edited volume and its deliberate staging of a range of perspectives, approaches, and voices). Rather, in moving across case studies from the nineteenth century to the present day, this book works from the assumption that the case study should play a crucial role in generating debate about the *dialogue* between "past" and "present," and the individual essays seek to reflect this spirit of enquiry.

Incorporating reassessments of figures we thought we knew (such as Helen Keller) alongside analyses, such as that of Candice Haddad, of emergent stars like Sri Lankan rapper M.I.A., this collection seeks to forge

---

16. John Corner, "Finding Data, Reading Patterns, Telling Stories: Issues in the Historiography of Television," *Media, Culture and Society* 25 (2003): 77.

17. Ibid., 275.

18. Andrew Scahill et al., "Introduction," in *The Velvet Light Trap*, 65 (Spring 2010): 1.

a greater conceptual, theoretical, and historical dialogue between celebrity studies and critical gender studies. We suggest that the need for an intellectual intervention of this kind is dramatized by the extent to which questions of gender have often been occluded in the rapidly expanding sphere of celebrity studies. Much like the cultural landscape of fame, the academic study of celebrity has become increasingly well populated. As P. David Marshall described in 2004:

> The academy has embraced the study of celebrity and fame over the last decade and it has accelerated in recent years. Sport stardom . . . film stardom . . . literary celebrity . . . journalism and celebrity . . . the psychology of fame . . . and media and the celebrity . . . have appeared as [topics for] full-fledged books with a regularity that echoes the celebrity system's own production process. This burgeoning interest in fame cuts across disciplinary study in surprising ways.[19]

The study of stardom and fame, associated in its earlier phases primarily with film studies, was initially reliant on a limited, while "classic," range of scholarly texts.[20] As discussed, the work of Richard Dyer situated the analysis of stars in the realm of ideology and representation.[21] Star "images" could be understood as semiotic "signs" and read as "texts" — dramatizing ideas of personhood, individualism, and class, gender, ethnicity, and sexuality at any one time. Dyer's *Heavenly Bodies* went on to offer a detailed conceptual framework for contextualizing the star image: situating it within the myriad of cultural, historical, and social discourses from which it emerged. Under the classical Hollywood studio system, close (if, inevitably imperfect) systems of control were in place to structure and maintain star personae, yet the contemporary era feels very different and it has become axiomatic that old verities about the stability of stardom and the chaos of celebrity no longer hold. The later expansion of "celebrity studies," as emerging from media, television, and cultural studies (as well as sports studies, popular music studies, work on digital culture, and beyond), has also widened the scope of analysis, not simply in terms of expanding the media focus, but with regard to critical, theoretical, and methodological approach. Within celebrity studies, a sphere which recognizes that the media contexts of fame have become less distinct and specific, the subject has been approached as a set of broader cultural and political processes.

Yet there currently exists no volume or collection that specifically focuses on the gendering of fame, and the particular ways in which female celebrity

19. P. David Marshall, "Fame's Perpetual Moment," *M/C Journal* 7(5), (November 2004).
20. Dyer, *Stars*; Dyer, *Heavenly Bodies*; John Ellis, *Visible Fictions: Cinema, Television, Video* (London: Routledge, 1982), Christine Gledhill (ed.), *Stardom: Industry of Desire* (London: Routledge, 1991), Richard deCordova, *Picture Personalities: The Emergence of the Star System in America* (Urbana: University of Illinois Press, 1990).
21. See Dyer's *Stars* and *Heavenly Bodies*.

is articulated. While recent books on celebrity often consider how star/ celebrity images are shaped by discourses of gender, race, or class, there has been no systematic or sustained attention to how the complex, multifarious, and deeply intertwined spheres of fame/gender intersect, nor has contemporary work on postfeminism often offered a sustained engagement with the subject of celebrity. To be sure, this is not to deny the long-standing — and ongoing — relationship between star/celebrity studies and feminism: from Jackie Stacey's *Stargazing: Hollywood Cinema and Female Spectatorship*, Linda Mizejewski's *Ziegfeld Girl: Image and Icon in Culture and Cinema*, Diane Negra's *Off-White Hollywood: American Culture and Ethnic Female Stardom*, Rachel Moseley's *Growing Up with Audrey Hepburn* and Adrienne McLean's *Being Rita Hayworth: Labor, Identity and Hollywood Stardom*,[22] to more recent interventions such as Catharine Lumby's work on young girls' relationships with fame culture,[23] Rebecca Feasey's work on the construction of femininity in *heat* magazine,[24] and the interventions of some contributors in volumes of Rutgers University Press' *Star Decades* series, fame has been understood as being shaped by gendered discourses of construction and reception. But on a general scale, gender has primarily factored in readings of specific canonical star images — as traditionally emerging from the approach pioneered by film studies. With the expansion of celebrity studies since this time, it is not unreasonable to suggest that celebrity studies and feminist media studies have failed to forge a visible, systemic or ongoing dialogue, meaning that the issues which concern us here have often fallen through the analytic cracks. Given that, according to a popular magazine show on British television, celebrity can be referred to as "the alternative C-word,"[25] the gendered dimensions of contemporary celebrity, and the ways in which they elucidate the promotion, testing, and negotiation of contemporary conceptions of femininity, require urgent interrogation.

As the reference above suggests, questions of terminology here are far from gender neutral. Although its meaning has changed over time, the term "celebrity" has a less prestigious lineage than the term "star" (although the

22. Jackie Stacey, *Stargazing: Hollywood Cinema and Female Spectatorship* (London: Routledge, 1994); Linda Mizejewski, *Ziegfeld Girl: Image and Icon in Culture and Cinema* (Durham, NC: Duke University Press, 1999); Diane Negra, *Off-White Hollywood: American Culture and Ethnic Female Stardom* (London: Routledge, 2001); Rachel Moseley, *Growing Up with Audrey Hepburn* (Manchester: Manchester University Press, 2003); Adrienne McLean, *Being Rita Hayworth: Labor, Identity and Hollywood Stardom* (New Brunswick, NJ: Rutgers, 2004); Ramona Curry, *Too Much of a Good Thing: Mae West as Cultural Icon* (Minneapolis: University of Minnesota Press, 1996).

23. Catharine Lumby, "Doing It For Themselves? Teenage Girls, Sexuality and Fame," in Redmond and Holmes (eds), *A Reader in Stardom and Celebrity* (London: Sage, 2007), 341–52.

24. Rebecca Feasey, "Get a Famous Body: Star Styles and Celebrity Gossip in heat Magazine," in Su Holmes and Sean Redmond (eds), *Framing Celebrity* (Oxford: Routledge, 2006), 177–94.

25. *Richard and Judy* (Channel 4, February 2, 2007).

contributors in this collection use these terms in different ways, depending on the context in hand). As Marshall outlines, by the nineteenth century "celebrity" had become a term that "announce[d] a vulgar sense of notoriety" and "some modern sense of false value."[26] In popular and academic discourse, this sense of a depreciated cultural value continues to structure the use of the term, and this in itself is inextricably linked to perceptions of work, worth, and "talent." For example, while stardom has long since been conceptualized as requiring an interaction between on-/off-screen selves ("work" self and "private" self), celebrity is often deemed to connote a representational structure in which the primary emphasis is on the person's "private" life or lifestyle. But as Christine Geraghty observed, this has meant that "celebrity" is a culturally gendered term, insofar as women are "particularly likely to be seen as celebrities whose working life is of less interest than their personal life":[27] women are more identified with the private sphere, and their status as workers has had to struggle for cultural legitimacy. Despite this, the media and cultural fascination with the "private" lives and identities of the famous has accelerated substantially since Geraghty was writing, and despite the fact that the apparently devalued currency of celebrity — laments regarding the decline of "talent" and "work" — have been articulated with increasing fervor, there has been little follow-on work interrogating the significance of Geraghty's important observations.

It is interesting to briefly consider why this might be the case. The study of stars, celebrity, and fame has increasingly become an accepted element of scholarly work in the academy since the first edition publication of Richard Dyer's work, yet it is fair to say that, even within academia, it is seen as residing at the most populist end of the conceptual spectrum of the "popular." To be sure, like many of the popular texts that film, television, and cultural studies have long since sought to treat as serious objects of analysis, an interest in celebrity can still be classed as a "guilty pleasure."[28] Indeed, in the opening to his 1994 book, *Claims to Fame*, Joshua Gamson asks the rhetorical question: "What were these people [the celebrities he was analyzing] doing in my life? . . . I was a PhD candidate from an established family!"[29] But as a potentially newer example of the apparent populism of academia, the study of celebrity has been repeatedly invoked in journalistic discourse as indicative evidence of a perceived drift toward cultural relativism and the supposed "dumbing down" of education (and with particular frequency in Britain). Sometimes appearing within an eclectic range of other subjects such as "surfing, beauty

26. *Celebrity and Power: Fame and Contemporary Culture* (Minneapolis: University of Minnesota Press, 1997): 5, 4.
27. "Re-Examining Stardom: Questions of Texts, Bodies and Performance," in Christine Gledhill and Linda Williams (eds), *Re-inventing Film Studies* (London: Arnold, 2001), 184.
28. Marshall, 4.
29. Joshua Gamson, *Claims to Fame: Celebrity in Contemporary America* (Berkeley: University of California Press, 1994), 4, cited in Turner, *Understanding Celebrity* (London: Sage, 2004), 92.

therapy, knitwear, circus skills, pig enterprise management, death studies, air guitar . . . and wine studies,"[30] the academic study of stardom/celebrity has become a favorite journalistic bête noire.

In one such account, the author makes particular mention of "academic courses on subjects such as the life of soccer player David Beckham,"[31] an indicative reference since Beckham has so often been placed as a highly *feminized* version of modern masculinity. Indeed, much of the journalistic derision directed at the study of stardom and celebrity is implicitly couched in gendered terms, given the dismissal of what is an apparently "trivial," "gossipy" and (in terms of the contours of its concerns) "private" sphere. Women/girls are also the primary imagined audience for the daily rhythms of celebrity culture (especially, for example, with regard to weekly celebrity gossip magazines). They are also, it would seem (at least in terms of our own undergraduate teaching experience), its most eager students. As teachers of university courses on stardom and celebrity, we have both consistently observed substantially skewed gender ratios in student enrolment, with male students seeming to operate on the principle that the material carries an emasculating tinge. Indeed, perhaps the relative paucity of concerted feminist interventions in celebrity culture might parallel the apparently "awkward" relationship between feminism and popular "women's" media once detailed with respect to soap opera. As Charlotte Brunsdon has observed: "In the popular imaginary, feminists are women who don't shave their legs, don't approve of page three girls, and don't like soap opera."[32] While in the context of feminist media and cultural studies — such an apparent polarity has long since been challenged and questioned, that is not to say that it has been rendered redundant. Given that, from a contemporary point of view, we encounter a celebrity culture on a daily basis that pivots, in large part, on the often punitive scrutiny, judgment and dissection of the female form (from constant weight surveillance to the apparently forensic interest in (for example) "close-up pap snaps of Lindsay Lohan's tit tape"),[33] it is little wonder that celebrity studies and feminist studies have not necessarily been seen as natural bedfellows. In this regard, although the acute study of gender politics, as well as the use of feminist critical/theoretical paradigms have certainly been part of star/celebrity studies, it is notable that many of the most visible and widely used texts in recent years have been produced by men.[34] This is not to endorse an essentialist view of the relationship between

30. Clark, cited in Su Holmes and Sean Redmond, "Editorial," *Celebrity Studies* 1(1), 2010: 2.
31. Reuters, "Mickey Mouse Degrees Face Funding Battle," September 23, 2009.
32. Charlotte Brunsdon, *Screen Tastes: From Soap Opera to Satellite Dishes* (London: Routledge, 1994), 29.
33. Matthew Bell, "Celebrity, the Cerebral, and Articles You Won't See in *heat*," *The Independent*, November 16, 2009.
34. Turner, *Understanding Celebrity*; Marshall, *Celebrity and Power*; Gamson, *Claims to Fame*; Chris Rojek, *Celebrity* (London: Reaktion Books, 2001).

authorship, gender, and gender politics, but this fact nevertheless contributes to a picture in which feminist media studies and celebrity studies have enjoyed a somewhat distant, or at best intermittent, relationship.

The efforts made here to forge tighter links between up-to-the-minute theoretical work on gender and historical and contemporary sites of female celebrity are undertaken in the hope that scholars will proceed apace. As Turner has recently noted,[35] the study of celebrity is not yet a truly inter-disciplinary enterprise, given that despite work indeed emerging across disciplines as diverse as law, marketing, sports studies, and literary studies, much of the most visible research is located within film, media, and cultural studies. In this respect, we hope that this book contributes to the furthering of interdisciplinary synergies and explorations and accordingly the contributors to this book seek to generate analyses that are clearly accessible and not unnecessarily weighted down by jargon — analyses that will be lucid to a range of scholars in the humanities and social sciences. Equally central to the work undertaken here is the belief that a feminist history of women's roles in popular culture must account for the complex and varied positionality of female stars and celebrities.

Bibliography

Bell, Matthew. "Celebrity, the Cerebral, and Articles You Won't See in *heat*," *The Independent*, November 16, 2009, 12.

Brunsdon, Charlotte. *Screen Tastes: From Soap Opera to Satellite Dishes*. London: Routledge, 1994.

Bullock, Chelsea. "*The Fame* of Lady Gaga: Affect, Assemblage, and 'Authentic Insincerity' in Contemporary Celebrity Transformation," unpublished essay.

Corner, John. "Finding Data, Reading Patterns, Telling Stories: Issues in the Historiography of Television," *Media, Culture and Society*, 25 (2003): 273–80.

Couldry, Nick. *The Place of Media Power: Pilgrims and Witnesses of the Media Age*. London: Routledge, 2000.

Cross, Steve and Jo Littler. "Celebrity and Schadenfreude: The Cultural Economy of Fame in Freefall," *Cultural Studies* 24(3), (May, 2010): 395–417

Curry, Ramona. *Too Much of a Good Thing: Mae West as Cultural Icon* (Minneapolis: University of Minnesota Press, 1996).

deCordova, Richard. *Picture Personalities: The Emergence of the Star System in America* (Urbana: University of Illinois Press, 1990).

Dyer, Richard. *Stars* (2nd edn). London: British Film Institute, 1998.

——. *Heavenly Bodies: Film Stars and Society*. Basingstoke: Macmillan, 1986.

Ellcessor, Liz. "People I Want to Know: Twitter, Celebrity and Social Connection," *FlowTV* 9(14), May 28, 2009. Available at: http://flowtv.org/?p=3954 (accessed July 4, 2010).

Ellis, John. *Visible Fictions: Cinema, Television, Video*. London: Routledge, 1982.

Fairclough, Kirsty. "Fame is a Losing Game: Gossip Blogging, Bitch Culture and Postfeminism," *Genders*, 48 (Fall, 2008). Available at: http://www.genders.org/g48/g48_fairclough.html (accessed June 29, 2010).

Feasey, Rebecca. "Get a Famous Body: Star Styles and Celebrity Gossip in *heat* Magazine," in Su Holmes and Sean Redmond (eds), *Framing Celebrity*. Oxford: Routledge, 2006, 177–94.

Gamson, Joshua. *Claims to Fame: Celebrity in Contemporary America*. Berkeley: University of California Press, 1994.

---

35. Graeme Turner, "Approaching Celebrity Studies," *Celebrity Studies* 1(1), 2010: 9.

Geraghty, Christine. "Re-examining Stardom: Questions of Texts, Bodies and Performance," in Christine Gledhill and Linda Williams (eds), in *Re-inventing Film Studies*. London: Arnold, 2001, 183–201.

Gledhill, Christine (ed.). *Stardom: Industry of Desire*. London: Routledge, 1991.

Holmes, Su. "Dreaming a Dream: Susan Boyle and Celebrity Culture," *The Velvet Light Trap* 65, (Spring, 2010): 74–6.

Holmes, Su and Sean Redmond. "Editorial," *Celebrity Studies* 1(1), 2010: 1–9.

Jermyn, Deborah. "Still Something Else Besides a Mother? Negotiating Celebrity Motherhood in Sarah Jessica Parker's Star Story," *Social Semiotics* 18(2), 2008: 163–76.

Kraszewski, Jon. "Coming to a Beach Near You! Examinations of Ethnic and State Identity in *Jersey Shore*," *FlowTV* 11(8), February 19, 2010. Available at: http://flowtv.org/2010/02/coming-to-a-beach-near-you-examinations-of-ethnic-and-state-identity-in-jersey-shore-jon-kraszewski-seton-hall-university/ (accessed July 4, 2010).

Lumby, Catharine. "Doing it for Themselves? Teenage Girls, Sexuality and Fame," in Sean Redmond and Su Holmes (eds), *A Reader in Stardom and Celebrity*. London: Sage, 2007, 341–52.

Marshall, P. David. *Celebrity and Power: Fame in Contemporary Culture*. Minneapolis, MN: University of Minnesota Press, 1997.

——. "Fame's Perpetual Moment," *M/C Journal* 7(5), November 2004. Available at: http://journal.media-culture.org.au/0411/01-editorial.php (accessed July 27, 2008).

McLean, Adrienne. L. *Being Rita Hayworth: Labor, Identity and Hollywood Stardom*. New Brunswick, NJ: Rutgers University Press, 2004.

McLean, Adrienne L. and David A. Cook. *Headline Hollywood: A Century of Film Scandal*. New Brunswick, NJ: Rutgers University Press, 2001.

Mizejewski, Linda. *Ziegfeld Girl: Image and Icon in Culture and Cinema*. Durham, NC: Duke University Press, 1999.

Moseley, Rachel. *Growing Up with Audrey Hepburn*. Manchester: Manchester University Press, 2003.

Negra, Diane. *Off-White Hollywood: American Culture and Ethnic Female Stardom*. London: Routledge, 2001.

——. *What a Girl Wants? Fantasizing the Reclamation of Self in Postfeminism*. London: Routledge, 2008.

——. "Picturing Family Values," *The Velvet Light Trap* 65 (Spring, 2010): 60–1.

Negra, Diane and Su Holmes. Introduction to the special issue "Going Cheap? Female Celebrity in the Reality, Tabloid and Scandal Genres," *Genders* 48 (Fall, 2008). Available at: http://www.genders.org/g48/g48_negraholmes.html (accessed June 29, 2010).

Reuters. "Mickey Mouse Degrees Face Funding Battle," STV, September 23, 2009, http://news.stv.tv/uk/125176-mickey-mouse-degrees-face-funding-battle/ (accessed June 29, 2010).

Rojek, Chris. *Celebrity*. London: Reaktion Books, 2001.

Scahill, Andrew, Curran Nault, Kevin Sanson and Lisa Schmidt. "Introduction", *The Velvet Light Trap* 65 (Spring, 2010): 1–2.

Scott, A. O. "Prince of Intensity With a Lightness of Touch," *The New York Times*, January 24, 2008.

Stacey, Jackie. *Stargazing: Hollywood Cinema and Female Spectatorship*. London: Routledge, 1994.

Turner, Graeme. *Understanding Celebrity*. London: Sage, 2004.

——, "Approaching Celebrity Studies," *Celebrity Studies* 1(1), 2010: 1–14.

Weber, Brenda. R. *Makeover TV: Selfhood, Citizenship and Celebrity*. Durham: Duke University Press, 2009.

Williams, Alex. "Boys Will Be Boys, Girls Will be Hounded by the Media," *The New York Times*, February 17, 2008. Available at: http://www.nytimes.com/2008/02/17/fashion/17celeb.html (accessed June 29, 2010).

1

"Mrs. Langtry Seems to Be on the Way to a Fortune"

The Jersey Lily and Models of Late Nineteenth-Century Fame[1]

CATHERINE HINDSON

THE ROYAL ACADEMY OF ART'S 1878 ANNUAL EXHIBITION attracted thousands of visitors to London's Piccadilly. Amid the estimated 1,200 exhibits on display at Burlington House, three portraits of a young woman from Jersey attracted, and sustained, the attention of the press and the public. The model was Lillie Langtry (1853–1929), a young married woman who had arrived in London in 1876 and "startled" the city with the "finish of her features and the fineness of her complexion."[2] By the opening of the 1878 Academy exhibition, Langtry was London's "reigning beauty"; a style icon and *the* female celebrity of her day.[3] Langtry was to remain a creature of notoriety until her death in 1929: as a beauty, an actress, and a business-woman, her public identity encapsulated the leisure industries of modernity and forged a new and enduring model of female celebrity.

Yet, on her arrival in London in January 1876, Langtry was a social out-sider. Born Emilie Charlotte Le Breton, she was the only daughter of the Dean of Jersey and had rarely left the Channel Islands before her 1874 marriage to Edward Langtry.[4] For an upper-middle-class young woman of the

---

1. *Moonshine* June 23, 1888, 290.
2. "London and Paris Gossip," *Trewman's Exeter Flying Post*, May 8, 1878, 8.
3. *The Newcastle Courant*, May 3, 1878, 6.
4. The Dean of Jersey acts as the leader of the Church of England in Jersey. Langtry's father, William Corbet le Breton (1815–1888) held the post from 1850–1883. Biographical information for this essay comes from a range of sources. Langtry's autobiography *The Days I Knew: The Autobiography of Lillie Langtry* (London: Futura, 1978), provides evidence of her character and celebrity construct. However, the details it offers are frequently incorrect. Laura Beatty's *Lillie Langtry: Manners, Masks and Morals* has supplied useful information and this has been used alongside material from the Victoria & Albert Theatre Collection's Lillie Langtry Biographical File and a range of press accounts, interviews and obituaries.

mid-nineteenth century, Langtry was relatively well educated. She had been tutored at home in the necessary "feminine skills" of French, German, music, and drawing, but she had also joined her five brothers' evening tutorials in Latin, Greek, and mathematics.[5] While her father's clerical vocation had made philanthropic activities and small-scale social entertaining familiar, Langtry had scant experience or knowledge of the social etiquette and practices of fashionable metropolitan life. After an uneventful first year in London, a chance encounter with a Jersey acquaintance, Lord Ranelagh, launched Langtry into the fashionable bohemian circles he patronized and entertained. At garden and dinner parties, salons and balls, she encountered the artists, writers, and aristocrats who were to aid her in the creation of a public identity and spread her celebrity. By the close of the 1877 season, Langtry's dark-haired, violet-eyed beauty had secured her widespread fame and popularity. Moreover, as the acknowledged mistress of the Prince of Wales she had become a fixture on the guest lists of the British social calendar's most exclusive events.

Celebrity identities operate in a complex dialogical relationship with culture: as Jo Burr Margadant has noted, "no one 'invents' a self apart from the cultural notions available to them in a particular historical setting."[6] As a model, a mistress, an actress and a celebrity, Langtry maintained a persona rooted in rapidly evolving concepts of gender, popular entertainment, and commercial culture. In Langtry's era urbanization and industrialization were unsettling dominant ideologies and constructs of masculinity and femininity struggled to incorporate the changing roles of men and women in the modern city, while the growth of popular culture prompted new attempts to redefine and entrench a sustainable division between "high" and "low" cultural categories. Langtry's public identity distilled these debates, locating her as a symbol of a threatening "low," "feminized" celebrity culture.

Mid-Victorian gender classifications were underpinned by a belief in innate differences between men and women.[7] A set of domestic ideologies affiliated women with the private world of the home, marriage, and spirituality, ostracizing them from the worlds of politics, industry, and the embodied experiences of public and modern life. Yet this ideal of domestic femininity was inevitably troubled by its inherent tensions and inconsistencies. Women were "spiritual yet sexualized, the irresistible object of desire and a certain kind of especially contemplative subject"; the embodiment of a set of unsustainable dualities.[8] These internal tensions increased as the century

---

5. Laura Beatty, *Lillie Langtry: Manners, Masks and Morals* (London: Vintage, 2000), 21.
6. Jo Burr Margadant (ed.), *The New Biography: Performing Femininity in Nineteenth-Century France* (Berkeley: University of California Press, 2000), 2.
7. Sonya O. Rose, *Limited Livelihoods: Gender and Class in Nineteenth-Century England* (London: Routledge, 1992), 15.
8. Kathy Alexis Psomiades, *Beauty's Body: Femininity and Representation in British Aestheticism* (Stanford University Press, 1997), 6–8.

progressed and women became more necessary to commercial culture, both as workers and consumers. This construct of femininity — challenged and threatening to implode as the role of women changed — functioned as a particularly significant element of Langtry's celebrity identity. By 1877, she was sitting for Britain's most celebrated artists. At the same time, Langtry postcards, sketches, prints, and photographs filled London's shop windows, attracting crowds that blocked the pavements as they struggled to see and purchase the latest representations of London's newest celebrity. Langtry's face was ubiquitous: as she recalled in her autobiography, people were "so familiar with my features that wherever I went — to theatres, picture galleries, shops — I was actually mobbed."[9] Her features presented a recognized ideal of female beauty to aesthetes *and* to consumers: she was simultaneously an icon of femininity and a modern metropolitan woman. Symbolically, the public and the private collided in Langtry's image. This complex dichotomy was at the core of Langtry's success: as a beautiful middle-class woman and daughter of a clergyman, her background made her a paragon of feminine ideals. Yet her public profile, the consumption of her image and her extra-marital affairs clearly removed her from the private space of the home and rejected the sanctified state of marriage and the role of the wife. Langtry's social and celebrity status thus spanned the unsettling dualities of modern life.

The Lillie Langtry phenomenon was greeted with adoration and trepidation. The scale of her celebrity, the "magnetism of her living presence" and the extent of her social and cultural influence was to provoke wonder and concern well into the twentieth century.[10] In spite of her notoriety, her fan base was diverse: as *The Sketch* noted, "there are few women whose individuality appeals to a constituency so varied and so extensive."[11] The scale of the Langtry model of fame was new. Richard Schickel has suggested that "there was no such thing as celebrity prior to the beginning of the twentieth century," arguing that earlier well-known figures were successful individuals and it was to this success that they owed their fame.[12] Yet the construction and circulation of Langtry's celebrity disputes this. Prior to attaining fame Langtry had no social position and no vocation, as illustrated by the magazine *Moonshine*'s 1888 comment that "Mrs. Langtry seems to be on the way to a fortune, thanks to her good *start as a celebrity*" (my emphasis).[13] When viewed in relation to Schickel's assertion, Langtry's celebrity status

9. Lillie Langtry, *The Days I Knew: The Autobiography of Lillie Langtry*, 40–1. Published in 1925, Langtry's autobiography is an erratic, absorbing, and heavily edited account of her friendships, her celebrity, and the opulent social events that she attended in her heyday.
10. *The Sketch*, October 31, 1928. Clipping Lillie Langtry Biography File, V&A Theatre Collections.
11. *The Sketch*, August 23, 1899, 182.
12. Cited in Graeme Turner, *Understanding Celebrity* (London: Sage, 2004), 10–11.
13. *Moonshine*, June 23, 1888, 290.

appears historically anomalous: a significant and influential precursor to fame's manifestations and representations in the twentieth and twenty-first centuries. Considering the two categories of public identity that Langtry occupied — the professional beauty and the professional actress — offers an insight into the emergence of a mass celebrity culture, the pervasive anxieties prompted by celebrity women and a model of fame that continues to shape patterns of responses to celebrity culture today.

"Rooms of the Lily": The Professional Beauty and the Royal Academy[14]

Langtry was mobbed when she arrived at the Royal Academy exhibition's star-studded private viewing.[15] Her attendance was a coup for the event's organizers; her presence at any social occasion secured valuable column space in the press and the public's attention.[16] On this occasion, however, Langtry brought critical and social commentary, as well as crowds. During May 1878, Burlington House — the home of the Royal Academy and London's bastion of high culture and the visual arts — became another site for reflection on the cultural implications of a previously unknown Jersey girl's rapid ascent to fame, sparking an outpouring of press coverage that ranged from gentle satire to outright condemnation. At the height of this press commentary the comic magazine *Fun* published a satirical ode, "Among the Pictures," that illustrates the centrality of the Langtry craze. Inviting the reader to accept "the arm of poet Fun" and "seek the house of Burlington, where Mrs Langtry reigns supreme," the ode offers a guided tour of the exhibition's most notable works in five stanzas:

> What noble efforts here there be —
> What noble efforts for our good!
> The crowd's so great we cannot see
> "The Road to Ruin" if we would.
> This woolly picture, called "May Dew,"
> May dew for others — not for us;
> (Of Mrs Langtry's portrait, too,
> There's some appear to make a fuss).

At the conclusion of each stanza, the reader is returned to Langtry's image, with the ode concluding that "*Fun* is proud of British art [. . .], Once more it's nobly done its part, (And Mrs Langtry's over all)."[17] Characteristic of the humorous strand of commentaries in newspapers, popular journals

---

14. "London and Paris Gossip," *Trewman's Exeter Flying Post*, May 8, 1878, 8.
15. "London Gossip," *Hampshire Telegraph and Sussex Chronicle*, May 11, 1878, 3.
16. *The Newcastle Courant*, May 3, 1878, 6.
17. *Fun*, May 15, 1878, 205.

and comic magazines, *Fun*'s satirical response barely conceals the cultural anxieties that underpin it.

In this context, Royal Academy portraits of Langtry were interpreted as disquieting engagements with a new celebrity species — the professional beauty. Emerging from London's social circles, the professional beauties were a sensation of the late 1870s. Headed by Langtry and Mary "Patsy" Cornwallis-West (1835–1917), they achieved a level of quintessentially modern, metropolitan celebrity founded entirely on their beauty and the new set of economic, social, and technological conditions that fostered the burgeoning commercial photographic industry. By "contriv[ing] to combine the two important modern agencies of advertisement and photography in their thirst for admiration,"[18] professional beauties sat for mass-reproduced, affordable postcards that made their image familiar to spectators across Britain, America and the colonial outposts of the British Empire. While the visual image of the professional beauty dominated, she also behaved according to a definable set of characteristics — in private and in public. It was essential that she was married and that her beauty was affirmed by a panel of "fashionable men of the faster sort"; generally those who circulated around the Prince of Wales. She was impetuous and habitually subverted social codes: the professional beauty would happily be led into dinner by a host, at the expense of guests whose social rank was higher than her own; at house parties she would borrow a horse and eschew a gentle sidesaddle ride for a vigorous gallop through the surrounding villages; she would instigate practical jokes and start food fights at dinner. Ensconced in the social arena, she disrupted its behavioral norms and occasioned a shift in notions of women in the public gaze, securing "an attention which used to be accorded to royalty only [. . .] the privilege of being unblushingly stared at is no longer confined to the blood royal."[19]

For many, the professional beauties' public image and reputation rendered them unfitting subjects for a work of art. Langtry, Cornwallis-West and their contemporaries were not anonymous materializations of female beauty. Rather they were women with distinct and modern public identities whose images blurred the distinctions between portraiture and photography, art and commerce. Inevitably the intersections between women, commerce and attainability embodied by professional beauties evoked the spectre of the prostitute. The extramarital affairs many professional beauties were involved in were well known. The expensive gifts of jewellery and clothing they received were itemized by the press to support the claim that "the trade of a professional beauty must be an uncommonly paying one."[20] *What* the professional beauty was "trading" was the unspoken anxiety that haunted

---

18. "Professional Beauties," *Aberdeen Weekly Journal*, September 3, 1979, 2.
19. Reprinted in *Aberdeen Weekly Journal*, September 3, 1879, 2.
20. *Sheffield and Rotherham Independent*, September 14, 1878, 1.

these accounts. Across the Channel, Paris' renowned courtesans symbolized the French capital's image as the international hub of modernity's pleasures and leisure forms. London's professional beauties remained distinct from their continental cousins because of their foregrounded married status. Nonetheless, they occupied a liminal position between acceptability and unacceptability. Visually the professional beauties were icons of femininity; their appearances conformed to current ideals of physical form and fashion. In reality their behavior was renowned for contraventions of the codes and conducts associated with their gender.

The professional beauties' admirers did not only proffer gifts, they also brought notoriety, further public and press attention, and access to wider and more exclusive social circles. In this context Langtry was of particular interest to the press. While discretion, prompted by the fear of legal retribution, resulted in the absence of explicit references to Langtry's relationship with the Prince of Wales in newspapers and journals, their relationship was well known and considered to be instrumental in Langtry's social — and thus celebrity — success.[21] As the art critic and fiction writer Frederick Wedmore (1844–1921) noted slyly in his 1912 *Memories*, by 1880 "the cordial appreciation of Royalty had already done much to make Mrs Langtry famous."[22]

Concerns about Langtry's celebrity and the figure of the professional beauty were also projected onto the three artists who produced Langtry portraits for the 1878 Royal Academy exhibition. Popular portraiture drew upon emergent concepts of individuality and personality and was aligned with the mass reproduction of images by the postcard industry and print media. It became a site that was seen to be particularly susceptible to the problems and faults of society's developments, a genre at the whim and peril of fashion and popular culture. Unlike the moral narrative paintings popular at this time, Millais, Poynter, and Weigall's handling of their subject matter did not clearly intervene in, or critique, the troubling elements of metropolitan life it displayed. Indeed the artists' submissions appeared to endorse and celebrate London's new celebrity paradigm and critics focused on this, at the expense of detailed considerations of the portraits themselves.

Millais' image of Langtry, entitled "A Jersey Lily," proved so popular with visitors to the 1878 Academy exhibition that it "had to be roped around to preserve the portrait from injury by the crowd which constantly

---

21. Discretion was wise. In December 1879 Langtry and her husband sued the popular society journal *Town Talk* for libel. The fashionable weekly had stated explicitly, in print, that Langtry's husband had filed for divorce on the grounds of his wife's infidelity. The sociopolitical context is significant. Gossip concerning Langtry's affair with the Prince of Wales brought the royal family unwanted press attention. The skill of the actress's legal team was observed by the press, although no publication ventured to suggest in print who might be funding Langtry's defense. Adolphus Rosenberg, editor of *Town Talk*, was imprisoned for 18 months when his publication made mention of the affair, sending a stark warning to the press industry.

22. Frederick Wedmore, *Memories* (London: Methuen, 1912), 84–5.

surged about it."[23] Yet, in spite of (or perhaps because of) the portrait's public success, critics deemed the image's positive reception unwarranted. Several critics compared "A Jersey Lily" with the second Millais portrait in the exhibition, an image of the politician and social reformer "The Earl of Shaftesbury" (1801–1885). The latter was considered to be a superior work, if only because — as several publications note — the Langtry portrait was unfinished when it was first displayed. Its superiority, however, did not secure the public's attention. As the art critic for the *Daily News* noted "Mr Millais's portrait of Lord Shaftesbury [. . .] is far and away the finest portrait in the Academy [but] Lord Shaftesbury cannot expect to be as much talked about as Mrs Langtry."[24] Critical consensus was that it was easier for an artist to achieve success when their themes were beauty and celebrity; that less skill and originality were required if a portrait's subject already held the public's favor. Moreover, an assumption that the celebrity's popularity lowered the cultural worth of the image by association pervaded reactions to the Langtry portraits. They were interpreted as being tainted by the troubling status of their model. The images of Langtry that hung in Burlington House could not be separated from her celebrity identity in the modern city; the images were in constant dialogue with her fame and the set of critical and cultural responses it prompted. Beauties were certainly not new to the walls of the Royal Academy, but Langtry represented a *new* beauty, beauty that had been harnessed to celebrity culture in a burgeoning commercial leisure industry.

As a professional beauty Langtry was not a passive muse; she was an active creator of a public personality. While her appearance attracted artists and resulted in the first flurries of fame, it was her personality that sustained aesthetic and public interest in a celebrity image that she was to sustain and refresh over the next forty years. The perceived power of her influence and her ubiquitous presence came to represent the 1870s and 1880s' clearest and most troubling example of "para-social interaction." Press coverage and representations of Langtry's image made the celebrity seem accessible; they fostered a sense of intimacy "constructed through the mass media rather than direct experience and face to face interaction."[25] The prospect of Langtry as an attainable figure proved to be of particular concern to those who worried about her popularity with female spectators and consumers. Social commentators were keen to stress that Langtry's image and behavior should not influence, or form an aspiration for, other women. She was frequently used as a means of instructing other women: her name awakened the dangers of the overexposure of female celebrities and was used as a shorthand reference for anxieties concerning the role of women in the public life of the modern city. Writing during the Academy Exhibition of

23. Lillie Langtry, *The Days I Knew: The Autobiography of Lillie Langtry*, 50.
24. *Daily News*, May 4, 1878, 3.
25. Chris Rojek, *Celebrity* (London: Reaktion, 2001), 110.

1878, the "London Correspondent" for the *Western Mail* offered an overview of current press responses to Langtry coupled with sage advice for other women who aspired to the Jersey Lily's level of fame, concluding: "I should certainly advise other beauties, if they do not wish to vulgarise their name, to keep their photographs out of the shops, and to content themselves with two portraits per season in the Academy."[26] Such criticism and concern offered Langtry a challenge and a resource. By appropriating the archaic and modern models of femininity that haunted these commentaries and operated at their perimeters and in the spaces between them, she constructed a celebrity identity that endured, adapted and appealed to women: an identity that enabled Langtry the professional beauty to become Langtry the successful actress.

"The Langtry" Takes to the Stage

> Mrs. Langtry intended, we suppose, by this performance to put herself up for hire to the highest managerial bidder in the theatrical market, and therefore we are justified in strongly and honestly reminding her that, without positive genius, there is no royal road to eminence even in the histrionic art.[27]

In 1881 — five years after their arrival in London — Langtry and her husband were declared bankrupt. The couple were estranged and Langtry was heavily pregnant; her relationship with the Prince of Wales had faded and creditors had been called in to her London home. Langtry was forced to face her penury and explore her future options under the intense scrutiny of the public's gaze. Then — as now — the downfall of a celebrity attracted the fascination of both fans and critics. Acclaim as a professional beauty had brought Langtry fame, gifts, occasional royalties and a succession of wealthy lovers, but it had not secured her a significant personal income. With the need to earn paramount, Langtry turned to the commercial stage for, as *Punch* suggested, the theater presented a gainful financial pathway if she could manage the transition to actress successfully.

The context of Langtry's attempted transition was significant for the popular entertainment industry was flourishing in the last decades of the nineteenth century. Across America and Europe growing cities offered new urban sites and audiences, setting in motion a theater and music hall building boom. In Britain, the Theatres Act of 1843 had led to the emergence of a diverse range of modern entertainment spaces in London, carefully designed venues that had been purpose built or revamped to attract and cater for the metropolis's increasing population and to compete within an international leisure industry. Improved travel networks and advances in

---

26. "London Correspondence," *Western Mail*, May 31, 1878, 2.
27. *Punch*, December 24, 1881, 297.

communication technologies produced and multiplied bodies of spectators over and above urban resident populations. Tourists and commuters joined local citizens in the audiences of many venues, changing the spectatorial demographic.

Theater was at the heart of mid-Victorian society. As Baedeker's 1878 edition of *London and its Environs: A Handbook for Travellers* surmised, "a visit to the whole of the fifty theatres of London [. . .] would give the traveller a capital insight into the social life of the people."[28] The commercial stage reflected the lives of those it entertained and responded to their demands, desires, and fashions. For many spectators the appeal of the stage lay in its opulent spectacle, its contemporaneity, and the familiarity of its celebrity casts. The lure of the star performer formed a key factor in the success and longevity of many companies and productions. It is clear that there were obvious comparisons to be drawn between the roles of actress and professional beauty in late-Victorian Britain, and these were duly noted by the press. As *Bell's Life in London and Sporting Chronicle* reported: "[B]efore Mrs Langtry took to the regular boards she was already a practised actress upon the world's stage, and played one of the most difficult roles in the real-life modern comedy of manners."[29]

Langtry had won public favor, proved her ability to enthral large audiences and handled the day-to-day processes and ramifications of mass celebrity before she appeared as an actress. As an established celebrity she was ideal — and unusual — raw material for the commercial theater of the early 1880s. Nonetheless, she chose to make her theatrical debut outside London, on the amateur stage, at a small-scale charity event at Twickenham Town Hall. In the closing decades of the nineteenth century, charity and the stage were closely linked, with performers frequently working on- and off-stage to benefit charitable bodies and institutions. For Langtry the approved, public, amateur performance space that philanthropic activity had created was a crucial element in framing her identity as an actress. It simultaneously distanced her from enduring ideas about the morally dubious status of the professional actress, affirmed her middle-class status and offered a degree of protection from theater critics and social commentators. The pervasive connections between high-profile women and prostitution noted earlier were particularly strong in relation to the actress; they plagued women who opted for a stage career in the nineteenth century.[30] In the Victorian city anxieties about the increasing divergence between the domestic ideal of femininity and the role of urban women deepened the anxieties inscribed on the actress's body. As Tracy C. Davis has noted, "acting and whoring were

---

28. Karl Baedeker, *London and its Environs: A Handbook for Travellers* (London: Baedeker, 1887), 60.
29. *Bell's Life in London, and Sporting Chronicle,* January 21, 1882, 11.
30. See Kirsten Pullen, *Actresses and Whores: On Stage and in Society* (Cambridge: Cambridge University Press, 2005).

the occupations of self-sufficient women who plied their trade in public places."[31] For Langtry — a royal mistress — these associations were significant: she owed her celebrity to her status as a professional beauty and her salacious identity as a royal consort. By presenting her move into theater as a charitable act of amateur dramatics — a popular and approved pastime for society women — Langtry evaded some of the correlations that could have been drawn between her previous public identities and her new identity as an actress.

Langtry's amateur stage debuts were greeted by dissension. There was a general sense that to critique a performance given for charity was unfair. In Langtry's case this was complicated by the consensus that it "appear[ed] to be an open secret that the lady's metropolitan debut as an amateur took the form of a trial to ascertain her ability, capacity, and fitness for the career of a professional actress."[32] In this context, a professional critical response was needed, albeit a tempered one. Overall the reviews were gracious and guarded, a tone that immediately changed on the confirmation that the professional beauty was to become a professional actress. Shortly after her Twickenham appearance, Langtry agreed to take part in a second charity event. Ostensibly another amateur performance, this second appearance effectively constituted her professional stage launch. London's well-known actor-manager couple, Squire and Lady Bancroft (1841–1926 and 1839–1921), the proprietors of the fashionable, West End Haymarket Theatre, had agreed to host the Royal General Theatrical Fund's annual benefit matinee. On this occasion, Langtry played Kate Hardcastle in *The School for Scandal*, taking on a popular role for contemporary actresses and appearing alongside a cast of celebrated, professional actors. Her first Haymarket audience was a microcosm of fashionable society, headed by the Prince and Princess of Wales. Press hype had surrounded her appearance and a four hundred pound profit was made from the subsequent demand for tickets. In the week leading up to the performance, seats in the stalls were selling at ten guineas apiece and rumors flourished that disreputable individuals had block-booked seats and were now selling them at a five hundred percent profit.[33] Langtry's earliest theatrical appearances occurred in a space between the amateur and professional, and the private and the public: liminal terrain that mapped the further complication of her public identity caused by her decision to take to the stage.

Critical responses to Langtry's second performance judged it mediocre, but the acclaim she won for it secured her a professional contract with the Bancrofts.

---

31. Tracy C. Davis, *Actresses as Working Women: Their Social Identity in Victorian Culture* (London: Routledge, 1991), 100.
32. "The Stage," *Bell's Life in London and Sporting Chronicle*, December 17, 1881, 11.
33. *The County Gentleman: Sporting Gazette and Agricultural Journal*, December 17, 1881, 1341.

Rumors concerning the "absurd" salary she was receiving abounded in the press. Figures varying from sixty to one hundred pounds a week, to a pay packet equal to that of the prime minister were bounced back and forth.[34] On one thing journalists and critics concurred. Langtry's engagement — and its cost — had nothing to do with her talent and everything to do with economics. Bancroft "is a man of business," asserted one drama critic, "and it may be assumed that Mrs Langtry's engagement rests on some commercial principles, on the same principles, indeed, which induced Mr Bancroft to make his theatre comfortable to sit in and agreeable to look upon."[35] In the eyes of many, the entrepreneurial manager was simply responding to the whim of the public by hiring Langtry. As *Reynolds's Newspaper* disparagingly concluded, "silly flatterers" have "persuaded [Langtry] that she is a born actress," and her success was merely an illustration of "the follies of which fashion can be guilty."[36]

To assume that fashion's follies were sufficient to secure and maintain a stage career was to underestimate the competitive complexity of London's theater industry. In the case of Langtry, the critics' sense that as long as her beauty continued to seduce the capital she would remain onstage was misplaced. By May 1882 the Bancrofts had released her from her contract at the Haymarket Theatre. Langtry's novelty value as an actress in London was fading and later in the year she went on her first provincial tour, appearing in a repertoire of classic and new material and offering Britain's other major cities the opportunity to see Langtry the actress. The experience was liberating; selecting roles offered Langtry the opportunity to "be my own manager, my own mistress, and free from unaccustomed control, changed my point of view entirely."[37] Later the same year she returned briefly to London, appearing as Rosalind in *As You Like It* and in *An Unequal Match* at the Imperial Theatre, to average reviews. In October 1882, she set sail for New York and remained in America for the next two years undertaking extensive tours of the country. Langtry spent the rest of her career between Britain and America, touring until 1913 in a stage career that spanned four decades. Yet, in spite of her enduring stage success, Langtry never escaped her connections with the world of the professional beauty and the accompanying conviction that she was a cultural interloper who was only interested in the financial rewards offered by the theater. Her celebrity status constrained and shaped the critical reception of her work, revealing a pervasive tension surrounding women, financial independence, business acumen and celebrity.

Funny Folks laid out the challenges Langtry faced early on in her stage

---

34. *The County Gentleman: Sporting Gazette and Agricultural Journal,* January 7, 1882, 5; *Moonshine,* December 31, 1881, 314.
35. "The Stage," *Bell's Life in London, and Sporting Chronicle,* January 21, 1882, 11.
36. *Reynolds's Newspaper,* January 1, 1882, 5.
37. Lillie Langtry, *The Days I Knew: The Autobiography of Lillie Langtry,* 149.

career. "The probability is that the public, should the Queen of 'Pro' Beauties become an actress, will think much more of her looks than her acting." "It will be for Mrs L. to show that she has positive as well as 'negative' attractions."[38] The identification of Langtry's looks as "negative" attractions was accurate; her public role as a beauty dictated responses to her performances and directed the roles that she was offered. Many critics viewed her performances as a costume parade; a pageant of beauty. *Pick Me Up*'s response to *The Queen of Manoa* at the Haymarket Theatre in 1892 (a decade after her stage debut) noted that it was "distinctly modern" in many ways, but that it "may nevertheless be considered as a costume-piece as far as the chief performer was concerned, since it afforded Mrs Langtry the opportunity to introduce four new dresses, a dainty wrapper, a diamond tiara, and some second-rate acting."[39] The focus on spectacle and costume design was characteristic of the popular entertainments of the day; neither the role nor the costumes were specific to Langtry. Nonetheless, reports of Langtry's acting throughout the 1880s and 1890s struggled to present anything other than a walking, talking, postcard image, available in the flesh for the price of a ticket.

The impact of these negative connections between Langtry's beauty and her acting can be traced in associations between her identity and commercial culture. The success of her stage career came to be judged primarily on its considerable financial rewards. By 1882 "Mrs Langtry [was] literally coining money," reported the comic magazine *Judy*, "they say her net profit one week amounted to over £1,400."[40] A cartoon printed by the journal in a slightly later issue characterized current opinion of Langtry's position as the embodiment of commercial theater versus cultural worth. The actress is shown wearing her trademark silk toque hat with a grim expression on her face and clutching two large money bags each marked £100,000. The caption made direct reference to current plans to form a vocational School of Dramatic Art, supported by many actor-managers and minor aristocrats: "They want an Academy of Acting! What to learn? Not to make money."[41]

The Jersey Lily's success — the culmination of a celebrity culture that enabled a stage career with average talent and no training — was read as symptomatic of the mass culture of Langtry's day: a threat to "high" culture and the aesthetics of taste that were represented by the vision of a School of Dramatic Art. These enduring prejudices and assumptions surfaced again in the prevailing sense that Langtry was suited to comedy, and not tragedy. Of her role as Lady Teazle in *The School for Scandal* (Prince's Theatre, London, 1885), the well-known critic Austin Brereton noted that "it would be idle to

---

38. *Funny Folks*, February 5, 1881, 35.
39. *Pick-Me-Up*, October 15, 1892, 33.
40. *Judy*, August 2, 1882, 57.
41. *Judy*, August 23, 1882, 88.

And yet they want an Academy of Acting!
What to learn? Not to make money.

Figure 1.1 **"What to learn? Not to make money."** An 1882 cartoon of Lillie Langtry.

suggest that she made a distinct dramatic success in the part." Nonetheless, "her charm of voice and manner certainly captivated the spectators. [. . .] [I]n short the comedy of Lady Teazle's character was quite excellently shown by Mrs Langtry, but the dramatic side of the character was completely ignored.[42] The guarded praise adheres to the sense that Langtry was representative of low culture: she could manage comedy, but not the intellectual remit of theatrical tragedy. Wider value judgments about celebrity and culture reverberate in the comment, ideas that echo the sentiments expressed by art critics that Millais's choice of a professional beauty as a model had made it easier for him to produce a successful portrait.

Langtry appealed to a new, wider audience; she embraced the new mass entertainment industry, increased representation from different audience members in theatres and unsettled the cultural norms surrounding theatre-going. Alongside the cartoon of Langtry and her money bags, *Judy* noted that:

> So Mrs Langtry, although she "can't act" as all the clever ones kept on saying, has already made a fortune [. . .] I know for a fact that, during her tour, many people have gone to the theatre to see her, who have never before gone to theatres, whatever attraction may have been offered.[43]

Like the majority of actors of her day, Langtry succeeded because her acting skills were combined with beauty, notoriety, and keen business sense. Unlike many she did not seek to conceal her affiliations with the period's new commercial industries. By aligning herself with the public, rather than society's

---

42. Austin Brereton, *Dramatic Notes: A Year Book of the Stage* (London: Carson and Comerford, 1886), 11.
43. *Judy*, August 23 1882, 88.

self-appointed "clever ones," Langtry's social and cultural influence grew throughout the last three decades of the nineteenth century. It extended beyond the readers who followed her movements in the press and the spectators who watched her onstage and offstage to include the consumers who bought merchandise that affiliated them with their idol.

"The Greatest Beautifier in the World": Lillie Powder and the Langtry Brand

Langtry used her image to inspire and market commercial products from early in her celebrity career and "The Langtry" was a familiar brand by the end of the 1870s. Langtry merchandise spanned the fashion, health, and cosmetics industries and included dresses, accessories, and beauty products that she created, inspired, or endorsed. These items drew on and reinforced Langtry's identity. Their commercial success depended on a press and public obsession with the fashions followed by Britain's leading female celebrities. Detailed descriptions of gowns and accessories worn by society's leading ladies were commonplace in newspapers and magazines, but Langtry's outfits rapidly began to receive more column space than those of her contemporaries. A plain, black gown had consistently characterized her early London social appearances. It was this "outsider" style that Millais had immortalized in "A Jersey Lily," but glamorous and opulent designs quickly became more customary for Langtry. There was a degree of originality and novelty to Langtry's dress in the late 1870s and the 1880s that drew frequent comment. Although she wore well-known designers, including Worth and Doucet, she opted for bold colors, including scarlets and blues, close-fitting designs and unusual fabrics and ornamentation. Her hair remained undressed, by contemporary standards, tied loosely in a low chignon and unornamented with jewels, feathers or fabrics. Rather than showcasing current trends, the designs Langtry favored were statement pieces; as she told an interviewer for *The Sketch* in 1893, "I prefer to have something original and individual to myself about my gowns."[44]

Langtry's sartorial style conveyed an individuality that enhanced her status as an icon. The originality of her choices reflected and played with her ambiguous social position: while they were sufficiently distinct to be admired and of note, they were not so removed from the fashions of the day to suggest a complete transgression of current fashions and ideas surrounding dress and femininity. This appealed to her female fans and press reports reveal an aspirational relationship between Langtry and late nineteenth-century women that is inconsistent with the tone of caution adopted by social commentators debating her celebrity. For many women Langtry was a role model, if not in behavior then certainly in appearance. In 1885 the *Pall*

---

44. *The Sketch*, February 8, 1893, 67.

Mall Gazette recorded that the peacock-feather trimmed, green plush dress Langtry chose for one event "seemed to reflect its colour in the eyes of all the ladies who beheld it."[45] The following year, the *Daily News* noted that the actress's dark blue velvet brocade and brown bonnet "was a sight to inspire one sex with delight and the other with despair."[46] Press reports suggest that women envied, and strove to emulate, Langtry's "look": they focused primarily on the elements of her identity that they could emulate, rather than aspiring to achieve the beauty that she was famed for.

Langtry set a standard for modern dress, eschewing trends to demarcate an individual style, but her influence on contemporary fashion and women was not restricted to the admiration and emulation of her outfits. Her style experimentations also led to the creation, production, and marketing of new designs. Sixty years before "star imitation" drove America's ready-to-wear fashion industries, British and American women could create the "Langtry look" for themselves. As with the Hollywood-inspired fashion industry that was to flourish in the 1930s, consumers did not attempt to replicate Langtry's image completely. The "practicality as much as the frivolity" of emulating her celebrity was stressed.[47] Small items and accessories — shoes, hats, jackets, and jewellery — became the best-selling items of Langtry merchandise: accessories that acknowledged the celebrity and announced the wearer's "up-to-dateness" as a fan.

The most popular and enduring of these items was the Langtry hat. Originally a small, silk toque dressed with feathers, velvet and plush versions of the hat became popular in Britain and America in the 1870s and remained fashionable throughout the 1880s. Department stores and millineries offered the accessories in a range of fabrics and colors, at different prices, in store or by mail order. Buying and wearing the Langtry hat enabled women to align themselves with the professional beauty, and later with the actress. The fashion industry understood the multifarious nature of Langtry's fan base and the potential range of consumers for merchandise that was stamped with her name and style. The hat's wide availability suggests that a diverse body of consumers in different locations with a range of incomes sought to adopt this signifier of fashion, celebrity, and aspiration.

Alongside the success and longevity of Langtry merchandise the actress worked with the new advertising industry, modeling for advertising campaigns and endorsing health and beauty products. Her extended contract as the face of Pears soap in the 1880s and 1890s remains the most familiar example of her advertising work. Pears was a modern company that

---

45. *Pall Mall Gazette*, May 2, 1885, 3.
46. *Daily News*, May 3, 1886, 2.
47. Charlotte Cornelia Herzog and Jane Marie Gaines, "Puffed Sleeves Before Tea-Time: Joan Crawford, Adrian and Women Audiences," in Christine Gledhill (ed.), *Stardom: Industry of Desire* (London: Routledge, 1991), 74–91, 74, 83. See also Jackie Stacey, *Star Gazing: Hollywood Cinema and Female Spectatorship* (London: Routledge, 1994).

embraced the new advertising industry and explored revolutionary ideas about brand image and the potential of celebrity endorsement.[48] For a period of over twenty years Pears used written commendations, photographs, and prints of Langtry, depending on her celebrity to sustain and increase its leading market share. In America she entered into a similar relationship with Hunters, advertising their Invisible Face Powder.[49] In both campaigns Langtry was presented as a "natural" beauty: Pears Soap and Hunters Invisible Face Powder were marketed as opposites of the make up and artifice associated with the stage. Kathy Peiss has noted that patent cosmetics "quite literally represented the corrosive effects of the market economy" at the end of the nineteenth century. "Associated with social climbers and urban sophisticates" they represented a sector of society more concerned "with making a good appearance than leading a virtuous life."[50] Pears Soap and Hunters Invisible Face Powder sought to simultaneously offer a modern brand and counter any dubious associations by offering patent products that foregrounded a "natural," often domestic, image of female beauty, supplied by a leading actress.

Langtry's relationship with Pears and with Hunters were symbiotic. Through endorsement, Langtry was positioned as a modern, international star. She was aligned with products that emphasized an accepted "femininity" that was distinct from the image of the actress, and her appeal was widened still further. In 1899 she developed her involvement with the health and beauty industries by becoming directly involved in the marketing and sales of an existing product, "Lillie Powder." This soothing and nourishing colored face powder had been available since the mid-1880s, marketed by William

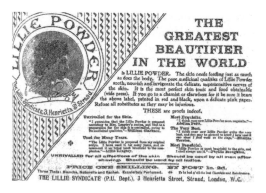

Figure 1.2 **A 1900 advertisement for Langtry's cosmetic product "Lillie Powder."**

48. *The Graphic*, January 15, 1887, 71.
49. Kathy Peiss, *Hope in a Jar: The Making of America's Beauty Culture* (Henry Holt and Company, 1998), 48.
50. Ibid., 20–2.

Clarkson, the proprietor of a theatrical wigmakers just off the Strand. Aimed at the professional theatrical market, it was advertised primarily in the theatrical trade journal *The Era* throughout the 1880s and 1890s and proved popular with an "army of actresses."[51] Langtry's involvement with Lillie Powder marked a shift in its brand identity and an attempt to increase its consumer base. Under the control of Langtry's newly formed Lillie Syndicate (a company that promoted merchandise directly connected to her), the product was advertised and endorsed as "pure Langtry." It was sold as a powder that she had used for many years, "prepared from [her] original recipe." William Clarkson remained involved in the enterprise, but now the theatrical wigmaker was attributed with the wisdom of the chemist as he spoke of the health benefits of "Lillie Powder" (see Figure 1.2). Advertisements were sealed with Langtry's profile, intersecting with the imagery that was being funded and distributed by Pears and Hunters.[52] Having worked with the masters of modern advertising, Langtry also employed testimonies from other celebrity performers including the actresses Ellaline Terriss (1872–1971) and Phyllis Broughton (1862–1926) and the opera singer Adelina Patti (1843–1919).

The creation, purchase, and use of Lillie Powder reflects Kathy Peiss's assertion that the emergence of beauty culture represented a "system of meaning [...] that helped women navigate the changing conditions of modern social experience."[53] The advertising strategies employed to market Lillie Powder after the formation of the Lillie Syndicate clearly aligned everyday women with celebrities. Alongside the other available Langtry merchandise, the powder discloses the complexities of the relationships between women fans and female celebrities in mid- to late Victorian Britain. The objects and products inspired by the Langtry brand brought together facets of Langtry's celebrity and made them desirable, attainable, and appropriate for many women fans and consumers. Charlotte Herzog and Jane Gaines have noted that the fashions inspired by early Hollywood cinema, "worked to elicit women's participation in star [...] myth-making."[54] This echoed the dynamics at play in the purchase and use of Langtry merchandise, when consumers were involved not only in the creation of star myths, but in the creation and modification of myths about women.

---

51. *The Licensed Victuallers' Mirror,* December 2, 1890, 570.
52. *Pick-Me-Up,* September 1, 1900, iii.
53. Kathy Peiss, *Hope in a Jar: The Making of America's Beauty Culture,* 6.
54. Charlotte Cornelia Herzog and Jane Marie Gaines, "Puffed Sleeves Before Tea-Time: Joan Crawford, Adrian and Women Audiences," 87.

A Woman More Famous for Beauty than For Either Talent or Virtue[55]

Amid fragile, threatened, and consequently more fluid, constructs of femininity, Lillie Langtry constructed a celebrity identity that offered access to a nexus of ideas about culture, society, and engagements between fans and celebrities in mid- to late Victorian Britain. As an astute businesswoman, her involvement in advertising and merchandising was accompanied by a broadly increased amount of theatrical management activity during the 1880s and 1890s; organizing tours, leasing theaters and commissioning plays. Nonetheless, Langtry's celebrity identity, public image, and private life have removed her from the circle of women who have been acknowledged as changing notions about femininity and women during this period, Indeed, Langtry has been frequently disregarded, or dismissed, by her contemporaries and by those who have followed her. Her celebrity has been classified as ephemeral and disposable; the folly of the Victorian mass audience; a nostalgic whim.

An established star when she took to the stage, Langtry extended and transformed her celebrity identity as a professional beauty to fit her new career as an actress. She appalled many of her contemporary female performers; in particular those actresses and managers whose work has been reclaimed and identified as proto-feminist. For them Langtry was viewed as using a distinct construct of femininity; manifesting an identity that was understood to be at odds with, and at worst a danger to, the identity of the professional actress. The actress-manager Elizabeth Robins (1862–1952) clearly aligned herself with this view, noting in her autobiography *Both Sides of the Curtain* that in spite of Oscar Wilde's advice that she emulate her contemporary Langtry, "I obviously couldn't emulate Mrs Langtry. I didn't want to. I wanted to act."[56] For Robins and for others committed to improving the status of the actress and increasing her business and artistic opportunities, Langtry could be — and generally was — seen as a threat to their advances.

Considering the Langtry myth alongside evidence of Langtry's role as a professional beauty, actress and commercial entrepreneur offers a unique insight into an influential late nineteenth-century female celebrity who existed and thrived at the boundaries of contemporary female representation. The Hollywood film industry is regularly cited as the point at which a recognizable celebrity culture emerged, but this industry absorbed and reflected an existing celebrity culture from the popular stage. Indeed, many actresses from the first generation of Hollywood stars performed on both stage and screen.[57] As a pre-celluloid mass celebrity, with an international level of fame, Langtry carved out a role for female celebrity that was filled by the next generation of actresses and film stars. The legacy of her identity

---

55. "London Correspondence," *Western Mail*, May 31, 1878, 2.
56. Elizabeth Robins, *Both Sides of the Curtain* (London: Heinemann, 1940), 16.
57. See Graeme Turner, *Understanding Celebrity*, 12.

perpetuates as the concerns her presence evoked persist. Indeed the industrial and cultural feminization of the "ambiguity/instability of contemporary celebrity" that Holmes and Negra argue for in this volume's introduction is rooted in the fame of Langtry and her late nineteenth-century contemporaries.[58] Assumptions about beauty and talent, judgments of financial success, and the low cultural status assigned to contemporary female celebrities continue to mark responses to their fame. While the personalities, their audiences, and the media that create and sustain fame have changed, patterns of female celebrity culture have persisted throughout history: the concerns of our mid-Victorian ancestors remain — in many ways — peculiarly familiar today.

Bibliography

Armstrong, Nancy. "Modernism's Iconophobia and What it Did to Gender," *Modernism/Modernity* 5(2), 1998: 47–75.

Baedeker, Karl. *London and its Environs: A Handbook for Travellers*. London: Baedeker, 1887.

Beatty, Laura. *Lillie Langtry: Manners, Masks and Morals*. London: Vintage, 2000.

Brereton, Austin. *Dramatic Notes: A Year Book of the Stage*. London: Carson and Comerford, 1886.

Davis, Tracy C. *Actresses as Working Women: Their Social Identity in Victorian Culture*. London: Routledge, 1991.

Gale, Maggie B. and John Stokes (eds). *The Cambridge Companion to the Actress*. Cambridge: Cambridge University Press, 2007.

Gledhill, Christine (ed.). *Stardom: Industry of Desire*. London: Routledge, 1991.

Herzog, Charlotte Cornelia and Jane Marie Gaines, "Puffed Sleeves Before Tea-Time: Joan Crawford, Adrian and Women Audiences," in Christine Gledhill (ed.), *Stardom: Industry of Desire*. London: Routledge, 1991, 74–91.

Langtry, Lillie. *The Days I Knew: The Autobiography of Lillie Langtry*. London: Futura, 1978.

"London and Paris Gossip," *Trewman's Exeter Flying Post*, May 8, 1878, 8.

"London Correspondence," *Western Mail*, May 31, 1878, 2.

"London Gossip," *Hampshire Telegraph and Sussex Chronicle*, May 11, 1878, 3.

Luckhurst, Mary and Jane Moody (eds). *Theatre and Celebrity in Britain, 1660–2000*. Basingstoke: Palgrave Macmillan, 2005.

Margadant, Jo Burr (ed.). *The New Biography: Performing Femininity in Nineteenth-Century France*. Berkeley: University of California, 2000.

Modjeska, Helena. *Memories and Impressions of Helena Modjeska*. London: Macmillan, 1910.

Negra, Diane and Su Holmes. Introduction to *Genders* 48 (2008). Available at: http://www.genders.org/g48/g48_negraholmes.html (accessed November 8, 2010).

Peiss, Kathy. *Hope in a Jar: The Making of America's Beauty Culture*. New York: Henry Holt and Company, 1998.

"Professional Beauties," *Aberdeen Weekly Journal*, September 3, 1979, 2.

Psomiades, Kathy Alexis. *Beauty's Body: Femininity and Representation in British Aestheticism*. Stanford, Stanford University Press, 1997.

Pullen, Kirsten. *Actresses and Whores: On Stage and in Society*. Cambridge: Cambridge University Press, 2005.

Robins, Elizabeth. *Both Sides of the Curtain*. London: Heinemann, 1940.

Rojek, Chris. *Celebrity*. London: Reaktion, 2001.

Rose, Sonya O. *Limited Livelihoods: Gender and Class in Nineteenth-Century England*. London: Routledge, 1992.

---

58. Diane Negra and Su Holmes, "Introduction," *Genders*, 48 (2008).

Stacey, Jackie. *Star Gazing: Hollywood Cinema and Female Spectatorship.* London: Routledge, 1994.

"The Stage," *Bell's Life in London and Sporting Chronicle,* December 17, 1881, 11.

Turner, Graeme. *Understanding Celebrity.* London: Sage, 2004.

Wedmore, Frederick. *Memories.* London: Methuen, 1912.

2

Helen Keller, Hollywood and Political Celebrity

ABIGAIL SALERNO

THIS ESSAY WILL CONSIDER the deaf and blind American author and activist Helen Keller (1880–1968) as a celebrity within modern media culture, a woman who used the media of her time — especially film and photography, personal appearance and public speaking — to share her radical, socialist politics with the American public. To examine Keller's political celebrity, I will draw upon recent scholarly work in film studies, not just because Keller appeared on film throughout her life, in two feature films and countless newsreels, but because film studies emphasizes the ways in which public culture is and was, in the Progressive Era, intimately dependent upon the presence and performance of the human body. Keller's political speeches and public statements, and the two films in which Keller performed as herself, do not reveal the "real" Keller any more than the better-known (and better-preserved) autobiography *Story of My Life,* which established its author as a disabled prodigy, sentimental heroine and incurable optimist. However, the speeches and films, and the performances that they index, demonstrate the ways in which Keller, throughout her life, participated in a celebritized popular culture and a political culture in which the body mediated public sentiment. Keller's celebrity body was understood in various ways throughout her lifetime: as an innocent, childish body to be saved, as a heroic (and still childish body) to be emulated, and as a body that fascinated the public with its extraordinary abilities and disabilities. Keller mobilized this last incarnation — her extraordinary body — in the silent film *Deliverance* (1919) and in her socialist speeches from the same period. She used her body — physically and metaphorically — to support her political commitments and this strategy aligned her not only with the labor movements she advocated for, but also with feminist activists of the period, whose bodies also performed extraordinary political acts.

The Politics of Helen Keller's Body, 1880 to the Present

At the age of 28, Helen Keller published a volume of essays entitled *The World I Live In*. The essays had been commissioned by the popular *Century Magazine* and published serially from 1904–1908. Relative to the earlier *Story of My Life*, the narrative of Keller's early childhood education, the essays of *The World I Live In* are more contemplative; it was, at the time, considered her most philosophical work and it has since been described as phenomenological.[1] But in her preface to the collection Keller explains her frustration with the autobiographical essays:

> Mr. Gilder [the editor of the *Century Magazine*] suggested the articles, and I thank him for his kind interest and encouragement. But he must also accept the responsibility which goes with my gratitude. For it is owing to his wish and that of other editors that I talk so much about myself. Every book is in a sense autobiographical. But while other self-recording creatures are permitted at least to seem to change the subject, apparently nobody cares what I think of the tariff, the conservation of our natural resources, or the conflicts which revolve around the name of Dreyfus. If I offer to reform the educational system of the world, my editorial friends say, "That's interesting. But will you please tell us what idea you had of goodness and beauty when you were six years old?"[2]

Keller's frustration, here directed at the magazine editor, is part of her life-long negotiation of a celebrity that was defined by, and dependent on, the public's fascination with her deaf and blind body. The essays in *The World I Live In* are Keller's adult reflections on sensory experiences, art and nature, and intimate friendships and the apparently apolitical nature of the work was, Keller suggests, unsatisfying to her as a college-educated woman who was increasingly engaged in the politics of the Progressive Era.

Keller had serious political ambitions in the first decades of the twentieth century, and this essay will investigate the connections between this political life and Keller's celebrity. Disability studies has explored the legacy of Keller's political career and Keller has been described as a "problematic icon,"[3] troublesome to both the politics of her time, and ours. Historian Kim Nielsen explains that, in her lifetime, Keller was routinely denied claims of civic fitness, as a person with disabilities and as a woman. Much of Keller's writing from the early decades of the twentieth century, like the preface to *The World I Live In*, contains explicit arguments for her right to write (and speak) as an informed political subject. Nielsen also sees Keller as

---

1. Diana Fuss, *The Sense of an Interior* (New York: Routledge, 2004), 118.
2. Helen Keller, *The World I Live In* (1908; reprint, New York: New York Review of Books, 2003), 7.
3. Liz Crow, "Helen Keller: Rethinking a Problematic Icon," *Disability and Society*, 15(6), (2000), 845.

intentionally isolating herself from other people with disabilities, and their communities and movements, and for Nielsen, the political consequences of this are far-reaching:

> Keller's isolation not only contributed to her inability to successfully politicize disability as an issue of rights, prejudice or discrimination, but also limited her actions. She neither experienced, nor saw herself as part of a minority or oppressed group, only as an individual who had difficulties . . . For her to have argued that blind people comprised a political category comparable to class, and that the myriad of disability experiences resulted in a shared political identity, would have been truly revolutionary.[4]

According to Nielsen, Keller did not contribute to the emerging identity politics of the period, and, in addition to this, Nielsen suggests, the politics that Keller did choose to participate in — her radical, socialist politics — further isolated her from mainstream political activity.

Literary historian Mary Klages sees Keller as liminal, rather than isolated, living in a multi-medial context of sentimental fiction and political reality, during a historical transition from Victorian to modern discourses of disability. For Klages, "Keller, and the popular cultural accounts of her, demonstrated her capacity to arouse others' concern, her power to act to relieve others' suffering, and her successful efforts to establish herself, through autobiographical writing, as an authorial subject."[5] According to Klages, sentimental Victorian representations of disability confined disabled subjects to only the first of these activities, arousing others' concern and inspiring others' action, without political (or emotional and/or intellectual) agency of their own. Scholars of sentiment and the public sphere, including Jane Tompkins and Lauren Berlant,[6] have focused their attention on nineteenth-century American literary culture, the contributions of women to that culture, and the legacy that culture has given to the twentieth century. The "sentimental power" that Klages recognizes in Keller has been identified as a gendered form of power that brought women into the nineteenth-century public sphere. Indeed, women had a significant role in the philanthropic culture that contributed to Keller's education and that Keller, in turn, contributed to as a woman and a person with disabilities.

Keller's literary work is, for contemporary scholars, less fraught than her

---

4. Kim Nielsen, *The Radical Lives of Helen Keller* (New York: New York University Press, 2004), 11.

5. Mary Klages, *Woeful Afflications: Disability and Sentimentality in Victorian America* (Philadelphia: University of Pennsylvania Press, 1999), 177.

6. Jane Tompkins, *Sensational Designs: The Cultural Work of American Fiction, 1790–1960* (New York: Oxford University Press, 1986) and Lauren Berlant, *The Female Complaint: The Unfinished Business of Sentimentality in American Culture* (Durham, NC: Duke University Press, 2008).

political legacy. Author and disabilities scholar Georgina Kleege describes *The World I Live In* as "a book that chafes at the shortcomings of the genre [Keller] helped to invent, exposes the limitations of the language that is her chosen medium, and experiments with a new approach to self-representation that was well in advance of her times."[7] Keller's literary style, and the possibilities and limitations of her political contributions comprise part of my analysis here, but this essay will study Keller primarily as a media celebrity. Celebrity has been described as "a product of capitalism [with] a particular connection to the historical evolution of public visibility, and its relations with the mass media and changing notions of achievement"[8] and this definition emphasizes important elements of Keller's turn-of-the-last-century celebrity. Each of her educational achievements was widely reported and publicized in the mass media, while, at the same time, her educational opportunities were deeply indebted to the industrializing wealth of the nation, and the philanthropy this wealth created. As a child, Keller gained a public visibility that she later used, in the 1910s especially, for her own political purposes, which at that time centered upon a pacifist, socialist agenda.

Helen Keller's childhood image — posed photographs of a small girl with curly hair, dressed in white lace, spelling with her teacher, sitting with her dog — circulated widely after 1887, when her education began with the arrival of Anne Sullivan at the Keller home. The headmaster of the Perkins Institution for the Blind, where Sullivan, who lived with visual impairment all her life, had been educated, meticulously chronicled Keller's education in the Institution's annual reports from 1887–1895. Alexander Graham Bell, a mentor of Sullivan's, sent a photograph of Helen Keller and a copy of one of her letters to him (Sullivan made letter writing a key part of Keller's early education) to a New York newspaper in 1888. An autobiographical account of Keller's childhood — an early version of *The Story of My Life* — was published by the popular young people's magazine *Youth's Companion* in 1894. This was only a fraction of the media attention she commanded, and from these representations emerged Keller's early celebrity persona, that of an innocent young girl, afflicted by sensory disabilities, saved by educational and institutional intervention, and heroic in her own efforts to communicate.

Mary Klages sees numerous fictional Victorian precursors that anticipated Helen's childhood celebrity. In novels for young girls, like *Elsie Dinsmore* (a series published between 1867–1905) and *What Katy Did* (1872), young heroines (often illustrated in striking detail) live through illness, triumph into

---

7. Georgina Kleege, "Helen Keller and the Empire of the Normal," *American Quarterly*, 52(2), (2000): 325.

8. Su Holmes and Sean Redmond, "Introduction: Understanding Celebrity Culture," in *Framing Celebrity* (London: Routledge, 2006), 11.

true, generous womanhood, and teach readers a lesson in empathy; Leslie Fiedler identified this body of literature as part of the "Good Good Girl" genre.[9] It was in such a media environment that Keller's celebrity emerged, and the public's fascination with her early childhood persisted in media representations all her life; the film *The Miracle Worker* (1962), starring Patty Duke as 7-year-old Helen was made when Keller was 82 years old.[10]

Keller's early celebrity depended, financially, on late nineteenth-century philanthropy and its ideological commitment to education. Keller left home to attend the Perkins Institute in Boston and, later, the Wright-Humason School for the Deaf in New York City. Mark Twain contributed to a fund for her college tuition at Radcliffe, as did other intellectual celebrities and philanthropic leaders of the period. Klages understood the education of Helen Keller (and, before her, deaf and blind Laura Bridgman, who was also educated at Perkins) as subject to "a combination of Christian ethos of charity and sympathy and the Enlightenment interest in education and improvement [which] resulted in [a] new context and cultural meaning for disability, that of suffering humans trapped within defective bodies and needing to be rescued by the earnest efforts of educators."[11] Keller acted as both the object of, and an active political subject within, the changing philanthropic ideologies of this period. In 1903, following the publication of *The Story of My Life*, and just before her graduation from college, Keller wrote "My Future as I See It" for the *Ladies Home Journal*, an essay that outlined the possible roles that she, as an educated woman with "limitations," might assume in the political life of the Progressive Era. Keller lists, among other possibilities for her future career, teaching, writing, promoting a system of education that will allow for the "self-support" of the blind, and founding a "magazine of high quality and varied interest like the best periodicals for those who see." As a young woman, Keller imagined that she would, through education, liberate herself and others, from their defective bodies.

But her early political ambitions extended beyond disability issues. In the same essay, Keller also describes, at length, the appeal of settlement work,

> I hear every day of young girls who leave their homes and pleasures to dwell among the poor, and brighten and dignify their lives, and the impulse within me to follow their example seems at times too strong for me to restrain.[12]

---

9. Leslie Fiedler, *Love and Death in the American Novel* (New York: Dell, 1966).
10. *The Miracle Worker* was originally written as a play. At the time of writing (Spring 2010), it is being performed on Broadway as a revival; an actor without sensory disabilities plays the part of Helen Keller. After criticism from disabilities activists, an actor with visual impairment has been selected as an understudy.
11. Klages, *Woeful Afflictions*, 11.
12. Keller, "My Future as I See It," *Ladies Home Journal* 20, (November 1903).

At this time, Jane Addams' Hull House was nationally famous and Addams had gained visibility for her work by lecturing publically, and by drawing around her a community of activists and reformers. In 1902 Addams published *Democracy and Social Ethics*, a book of essays based on lecture series she'd given to college students. Addams served as an inspiration for Keller's generation of college-educated women and Addams' political celebrity — a combination of public speaking, publication, and public service on behalf of wider reforms — appears to have been very similar to the political career Keller pursued in this period.

After graduating from college, Keller studied, wrote and spoke about, and lobbied for public health issues and educational issues of particular interest to the deaf and blind. But in 1908, she also joined the Socialist Party. Biographer Joseph Lash describes her socialism as an "ideological earthquake"[13] while Neilson explains simply, "Keller's study of blindness contributed to her indictment of capitalism."[14] Nielsen's interpretation of events follows Keller's own account of her political transformation, one that can be seen in her published writing from the period. In an essay, "The Social Causes of Blindness," from 1911, Keller cites the overcrowded and unsanitary living conditions of workers' tenements, and the frequency of industrial accidents as preventable causes of blindness, brought about by an industrial economy that abuses and exploits its workers. An essay written for the *Ziegler Magazine for the Blind*, also from 1911, entitled "The Unemployed," begins with a letter from an underemployed textile worker with a hearing impairment, who has written to Keller for advice. She moves from his personal appeal, to a discussion of the larger economy in which the textile worker finds himself,

> There are, it is estimated, a million laborers out of work in the United States. Their inaction is not due to physical defects or lack of ability or of intelligence, or to ill health or vice. It is due to the fact that our present system of production necessitates a large margin of idle men . . . The means of employment — the land and the factories, that is, the tools of labor — are in the hands of a minority of the people, and are used rather with a view to increasing the owner's profits than with a view to keeping all men busy and productive.[15]

Nielsen's assessment, cited earlier, of Keller's disinterest in issues of "discrimination" seems accurate here; Keller does not identify herself, nor her correspondent, as part of a disabled minority group whom she might represent. Keller's rhetoric calls for an economic analysis of exploitation

---

13. Joseph Lash, *Helen and Teacher* (New York: Delacorte Press, 1980), 366.
14. Nielsen, *The Radical Lives of Helen Keller*, 23.
15. Keller, "The Unemployed," in John Davis (ed.), *Helen Keller* (New York: Ocean Press, 2003), 21.

and an organized and unified opposition to the structural inequalities of wealth and labor in the US, rather than the representation of minority rights within American society. During this period, Keller also declined to support political representation for women, and she valued workers' rights over women's right to vote; in her essay "To an English Woman-Suffragist" she argues, "The majority of mankind are working people. As long as their fair demands — the ownership and control of their lives and livelihood — are set at naught, we can have neither men's rights nor women's rights."[16] Keller had been asked to write on disability and gender (in a magazine for the blind, on "the question of woman-suffrage") but she uses these opportunities to redefine her political project; she garners attention from the press as a deaf-blind woman, but she diverts that attention to her chosen political commitments. In 1912, when Keller more directly confronted newspaper rumors regarding her socialist politics, she wryly suggested, "Even notoriety may be turned to beneficent uses, and I rejoice if the disposition of the newspapers to record my activities results in bringing more often into their columns the word socialism."[17] In this period, Keller deliberately used her celebrity — earned as a child prodigy and maintained as a college-educated activist and author — in the service of her now more radical politics.

"I Make Believe I Am an Actress"[18]

In the 1910s, when Keller was in her thirties, she took on two significant projects that seem, to Keller biographers and scholars, unrelated: she regularly published and spoke in support of socialist causes and she agreed to star, as herself, in a Hollywood film, entitled *Deliverance* (1919). But both of these projects exploited Keller's celebrity and, more specifically, the public's fascination with her disabled body. Helen Keller used her celebrity — a celebrity based, in the film and in her public appearances, in the sensational appeal of her body — to convey her socialist message. Thus, the context in which it was possible for Keller to exploit her own celebrity is best illuminated through an analysis that attends to recent developments in the study of early film melodrama and the function of female celebrity in the silent-film era. Examining Keller's celebrity from a film studies perspective reveals that her political activism and her filmmaking project were both deliberate engagements with a media culture fascinated by her disabled body — a fascination with the body that was part of film culture and political culture alike.

---

16. Keller, "To an English Woman-suffragist," in Philip S. Foner (ed.), *Helen Keller, Her Socialist Years: Writings and Speeches* (New York: International Publishers, 1967), 33.
17. Keller, "How I Became a Socialist," in John Davis (ed.), *Helen Keller* (New York: Ocean Press, 2003), 27.
18. This is Keller's title for a chapter on her Hollywood experiences in the autobiography *Midstream* (New York: Doubleday, Doran and Company, 1929), 186.

Although made when Keller was 39, *Deliverance* still represents Keller as a child, at least in the first third of the film. In an essay on Mary Pickford "and the pedophilic gaze" film historian Gaylyn Studlar traces the persistence of Leslie Fiedler's "Good Good Girl" genre within silent-era film culture; as an adult woman, Pickford played *Rebecca of Sunnybrook Farm* (1917) and *Pollyanna* (1920), two adolescent girls marked by "altruism and illness"[19] whose developing sexuality and sense of duty to others provides a narrative arc to their respective films. Keller's childhood, as represented in the first third of *Deliverance* (1919), adheres to this formula. Helen (played by a child actor) flirts with the boy next door,[20] learns to play nicely with little (somewhat fictional) Martha Washington, the daughter of the Kellers' black housekeeper, and is, eventually, held up as an example of virtue to Nadja, an impoverished, sullen (and entirely fictional) white immigrant girl, who also lives nearby. All the while, Helen is also completing the trajectory, familiar from *The Story of My Life*, from a violent, isolated, deaf and blind child to a disciplined young woman who uses her hands for communication with family and friends. Keller's film, in its first act "Childhood," adheres to conventions — both literary and cinematic — of appropriate embodiment for its disabled, feminine heroine.

But when Keller agreed to make a motion picture based on her life, she did not want to make a picture that told, again, her affecting childhood story; instead, she wanted the film to extend the reach of her adult political work. She wrote to the filmmakers, "the interest of our life-drama will not be confined to the events of my life, but will be spread out all round the world ... and bring many vital truths home to the hearts of the people, truths that shall hasten the deliverance of the human race."[21] This lofty rhetoric becomes more pointed in the context of Keller's socialism. But, in its representations of Keller's political work and ideals, *Deliverance* ultimately represented a compromise. To cite Keller's own critical account of the film,

> Towards the end we seem to have fallen down somehow. For instance, there is a scene called "The Council Chamber," where all the great generals, kings and statesmen are assembled in a sort of peace conference. I enter in a queer medieval costume and proclaim the Rights of Man rather feebly. There is no foundation in fact for such a scene, and the symbolism is not apparent. We want it omitted. This scene is followed by a Pageant with me on horseback, leading all the peoples of

---

19. Gaylyn Studlar, "Oh, 'Doll Divine': Mary Pickford, Masquerade, and the Pedophilic gaze," in Diane Negra and Jennifer Bean (eds), *A Feminist Reader in Early Cinema* (Durham, NC: Duke University Press, 2002): 352.
20. *Deliverance* contains rare representations of Keller as a romantically desiring subject: in addition to this childhood flirtation, she laments her single status in "Girlhood" and she has a fantasy romance with the character of Ulysses.
21. Helen Keller to Francis Trevelyan Miller, April 10, 1918, Helen Keller Papers, American Foundation for the Blind.

the world to freedom — or something. It is altogether too hilarious to typify the struggles of mankind . . . According to our contract, we have the right to reject the picture if it does not satisfy us.[22]

Essentially, in this correspondence with an influential friend, Keller is requesting that the film's financiers apply pressure to the filmmakers who have "sadly disappointed" her. Despite Keller's efforts, the extant version of the film includes much of the footage that Keller found objectionable and it actually opens with the scene in "The Council Chamber." The pageant with her on horseback provides the film's finale. Archived correspondence reveals that the filmmakers did not intend to honestly represent Keller's politics; scenarist Francis Trevelyan Miller, who first approached Keller with the idea for the film, was a popular military historian who had recently published a highly lucrative *Photographic History of the Civil War*. Miller, and director George Platt, complained to Keller that her speeches and public appearances at political rallies and meetings threatened the film's commercial success. Among themselves the filmmakers agreed that they wanted the film's message to support the US entry into World War I.

To tell its tale of patriotic duty, *Deliverance* introduces the fictional Nadja into Keller's Alabama childhood. Scenes from Nadja's life, a story of poverty and hardship, are cross-cut with scenes from Keller's biography, performed by actors representing Keller in her childhood and teenage years. The characters of Nadja and Helen reunite after Nadja's son returns from war blinded and she seeks Keller's aid; in this portion of the film, Keller plays herself, as an adult. The film includes no direct representations of Keller's socialist political work or speeches. Instead, Nadja's story carries an explicitly patriotic, pro-war message very much at odds with the anti-militarism that was part of Keller's socialist commitment, and, specifically, her speech "Strike Against War" (which I discuss in detail later in this essay). In one scene, set in a sweatshop where poor, widowed Nadja works, the other workers chide Nadja for refusing to send her son to war and the crowd insists on the patriotic duty of mothers in wartime.

Sensational Melodrama and Extraordinary Bodies in the Silent-Film Era

The fictional story of Nadja conforms to many of the popular narrative conventions that film scholar Miriam Hansen recognizes in the patriotic and pedagogical "Ghetto films" of the period — including "family separation and reunification," and "conflicts between traditional values and American

---

22. Helen Keller to Mrs. Thaw, April 16, 1919, Helen Keller Papers, American Foundation for the Blind.

customs and attitudes."[23] If Lewis Jacob's 1939 description of the ideological work of silent-era Hollywood film seems overly simplistic, that is, to give "newcomers a respect for American law and order, an understanding of civic organization, pride in citizenship and in the American commonwealth"[24] it would appear that *Deliverance* attempted to do exactly that in the parallel narratives of Nadja and Helen. But to be historically accurate, it is not the dramatically cross-cut and pathos-filled narrative of Helen and Nadja (whose encounters highlight Helen's spiritual triumphs and Nadja's romantic and maternal tragedies) that qualifies this silent-era film as a melodrama of the teens.[25]

Film historian Ben Singer's work on the meaning of melodrama in the silent-era argues that tales of love, loss, and redemption, despite their narrative and affective similarities to what came to be understood as melodrama in the mid-century studio era, weren't generally considered melodramas in silent-era Hollywood. They were "Tear Drenched Dramas" and sentimental stories, but they were not called — in the press or within the film industry — melodramas. Melodramas, or, as Singer more precisely calls them, "sensational melodramas," were, by and large, films structured by lots of action, violence, and dare-devil stunts, starring plucky, resourceful, often orphaned heroines whose adventures invoked "certain qualities of corporeality, peril and vulnerability associated with working-class life."[26] In Singer's analysis, the bodies of the daring and extraordinarily skilled heroines are intimately bound (if not identical) to the imperiled, vulnerable bodies of the modern filmgoers that attend the theaters. For Singer, the locations — the train tracks, the western mine and the city streets; the action — "insensible" girls (blindfolded, etc.) in peril who triumph by their wits; and the entire moral and phenomenal universe of the "sensational melodramas" correlated with perceived experiences of an urban mass culture of capitalist modernity. The heroines of the sensational melodramas triumphed in a physically dangerous world, despite their vulnerabilities and brushes with danger and death. Keller's own, literally, "insensible" body, her heroic triumphs, her presumed vulnerabilities, and her fascinating sensational experiences, as represented in *Deliverance*, are an extreme production of the same media culture that produced and consumed the generic sensational melodramas.

The "serial queen melodramas" that Singer investigates have attracted further study, and Jennifer Bean's essay "Technologies of Early Stardom and

---

23. Miriam Hansen, *Babel in Babylon: Spectatorship in American Silent Film* (Cambridge, MA: Harvard University Press, 1991), 71.

24. Lewis Jacobs, *The Rise of the American Film* (1939; reprint, New York: Teachers College Press, 1968), 12.

25. The film is over two hours long and, in many ways, it is a fairly conventional film of the silent era: the fantasy sequences, motivated by scenes of Keller reading and daydreaming and the scenes of historical pageantry (however frustrating they were to Keller) would have been familiar to audiences of the period.

26. Ben Singer, *Melodrama and Modernity* (New York: Columbia University Press, 2001), 53.

the Extraordinary Body" makes it particularly clear how *Deliverance* might be considered one of the "sensational melodramas" of the period and Keller one of its extraordinary heroines. Bean's study of the same serial films addresses the indexical appeal of a particular kind of celebrity performance in the silent cinema of the teens, the very physical, active "stunting" of the girl heroines in the serial films. Considering the work of such "daredevils" as Pearl White, Helen Gibson, Anita King, Marie Dressler, and Mabel Normand, Bean writes, "Each of these star personae stood for a particular synthesis of femininity, athletic virility, and effortless mobility."[27] Stars of the serials scaled mountains, plummeted into bodies of water, flew airplanes and handled wild horses, lions, and other untamed creatures as part of what Bean identifies as a "phenomenology of performance"[28] that depended on the "believability of real peril to the player's body" to produce a "thrilling realism."[29] A film like *The Race* (1916), which followed Anita King's cross-country motor trip, was, in Bean's words, "billed as quasi-documentary."[30] Films of this kind depended on a fascination with the extra-cinematic, ostensibly real — with the perilous event, with the physical setting, with the extraordinary body of the female celebrity — for their appeal.

But Bean explores a twist in the logic of the "thrilling realism" of the cinema of the teens: the stars, and the star discourse, make the strongest claims for early melodrama's believability. Its star personae collapsed distinctions between actress and character, as actresses assumed their characters' names as stage names, and characters were named after actresses. The star discourse, namely, the press, produced "star testimonials" that offered "meaning unavailable to or . . . occluded by sight" in the "contradiction between image and experience."[31] These testimonials followed a formula in which the star denied the actual danger of certain stunts that might look dangerous in the film, while emphasizing the danger of other scenes. Bean's analysis of the function of female stardom, in this media culture, suggests that film and its moving images could not, alone, provide the necessary thrills. The real body of the female celebrity was required, in the film, and in the world outside the film.

Deliverance participates in this genre of "thrilling realism" and "extraordinary bodies" in a number of ways: Publicity for the film billed Keller's celebrity and her appearance as herself in the film above all else, calling audiences to "See HELEN KELLER in this Photoplay of Photoplays and Be Convinced,"

---

27. Jennifer Bean, "Technologies of Early Stardom and the Extraordinary Body," *Camera Obscura* 16(3), (2001): 11–12.

28. Ibid., 13.

29. Ibid., 19–21.

30. Ibid., 24. Bean is writing for contemporary film scholars; the idea of films as "documentary" came into being well after the teens.

31. Ibid., 26.

adding, "Miss Keller will be present at the OPENING PERFORMANCE."[32] Within the film, Keller's body was ostensibly put into "real peril" in ways conventional for the serials; *Deliverance* includes sequences of Keller on horseback and taking her first plane ride. And like the serial daredevils, Keller assumes the responsibility, in the press and in her own published accounts of the filmmaking, of, as Bean puts it, "resignify[ing] the visual referents,"[33] that is, describing her own experience of the making of the film and its stunts. Of the plane ride, Keller wrote, "The pilot told me afterwards that I myself was in danger for a few minutes in what was to me the most thrilling event connected with the picture — my ride in an aeroplane."[34] Keller insists on the status of the plane ride as the "most thrilling event," while she simultaneously reveals the extra-cinematic "danger" vouched for by the pilot. She tells a similar story about the scene on horseback. In the case of Keller, the contradictions between the film image, as seen by the audience, and the daredevil experience of the filmmaking, are mediated by Keller's performance of disability.

Keller's account of the studio filming, described similarly in publicity pieces in *The New York Times* and *Moving Picture World*, is as follows:

> [The director] devised a signal system of taps that I could follow. . . . After general directions had been spelled into my hand, I was supposed to go through the action with the help of signal taps. "Tap, tap, tap" — walk toward the window on your right. "Tap, tap, tap" — hold up your hands to the sun (a blaze of heat from the big lamps). "Tap, tap, tap" — discover the bird's cage; (I had already discovered the cage five times). "Tap, tap, tap" — express surprise, feel for the bird, express pleasure. "Tap, tap, tap" — be natural. In my hand impatiently: "There's nothing to be afraid of; it isn't a lion in the cage — it's a canary."[35]

Here, Keller provides a testimonial to the physical challenges of performing and filming everyday actions, rather than daredevil stunts. Some of the gestures and movements she describes, and others like them, appear in "Act Three Womanhood" of the film, when the film's biographical narrative (and the fictional Nadja story) are temporarily halted to incorporate scenes that explore Keller's sensory experiences. She describes other scenes,

> I danced for the camera, I poured tea for callers and after the last guest was sped, there came the "tap, tap, tap" from the director: "Lift up your hands and let them fall, express relief that the last bore has left." There was a bedroom scene in which I was directed to show the curious public that I could dress and undress myself alone and that I closed my eyes when I went to sleep."[36]

32. *New York Times* (advertisement) August 17, 1919.
33. Bean, "Extraordinary Body," 27.
34. Keller, *Midstream*, 199.
35. Ibid., 189.
36. Ibid., 193.

Figure 2.1 **Keller performs her extraordinary abilities and disabilities in *Deliverance* (dir. George Platt, 1919).**

Keller's account suggests that at least part of the film's appeal, like that of the serials, relied on the effortless mobility of an extraordinary body. But, as Keller's joke[37] about the confusion between lion and canary implies, her disabled body is made to appear extraordinary in the competent performance of very ordinary actions — dancing, pouring tea, moving through a room, touching a bird. The actions, in themselves, are not difficult or thrilling for Keller. However, performing for the camera, and for sighted filmgoers, transforms them into daredevil feats. And performing these for the camera is what Keller claims is the real challenge.

Throughout her life, and to her own frustration, Keller was repeatedly asked — as in the essays in *The World I Live In* — to describe her sensory experiences and narrate her biography. This form of celebrity, it would seem, granted Keller authority only over her subjective, physical experience as a disabled body. But Keller also assumed the responsibility of speaking on issues she understood to be related to the experience of disability — poverty, education, and public health — as well as issues that she felt strongly about because she spoke as an informed citizen — she wrote and spoke in support of Eugene Debs, socialist newspaper editor Fred Warren, and the International Workers of the World, and against police brutality towards striking workers, the "militarist program" of US entry into WWI, and the blockade of Russia. Keller's political celebrity eclipsed the political message of *Deliverance* at the time of the film's release, but it is not simply a question of righting the film's misrepresentations of her politics. The film exploited the public's fascination with Keller's disabled body, but Keller did too, and used her celebrated body to attract attention to the political movement she supported.

---

37. Although the joke is, in Keller's account, made by the director, I attribute it, here, to Keller herself. It is characteristic of her literary style — she often makes dry jokes at her own expense about her perceptions and misperceptions.

Political Performances in the Progressive Era

Keller's political writings and speeches from the teens are at odds with the cinematic representation of her politics in *Deliverance* even as these works rely on the sensational treatment of her disability that characterized the film. During the period of the filmmaking project, and throughout her life, Keller used language and metaphors that invoked her disabled body. If part of the appeal of *Deliverance* is Keller's body, Keller exploited this fascination for her own political purposes. Her strategic use of bodily metaphors did not limit her to the personal, experiential discourse of many of the essays in *The World I Live In*, but rather allowed her to make expansive political appeals that criticized nationalist, militarist, and capitalist ideologies. Rhetorical analyses of her socialist speeches and writing reveal the complexity of this strategy — to use her disabled body to represent the oppression of labor under capitalism — but it was not just a question of Keller's use of language. Physical risk and bodily performance were a significant element of political action in the Progressive Era, and, I will argue, Keller's use of her celebrity body for political causes in the Progressive Era was part of a larger political culture.

Keller's rhetoric of political embodiment, in the service of her socialist message, is particularly vivid in her 1912 essay "The Hand of the World." She deliberately moves from descriptions of the significance of touch, in her own life, to a discussion of manual labor, to the potential of mechanized labor — in which the hand "projects, and multiplies itself in wondrous tools" to, finally, her commitment to "the coming of that commonwealth in which the gyves shall be struck from the wrist of Labour, and the pulse of Production shall be strong with joy." The hands Keller calls our attention to are the hands attached to her deaf and blind body, the prosthetic hands of modern technology, whose abilities all workers can benefit from, and the metaphorical hands of united workers. Keller appreciates the celebrity that her own hands have earned her — the hands of a disabled child who learned to communicate using a manual alphabet — but the hands she is describing here are clearly not just her own.

In her speech, "Strike Against War," given at New York City's Carnegie Hall to the Women's Peace Party and Labor Forum in 1916, Keller again invokes her body and unites it with the bodies of the audience to whom she makes her appeal. The speech closes with a call,

> Strike against all ordinances and laws and institutions that continue the slaughter of peace and the butcheries of war. Strike against war, for without you no battles can be fought. Strike against manufacturing scrapnel and gas bombs and all other tools of murder. Strike against preparedness that means death and misery to millions of human beings. Be not dumb, obedient slaves in an army of destruction.[38]

---

38. Keller, "Strike Against War," in Philip S. Foner (ed.), *Helen Keller, Her Socialist Years: Writings*

The call for a strike is in itself an acknowledgment of the power of using one's body for the cause of political resistance. Keller's description of the very nature of a strike, "for without you no battles can be fought," draws attention to the way in which bodily risk was widely understood by activists, including militant suffragists and workers to be the very basis of political resistance to the capitalist and nationalist regimes that depended upon the physical exploitation of their bodies. Answering the question "What is the IWW?" in the *New York Call*, Keller wrote, "The IWW is a labor union based on the class struggle . . . Its battlefield is the field of industry. The visible expression of the battle is the strike, the lockout, the clash between employer and employed."[39] John Davis and Karen Fletcher, in their introduction to a collection of Keller's political writings explain that "Keller's dissatisfaction with the primarily electoral activity of the Socialist Party and her growing preference for industrial direct action tactics are evident as early as 1911"[40] and Keller's own words make plain the appeal of embodied political action.

Keller's right to participate in US socialism was widely contested (by skeptical newspaper editors and activists alike) and her exclusion was justified, in her critics' accounts, by the disabilities of her body. Her bodily experience of disability was considered the only legitimate topic on which she should publicly speak or write. Keller's speech "Strike Against War" addresses her critics' assumptions and defends her right to participate in broader political discourse,

> Some people are grieved because they imagine I am in the hands of unscrupulous persons who lead me astray and persuade me to espouse unpopular causes and make me the mouthpiece of their propaganda. Now, let it be understood once and for all that I do not want their pity; I would not change places with one of them. I know what I am talking about. My sources of information are as good and reliable as anybody else's. I have papers and magazines from England, France, Germany and Austria that I can read myself. . . . Let them remember, though, that if I cannot see the fire at the end of their cigarettes, neither can they thread a needle in the dark. All I ask, gentlemen, is a fair field and no favor. I have entered the fight against preparedness and against the economic system under which we live. It is to be a fight to the finish, and I ask no quarter.[41]

Again, Keller's celebrated body is the site of a great deal of attention, both in her own statements, and those of her critics. The implication of her

---

and Speeches (New York: International Publishers, 1967), 81.

39. Keller, "What is the IWW?" in John Davis (ed.), *Helen Keller* (New York: Ocean Press, 2003), 37.

40. John Davis and Karen Fletcher, "Introduction," in John Davis (ed.), *Helen Keller* (New York: Ocean Press, 2003), 6.

41. Keller, "Strike Against War," 75. The essay "How I Became a Socialist" makes this same argument and Keller's answer to the question in the title is, "By reading."

critics is that her gendered and disabled body excluded her from meaningful knowledge of the political world. Keller, in her rebuttal, insists that her ability to read Braille and Brailled foreign language papers, gives her equal agency to those who might make political claims based on visible evidence or accessibility to traditional print or visual media. Keller does not avoid metaphors of the body, here, the metaphor of her own dexterity. Rather, she relies on them again and again to assert her political arguments. Keller exploits the fascination of the public for her disabled body, as she uses this body to discuss, and to communicate with the world beyond that of her own sensory experience.

In the close of "Strike Against War" Keller invokes "dumb, obedient slaves" as apolitical subjects; often she equates "blindness" with folly, and "deafness" with insularity. Keller invokes the abilities and disabilities of her body, clearly on display as she speaks in front of her audience, while at the same time denying, or rather, reassigning the cultural meanings that might label that body. She insists on the metaphorical use of the terms "deaf," "blind," and, here, "dumb," as opposed to the use of these terms as a literal description of disability. Instead of identifying her own body as disabled, Keller describes the epistemological experience of all politically active subjects in a mediated world, informed by representations which are none the less politically compelling as representations. But Keller's political use of her body was not unique; as I have suggested it was a popular political strategy of the period and one that was, increasingly, seen as quite threatening.

That Keller should have thought her radical politics might be able to be shared with the public by a Hollywood film is not surprising, given the cinema history of the period. Kay Sloan's *Loud Silents* is a history of the ways in which many commercial films, in the period before World War I served as "vehicles for overtly presenting social problems to the public."[42] Films were sponsored by the National Child Labor Committee and the National American Woman Suffrage Association, Progressive reformers like Upton Sinclair and Jane Addams participated in filmmaking projects, and there were film companies that were created expressly for the purpose of making films that advanced women's rights and labor rights, among other causes. Keller was not unique in thinking that film might help extend the reach of her political work and the presence of activists in film in this period became controversial.

A particularly interesting tension surrounded the release of the film *Birth Control* (1917), in which women's rights advocate Margaret Sanger appears as herself, a "'placid, clear-eyed, rather young and certainly attractive propagandist'," in the words of a critic of the day, in a film that used flashbacks, fictional scenarios and re-enactments of Sanger's trial for violating obscenity laws because she distributed literature about contraception, all to make

---

42. Kay Sloan, *Loud Silents: Origins of the Social Problem Film* (Urbana, IL: University of Illinois Press, 1988), 4.

"an emotional as well as a reasoned case for birth control."[43] This film was censored by the New York Motion Picture License Commissioner, as was *The Hand that Rocks the Cradle* (1917) by Lois Weber, a film which was based more obliquely on Sanger's life and work. In the previous year, the commissioner had allowed the screening of Weber's *Where are My Children?* (1916), another abortion-issue film with a more moralistic and dramatic approach; the National Board of Review had taken the opposite attitude towards these three films, passing *Birth Control* and *The Hand that Rocks the Cradle* and censoring *Where are My Children?* Film historian Shelley Stamp understands these seemingly contradictory decisions as part of "a struggle over how the cinema itself should be viewed, whether as an informational medium akin to the press and therefore subject to guarantees of free speech, or as a commercial entertainment medium entitled to regulations governing theatrical presentations."[44] Within this contested territory of cinema as public speech and entertainment, the presence of a political subject — Sanger's "attractive" and persuasive celebrity body — within the film's diegesis was particularly disruptive. Indeed, the power of a political performance by a film's actors was very real, and seen as, potentially, quite threatening — in the Sanger films, and in the case of *Deliverance* as well.

In the production of *Deliverance*, Keller and Sullivan had repeatedly requested that the film include footage of hospitals for blinded veterans, where Keller and Sullivan had been working to raise money and draw attention to the difficulties returning veterans faced in finding rehabilitation and employment. This kind of representation would have been more in tune with Keller's political views, of a war that would take "the lives of millions of young men; other millions crippled and blinded for life; existence made hideous for still more millions of human beings."[45] While the film does contain a fictional blinded veteran, triumphant in the scene on horseback, the reality of injured soldiers would have been far more disruptive to the patriotic fiction, or at least the filmmakers thought so, and resolutely excluded such footage.[46] Keller's appearance, Sanger's, and the appearance of disabled

---

43. Ibid., 87. The first quotation comes from the 1917 *Variety* film review, the second comes from Sloan.
44. Shelley Stamp, "Taking Precautions, or Regulating Early Birth Control Films," in Bean and Negra (eds), *A Feminist Reader in Early Cinema*, 291.
45. Keller, "Strike Against War," 79.
46. Consider also two films from the classical Hollywood cinema: *The Men* (Fred Zinneman, 1950) and *The Best Years of Our Lives* (William Wyler, 1946). These films represent two different approaches to "real" disability and the injuries caused by combat. In *The Men*, the collective hospital setting is the historical real — the film was made at the Birmingham Paraplegic Hospital in Los Angeles and was based on individual accounts of post-WWII injuries, trauma and therapies and the work of the Paralyzed Veterans Association; it stars Marlon Brando, who learned to use a wheelchair for the film. The use of non-professional, disabled actor, Harold Russell, in *Best Years of Our Lives* places a historically real individual subjectivity, and one with an extraordinary body, at the center of a cinematic fiction set in the post-WWII period.

war veterans had a sensational appeal, and, in these figures, this sensational appeal was paired with a serious political message.

The substitution of Keller's heroism for a story in which the injured soldier is a protagonist can also be understood as a film convention in the period. In Bean's argument, the "nervy movie lady" is not just part of an exciting "fantasy of a body revised" in technological modernity. The sensational heroine has an army of dark, vulnerable doubles, the "mutilated male bodies and psyches" on the "battlefields of the First World War"[47] that she displaces from the minds of her audiences. Although intimately bound in the imaginations of period audiences, disabled and extraordinarily-abled figures rarely appear side by side in films of the period[48] and the wealth of silent films produced in the teens about World War I soldiers and veterans are not necessarily part of Bean's study. Fantasies of extraordinary physical ability and disability seem inevitable in wartime and to address the relationship of bodies on-screen and off, we might, at the present moment, be tempted to call the extraordinarily abled bodies avatars, fantasy bodies that replace and displace our vulnerable material bodies.

These vulnerable bodies, however, index the experience of bodies in the real, social world outside the sensational melodrama — the world of war, industrialized labor, and political protest. It seems possible, too, that the daredevil bodies of the sensational film heroines of the teens mediated, in the imaginations of the period audience, the physically imperiled and politically threatening bodies of the militant suffragists — who performed stunts of their own, which included hunger strikes, demonstrations, and theatrical performances, violent confrontations with the police. These included, perhaps most famously, the fatal protest of British suffragist Emily Davison at the Epsom Derby, captured on film in 1913. Davison, who had justified her 1912 hunger strike on the grounds that "by nothing but the sacrifice of human life would the nation be brought to realize the horrible torture our women face"[49] was trampled to death when she tried to hang a banner for the Women's Social and Political Union on the king's horse at the derby, during the WSPU's 1913 summer fundraising festival.

When Keller's attempt to control the financing, content, and release of the film ultimately failed, she boycotted the premiere and her extraordinary body was not, in fact, present at the Lyric Theater in New York on the opening night to vouch for the film's thrilling realism. According to Keller's

47. Bean, "Extraordinary Body," 76.
48. Martin Norden identifies a silent-era sleuth named Kirby as an early cinematic super-crip, or, as he puts it, a "Civilian Superstar: a resourceful, adaptive, and courageous individual who happens to have a disability." Kirby was the hero of only one film, *Chelsea 7750* (1913); the role of Kirby quickly developed into that of wheelchair-bound father to the crime-solving Kate Kirby, a serial melodrama heroine like those Bean and Singer studied. In *The Cinema of Isolation: A History of Physical Disability in the Movies* (New Brunswick, NJ: Rutgers University Press, 1994), 51.
49. Emily Davison, "Letter to the Editor." *Pall Mall Gazette*, September 19, 1912.

correspondence, she refused tickets to the premiere because the screening coincided with an actors' strike and she understood her picture to be acting as a technological strikebreaker. *New York Times* coverage included both reviews of the film and reports of Keller's participation in the parades and meetings of the strikers. The *Times* report, characteristically, suggests her physical presence among the strikers, and an extant photograph of Keller, surrounded by striking actors holding a strike banner provides some visual evidence for this.[50]

Extraordinary Bodies and Documentary Film

Disability historian and literary scholar Rosemarie Garland-Thomson has claimed that photography has allowed for the continuation, and trans-formation, of a nineteenth-century fascination with "a spectacle of bodily otherness."[51] This spectacle depends on the confrontation between "real people with extraordinary bodies" and real people whose bodies are defined in opposition to those seen through the medium of the photograph and its encounter. For Garland-Thomson, the nineteenth century defined norm-ative and non-normative bodies through the live spectacle of the freak show, while twentieth-century photographic representations of extraordinary bodies continue to enable the social ritual of staring at disability, in new cultural contexts in which the audience can literally see disabled bodies displayed in photographs. An example of one such encounter might be the modernist audience for Paul Strand's 1916 photograph "Blind Woman" — Strand even had a trick camera with mirrors and false lenses that, he hoped, would deceive photographed subjects into believing that they were outside of the camera's frame, that they were not being photographed. Strand's technique allowed his audience — who might be caught somewhere bet-ween Victorian sentimentality and modern estrangement — to stare at the disabled and impoverished subjects of his "New York" photographs, while they appear unaware of the photographic experience or the performance solicited from them.

It seems to be coincidence that Garland-Thomson and Bean both use the exact same term, "the extraordinary body," to describe bodies made visible by photographic technology at the beginning of the twentieth century; their bibliographies do not substantially overlap. But Keller's appearance in *Deliverance* suggests historical connections between silent-era sensational

---

50. "Hint at Closing all the Theaters," *New York Times*, August 18, 1919 and "Stage Hands and Musicians Strike; 16 Theaters Dark," *New York Times*, August 17, 1919. Photograph is at Helen Keller Archives, American Foundation for the Blind.
51. Rosemarie Garland-Thomson, "The Politics of Staring: Visual Rhetorics of Disability in Popular Photography," in Garland-Thomson, Sharon Snyder and Brenda Bruggemann (eds), *Disability Studies: Enabling the Humanities* (New York: Modern Language Association of America, 2002), 56.

melodrama, its indexical fascination with super-abled, female bodies, and photography and its construction of disabled bodies in the social world. Rather than understanding a "normal" body to exist between an opposition of super-abled and disabled, however, I find that the term "extraordinary body" describes a broad variation of human bodies brought into being by film. The use of the term in nonfictional and fictional contexts, and in cinematic and photographic territory that is both nonfictional and fictional (or neither), also justifies the term "extraordinary."

David Mitchell and Sharon Snyder have persuasively argued that disabled bodies are necessary for the affective experience of Hollywood's genre films. Following film theorist Linda Williams, they take up the concept of "body genres" and argue that while body genres rely on extreme sensations, not just women's bodies, but "disabled bodies have been constructed cinematically and socially to function as delivery vehicles in the transfer of extreme sensation to audiences."[52] They list the familiar bumbling fool of comedy, the disabled avenger of horror and the long-suffering victim of melodrama as the delivery vehicles for the sensational effects of film; Mitchell and Snyder, here are primarily concerned with films from the Hollywood studio-era and after. In a longer film history, extraordinary bodies — marked by their abilities and disabilities — were also necessary for the sensational melodramas of the teens. Keller's extraordinary body, and its stunts (as well as a plot in which independent, accomplished Keller saves the day) reveal *Deliverance's* affinity with the silent-era genre of sensational melodrama, and the media culture that produced these. But Keller's cinematic performance of her own disability, the "thrilling realism" it produces, and the political arguments both she and the film make, also inform the history of documentary and nonfiction film. Bodily performance, and its sensational effects are essential to many forms of nonfiction and documentary film. And in nonfiction film, from the earliest celebrity actualities to direct cinema to contemporary bio-pics, a strong fascination with raced, gendered, national, and/or extraordinarily talented bodies is evinced.[53]

---

52. Mitchell and Snyder, *The Cultural Locations of Disability* (Chicago, IL: University of Chicago Press, 2006), 163.

53. In early actualities: political figures like McKinley, Queen Victoria, Gladstone, and Emily Davison, and actors like Mary Irwin, John Rice, and Sarah Bernhardt; at mid-century: *Bernstein in Israel* (1956) — an American-Jewish conductor visiting Israel, and *The Day Manolete Was Killed* (1957) — a Spanish bullfighter's controversial death during the Franco regime; in the direct cinema of the sixties and seventies: the celebrity subjects of the Maylses brothers, Richard Leacock and D. A. Pennebaker. In recent mainstream documentaries: Robert McNamara, Michael Moore, Morgan Spurlock, *Zidane* (2001), *Derrida* (2002), *Zizek!* (2005), *Judith Butler* (2007), and *Joan Rivers: A Piece of Work* (2010).

One Final Performance

As a celebrity, Keller had more success in influencing the form and content of the biographical documentary *The Unconquered* (1954) than she had with *Deliverance*. When, late in Keller's life, her friends wanted to have a film made to honor her life and work, filmmakers no less renowned than Robert Flaherty and Francois Truffaut both expressed interest in directing it. However, Keller and her colleagues were not comfortable with either — both seemed more interested in their own vision (or careers) than in creating a meaningful representation of Keller's life and work. Keller's celebrity and the respect afforded her by her friends, prevented her from becoming the subject of a film like Truffaut's *L'enfant Sauvage* (1970) (which treats its nonfictional subject primarily as the philosophical and aesthetic problem he was considered, in Enlightenment France) or Flaherty's portraits of exoticized and infantilized "primitive" cultures. *The Unconquered* was finally made on a tiny budget, and directed by Keller's personal friend and neighbor, a woman named Nancy Hamilton, for whom *The Unconquered* was her first and only film.

The Unconquered is not a particularly radical or sophisticated political project. Indeed, it was made after Keller put aside her socialist politics to represent the mission of the American Foundation for the Blind (AFB) and to serve as its spokesperson and fundraiser, a position that Keller felt deeply ambiguous about. In 1924, the year Keller accepted a salary from the AFB, she wrote an explanation for her withdrawal from socialist politics to the Farmer–Labor presidential candidate Robert La Follette. She expressed her anxieties about entering into a career in philanthropy, where "superficial charities make smooth the way of the prosperous" and socialist economic critiques and utopian visions were unwelcome.[54] Still, the non-professional production of *The Unconquered* allowed for a number of decisions that constructed a very different, but nonetheless extraordinary body in the later film. *The Unconquered* shares with its audience Keller's manual communication and her speaking voice, two elements of her extraordinary body that the silent film — and the photographic archive, and the literary legacy of Keller's life — did not, could not, or would not include.

In her study of Keller, Klages suggests that Keller's celebrity depended upon her participation in very specific forms of representation. In her literary work, and in still photography according to Klages, Keller could pass as "normal," because of her use of visual and aural language and her disciplined body. However, Klages notes, "when she spoke, of course, her speech patterns (as well as her sign language) marked her incontrovertibly as deaf, just as her movements and her need for a guide marked her physically

---

54. Keller, "To Senator Robert M. La Follette," in Foner, 113.

as blind."[55] Keller's ability to appear more or less disabled is quite striking, when the rich archive of photographs of her life is examined. But Keller never restricted herself to a life of literary work or hid from public view, and this essay emphasizes her public appearances, her film appearances, and her speeches despite the fact that the full impact of these is no longer accessible to researchers. For Nielsen, too, Keller's visibility has political potential, and she writes, "Whether she intended it or not, being seen, disrupting the visual field, became a radical move."[56] *The Unconquered* is, in this way, a disruptive film; its representation of Keller is remarkably different from that preserved in the AFB photographic archive, and published and republished in *Story of My Life*. In *The Unconquered* sound and image manage to represent something of Keller's embodiment as a comfortable, capable, and extremely disabled elderly woman.

The film includes a fraction of the newsreel footage in which Keller appeared, in her long career with the AFB, and this footage reminds viewers that Keller did not necessarily restrict herself to those media that allowed her to pass as normal, and are best preserved by her archives — writing and photography. *The Unconquered* shows Keller touching the faces and hands of her friends and acquaintances; she makes one guest visibly uncomfortable. She follows conversations by touching her acquaintance's moving lips, and she is seen communicating, quickly and efficiently (but never invisibly) via the manual alphabet with her friends and colleagues. *The Unconquered* also includes Keller's own voice, speaking directly to the film's audience, as well as footage, with original sound, of public speeches made with Polly Thompson, Keller's companion after the death of Anne Sullivan. Keller and Sullivan appear together, again with original sound, performing (during their vaudeville period)[57] a demonstration of how Keller learned to enunciate words though touch. The film does not deny Keller a voice, either literally, or figuratively, but instead explores the ways in which her eloquence was spoken with and through her relationships with others.

Conclusion

In a review of the centennial edition of *Story of My Life*, Michael Bérubé noted that "all too often, Keller's intellectual legacy has been treated as a matter of debits and credits"[58] and, to some extent, my brief analysis here

55. Klages, *Woeful Afflictions*, 193.
56. Nielsen, *The Radical Lives of Helen Keller*, 136.
57. After the commercial failure of *Deliverance*, Helen Keller and Anne Sullivan performed on the vaudeville stage, which Keller preferred to film performance, she said, because of her sense of the live audiences' presence. For a comparison of Keller and Sullivan's performance to freak show conventions of the period, see Susan Crutchfield, "Playing Her Part Correctly: Helen Keller as Vaudevillian Freak," *Disability Studies Quarterly* 25(3), (2005).
58. Michael Bérubé, "Written in Memory," *The Nation*, August 4, 2003.

of *The Unconquered* falls prey to that impulse. But the film is part of Keller's celebrity and its contributions are important for more than evaluation. Not only does *The Unconquered* explore the ways in which a politically and socially active (though censored) Keller uses her abilities and disabilities to communicate, the filmmaking project demonstrates that Keller's celebrity late in life depended, as ever, upon her canny participation in a visual culture, and a public culture, from which she was often assumed to be excluded. Including Keller's work in the film history of the silent era, and the long history of nonfiction film sharpens our attention to the political dimensions of the long, intimate, and uneasy relationships of the material world, the human body, and film technology.

Finally, expanding the study of Keller's life and work to include analytical frameworks from film studies reveals the specific political function of Keller's celebrity in the Progressive Era. The history of sensational melodrama, and its celebrity culture reveal the connections between Keller's political speeches and writings, and her appearance in a Hollywood film; namely, both projects (nearly simultaneous in her life but treated very differently by biographers) exploited a public fascination with her deaf and blind sensorium and depended upon her extraordinary body for their appeal, a process in which she was a creative participant. In the Progressive Era, Keller used her celebrity, which was based on the public fascination with her disabled body, to embody a collective public and its resistance to the industrial exploitation of the Gilded Age. In turn, an analysis that takes the Keller films seriously places Keller's political negotiation of visual media and her own extraordinary body in a broader historical context. Keller's ability to exploit the fascination with her body for a political cause is not specific to her: it is part of the intersection of celebrity, politics, and visual media in the public culture of the Progressive Era, and after.

Works Cited

Bean, Jennifer. "Technologies of Early Stardom and the Extraordinary Body," *Camera Obscura* 16(3), (2001): 8–57.

Berlant, Lauren. *The Female Complaint: The Unfinished Business of Sentimentality in American Culture.* Durham, NC: Duke University Press, 2008.

Bérubé, Michael. "Written in Memory," *The Nation*, August 4, 2003.

Crow, Liz. "Helen Keller: Rethinking a Problematic Icon," *Disability and Society* 15(6), (2000): 845–59.

Crutchfield, Susan. "Playing Her Part Correctly: Helen Keller as Vaudevillian Freak," *Disability Studies Quarterly* 25(3), (2005), http://www.dsq-sds.org/article/view/577/754 (accessed November 22, 2010).

Davis, John and Karen Fletcher. "Introduction," in John Davis (ed.), *Helen Keller.* New York: Ocean Press, 2003.

Davison, Emily. "Letter to the Editor," *Pall Mall Gazette* (London), September 19, 1912.

Deliverance. Directed by George Platt. Helen Keller Film Corporation, 1919. 16mm film.

Fiedler, Leslie. *Love and Death in the American Novel.* New York: Dell, 1966.

Fuss, Diana. *The Sense of an Interior.* New York: Routledge, 2004.

Garland-Thomson, Rosemarie. "The Politics of Staring: Visual Rhetorics of Disability in

Popular Photography," in Rosemarie Garland-Thomson, Sharon Snyder and Brenda Bruggemann (eds), *Disability Studies: Enabling the Humanities*. New York: Modern Language Association of America, 2002, 56–75.

Hansen, Miriam. *Babel in Babylon: Spectatorship in American Silent Film*. Cambridge, MA: Harvard University Press, 1991.

"Hint at Closing all the Theaters," *New York Times*, August 18, 1919.

Holmes, Su and Sean Redmond. "Introduction: Understanding Celebrity Culture," in Su Holmes and Sean Redmond (eds), *Framing Celebrity*. London: Routledge, 2006, 1–16.

Jacobs, Lewis. *The Rise of the American Film* 1939. New York: Teachers College Press, 1968.

Keller, Helen. Helen Keller Papers. American Foundation for the Blind.

——. "How I Became a Socialist," in John Davis (ed.), *Helen Keller*. New York: Ocean Press, 2003.

——. *Midstream*. New York: Doubleday, Doran and Company, 1929.

——. "My Future as I See It," *Ladies Home Journal* 20, (November 1903).

——. "Strike Against War," in Philip S. Foner (ed.), *Helen Keller, Her Socialist Years: Writings and Speeches*. New York: International Publishers, 1967.

——. "The Unemployed," in John Davis (ed.), *Helen Keller*. New York: Ocean Press, 2003.

——. *The World I Live In*. 1908. New York: New York Review of Books, 2003.

——. "To an English Woman-suffragist," in Philip S. Foner (ed.), *Helen Keller, Her Socialist Years: Writings and Speeches*. New York: International Publishers, 1967.

——. "What is the IWW?" in John Davis (ed.), *Helen Keller*. New York: Ocean Press, 2003.

Klages, Mary. *Woeful Afflications: Disability and Sentimentality in Victorian America*. Philadelphia: University of Pennsylvania Press, 1999.

Kleege, Georgina. "Helen Keller and the Empire of the Normal," *American Quarterly* 52(2), (2000): 322–5.

Lash, Joseph. *Helen and Teacher*. New York: Delacorte Press, 1980.

Mitchell, David and Sharon Snyder, *The Cultural Locations of Disability*. Chicago, IL: University of Chicago Press, 2006.

New York Times (advertisement) August 17, 1919.

Nielsen, Kim. *The Radical Lives of Helen Keller*. New York: New York University Press, 2004.

Norden, Martin. *The Cinema of Isolation: A History of Physical Disability in the Movies*. New Brunswick, NJ: Rutgers University Press, 1994.

Singer, Ben. *Melodrama and Modernity*. New York: Columbia University Press, 2001.

Sloan, Kay. *Loud Silents: Origins of the Social Problem Film*. Urbana, IL: University of Illinois Press, 1988.

"Stage Hands and Musicians Strike; 16 Theaters Dark," *New York Times*, August 17, 1919.

Stamp, Shelley. "Taking Precautions, or Regulating Early Birth Control Films," in Diane Negra and Jennifer Bean (eds), *A Feminist Reader in Early Cinema*. Durham, NC: Duke University Press, 2002, 270–97.

Studlar, Gaylyn. "Oh, 'Doll Divine': Mary Pickford, Masquerade, and the Pedophilic Gaze," in Diane Negra and Jennifer Bean (eds), *A Feminist Reader in Early Cinema*. Durham, NC: Duke University Press, 2002, 349–73.

Tomkins, Jane. *Sensation Designs: The Cultural Work of American Fiction, 1719–1960*. New York: Oxford University Press, 1986.

The Unconquered: Helen Keller in Her Story. Directed by Nancy Hamilton, 1954. American Foundation for the Blind, 1992. Videocassette (VHS).

3

Bloody Blondes and Bobbed-Haired Bandits

The Execution of Justice and the Construction of the Celebrity Criminal in the 1920s Popular Press

APRIL MILLER

"**D**EAD!" That single word, printed below the infamous photograph of her execution, brought to an abrupt end the American public's year-long obsession with one of the most well-known celebrity criminals of the 1920s: Ruth Snyder. The blurry photograph of Snyder, who conspired with her lover, Judd Gray, to bludgeon her husband to death with a sash weight, took up the entire front page of the *New York Daily News* on January 13, 1928, the morning after her execution. Thomas Howard's incredible photograph, which showed Snyder sitting in the electric chair with a black leather mask over her face and broad straps around her chest, waist, torso, arms, and ankles, created an unprecedented demand for the *Daily News* and a firestorm of controversy. On the following day, the newspaper ran the photograph again and the accompanying report described the snapshot as "the most talked-of feat in the history of journalism."[1] Just as thousands of readers rushed to purchase their own copy of Snyder's final image, many reporters condemned both Howard and the *Daily News* for "flaunting" this image of Snyder's death and catering to the public's voracious appetite for news about Long Island's infamous "marble woman," so called due to her seemingly emotionless deportment during the court proceedings.[2]

---

1. The *New York Daily News* published the photograph in an extra edition on January 13, and then printed it again on January 14, 1928. Together, the two editions sold more than half a million extra copies. A few years later, Warner Bros. Studios also capitalized on the uproar created by the photograph, releasing Lloyd Bacon's *Picture Snatcher* (1933), starring James Cagney as an ex-convict turned reporter who takes a photograph of an execution. For an historical analysis of the tabloid coverage surrounding the Snyder-Gray trial and execution, see Jessie Ramey, "The Bloody Blonde and the Marble Woman: Gender and Power in the Case of Ruth Snyder," *Journal of Social History* 37(3), (Spring 2004): 625–50.
2. Thomas S. Bosworth describes both the pains Howard suffered in capturing the shots and the questionable ethics of the *Daily News*'s decision to print it in "Snapshot," *New Yorker*, January 28, 1928, 9.

Figure 3.1   **The cover of the *New York Daily News* the day after Ruth Snyder's execution, January 13, 1928.**

In fact, Howard's surreptitiously snapped photograph, which has since become famous in its own right, provides an elucidating snapshot of something much bigger than the final moments of a much-talked-about female offender.[3] It speaks to the public's rising obsession during the period with the female criminal celebrity and anxiety over women's propensity for violent crime. Though middle-class Ruth Snyder was perhaps the most sensational of the female offenders to receive sustained attention from the 1920s popular press and its readers, others like Celia Cooney, Brooklyn's working-class "Bobbed-Haired Bandit," who in the spring of 1924 sported a fashionable hairdo while robbing New York grocery stores with her "baby automatic," also temporarily dominated the nation's newspaper headlines. While the differences between their cases are substantial — Cooney was accused of armed robbery, not murder, and ultimately sentenced to ten years in prison but released in just over five years — both Snyder and Cooney's narratives reflect a strong public engagement with celebrity female offenders and the

---

3. In his article celebrating the 80th anniversary of "one of the most famous front pages in history," David J. Krajicek quotes an unnamed expert who called Howard's photograph "the most famous sneak shot in journalism," "Ruthless Ruth", *New York Daily News*, January 20, 2008, 42.

debates over gendered justice that their trials often inspired. In fact, the fourth estate quickly realized that such stories could easily compete with the celluloid stars coming out of Hollywood as the general public increasingly began to view real-life female criminals as top-shelf entertainment.

By publishing the intimate details of the offender's life, criminal activity, and trial proceedings, newspapers could not only add to her celebrity status, but also suggest causes for her criminal behavior and provide justifications for her punishment. An examination of the public's response to these famous offenders also reveals the tensions specific to the celebrity criminal: the reporting on the Snyder and Cooney cases, with its tendency to present the criminal as glamorous and able to attract an enthusiastic fan base, mirrored the public's dual desire to both condemn and venerate the female offender. Certainly, male criminals were also receiving their fair share of media attention throughout the 1920s; newspapers frequently profiled male gangsters like Al Capone and John Dillinger and Hollywood studios were tapping into public interest by producing a steady stream of gangster films like Josef von Sternberg's *Underworld* (1927) and, later, William A. Wellman's *The Public Enemy* (1931). However, the public's particular fascination with the high-profile female offender focused on specifically gendered social issues. While the male criminal often inspired questions about urban growth and development, law-enforcement methods, and federal and municipal government policy, the celebrity female offender became a foundational figure for debating issues of women's rights and the once-deemed "weaker sex's" propensity for acts of physical violence. The female offender's popularity resided in her status as a contentious but powerful symbol of women's shifting legal status and changing social roles.

Readers of these newspaper narratives responded to them with tremendous enthusiasm, arriving by the thousands to catch a glimpse of Snyder and Cooney as they passed through the streets or sat in packed courtrooms. While the brutality of Snyder's crime inspired venomous calls for her electrocution, the laudatory descriptions of her remarkable beauty and glamour also encouraged public admiration. In Cooney's case, reports exhibit a similar interest in seeing the fashion-forward criminal be punished, but also express a desire for clemency given the girl's troubled upbringing. One might ask whether the crowds who mobbed the courthouses and train stations through which Cooney and Snyder passed were expressing admiration for their rebelliousness or simply trying to catch a glimpse of the women so that they might better relish the offenders' eventual condemnation. Or, as is perhaps more likely, were their fans simultaneously venerating and condemning these remarkable women?

Using these two particularly notorious 1920s female celebrity criminals, this essay considers how mediated visibility led to the celebritization of the female offender. Their presence in the popular press tried these women before the court of public opinion and transformed the popular understanding of women's propensity for and desire to commit criminal acts. In fact, the extensive coverage of cases like the Snyder murder and the Cooney robberies contributed to a Foucauldian reversal of the axis of individuation whereby the most intimate details of a female criminal's life were made a matter of public record — and the legal decisions surrounding her fate were made material for public debate. In *Discipline and Punish,* Foucault argues that disciplinary methods, particularly the "observing hierarchy" and "normalizing judgment" of the examination, extend the biographical process to the everyday individual, rather than confining it to the lives of the great.[4] I argue that the popular press's coverage of these women's crimes became just such a disciplinary tool by which the individual could be, to use Foucault's words, "described, judged, measured, compared with others . . . trained or corrected, classified, normalized, excluded, etc.," and that these methods of measuring and disciplining became even more loaded with gendered assumptions about femininity when they were applied by both the official legal system and the unofficial disciplinary processes of the public press.[5] By turning female offenders into celebrities, the press provided a venue for managing the modern female offender and critiquing the obvious gendered inequalities of the penal system.[6] The mediated spectacle of the female offender contributed to a process of celebritization that simultaneously celebrated women's rejection of legal and social norms and discouraged such a dangerous disregard for social and legal standards by trying her before a court of public opinion. Ultimately, the press's presentation of the celebrity female offender encouraged readers to debate one of modernity's most perplexing questions: given that women were not yet equal before the law, should they be condemned or celebrated for refusing to play by the law's rules?

---

4. Michel Foucault, *Discipline and Punish: The Birth of the Prison,* translated by Alan Sheridan (New York: Vintage Books, 1995), 184.

5. Ibid., 191.

6. Certainly, suffrage had eradicated the most egregious legal inequalities by 1920, granting women the right to vote, the right to hold property, access to education, and the right to practice most professions. However, the Nineteenth Amendment did not protect women from courtroom inequities as most states continued to deny women the right to participate in civic activities, including jury duty. Despite the Amendment, the right of trial by jury continued to be defined by English common law: "twelve good and lawful *men.*" As Christina M. Rodriguez explains, the possibility of a gendered justice, or the belief that "women as women would perform their duties as jurors differently from their male counterparts," inspired fierce "opposition to female jury service even as female suffrage remained grudgingly accepted." "Clearing the Smoke-Filled Room," *Yale Law Journal,* 108(7), (May, 1999): 1805–44. As a result, well into the 1920s the courtroom was often viewed as a particularly glaring arena for gender inequality. Women were repeatedly denied representation on juries across the United States late into the 1920s. And those states that did allow women to serve as jurors did not protect women from inequities in the process by which jury pools were established. In 1927, when Ruth Snyder stood trial, 19 states allowed women to serve on juries, New York noticeably absent among them. In some states, the right to jury service was not won until the 1950s. Not until 1975 were women eligible for jury duty in all federal and state courts.

Stardom, Celebrity, and Criminal Infamy

Though the term certainly occupies a contested terrain, stardom is often attributed to the individual based on his or her perceived accomplishments in a given field such as stage or screen performance, sports, singing, or dance. In fact, the hegemonic definition of fame is an inherently positive one whereby to be famous is to achieve something desirable and admirable. As has been well mapped out by Richard deCordova in *Picture Personalities*, the origins of the star system began to emerge very early in the twentieth century. Nonetheless, in the mid-1920s, when Cooney and Snyder's criminal exploits started dominating the headlines, the body of public knowledge that regulated the actor and defined the star was reaching new cultural prominence. No longer was knowledge of the actor confined to his or her on-screen performance via a highly regulated "picture personality"; rather, the star came to be known through a "thoroughgoing articulation of the paradigm professional/private life" that gave fans unprecedented access to a wealth of information about stars' off-screen lives.[7] Though this body of knowledge about the star came from a wide range of sources — personal appearances, sheet music tie-ins, signed photographs distributed to fans, posters — deCordova emphasizes the role of journalism, which "provided the institutional setting for much, if not most, of the discourse on stars. The trade press, fan magazines, the popular press, and newspapers all constituted specific positions from which to speak of the star."[8] As Richard Dyer explains, the star image emerged out of the complex, and often contradictory, nexus of information available on the star. As fans began to engage with an ever-increasing body of information — on-screen performance, fan magazines and trade publications, posters and other promotional materials, national newspaper columns and film reviews — a new intertextual star identity emerged.

Though it has an equally complex and contentious history and scholars use the term in different ways, the celebrity, unlike the star, is relatively unconnected to the sphere of professional work, excellence, or ability. As Irving Rein explains, celebrity is not something bestowed on the individual because of a measurable talent or skill; rather, celebrity is often something that first happens *to* an individual who, "once made by the news, now makes news itself."[9] One might further refine this definition by turning to Daniel Boorstin's 1961 claim that a "celebrity is a person who is well-known for their well-knownness."[10] In short, some suggest that the celebrity connotes

7. Richard deCordova, "The Emergence of the Star System in America," in Christine Gledhill (ed.), *Stardom: Industry of Desire* (New York: Routledge, 1991), 26.
8. Richard deCordova, *Picture Personalities: The Emergence of the Star System* (Urbana, IL: University of Illinois Press, 2001), 12.
9. Irving Rein, Philip Kotler, and Martin Stoller, *High Visibility: The Making and Marketing of Professions into Celebrities* (New York: McGraw-Hill, 1997), 14.
10. Daniel Boorstin, *The Image: A Guide to Pseudo-Events in America* (New York: Vintage Books, 1992), 57.

the state of simply *being* famous. Despite their often dubious talents and problematic behavior, the esteem with which fans view stars and celebrities is largely accepted as a questionable but relatively harmless byproduct of our fame- and celebrity-driven culture.[11] However, when the object of the fan's veneration is famous, or shall we say infamous, for having committed violent crimes, then the fan's veneration poses some particularly vexing problems.

In what I see as a particularly telling move, Leo Braudy begins his expansive study of fame, *The Frenzy of Renown*, with a murderer's complaint to the Wichita police, "How many times do I have to kill before I get a name in the paper or some national attention?"[12] In the case of Ruth Snyder, the answer was "once." With one single but particularly shocking criminal act, Snyder was propelled into the spotlight where she quickly came to represent modernity's seemingly new image of womanhood: the celebrity "murderess." In fact, many critics eventually turn to criminals when trying to map out the differences between stars and celebrities, a not-surprising strategy given that many contemporary serial killers, for example, express a strong desire, like Braudy's Wichita murderer, to achieve fame and notoriety through their criminality. In *Celebrity*, Chris Rojek argues that "[c]riminals are frequently driven by the overwhelming compulsion to be different, to possess fame, to break boundaries, to be a star — something literally, distinctively transcendent. [. . .] Criminality is, in part, the expression of the quest for one-upmanship, the desire to outsmart others and take people for a ride so as to confirm one's inner sense of superior gamesmanship."[13]

In fact, the public obsession with high-profile female offenders like Snyder and Cooney reflects the celebrity's ability to integrate what, as Rojek explains, are usually viewed as polarized terms: the favorable public recognition associated with glamour and the unfavorable public recognition associated with notoriety.[14] Although David Schmid turns to the "iconic status of serial killers in contemporary American culture" as proof of the collapsing boundary between fame and notoriety, the press's presentation of Snyder and Cooney's narratives suggests that these two terms became conflated long before the rise of the contemporary serial killer.[15] Braudy claims that, particularly since World War II, the "concept of fame has been grotesquely distended, and the line between public achievement and private pathology grown dimmer."[16] Critics like Braudy and Rojek often focus their analyses of

11. Rojek presents an exception to this rule in the chapter "Celebrity and Religion," in which he discusses the "obsessed fan" and the worship of celebrity as idolatry. Chris Rojek, *Celebrity* (London: Reaktion Books, 2001), 51–100.
12. Leo Braudy, *The Frenzy of Renown: Fame and its History* (New York: Vintage Books, 1986), 3.
13. Rojek, *Celebrity*, 151.
14. Ibid., 10.
15. Schmid, David, "Idols of Destruction: Celebrity and the Serial Killer," in Su Holmes and Sean Redmond (eds), *Framing Celebrity: New Directions in Celebrity Culture* (New York: Routledge, 2006), 297.
16. Braudy, *The Frenzy of Renown*, 3.

celebrity criminals on the high-profile, usually male, serial killer who publicizes his desire to outwit law enforcement officials and go down in history for high body counts. In contrast, an examination of the media's response to Cooney and Snyder's crimes suggests a less intentional acquisition of celebrity through criminal activity. In fact, these women's celebrity status emerged as an unexpected byproduct of their legal offenses, only later escalating into a desirable form of public recognition that the offenders seemed to savor and provoke. During the first few decades of the twentieth century, the celebrity, when she appears in the form of a high-profile female offender, often traded in a combination of glamour, fame, *and* notoriety. And, at the same time that the star system outlined by deCordova was emerging, so too was a new corpus of criminological knowledge as anthropologists measured the criminal's body, psychologists evaluated the criminal's mind, and sociologists examined the criminal's environment. These two nascent discourses merged in the early 1920s as Hollywood suffered the impact of a series of high-profile legal scandals, which caused the still-new star system to experience a noticeable blurring of the line between glamorous star and notorious criminal.[17]

The Rise of the Female Offender

During the first two decades of the twentieth century, countless newspaper articles (often within the context of debates about the onset of modernity) decried the decreased moral standards of American citizens, citing rising crime rates as evidence of this moral backsliding. One *Boston Globe* article suggests the urgency of the crime problem by emphasizing the cost in both lives and dollars: "With murders at the rate of 1 a day in Chicago and New York, with robberies and embezzlements costing the business men of the country $3,000,000,000 annually, there is urgent need that this social menace be dealt with by constructive thought."[18] Newspapers often described a general rise in crime rates without providing hard numbers to back up the claims, maintaining a particularly precipitous rise in women's criminal activity. Although there was not yet a federal apparatus for collecting data on crime rates, local police departments occasionally publicized statistics that showed that rates of arrest and incarceration among women, while still considerably lower than rates among men, began rising in the 1910s and continued to rise throughout the 1920s and 1930s.[19] Such reports rarely disclosed actual

---

17. To name but the most high-profile crimes that rocked Hollywood in 1922, Fatty Arbuckle was accused of rape and manslaughter, William Desmond Taylor was murdered and many believed the crime was committed by a Hollywood insider, and Wallace Reid died of a drug overdose. For a more detailed examination of these criminal cases, see Adrienne L. McLean and David A. Cook's *Headline Hollywood: A Century of Film Scandal* (New Brunswick, NJ: Rutgers University Press, 2001).
18. "Fr. Corrigan, S. J., Shows the Defects of Educational System," *Boston Daily Globe*, August 24, 1925, A16.
19. Ellen C. Potter, "The Problem of Women in Penal and Correctional Institutions," *Journal*

incarceration numbers, instead speaking in vague and often contradictory terms about the rise in criminal behavior. Yet, some bureaus would release information that attempted to quantify this statistical change in the criminal population. For example, a study of arrest cards in the Record Bureau of the Detroit Police Department, a rare early attempt to quantify the rise in female criminality, showed that female arrests for various crimes increased from 2,110 in 1913 to 9,799 in 1919.[20] Similarly, a 1921 *Los Angeles Times* report claimed that "offenses committed by women in Los Angeles have nearly trebled in one year."[21] While there exists little statistical evidence to support such reports of a female "crime wave," the pervasiveness of these claims suggest that both law enforcement officials and the reading public were troubled by women's increasing criminal propensities.[22]

In addition to decrying the sheer increase in the number of female offenders, reports like the following one by Frederick J. Haskins also lamented women's increasing social autonomy and the wider range of criminal roles afforded by that independence:

> Experts who have been studying what is popularly referred to as the present "crime wave" in the United States agree that there has been a startling increase in the number of female lawbreakers within the last few years. Bobbed-haired bandits and gun-women are breaking into the front pages of the newspapers almost daily with their spectacular exploits and where formerly the women of the criminal underworld did little more than associate with men crooks they now seem disposed to go out and make careers of their own in crime.[23]

In fact, such reportage suggests that a "bandit queen who called the shots and was the 'Boss over Men'," as one headline put it, was a novelty signifying a new way of understanding women's potential roles in 1920s America. The idea of a woman committing armed robbery or violent murder seemed to be one stolen from the Hollywood playbook; Celia Cooney's first victim, the manager of a grocery store, refused to believe a woman had actually committed the crime, saying "it must have been a man dressed up in girl's clothes," because "who the hell ever heard of a girl bandit except in the movies."[24]

---

of Criminal Law and Criminology 25(1), (May–June 1934): 65–75.

20. Arthur Evans Wood, "A Study of Arrests in Detroit, 1913–1919," *Journal of the American Institute of Criminal Law and Criminology* 21(2), (Aug 1930): 168–200.

21. "Women's Crime Growing Fast," *Los Angeles Times*, October 9, 1921, 13.

22. It is important to note that the Federal Bureau of Investigation did not begin to collect national statistics on crime until 1930 when it launched the Uniform Crime Reporting Program (UCRP), which collects, publishes, and archives the statistics voluntarily provided by city, county, and state law enforcement agencies. Prior to the introduction of the UCRP, crime statistics were collected only on state and municipal levels and, therefore, any claims to large increases in criminal activities are very difficult to substantiate.

23. Frederick J. Haskin, "Breaking into a Penitentiary," *Los Angeles Times*, January 10, 1926, L10.

24. Stephen Duncombe and Andrew Mattson, *The Bobbed-Haired Bandit: A True Story of Crime*

This remarkable new trend also created considerable anxiety as news of copy-cat "girl bandits" spread throughout the country, thus reinforcing the belief that one woman criminal would lead to a plague of gun-toting bob-haired bandits. As one judge explained after arraigning two teen-aged girls for holding up a store, "unaided by man's guiding hand," "This is serious. If such things are allowed to go on, many a good stick-up man is liable to lose his job. Women are evidently coming into their own. This is the first case that has come to my attention in which girls have held up and robbed a store unaided. It looks like the dawn of a new era."[25] While on the one hand this assessment of women's criminal propensities makes light of women's increasing independence in the underworld, it also aligns the female criminal with another type of female offender. And while the facetious assessment of "thieving" may seem humorous in this 1920s context, many critics feared that female emancipation would inspire iniquitous desires for material goods that would inspire women to steal the jobs of both the working man and the common criminal alike, a fear that would turn deadly serious with the onset of the Great Depression.[26]

These sensational descriptions of women's criminal activity suggest that women's emancipation was not only giving women increased access to legitimate professional and social pursuits, but also more illegitimate ones. As Nicole Rafter and Mary Gibson explain, it's no coincidence that studies of female criminality, like Cesare Lombroso's *The Female Offender*, first published in Italian in 1893 and translated into English in 1895, appeared "during a period when members of the women's movement were vociferously demanding access to education, entrance to the professions, equality within the family, and the right to vote."[27]

Lombroso, who published the first study focusing on the woman criminal, popularized theories of a physiological criminal type that would influence many scientists' and laypeople's understanding of crime and the criminal body. Ultimately claiming that the female offender's "moral physiognomy" was more primitive than her law-abiding counterpart, Lombroso concluded that the female criminal's "atavistic diminution of secondary sexual characteristics" caused her to exhibit very masculine qualities — excessive eroticism, an ability to dominate weaker beings, and a taste for violence

and Celebrity in 1920s New York (New York: New York University Press, 2006), 35.

25. "Growing Proficiency Among Girl Bandits May Drive Men Out," *The Atlanta Constitution*, January 22, 1924, 3.

26. By the mid-1920s, women made up almost one-quarter of the labor force and they were increasingly accused of stealing jobs from able-bodied male workers, accusations that only increased with onset of the Great Depression. See Laura Hapke's *Tales of the Working Girl: Wage-earning Women in American Literature, 1890–1925* (Toronto: Maxwell Macmillan Canada, 1992).

27. Nicole Hahn Rafter and Mary Gibson, "Editors' Introduction," in Nicole Hahn Rafter and Mary Gibson (eds), *Criminal Woman, the Prostitute, and the Normal Woman* (Durham, NC: Duke University Press, 2004), 16.

Figure 3.2 **Photograph of the bobbed-haired bandit, Celia Cooney, and her husband, Edward Cooney, taken after their arrest in Florida. Published April 24, 1924.**

— and a deficiency in traditionally feminine qualities — weak maternal and moral instincts.[28] The influence of this Lombrosian model continued to hold until World War I, when researchers began to slowly move away from such biological models that emphasized intelligence and physical characteristics when determining the individual's propensity for criminal behavior. By the mid-1920s, such a reliance on biological determinism began to wane as researchers placed an increasing emphasis on social and environmental influences.[29] Although Lombroso's biological interpretations of crime were under attack by the time that Cooney and Snyder came to the public's attention, a Lombrosian proclivity for cataloguing the anatomical markers of the criminal seems to have influenced the media's laborious physical descriptions of these notorious celebrities.

The photographs of Celia Cooney and her husband, Edward, taken after their arrest in Florida speak to their celebrity status. These are certainly *not* mug shots. Instead, they bear much in common with the photographs of movie stars that also appeared in national newspapers. Celia smiles slightly for the camera, her hands crossed at her pelvis, her right foot extended slightly to better show off her stylish shoes. Her infamous bobbed hair

28. Caesare Lombroso and William Ferrero, *The Female Offender* (New York: D. Appleton and Co., 1909), 187.
29. See Estelle B. Freeman, *Their Sisters' Keeper: Women's Prison Reform, 1830–1930* (Ann Arbor, MI: University of Michigan Press, 1984), 111.

is tucked under a hat that also shields her left eye slightly. Eddie stands beside her in a similarly relaxed pose, his hands in his pockets and a smile on his face. These are not criminals trying to hide from the press's prying eyes. These are two people who are very conscious of their public image and their star status. Even the caption used below the photo speaks to this celebrity status, proclaiming "First photo to be received in Washington of bobbed-haired bandit, Celia Cooney, and her partner-husband, Edward Cooney."[30] The caption above the photo also spoke to a marked shift in the celebrity status of the female criminal in that Celia was front and center: "The Bobbed-Haired Bandit and Mate." The woman criminal is the primary focus here, while her husband is the sidekick. This, too, was in keeping with a new shift in understanding of women's criminal propensities. It was not necessarily the man who was leading the woman into a life of crime. In fact, the men were often described as hapless ride-alongs who were coerced into committing crimes by their much more aggressive and crime-prone wives and lovers. This same notion was put forward with Ruth Snyder, whose lover was often "feminized" and disempowered by the popular press.

Though many photographs of Snyder circulated in the press, journalists still included detailed descriptions of her appearance in their reports, creating lists of physical characteristics that seemed to belie her hard-hearted criminal tendencies. A *Los Angeles Times* writer, for example, claims that photographs, which made her look heavy-jowled and "button nosed" could not possibly do her justice:

> On the contrare [*sic*], she is very good looking and seems younger than her thirty-three years. Her mouth seems to me to be hard and cold; her closed lips form a straight, tight line, and her eyes are not merely blue; they are more than blue; they are pale blue stones that have become alive and alert. Otherwise there is nothing remarkable about her appearance. Her type is so conventional that one constantly meets women who look like her. As I studied her features I thought of three women of my acquaintance who resemble her closely. One of them, who is almost her living image, has high social position and is a perfect pattern of philanthropy and propriety.[31]

Ironically, these details both suggest Snyder's remarkable beauty — a beauty often employed in futile attempts to influence jurors — and her ordinariness, her astonishing resemblance to countless other women, including the jury foreman's wife.[32]

Such detailed descriptions of women's bodies suggest something of the

---

30. "Photo Standalone 1," *Washington Post*, April 23, 1924, 3.
31. W. E. Woodward, "Author Tells of Details at Snyder-Gray Trial," *Los Angeles Times*, April 19, 1927, 2
32. "Resemblance to Jury's Foreman to Mrs. Snyder Said to Have Been Remarked," *Washington Post*, April 25, 1927, 1.

disciplinary process outlined in Foucault's *Discipline and Punish*. He describes how the disciplinary methods of surveillance created a reversal of the axis of individuation whereby the life of the "ordinary" individual suddenly met the "threshold of description":

> To be looked at, observed, described in detail, followed from day to day by an uninterrupted writing was a privilege. The chronicle of man, the account of his life, his historiography, written as he lived out his life formed part of the rituals of his power. The disciplinary methods reversed this relation, lowered the threshold of describable individuality and made of this description a means of control and a method of domination. It is no longer a monument for future memory, but a document for possible use. [. . .] This turning of real lives into writing is no longer a procedure of heroization; it functions as a procedure of objectification and subjection. The carefully collated life of mental patients or delinquents belongs, as did the chronicle of kings or the adventures of the great popular bandits, to a certain political function of writing.[33]

The media's cataloguing of the celebrity criminal's biography rendered every aspect of her life a matter of public record. Much like the examination outlined by Foucault, these media accounts created a reversal of the axis of individuation that allowed both the few, the official members of the penal system, and the many, the "fans" who eagerly read about her exploits, to evaluate the criminal's guilt and punishment. These mediated spectacles became tools by which the few could discipline both the individual female criminals actually on trial and the many women who would read about them. When Cooney was commissioned by William Randolph Hearst to write the story of her life, thus earning her first "honest" $1,000 for the piece, the narrative was presented as a warning against this new "era" of female offenders. Cooney's first-person account of her life of crime was serialized and distributed via newspapers across the country and even used in the courtroom to help explain the motive for her crimes, an explanation that one reporter felt would surely deter other women from following her example: "Before Judge Martin sentenced Brooklyn's bobbed-haired bandit and her husband to terms of 10 to 20 years in prison this week, he read one of the most remarkable reports ever made by a probation officer. It is not only a story about Celia Cooney — it is a message to every girl who is inclined to waywardness, who would seek notoriety as she gained it — and a message to those of us who sit complacently by and say, 'Wasn't she awful'."[34] Just as readers were being encouraged to take pleasure in Cooney's biography and the punishment to which she was subjected, such a story could also have a panoptic effect, reminding the female reader that she, too, could languish

---

33. Foucault, *Discipline and Punish*, 192.
34. "Side of Bob-Haired Bandit's Story," *Boston Daily Globe*, May 11, 1924, A7.

in prison if she were to seek out this same kind of notoriety.

Much like the actor who "cannot be viewed simply as a real individual," the celebrity offender, whose every appearance before the public is meticulously recorded and disseminated via photographs, trial transcripts, and sensationalized reporting, ceases to be simply an individual.[35] And yet I want to suggest that the process of celebritizing that surrounded these high-profile female offenders served more than just a disciplinary function. While their stories certainly held tremendous sensational appeal, the exploits of Cooney and Snyder, and other female offenders, were described in a manner intended as warnings; these were figures that women should avoid emulating, and men avoid marrying, at all costs. However, just as fans will continue to imitate and emulate stars of questionable repute, many followers found something to admire in the celebrity female offender. The image/text of the celebrity female offender served a complex and often contradictory function, simultaneously warning women against legal infractions and highlighting the subversive potential of a blatant disregard for legal- and gender-based restrictions on women's behavior. In *Discipline and Punish,* Foucault explains how the examination process serves as a disciplinary function:

> The examination leaves behind it a whole meticulous archive constituted in terms of bodies and days. The examination that places individuals in a field of surveillance also situates them in a network of writing; it engaged them in a whole mass of documents that capture and fix them. The procedures of examination were accompanied at the same time by a system of intense registration and of documentary accumulation.[36]

With a disciplinary system that leaves the many constantly under examination by the few, a vast archive of information is collected in an attempt to render the criminal identifiable and controllable.

This technique is most evident in the reportage about Ruth Snyder, which very clearly sought to show how her previous behavior served as evidence of her criminality. Her interest in dancing and drink, her desire to socialize and spend time with men other than her husband, her possession of an address book with the names of 28 strange men — behavior that was certainly legal — were all used as evidence of her later crime. Descriptions of a criminal's personal history seek to find evidence of criminality, or to show how the "individual already resembles his crime before he has committed it."[37] This background information, often provided by expert psychiatric opinion, creates a "kind of reconstruction of the crime itself, in a scaled-down version,

---

35. deCordova, *Picture Personalities,* 19.
36. Foucault, *Discipline and Punish,* 189.
37. Michel Foucault, *Abnormal: Lectures at the Collège de France 1974–1975,* translated by Graham Burchell (New York: Picador, 1999), 19.

before it has been committed. [. . .] In this parapathological, sublegal series below the threshold, the subject is present in the form of desire. Expert psychiatric opinion shows how the subject is present in the form of criminal desire in all these details and minutiae, in all these vile deeds and things that are not quite regular."[38] In the case of Snyder, her ability to mentally overpower a male co-conspirator who was only too willing to "hide behind her skirts," her love of drinking and dancing, and her consumerist desire for more than her husband's $115 a week paycheck were all presented as evidence of her criminal desires, as details of her biography that could be deemed "not quite regular" and thus used as further evidence of her criminal guilt. In a period of great social concern over women's expanded access to leisure pursuits, Snyder's lifestyle served as evidence of the dangerous repercussions of women's increased mobility, raising questions that it might transform not just the political system but also the very notion of "woman" itself.

The Corporeality of Fame and the Spectacle of Execution

Armchair psychologists and news reporters would have been hard-pressed to find a more sensational criminal subject than Ruth Brown Snyder, the one-time switchboard operator and secretary who married her boss, Albert Snyder, and eventually conspired with her lover to bludgeon her husband to death. Known by many of her friends as "Tommie" and described by newspapers as a party-loving "ingénue Lady Macbeth," Snyder later became the inspiration for many of film's most influential femmes fatales.[39] Although other stories of female murderers appeared regularly in the nation's newspapers, Snyder's criminal celebrity grew to an unprecedented, fever-pitch popularity. Over 180 reporters from across the nation were assigned to cover the case, and by May 5, 1927 the *Evening Post* reported that "Approximately 1,500,000 words about the Snyder story" had been "filed on press wires," and the *New York Times* ran daily articles on the trial from the morning of the murder to the night of the execution almost ten months later.[40] For the thousands of eager spectators who were denied access to the courtroom, the newspapers recreated the trial in phenomenal detail. In fact, the press coverage of the crime "encouraged readers to see Ruth Snyder as an actor in a film" with an abundance of "star quality" that helped ensure her iconic status while also calling into question the supposed authenticity of the news reporting.[41]

---

38. Ibid., 20.
39. The Snyder-Gray murder case was most famously recounted by director Billy Wilder in *Double Indemnity* (1944), though Tay Garnett's 1946 film, *The Postman Always Rings Twice*, and Lawrence Kasdan's 1981 neo-noir, *Body Heat* also present versions of the same crime.
40. *Evening Post*, May 5, 1927, 6.
41. V. Penelope Pelizzon and Nancy M. West, "Multiple Indemnity: Film Noir, James M. Cain

As a reporter for the *New Yorker* explains, the legal system was even being forced to develop new legal guidelines and procedures due to the female offender's rising celebrity status: "Justice Scudder has announced that photographers and lunch-baskets will not be permitted at the Snyder-Gray trial. These days a judge who can distinguish between a murder case and a picnic is as rare as a Button Gwinnett autograph."[42] While the increasing number of women accused of crimes inspired questions about women's interest in and capacity for violence, these packed courtrooms speak to the female offender's tremendous celebrity status and the public's paradoxical relationship with the criminal woman. While social critics expressed growing concern over the female offender, often linking women's growing presence among the criminal classes to their increasing mobility, the popular consumption of female-centered crime narratives in a wide range of venues also suggests the female criminal's expanding cultural cachet.[43]

Certainly, the thousands of citizens who strained to catch a glimpse of female celebrity newsmakers Snyder and Cooney made no distinction between them and the latest Hollywood star or political figure. In fact, numerous newspaper reports described how Cooney stole the President's thunder when he visited New York City as Coolidge's public quickly abandoned him in favor of the Brooklyn Bandit. A reporter, in trying to explain the public's preference, stated: "There have been thirty presidents of the United States, but only one bob-haired girl bandit. Probably that was the reason why Celia Cooney, the pretty little ex-laundress who terrorized the shopkeepers of Brooklyn and made monkeys out of thousands of coppers during her amazing string of chain-store holdups, took the show away from Calvin Coolidge when she was brought into competition with the president as an attraction at the Pennsylvania station here Tuesday afternoon."[44] Reportedly, more than "a thousand persons jammed the corridors long before the arrival of the Cooneys and this throng was augmented by hundreds of others who raced from the railroad terminal" as Cooney's fans strained to get a glimpse of the woman behind the headlines.[45] Public interest did not wane even after the Cooneys pled guilt to their crimes. In fact, later newspaper reports that

and Adaptations of a Tabloid Case," *Narrative* 13 (3), (2005): 218–19.

42. "Comment," *The New Yorker*, April 16, 1927, 17.

43. Snyder's story provided the basis for a well-received 1928 Broadway play by Sophie Treadwell, *Machinal*. And, while this essay focuses specifically on Ruth Snyder and Celia Cooney, many other celebrity female offenders emerged in the popular press during the 1920s and provided the inspiration for numerous Hollywood films. Further evidence of the female offender's cultural cachet can be seen in Tod Browning's numerous films depicting the working-class female criminal, Dorothy Davenport Reid's portrayal of prostitute-turned-murderer Gabrielle Darley in *The Red Kimona* (1925), and, perhaps most famously, in the glamorous celebrity female offenders in Frank Urson and Cecil B. DeMille's *Chicago* (1927). These are all works that I explore in a larger book manuscript entitled *Offending Women: Modernism, Crime, and Creative Production*.

44. "Bobbed Bandit Steals Eye of Public," *Atlanta Constitution*, April 23, 1924, 22.

45. Ibid.

detailed Celia's hard-luck childhood of panhandling and living in poverty only increased public sympathies by creating a kind of populist working-class sense of affiliation with the non-murderous Brooklyn offender.

In contrast, Ruth Snyder's personal story of "marrying up" into middle-class society, and her continued dissatisfaction with that social status, caused the public to judge her far more harshly. Yet the public responded with similar freneticism to the Snyder-Gray murder trial, with the *New York Times* reporting "mobs" a thousand deep lining up outside the courtroom in the hopes of gaining admittance to the trial "show." Even after she was convicted and sentenced to death, Snyder's fans continued to appear outside of her Sing Sing cell where the "Bloody Blonde" held court like the highest profile Hollywood star:

> Mrs. Snyder did not disappoint the mob that gaped. At 5 p.m. she made a sudden appearance at her cell window, her blonde hair fanned by the breeze, her white sweater making her an easy target for the gaze of the curious. Instantly staid looking citizens with their wives and children stampeded the prison courtyard. She stared down at them for a moment, smiled and withdrew. Hopeful of another glimpse of the murderess the crowd waited until dark, but in vain.[46]

Whether this reporter's account of Snyder's appearance is accurate, or merely a melodramatic conception of the supposedly "steel-eyed" and "fame-hungry" bloody blonde is, I would argue, beside the point. His account clearly displays the female offender's cultural currency and ability to attract and entertain adoring fans.

W. E. Woodward describes the press of bodies outside the prison, detailing the crowds vying to see the infamous murderess:

> In the crowd outside in the street a woman touched my arm and asked me to get her into the Courthouse. I told her that I could barely squeeze myself in. Then she explained that she and her friend — a woman who stood nearby — lived in Southold, L.I., and that they had risen at 3 o'clock in the morning to catch the train for Long Island City and how, after all that trouble, they were not allowed even to have a glimpse of Mrs. Snyder.
>
> "If we could have only one glimpse," they said in chorus.
>
> "Why not go around to the jail?" I suggested. "Maybe the jailer would let you see her."
>
> "We did," they said, "but he wouldn't let us" — and they wept a little.
>
> I had not gone ten steps before two other women stopped me and prayed for intercession.
>
> "We have a right in there," one of them said.[47]

---

46. "Still Loves Judd Gray, Ruth Snyder protests," *Washington Post*, May 16, 1927, 8.
47. "Author Tells of Detail at Snyder-Gray Trial," 2. Emphasis mine.

The reporter presents these two would-be female spectators as over-eager fans waiting for hours outside of a stage door in the hopes of catching even a glimpse of the object of their adoration. And perhaps most striking is the one woman's claim that to deny them access to their sought-after celebrity is to deny them a basic "right," a claim that seems doubly telling given that women were still not given the right to officially bear witness to another woman's crimes via the jury box.

Similarly, although only 24 witnesses were permitted inside the execution chamber, hundreds of people applied to see the Snyder-Gray deaths. In an attempt to sate the desires of these disappointed potential spectators, numerous newspapers printed macabre and highly detailed descriptions of Snyder's execution. While other newspapers' coverage of the execution paled in comparison to Howard's photographic scoop, they presented equally explicit renderings of the execution process and supplied pains-taking details about the emotional and physical effects of death row on the prisoners. Reports such as one by Sid Sutherland of the *Chicago Daily Tribune* reenact Snyder's death, describing the hours leading up to the execution, including what she ate as her last meal, how many steps she took while walk-ing to the execution chamber, and, perhaps most important, how her body responded to the flipping of the executioner's switch:

The woman about to die was garbed in a shapeless dark green gingham dress and a cheap brown smock. [. . .] On her blonde head was an apparatus that looked like a leather football headgear, inside of which the wire mesh and sponge electrode pressed against a bald spot where they had clipped her hair. Against her right ankle was another electrode. In a little alcove across the room stood Robert G. Elliott, the state executioner. Without a signal from anyone, he suddenly threw in his switch. It was exactly 11:02 o'clock. Ruth's body straightened, writhed for a fleet-ing moment, and then was arched forward in its death throes, tugging vibratingly against the bonds. In the void of quietness there was a curious humming sound, a whine that rose to a low, ominous pitch, and held that note. It was the 2,000 volts and 10 amperes of alternating current ebbing and flowing through the woman's body. At 11:04 the voltage was decreased. At the end of three minutes the current was turned off, and Dr. C. C. Sweet, prison physician, examined the woman. [. . .] At 11:07 Dr. Sweet turned to the witnesses and said: 'I pronounce this woman dead.'[48]

---

48. Sid Sutherland, "Electrocute Ruth and Gray," *Chicago Daily Tribune*, January 13, 1928, 1. It is worth noting that Sutherland did not present a similarly detailed reconstruction of Gray's execution. He simply described how "the guards started forward, grasped the doomed man by the arms, and seated him. The straps and electrodes were quickly adjusted. The guards then returned to their post, and the executioner, from his place across the room, at once pressed the switch. The current was turned on at 11:10 o'clock, and in three minutes was shut off. A minute later Gray was pronounced dead." In contrast, the *Atlanta Constitution* kept the description of Snyder's death short while detailing Gray's execution: "Gray's body seemed to be lifted upward and outwards as though he was about to rise out of the chair. He remained in this uncouth position while his left hand curled into a fist and his right

When combined with the aforementioned photograph of Snyder, these precise minute-by-minute accounts of the physical details of her death presented hyperrealistic, albeit sensational, play-by-plays of the murderer's last moments. Even in death, the rhetorical and visual aspects of her image dominated the public imagination like so many of the period's biggest Hollywood stars.

The journalistic accounts of Ruth Snyder's trial and execution and the eventual capture and trial of the elusive Bobbed Haired Bandit functioned as disciplinary tools within 1920s American society. By actively producing scandalous criminal identities and with newspapers marketing these identities to a hungry public, these celebrity offenders functioned as larger-than-life "others" against which women's normality could be measured. In an era in which women's expanded public roles were of increasing public concern, the female offender became a sign of the dangers of such emancipation. As their crimes and personal histories were placed front-and-center in the popular imagination, Cooney and Snyder, as celebrity female offenders, became representatives of the seismic changes in 1920s gendered behavior, criminal and otherwise. With women struggling for and obtaining greater autonomy in a variety of public spheres, from the workplace to the courtroom, the celebrity criminal became an emblem for debating the perils and pleasures of women's emancipation.

In his contemporaneous analysis of the Ruth Snyder trial, John Kobler emphasizes the destabilizing nature of such a gender-specific shift in the murderer's representation:

> No crime stings popular imagination so sharply as one that is essentially commonplace. [. . .] Psychotic freaks who go in for fancy dismemberment and other baroque horrors may momentarily titillate the old gentleman in carpet slippers, but when Mrs. Jones next door laces her husband's chowder with weed killer that same old gentleman is jounced off his perch. The thing is too near home, too understandable. Subconsciously he identifies with poor Jones. He may even view his own consort in fresh perspective — and wonder a little.[49]

As Kobler's comment suggests, countless newspaper reports on flapper bandits and housewives-turned-murderers threatened many long-held stereotypes about the female subject and foregrounded women's volatile relationship to the law.

Celebrity criminal cases like those of Cooney and Snyder became cultural

---

hand grotesquely relaxed. To the horror of the spectators, at 11:12 a small curl of smoke, such as might have come from a tobacco pipe, fantastically wreathed toward the ceiling from Gray's right temple." See Sam Love, "Jury Selected to Try Slayers of Art Editor," *Atlanta Constitution*, April 23, 1927, 2.

49. John Kobler, *The Trial of Ruth Snyder and Judd Gray: Edited with a History of the Case* (New York: Doubleday, 1938), 1.

events that inspired debates about many complex social questions, including a woman's right to face both a jury of her peers and the executioner's chamber. In 1923, the *Chicago Daily Tribune* published an editorial that lamented the tendency for juries to use leniency when hearing the cases of women criminals, in this case "Honey" Sullivan, the blonde bandit queen who was suspected of shooting a man:

> If she is found, she will travel the road of the law, which offers so many exits, the widest being the sex sentimentality which permits vicious women to defy justice so often in this country. Leniency to female criminals is a wrong not only for society but to women themselves. It encourages the wayward, who need restraint, not encouragement to crime. The slender girl bandit in the picture hat who is now hiding with husband's and father's life blood on her soul grew up in an atmosphere of contempt for law and its power of punishment. Undoubtedly she thought robbery a sporting way of getting what she wanted at small risk and if caught a good chance before a sentimental jury of males or a court easy with youth.[50]

In fact, the media spectacle inspired by these crimes often encouraged readers to engage in a highly controversial debate: "Can a woman be held to the same legal responsibility for murder or other crimes as a man?"[51] The published responses to the Snyder trial testify to the public's desire to participate in the judicial process by which such celebrity murderers would be punished. This interest can be seen most explicitly in a postcard signed by "The Public" and published June 2, 1927, by the *New York Times*. Intended for the Albany Court of Appeals that was considering the Snyder case, the postcard issued the following directive: "We will shoot you if *you* let that woman Snyder go free. She must be electrocuted. The public demands it. If she is not done away with, other women will do the same as she has. She must be made an example of. We are watching out."[52] And as historian Jessie Ramey has shown in her analysis of the Snyder case, men were not alone in this fear: 1,500 club women in New Jersey took a poll and wrote the *New York Daily News* in favor of Ruth's execution. Mrs. Maude Gossett, an officer of the Flushing, Queens branch of the Women's Christian Temperance Union, wrote: "If Ruth Snyder isn't electrocuted, then ladies will order sashweights by the dozens and men will never be safe."[53] In the public's cry for the execution

---

50. "Encouraging the Criminal," *Chicago Daily Tribune*, June 7, 1923, 8.
51. This question was posed by the *Chicago Daily Tribune* in its coverage of jury selection for the case of Eliza Nusbaum, who was tried for the murder of her husband Albert in 1926. Potential jurors who claimed they could not hang a woman were dismissed. "Jury Scruples Slow Trial," *Chicago Daily Tribune*, February 17, 1926, 5. Countless articles from the period address this same debate, often in response to yet another trial of a female murderer.
52. "Threat in Snyder Case," *New York Times*, June 2, 1927, 27.
53. Ramey, "The Bloody Blonde and the Marble Woman," 632.

of Ruth Snyder one can see both the destabilizing power of the murderous female subject and the public's desire to contain that power.

As their crimes and personal histories were placed front-and-center in the popular imagination, Cooney and Snyder, as celebrity female offenders, became representatives of the seismic changes in 1920s gendered behavior, criminal and otherwise. In fact, their presentation in the popular press effectively tried women before a court of public opinion and influenced popular understandings of women's propensity for and desire to commit criminal acts. The most intimate details of a criminal's life were made a matter of public record and that public record threatened to diminish any clear understanding of the person behind the personality. Ultimately, Cooney and Snyder's cases show how celebritization can become an integral component for critiquing and reinforcing the evolving system of penality used for managing the modern female offender. The media spectacle that surrounded these high-profile female offenders betrays the complexities of fame and fans' often-conflicted emotional response to the celebrities they so eagerly followed. Snyder and Cooney's followers included both supporters and detractors who called respectively for leniency and the harshest of punishment. Perhaps more disturbing is how these cases suggest that the public record fabricated by the media can be used to determine the offender's guilt or innocence — and the punishment to which she should be subjected. In turning high-profile female offenders into celebrities the press provided a venue for debating the merits of a still-gender-biased legal system, one that relegated women to the sidelines, one where to observe the celebrity criminal's trial and even execution was the only way to allow the female offender an audience of her peers.

Works Cited

Atlanta Constitution. "Bobbed Bandit Steals Eye of Public," April 23, 1924, 22.
——. "Growing Proficiency Among Girl Bandits May Drive Men Out," January 22, 1924, 3.
"Author Tells of Detail at Snyder-Gray Trial," 2.
"Bobbed Bandit Steals Eye of Public," *Atlanta Constitution,* April 23, 1924, 22.
Boorstin, Daniel J. *The Image: A Guide to Pseudo-Events in America.* New York: Vintage Books, 1992.
Boston Daily Globe. "Fr. Corrigan, S. J., Shows the Defects of Educational System," August 24, 1925, A16.
——. "Side of Bob-Haired Bandit's Story," May 11, 1924, A7.
Bosworth, Thomas S. "Snapshot," *New Yorker,* January 28, 1928, 9.
Braudy, Leo. *The Frenzy of Renown: Fame and its History.* New York: Vintage Books, 1986.
Chicago Daily Tribune. "Encouraging the Criminal," June 7, 1923, 8.
——. "Jury Scruples Slow Trial," February 17, 1926, 5.
"Comment," *The New Yorker,* April 16, 1927, 17.
deCordova, Richard. "The Emergence of the Star System in America," in Christine Gledhill (ed.), *Stardom: Industry of Desire.* New York: Routledge, 1991.
——. *Picture Personalities: The Emergence of the Star System.* Urbana, IL: University of Illinois Press, 2001.
Duncombe, Stephen and Andrew Mattson. *The Bobbed-Haired Bandit: A True Story of Crime and Celebrity in 1920s New York.* New York: New York University Press, 2006.

Foucault, Michel. *Discipline and Punish: The Birth of the Prison*, translated by Alan Sheridan. New York: Vintage Books, 1995.

——. *Abnormal: Lectures at the Collège de France 1974–1975*, translated by Graham Burchell. New York: Picador, 1999.

"Fr. Corrigan, S. J., Shows the Defects of Educational System," *Boston Daily Globe*, August 24, 1925, A16.

Freeman, Estelle B. *Their Sisters' Keeper: Women's Prison Reform, 1830–1930*. Ann Arbor, MI: University of Michigan Press, 1984.

Hapke, Laura. *Tales of the Working Girl: Wage-earning Women in American Literature, 1890–1925*. Toronto: Maxwell Macmillan Canada, 1992.

Haskin, Frederick J. "Breaking into a Penitentiary," *Los Angeles Times*, January 10, 1926, L10.

Kobler, John. *The Trial of Ruth Snyder and Judd Gray: Edited with a History of the Case*. New York: Doubleday, 1938.

Krajicek, David J. "Ruthless Ruth", *New York Daily News*, January 20, 2008, 42.

Lombroso, Caesare and William Ferrero. *The Female Offender*. New York: D. Appleton and Co., 1909.

Los Angeles Times. "Women's Crime Growing fast," October 9, 1921, I3.

Love, Sam. "Jury Selected to Try Slayers of Art Editor," *Atlanta Constitution*, April 23, 1927, 2.

McLean, Adrienne L., and David A. Cook. *Headline Hollywood: A Century of Film Scandal*. New Brunswick, NJ: Rutgers University Press, 2001.

New York Times. "Threat in Snyder case," June 2, 1927, 27.

Pelizzon, V. Penelope and Nancy M. West. "Multiple Indemnity: Film Noir, James M. Cain and Adaptations of a Tabloid Case," *Narrative* 13(3), (2005): 218–19.

"Photo Standalone 1," *Washington Post*, April 23, 1924, 3.

Potter, Ellen C. "The Problem of Women in Penal and Correctional Institutions," *Journal of Criminal Law and Criminology* 25(1), (May–June 1934): 65–75.

Rafter, Nicole Hahn and Mary Gibson. "Editors' Introduction," in Nicole Hahn Rafter and Mary Gibson (eds), *Criminal Woman, the Prostitute, and the Normal Woman*. Durham, NC: Duke University Press, 2004.

Ramey, Jessie. "The Bloody Blonde and the Marble Woman: Gender and Power in the Case of Ruth Snyder," *Journal of Social History* 37(3), (Spring 2004): 625–50.

Rein, Irving, Philip Kotler, and Martin Stoller. *High Visibility: The Making and Marketing of Professions into Celebrities*. New York: McGraw-Hill, 1997.

Rodriguez, Christina M. "Clearing the Smoke-Filled Room: Women Jurors and the Disruption of an Old-Boys' Network in Nineteenth-Century America," *Yale Law Journal*, 108(7), (May 1999): 1805–44.

Rojek, Chris. "Celebrity and Religion", *Celebrity*. London: Reaktion Books, 2001: 51-100.

Schmid, David. "Idols of Destruction: Celebrity and the Serial Killer," in Su Holmes and Sean Redmond (eds), *Framing Celebrity: New Directions in Celebrity Culture*. New York: Routledge, 2006: 295–310.

Sutherland, Sid. "Electrocute Ruth and Gray," *Chicago Daily Tribune*, January 13, 1928, 1.

Washington Post, "Photo Standalone 1," April 23, 1924, 3.

——. "Resemblance to Fury's Foreman to Mrs. Snyder said to Have Been Remarked," April 25, 1927, 1.

——. "Still Loves Judd Gray, Ruth Snyder protests," May 16, 1927, 8.

Wood, Arthur Evans. "A Study of Arrests in Detroit, 1913–1919," *Journal of the American Institute of Criminal Law and Criminology* 21(2), (August 1930): 168–200.

Woodward, W. E. "Author Tells of Details at Snyder-Gray Trial," *Los Angeles Times*, April 19, 1927, 2.

4

Rocket Scientist!

The Posthumous Celebrity of Hedy Lamarr

RUTH BARTON

BY THE TIME OF HER DEATH IN FLORIDA on January 19, 2000, Hedy Lamarr was an all-but-forgotten figure from Hollywood's classic era. Her neighbors were surprised to hear that the nearly blind old woman, who occasionally was spotted slipping down to check her mailbox, a scarf covering her features, or swimming late at night in her pool, had once been one of Hollywood's biggest attractions. For others, her name recalled a long-running gag in Mel Brooks' *Blazing Saddles* (1974) — "It's not Hedy, It's Hedley. Hedley Lamarr!" A few, if pressed, might have thought of her appearance in Gustav Machaty's controversial Czech modernist art-film, *Ecstasy* (*Extase*) from 1933, where, aged just 19, Hedy Kiesler, as she then was, performed an extended nude sequence, followed by another in which she simulated orgasm. Some might have been able to name one or two of her Hollywood films — *Algiers* (John Cromwell, 1938) perhaps, with Charles Boyer or what was effectively her swan song, Cecil B. DeMille's *Samson and Delilah* (1949). Since the 1960s, it seemed, Hedy Lamarr had only been in the headlines as a consequence of her multiple run-ins with the American legal system, most often on shoplifting charges, but also in connection with her provocative autobiography, *Ecstasy and Me: My Life as a Woman,* published in 1967.

Then came the obituaries; all ran through the official narrative of Lamarr's life — born in Vienna in 1914, fled to Hollywood from her munitions-baron husband, Fritz Mandl, five more marriages, known as "the most beautiful woman in the world," multiple film appearances in the 1940s, followed by a career decline, lawsuits, enforced retirement and finally, her death. Unexpectedly, however, a new narrative emerged that was almost as titillating as any of the details of Lamarr's life but, equally, complicated her legacy. For as obituarist after obituarist related, often with some incredulity, Hedy Lamarr was now regarded as a significant figure in the world of science and invention. On August 11, 1942, US patent number 2,292,387 was granted to Hedwig Kiesler Markey and George Antheil. Their invention,

Figure 4.1 **Headshot, Hedy Lamarr.**

titled "Secret Communication System," proposed a new, wireless torpedo guidance system to be used in the fight against the Germans. Since then, Lamarr and Antheil's design had been adapted, firstly during the Cold War, and subsequently to form the basis of our own mobile telephone technology. Hedy Lamarr, it was even suggested, might have been a genius.

In this chapter, I would like to examine the notion of posthumous celebrity, specifically in relation to Hedy Lamarr. Star studies has accustomed us to the concept of stardom as a process created through the intersection of top-down manipulation — studio-generated "news" items and celebrity gossip — and bottom-up expectation; that is, the public's pleasure in the melodrama of stardom, its rise and fall, its impossible glamour, wealth, and success and the titillating possibility of an equally precipitous fall from grace. Somewhere within this equation lurks the figure of the star herself, although often having only minimal influence on the projection of their identity, particularly in the case of stars from the classical Hollywood era. Rather evidently, the public perception of stars after their death is a matter in which they can play no part, but while writing on stardom often takes place after the star has died, little attention has been paid to the concept of "posthumous" fame, or the effect of death on a star's persona.

In the case of Hedy Lamarr, Diane Negra has analyzed her career as a metaphor for American interventionism and examined how the narrative of her escape from her first husband, and her embrace of American values came to symbolize America's rescue of a decadent but powerless old Europe.[1] Elsewhere, Jan-Christopher Horak has argued for the importance of the star's strong pre-war female characters, her "independent, sexually aggressive women of questionable morality," who always appeared morally ambiguous to middle-class viewers because they foregrounded rather than

1. Diane Negra, "Re-Made for Television: Hedy Lamarr's Post-War Star Textuality," in J. Thumin (ed.), *Small Screens, Big Ideas* (London and New York: I. B. Tauris, 2002), 103–35.

glossed over the exchange of sex for money.[2] The consequences of starring in *Ecstasy* for Lamarr's Hollywood career are the subject of Lucy Fisher's essay on the star in *Headline Hollywood: A Century of Film Scandal.*[3]

In my own biography of Lamarr, I have attempted to locate her within a narrative of exile that led to her intense sense of dislocation, of belonging neither in American culture, nor in postwar Europe. I have also charted how the American popular press increasingly vilified her as aged, as if she had sinned against some unwritten law by losing her beauty to time and poor plastic surgery.[4]

Here, however, I would like to focus on Lamarr's reputation as an inventor. As I hope to demonstrate, this aspect of her personality should not have emerged as new information after she had died, but was in fact in the public domain from the moment of the granting of the patent. My purpose is therefore to consider why the public "forgot" Lamarr's achievement in the years during and after World War II and why, from the 1990s onwards, she was gradually rehabilitated on the basis of her contribution to technological development, a process that only reached fruition with her death. A further issue is why Lamarr herself did not mention the Secret Communication System in *Ecstasy and Me*, preferring to focus instead on a reasonably factual account of her life and career interlaced with spicy tales of her sexual adventures and a transcript of her sessions with a psychiatrist. As well as discussing the part her status as a foreign national with a racy past played in the coverage of her role in the American war effort, I would like to explore how the public discourse on Lamarr's body worked to undermine any serious consideration of her intelligence. Ultimately what I would like to propose is that Lamarr had to "lose" her body in order to realize fully her status as an inventor, particularly one associated with the new "cool" technology of mobile communications.

Hedy Lamarr was viewed with some suspicion by patriotic Hollywood during the war years, although by the time of her arrival in America, in 1937, the star's credentials ought not to have been in question. She was Jewish by birth, but had converted to Christianity before her marriage to Fritz Mandl. The latter was by all accounts a remarkably unpleasant man with a taste for high society and political influence that had seen him support the right-wing Heimwehr, ally himself with Mussolini, and back the Austrian Fascist, Count Ernst Rüdiger von Starhemberg, in the latter's attempt to take over control

---

2. Jan-Christopher Horak, "High Class Whore: Hedy Lamarr's Star Image in Hollywood," *CineAction* 55, (2001): 34, 37.

3. Lucy Fisher, "*Ecstasy*: Female Sexual, Social, and Cinematic Scandal," in Adrienne L. McLean and David A. Cook (eds), *Headline Hollywood: A Century of Film Scandal* (New Brunswick, NJ: Rutgers University Press, 2001), 129–42.

4. Ruth Barton, *Hedy Lamarr: The Most Beautiful Woman in Film* (Lexington, KY: University of Kentucky Press, 2010).

of Austria.[5] While there is no evidence that Mandl even knew or supported Hitler, Lamarr does state in *Ecstasy and Me* that the Nazi leader was a guest at her husband's dinner table.[6]

Lamarr was careful, from her arrival in Hollywood, to put as much distance as possible between herself and Mandl. In interview after interview, she related how he had kept her locked up in his castle and how she had felt bought by him. She particularly distanced herself from his politics, which became conflated with a cartoon image of the industrialist and munitions manufacturer, so that Mandl soon evolved into a stereotypical fascist fat cat. Like other émigré stars, notably Marlene Dietrich, Lamarr threw herself into the war effort, working in the Hollywood Canteen and selling war bonds. Yet, she never managed to shake off her foreignness, nor did Hollywood bother to distinguish between the friends and enemies of Germany. Thus, for instance, when she challenged the pegging of her salary at $1,500 during the war, the *Hollywood Reporter* had this to say:

> The Hedy Lamarr thing is entirely out of line, as is Miss Lamarr with the filing of such action. It would seem to us that such a test case, if there is necessity for such action at this time, might far better be filed by one of our own people and not by a foreigner, nor even by a foreign-born American citizen. Miss Lamarr, with her action, tells the world she does not like our laws, that she resents the President or anyone else meddling with her $2,000-a-week salary, and wishes the court to straighten out the President, the Salary Stabilization Board, the Treasury, the Government and MGM. Each of these might well say, "Look who's talking," and suggest that if she does not like our way of doing things, she go back to her native country, try her talents on that government and question its rights, rather than offer criticism of this land in its war effort.[7]

The idea for the Secret Communication System almost certainly had its

---

5. Marie-Theres Arnbom, *Friedmann, Gutmann, Lieben, Mandl und Strakosch* (Vienna: Böhlau, 2002); Ronald C. Newton "The Neutralization of Fritz Mandl: Notes on Wartime Journalism, the Arms Trade, and Anglo-American Rivalry in Argentina During World War II," *Hispanic American Historical Review* 66(3), (1986): 541–79.
6. Hedy Lamarr, *Ecstasy and Me* (Greenwich: Fawcett Publications, 1967). This unsubstantiated claim was later taken up in a particularly unpleasant book, *What Almost Happened to Hedy Lamarr 1940–1967*, written by Devra Z. Hill, with "contributions" by Jody Babydol Gibson, and published in August 2008, which I have omitted in this discussion by virtue of its thorough speciousness. That the book is written to the structure of a soft-porn narrative ought to be no surprise given Jody Babydol Gibson's notoriety as the Hollywood brothel keeper whose tell-all publication, *Secrets of a Hollywood Super Madam*, named a string of high-profile celebrities as clients of her lucrative global escort agency. Hill herself, whose résumé includes master's and PhD degrees from unaccredited universities and a career as a self-help nutritionist, claims that the star asked her to write her biography. After Lamarr's arrest for shoplifting, Ms. Hill developed scruples and decided not to continue. See Devra Z. Hill. *What Almost Happened to Hedy Lamarr 1940–1967* (Corona Books, 2008).
7. W. R. Wilkerson, *The Hollywood Reporter*, undated clipping, Constance McCormick Collection USC Cinema-Television Library.

origins in Lamarr's days as Frau Mandl. According to Hans-Joachim Braun, a substantial contract was awarded to the German firm, Siemens and Halske, to develop missile guidance technology. It was around this time, just as war was about to break out, that the idea of frequency hopping was first mooted:

> [I]t was definitely discussed at a meeting in July 1939, and it seems likely that the notion had already come up in Fritz Mandl's conversations a few years earlier. Siemens and Halske was supposed to have a radio-control system ready by the end of 1939, but the outbreak of war redirected military R&D priorities, and the project went by the wayside amid continuing uncertainties about jamming, cumbersome transmitters, and underwater penetration.[8]

We can only guess that Lamarr carried this information with her to America. We know too that she enjoyed design and, to the end of her days, was always happy working on some or other invention. In her last few years, she was developing "a functionable, disposable accordian [sic] type attachment for and on any size Kleenex box" as the solution for used paper tissues.[9] She had a proposal for a new kind of traffic stoplight and some modifications to the design of Concorde. There were plans for a device to aid movement-impaired people to get in and out of the bath, a fluorescent dog collar, and a skin-tautening technique based on the principle of the accordion. After directing her on *Comrade X* (1940) and *H. M. Pulham Esq.* (1941), King Vidor remembered of Lamarr that:

> Her interest seemed to be divided between the part she was playing and another career as an inventor or discoverer of some fascinating new soft drink or useful invention. Although Hedy was a tremendous sex symbol to millions of moviegoers, she presented quite a different image to those working with her on the set.[10]

Still, Lamarr needed assistance if she was to realize the potential of Mandl's blueprints. This is where modernist composer George Antheil enters the story. Born in Trenton, New Jersey, Antheil was notorious for his aggressively modernist composition and performances of the *Ballet Mécanique* (premiered coincidentally by Lamarr's cousin, Frederick Kiesler, in Vienna in 1924). His reputation was cemented by his Paris concerts which were regularly attended by his friends from the modernist and surrealist set: Gertrude Stein, Ernest Hemingway, James Joyce, Ford Madox Ford, Ezra Pound, F. Scott Fitzgerald and Sylvia Beach. His Paris debut was in the Champs Elysées Theatre where

---

8. Hans-Joachim Braun, "Advanced Weaponry of the Stars," *Invention and Technology* (Spring, 1997): 16.
9. Letter to Hans Janitschek in *Hedy Lamarr: Secrets of a Hollywood Star*. DVD, directed by Donatello Dubini, Fosco Dubini and Barbara Obermaier (Germany, Canada, Switzerland, 2006).
10. King Vidor, *King Vidor on Film Making* (New York: McKay, 1972), 52.

he played three of his sonatas, an event filmed for and included in Marcel L'Herbier's *L'Inhumaine* (1924). Riots accompanied this, as they did his other public appearances; Antheil himself contributed to the reputation of these occasions by locking the doors of the concert hall before he performed and placing a revolver on the piano as he readied to play.[11] By the time he met Lamarr, however, his European career was over and he had returned to the United States where he was making a modest living through film scores and his agony aunt column ("Boy Advises Girl") for the *Chicago Sun* syndicate.[12] He was also an expert on the then fashionable discipline of endocrinology. In 1939, Antheil published *Every Man His Own Detective: A Study of Glandular Criminology*, its premise being that a glandular criminologist could solve a crime by analyzing forensic evidence to determine what hormonal type had committed the deed. He followed this in 1940 with *The Shape of War to Come*, on international strategy.

Antheil and Lamarr apparently met at a Hollywood party in 1940, where she sought advice from him on how to enhance her bust size. A dinner meeting was arranged. In his utterly unreliable memoirs, Antheil recalled the event:

> I sat down and turned my eyes upon Hedy Lamarr. My eyeballs sizzled, but I could not take them away. Here undoubtedly was the most beautiful woman on earth. Most movie queens don't look so good when you see them in the flesh, but this one looked infinitely better than on the screen. Her breasts were fine, too, real postpituitary.[13]

These memoirs, happily titled *Bad Boy of Music*, detail the course of their collaboration on Lamarr's initial proposal and have been widely used as a source for subsequent accounts of the invention, gradually accumulating the status of "fact." From the little we know of the details of the invention, they may well be reasonably accurate; according to Antheil, Lamarr enlisted his help in the development of a torpedo missile device. His contribution drew on his experience of using player pianos as part of his performance — by mimicking the operation of two synchronized player pianos, a message could be transmitted to a receiver in such a manner that it could not be decoded. The system used 88 frequencies, the number of keys on a player piano. Thus the missile could be launched and guided without interception. As well as explaining the basics of the invention, Antheil's other legacy, then, was to link the narrative of the technical development with Lamarr's alleged interest in breast enhancement. Judging by his writings and his unpublished letters (in the George Antheil papers archived at Columbia University), he

11. Linda Whitesitt, *The Life and Music of George Antheil 1900–1959* (Epping: Bowker, 1983).
12. These were written with his wife, Böski, niece of Arthur Schnitzler.
13. George Antheil, *Bad Boy of Music* (London and New York: Hurst and Blackett, 1945), 255.

greatly admired his co-inventor and, as we shall see, understood exactly how difficult it was for her to function in a society that refused to accept that beautiful women might also be intelligent. What is also noteworthy is that his memoirs were published in 1945, just a short period after the events they describe. Yet, at the time of their publication, for reasons that I will explore shortly, they went almost completely ignored.

Antheil was not betraying a state secret in describing his and Lamarr's collaboration. In October of 1941, before it had been completed, Col Lent of the National Inventor's Council leaked the story of the invention to the press. Their response to the news of Lamarr's achievement was one of enthusiasm: "Her invention, held secret by the government, is considered of great potential in the national defense program," the *Los Angeles Times* enthused.[14] Other papers agreed. In 1944, *Motion Picture Magazine* ran the story, wondering if perhaps it was her intelligence that had rendered the star an outsider in Hollywood:

> The enigma that is Hedy Lamarr has long puzzled Hollywood. Time after time she has caused studio personnel and writers to scratch their heads in bewilderment. Whether it is quoting Goethe or discovering a new headdress, she is constantly startling those who have just settled down to the idea that she must be another typical beauty with a negligible IQ.[15]

Lurking behind this analysis is the association between an intellectual European culture and the brashness of Hollywood. Here, unusually, being foreign is not a threat but an asset. On August 11, 1942, the patent was granted; the description is concise:

> This invention relates broadly to secret communication systems involving the use of carrier waves of different frequencies, and is especially useful in the remote control of dirigible craft, such as torpedoes. An object of the invention is to provide a method of secret communication which is relatively simple and reliable in operation, but at the same time is difficult to discover or decipher.

Despite the granting of the patent, the story died. The invention went no further, particularly after the Navy claimed that it was unworkable. I'm not qualified to assess just how practicable the Secret Communication System was. Judging by the available reading on the topic, it seems that, like so many inventions or discoveries, Lamarr and Antheil's was just one of many to emerge more or less simultaneously, in this case fed by wartime requirements. Whether it is even the direct ancestor of the mobile telephones we

---

14. "Hedy Invention Seen as Defense Aid," *Los Angeles Times*, October 11, 1941: 3.
15. Lou Ann Garrett, "Hedy's Secret Weapon," *Motion Picture Magazine* (November 1944); unpaginated press cutting, author's private collection.

all use is also beyond my expertise to judge with competence, though many claim this to be the case.[16]

What interests me in terms of Lamarr's celebrity is the media's swift and enthusiastic embrace of her invention (over time, Antheil's name became less and less associated with the Secret Communication System), and their equally abrupt dropping of the story. In one way, the invention accords with Lamarr's Mata Hari image. What other kind of female would have been capable of dreaming up such a clandestine scheme? Col Lent, by releasing its details to the media was also evidently hoping to "sex up" (to borrow a phrase from a later conflict) the war effort. But it was left to George Antheil to battle for acceptance of his and Lamarr's invention, indeed both their inventions as they were also working on a magnetic device designed to adhere to enemy aircraft before exploding. In a series of letters to his old friend, William C. Bullitt, the Special Assistant to the Secretary of the Navy, Antheil argued for the viability of the concept. When Bullitt was unforthcoming, Antheil turned to the National Inventor's Council, a body set up during World War II to encourage the citizenry of America to contribute their ideas to the fight against fascism:

> Likewise, a curiosity of this idea is that its co-inventor is Miss Hedy Lamarr, the motion picture actress (who is a good friend of mine), who, curiously enough, has had considerable experience of a second-hand nature concerning this subject. Her first husband, Fritz Mendel [*sic*], was once one of the largest munition [*sic*] manufacturers in Austria, besides which Miss Lamarr has a natural aptitude for the rather unfeminine occupation of inventor.[17]

Surely, here, Antheil had put his finger on the issue. Being an inventor was, indeed, a rather unfeminine occupation and certainly not one befitting an actress, a profession not often associated with intellectual ideas or technological know-how. Had she perhaps come up with a new design for nurses' uniforms or some such suitably "feminine" invention, Lamarr's contribution might well have been more acceptable.

The publication of Antheil's memoirs gave no further rise to discussion around the invention and the story died. So, quite swiftly, did Lamarr's career. In 1945, she formed Mars Film Corporation with Hunt Stromberg and Jack Chertok, producing and starring in two films, *The Strange Woman* (Edgar Ulmer, 1946) and *Dishonored Lady* (Robert Stevenson, 1947). The first was a moderate success, the second less so, and, now no longer under studio contract, there seemed little place in Hollywood for a star so associated with strong, dangerous, sexual roles. Only in Cecil B. DeMille's high camp *Samson*

---

16. For a populist account of the invention, see, for example, Rob Walters, *Spread Spectrum: Hedy Lamarr and the Mobile Phone* ([Great Britain]: BookSurge, 2005).

17. Letter to Mr. Reynolds, Antheil Collection, Columbia University archives.

Figure 4.2   **The Cut-Out Paper Doll and her Military Invention. (Courtesy of Filmarchiv Austria, Vienna.)**

and Delilah, was Lamarr cast (as Delilah) in a part that suited her persona, as a languid temptress, and her looks, with the Technicolor cinematography transforming her into a gleaming, exotic gem.

Lamarr's final film performance was in *The Female Animal* (Harry Keller, 1958); her television career lasted into the sixties.[18] By now, as I have already mentioned, she was becoming better known for her clashes with the legal system. A series of high-profile shoplifting cases, notably the case taken by Mays Department store in February of 1966, kept her in the news as did her action against her publishers. Filing a suit for $9.6 million against Bartholomew House, Lamarr claimed that the accounts of her love life in *Ecstasy and Me* were "fictional, false, vulgar, scandalous, libelous and obscene."[19] The case was settled out of court and the offending sections of the book remained in place.

It is unusual to complain that your own autobiography is inaccurate and libelous. Lamarr blamed the ghostwriters, Cy Rice and Leo Guild, although it is not at all clear whether they did invent the disputed passages, or whether she supplied the details when they were recording her and later regretted what she had said. In terms of how these events shaped Lamarr's celebrity image, what is telling is the judge's response to the case in front of him. The book was, Judge Nutter said, "filthy, nauseating and designed to exploit the

18. For an analysis of Lamarr's television career, see Negra, "Re-Made for Television," 105–17.
19. Howard Hertel, "But Calls it 'Filthy' and 'Nauseating,'" *Los Angeles Times,* September 27, 1966, 3.

worst instincts of human beings."[20] The prosecution case hinged on Lamarr's accumulated star persona; Attorney Pacht argued that her "reputation for morality, integrity and honest dealing was and is notoriously bad . . ."[21] Just what were his grounds for this argument, bearing in mind that Lamarr had been acquitted in the May Corporation case? The newspaper reports do not identify the basis for this assertion other than that Lamarr had been out of filmmaking for fifteen years and that "she was desperate," according to Pacht, "to revive her name in the public mind. The only thing she had to sell was her sex life." Pacht also reminded the court that Lamarr had been married six times and had "discarded" all her husbands. [22]

In a sense, Lamarr was the author of her own misfortunes insofar as she brought the case to court herself. Yet, she was also very evidently being judged by a patriarchal establishment on her screen reputation as much as on her actual life. Certainly her divorce cases had been widely profiled, and usually ended in court, usually in a dispute over assets. She had also been tried for non-payment of taxes and invoices. Even the title of the "autobiography" *Ecstasy and Me,* could be regarded as exploitative, recalling as it did Lamarr's much discussed role in Machaty's film. Despite the era — this was after all 1966 and supposedly the dawn of "free love" and female sexual emancipation — this was a "dirty" book and its subject was morally suspect.

Matters did not improve for Lamarr. That epitome of the counter-cultural movement, Andy Warhol's Factory, weighed in, also in 1966, with a 66-minute feature film that might have been scripted by Judge Nutter and Attorney Pacht. Entitled variously *Hedy* or *Lives and Loves of Hedy Lamarr* or *Hedy Goes Shopping,* and directed by Warhol's disciple, Ronald Tavel, the film featured transvestite Mario Montez in a series of enactments from the headlines. Montez, as Hedy, undergoes plastic surgery while insisting on her beauty, and is arrested and tried for shoplifting. Although the case could be made for the film being a parody of recent events (Lamarr had already sued a newspaper for reporting that she had had her nose altered), it did little to provide a counter-narrative to the public construction of her persona.

By the late 1970s Lamarr's star persona was deeply tainted. In June 1978, for example, the *National Enquirer* ran a story describing her as "old and ugly" and a "pathetic recluse" who "lives in an unkempt one-room apartment."[23] In part, this type of coverage reflects the contradictions engendered by the plastic surgery process. On the one hand, stars were to grow old "naturally" and not to engage in the undignified pursuit of youth. At the same time, they were derided and humiliated for having "lost their beauty." Plastic surgery in that era was primitive and, certainly in Lamarr's case, resulted in facial

---

20. Ibid.
21. Ibid., 26.
22. Ibid., 3, 26.
23. "Labeled 'Old', 'Recluse', Hedy Lamarr Sues," *Los Angeles Times,* April 11, 1979, A1.

features that could only be described as disfigured, with her skin pulled tightly in certain directions and then falling in folds in others. There seems little doubt that she was humiliated, both by the long-term damage of the surgery and the media coverage of her looks. After the move to Florida, she was reclusive, and particularly discouraged visits from anyone who might have remembered her from her screen heyday.

Only in the final years of her life did a counter-narrative of Lamarr's career and persona begin to emerge and now only as a consequence of the revival of public interest in the Secret Communication System. In fact, newspaper reports of the invention can be dated back to the 1970s. In 1973, for instance, National Inventors' Day was inaugurated in the US. The date, February 11, was selected to coincide with the birth of Thomas Edison and, in its second year, a nonprofit group, Intellectual Property Owners, Inc., released a list of inventions that it felt would intrigue the public. Lamarr was included on it, as was Lillian Russell who had patented a dresser-trunk in 1912. Another name designed to surprise the public was that of Dorothy Rodgers, wife of the composer, Richard Rodgers, who had invented the "Johnny Mop," a device for cleaning toilet bowls. Evidently, what distinguished Lamarr's invention from those of the other two women was that it was not based on practical domestic usage. Contacted by Intellectual Property Owners, Inc., Lamarr responded that she was unaware whether the invention was ever used.[24] At this point, Lamarr seems to have been indifferent to the invention. As I have already mentioned, she did not include it in *Ecstasy and Me*, presumably because she believed it had come to nothing, and presumably too because she considered that either the public would find the story incredible or that it was irrelevant to her own narrative of success and its aftermath.

It was not until 1997, three years before Lamarr's death, that the story of the Secret Communication System returned to the headlines in a systematic manner. In that year, the Electronic Frontier Foundation, a public policy organization concerned with digital communication, officially honored her for her patent. The story was reported with breathless incredulity and much, often highly sexist, referencing of Lamarr's screen career:

> With IQ numbers as impressive as her hip-and-bust measurements, she offers her mind to the war effort. But the military brass takes one look at her figure and face and decide that her contribution would be to prance around nightclub and vaudeville stages selling war bonds, which she does by the millions of dollars.[25]

Without wishing to dwell on this kind of reporting, it ought to be noted that Lamarr had almost no bust, a failing that was a considerable worry to MGM when she arrived in Hollywood and lends credence to Antheil's

---

24. "Edison's Day is for Hedy, Dorothy, Lillian, Too," *Los Angeles Times*, February 7, 1974, 2.
25. Ron Grossman, "Brainy Beauty," *Chicago Tribune*, March 31, 1997, 1, 4.

account of their first meeting. More important, it is apparent that, even by the late 1990s, the two discourses — of Lamarr as a classic Hollywood beauty defined by her corporeality, and her technology invention — were still largely irreconcilable.

With Lamarr now sequestered away in Altamonte Springs, her son, Tony Loder, stepped forward to speak on behalf of his mother. Loder is the family member who has most often intervened in the rehabilitation of Lamarr's reputation, both in the years immediately before her death and in terms of her posthumous celebrity. The narrative was to gain even greater currency when it emerged that Loder worked for a telephone store in Los Angeles and therefore was selling the mobile phones that had been designed on the basis of the Secret Communication System. In a sense he had become the inheritor of his mother's tech interests.

It was this specific development that facilitated Lamarr's resurrection. As one journalist exhorted: "The next time you pick up a cellular phone, give a brief thought to the improbable woman who first patented some of its underlying technology fifty-five years ago — 'the most beautiful girl in the world', actress Hedy Lamarr."[26] Since the early eighties, technophiles had been aware of the significance of the Lamarr-Antheil patent and one in particular, Robert Price, an electrical engineer from Lexington, Massachusetts, had twice unsuccessfully attempted to have Lamarr honored; on the first occasion by proposing her for an award from the Institute of Electrical and Electronics Engineers, and next for a Medal of Honor from Congress. The campaign was taken up subsequently by Colonel David Hughes and it was he who was behind the EFF's decision to recognize the invention in 1997. "Even today," he wrote in his citation,

> 44 years after this young woman, not operating out of a research or university center, grasped and articulated the novel technical ideas underlying spread spectrum, and which she pursued to the point of a formal US Patent, the offering of these ideas [*sic*] to the public, very few, even technically savvy Americans understand today how, and why spread spectrum works, or its significance in providing a revolutionary form of high speed, quite secure, non-interfering (shared spectrum) data communication.[27]

Hughes' particular interest is in enabling developing countries to access cheap and easy-to-use technology and he probably saw the potential in the Secret Communication System for this kind of usage.

Tony Loder accepted the award from the EFF on his mother's behalf, and

---

26. Elizabeth Weise, "Hedy Lamarr: A Sultry Screen Star Who Didn't Just Act — She Invented," *Classic Images* 265, (1997): C14.

27. In Richard Brem and Theo Ligthart (eds), *Hommage à Hedy Lamarr* (Vienna: Edition Selene, 1999), 79.

played a message that she had taped to the audience. She acknowledged them for honoring her; of her invention she said, "I hope it will do you good as well. I feel good about it and it was not done in vain."[28] It was widely reported that Lamarr's only response to this recognition was: "It's about time," a much less generous choice of words than those of her recorded acceptance speech.

The next development in Lamarr's celebrity re-imaging was her recognition in her home country of Austria. To coincide with her 85th birthday, an exhibition called *Hommage à Hedy Lamarr*, with photographs, film clips and other memorabilia toured Austria. The exhibition had opened in Linz in September 1998, as an installation at Ars Electronica, an international media arts festival concerned with promoting dialogue between the arts and the sciences, especially in the realm of invention and creativity. The overall theme of the 1998 exhibition was "Info War," and focused on the inter-relationships between military technologies and civilian society. *Hommage à Hedy Lamarr* consisted of monitors showing extracts from Lamarr's films and newsreel footage from World War II alongside projections of the work-ings of the Secret Communication System, now widely referred to in the terminology of its contemporary digital incarnation — spread spectrum technology. Illustrations demonstrated recent uses of the technology, and the whole exhibit took its rhythm from Antheil's modernist compositions, with a particular nod towards his multimedia opera installation, *Transatlantic* which premiered in Carnegie Hall in 1930.[29] Curd Duca, the Vienna-based, electronic musician, composed the soundtrack for the exhibit.[30] In 1997, Lamarr and Antheil (posthumously) also received the Bulbie Gnass Spirit of Achievement Award, as well as a prize presented by Milstar (the US gov-ernment satellite communications system). Loder also accepted the Victor Kaplan Award (Austria's most prestigious scientific honor for an inventor) on Lamarr's behalf in October 1998. This had been organized by Peter Sint who came across her name in an article in *The Economist* and vaguely remembered her image from old black-and-white films on television: "I sup-posed it would be useful if her country of origin gave her some recognition too," he said. "Actually she wanted to come to fetch the prize but she was already too ill."[31]

These awards are important, particularly the Austrian ones, because of Lamarr's longtime neglect in her country of origin, of which she always spoke with deep nostalgia. When I was researching newspaper coverage of her August 1955 visit to Vienna, her first since she had left for Hollywood in 1937, I found almost no mention of the occasion. This contrasts notably with

---

28. From audio clip emailed to the author by Colonel Hughes, August 18, 2009.
29. For more on this fascinating work see Cook, 1991.
30. See Brem and Licthart, *Hommage*.
31. Email exchange with the author, March 30, 2009.

her pre-exile days when, although she was only still a minor star, she received generous news attention. There are complex historical reasons for this, that I will pursue shortly, that also contribute to her rehabilitation.

Complicating what on the surface seems like a "happy ending" in terms of Lamarr's late-life recognition, was her own predisposition to litigation. In 1998, she sued the Corel Software Company for illegally using her image in their publicity and was awarded $5 million. She in turn invested this money in shares. In the same year, the Calgary-based technology company, Wi-LAN bought out 49 percent of her interest in the patent in return for shares in the company and the right to use her name in publicity. This money was to leave her, contrary to rumor, a relatively wealthy woman. Yet, the popular media was still reluctant to revise its punishing attitude to the star. An article headed, "Screen Siren Suing Software Manufacturer," reported that: "Canadian software giant Corel Corp. is being slapped with a civil suit filed by retired Hollywood sex siren Hedy Lamarr."[32] Counsel for the Corel Corp raised as part of its defense the old shoplifting charges, even though these had never been proven, or had been dropped.

It seems to me that the reinvention of Hedy Lamarr could only fully take place after she had died. Thus, I would like to conclude by making the case for an understanding of Lamarr's death as enabling a new form of her celebrity. This does not mean that she left behind her "screen siren" image, rather that both reputations — inventor and "sultry" star — began to accommodate each other and to be enabled by another aspect of her life's narrative, her escape from Mandl and fascist Austria.

It was important for Lamarr to die for several reasons. One was practical; with her passing, there was no longer any serious threat of litigation for anyone who reproduced her image. Neither Tony Loder, nor his sister, Lamarr's other child from her marriage with John Loder, Denise, seem to be litigious. The only family member who did invoke the law in connection with Lamarr was her adopted son, James Loder, who stated after her death that he was, in fact, her birth child. Although this assertion has never been legally substantiated, it did result in a successful claim for a portion of Lamarr's $3 million estate.[33] The immediate result of her death was a renewed interest in her life story, occasioned by the many obituaries that now appeared. Although, as I have demonstrated, the story of the Secret Communication System had long been in the public domain, and had accumulated greater visibility as a consequence of its adaptation for use in the mobile telephone industry, knowledge about Lamarr's and Antheil's invention was still largely limited to technology insiders. Nearly all the obituaries carried the story of the invention and some led with it; those that did not were corrected

32. Alex Finkelstein, "Screen Siren Suing Software Manufacturer," *Orlando Business Journal,* April 24, 1998.
33. For further on this, see Barton, *Hedy Lamarr.*

swiftly by letter-writers. All the major newspapers carried obituaries; this wave of attention was followed by the broadcast of a documentary in BBC's prestigious *Arena* slot in 2004. *Calling Hedy Lamarr* was a German/Austrian/ British co-production, directed by Georg Misch. It is an impressionistic piece of filmmaking that was structured around the conceit of having its interviewees talk on the telephone instead of to camera and featured Tony Loder centrally as he worked through his complicated relationship with his mother. Much of the emphasis was now on Lamarr's identity as an inventor. This was followed, in turn, by a proliferation of websites, blogs and other web-based activities dedicated to Lamarr, all of which devoted considerable space to the invention.

I don't believe, however, that it was just the occasion of Lamarr's death that excited the interest in her and Antheil's invention. It seems to me that Lamarr's identity, as an elderly, nearly blind "has-been," living in seclusion, rumored to be destitute, in Florida, constantly disturbed the smooth surface of the technology that had become associated with her. Only by being no longer corporeally present, could her intellectual reputation begin to eclipse her physical reputation. There is a very clear mind–body split in Lamarr's celebrity; there are also temporal issues at stake. Her persona, as we have seen was founded on her physical presence, notably her "imposs-ible" beauty. The influence of *Ecstasy* in determining this reputation cannot be underestimated, imbuing her, as it did, with an aura of intense, taboo sensuality. Although she played strong women in her pre-war films, these roles were ultimately defined by Lamarr's permissiveness rather than her intellect. As she grew older, this beauty became an embarrassment, as did her now uncontrollable body — she shoplifted, she was unable to disguise her aging, her plastic surgery was showing, her eyesight was failing.

In order then, for her to become part of tech culture, Lamarr had to lose her "real life" status and to be narrativized and fictionalized in a de-corporealizing manner. In particular, to take on the new role that she was to acquire after her death, that of role model for women in science, certain of the most widely publicized factors in her public persona had to be forgotten, or dropped from the narrative.

In 2003, Lamarr appeared on the cover of a publication aimed at encour-aging children to engage with science, and, specifically, to promote the figure of the female scientist. *Dignifying Science: Stories About Women Scientists* was written by Jim Ottaviani and illustrated by multiple illustrators. It is a comic book and contains sketches of the lives and work of: Lamarr, Marie Sklodovska, Lise Meitner, Rosalind Franklin, Barbara McClintock, Biruté Galdikas and Marie Curie. The section on Lamarr is illustrated by Carla Speed McNeil. The style particularly in the opening frames is dark, with a suggestion of menace, reflecting the setting in Vienna of 1933, where Fritz Mandl is seated at the phone in front of a massively enlarged image of Lamarr on screen holding her head in her hands, her mouth open. As he thunders on the phone, threatening to destroy the prints of *Ecstasy* (as he was rumored to have done in real life), Lamarr's face sinks into repose, as if she is falling asleep. The reference is unmistakably to the orgasm sequence in *Ecstasy*, although nothing in the dialogue suggests this. On the second page, the comic cuts to Lamarr sitting, arms defiantly folded, between the projector and the screen. "It hurts me, seeing you in this," Mandl tells her from off-screen. "Hurts you?" Lamarr thinks and the ensuing frames illustrate the shooting of the orgasm sequence, taken in detail from *Ecstasy and Me*.[34] There, she wrote:

> I was told to lie down with my hands above my head while Aribert Mog whispered in my ear, and then kissed me in the most uninhibited fashion. I was not sure what my reactions would be, so when Aribert slipped down and out of camera, I just closed my eyes.[35]

Machaty, in Lamarr's account, was not impressed. Mumbling about the stupidity of youth, he looked around until he found a safety pin on the table: "'you will lie here,' he said, 'I will be underneath, out of camera range. When I prick you a little on your backside, you will bring your elbows together and you will *react*!'"[36] The other narrative reference here is to the often-repeated story that Mandl obsessively bought up all the prints of *Ecstasy* he could lay his hands on, so disgusted was he with the film and his wife's role in it.

In McNeil's illustration, the lover has been removed from the frame, leaving it quite unclear as to why this sequence should be taking place; nor has Machaty's film yet been referred to by name. "'I don't care how you do it in the movies. That expression is not for the world to see,' a glowering Mandl tells his wife. 'You are mine now'?"[37] The scene moves on to Mandl's dinner table, where he is entertaining Mussolini, and showing off his trophy bride. First he projects the film for the dictator and then the conversation moves on to Mandl's munitions interests, specifically his long-range missile weaponry, which he acknowledges is imperfect. Mussolini is unimpressed with the fallible technology and various men are seen to attempt to work out a solution. As they scratch their heads, Lamarr's manicured nail lands on the blueprint. "Gentlemen, this is where I think my guidance sys—," she begins to say before being rebuffed. She storms out of the room. Time moves on to 1937 and Mandl is now entertaining Hitler. Again, following *Ecstasy and Me* closely, in the next sequence Lamarr tries to escape but the plan is foiled when she discovers her co-conspirator, Colonel Righter, is in fact in the pay of Mandl and he has been recording their conversations. Lamarr then drugs

---

34. Jim Ottaviani, *Dignifying Science* (Ann Arbor, MI: G. T. Labs, 2003), 16.
35. Lamarr, *Ecstasy*, 23
36. Ibid.
37. Ottaviani, *Dignifying Science*, 18.

her French maid and escapes Mandl, disguised as the maid, again a story taken directly from her own disputed autobiography.

In the next sequences, we see Lamarr's first encounter with MGM boss, Louis B. Mayer, who claims to be "the most important movie man in America, in the world."[38] The point is clear, Lamarr's early days were marked by a struggle to make her voice heard in a society run by crass, controlling men. She fights for a decent salary at MGM and is imagined sighing in the background as Mayer mispronounces her name. We see her gain a new husband (Gene Markey) and she finds herself surrounded by Hollywood noise, which segues into her listening to George Antheil play the piano. She instructs him to phone her (no mention now of breast enhancement), and at their first meeting, Lamarr is rendered as instructing Antheil, rather than collaborating with him. A skeptical navy representative pores over the plans but neither he, nor his colleague understands what is now seen as solely Lamarr's invention. Finally, in a complete departure from any of the existing accounts of Lamarr's wartime career, we see her attempt to hand in her resignation to Mayer so that she can work with the Inventor's Council. Instead, to her humiliation, he insists that she contribute to the war effort by kissing a crowd of men who line up to pay $50,000 per kiss. The final frame sees the plump Mayer pronounce, "Don't rush boys . . . Miss Lamarr's not going anywhere!"[39] In fact, Lamarr willingly participated in the "Stars over America" tour, just as she willingly helped out at the Hollywood Canteen. She is widely credited with selling $25 million worth of bonds during that tour. In one day alone, according to most accounts, she sold $7 million. Titus Haffa, a Chicago businessman, made the headlines by suggesting that he would buy a $25,000 war bond if Hedy kissed him; subsequently, he pronounced that, on the contrary, he would kiss her if she bought a bond to that tune.[40] Ottaviani provides notes to his sources at the end of the book, which explain the orgasm sequence and connect the wartime invention to its adoption by the mobile telephone industry.

The image on the front cover of *Dignifying Science* features Lamarr, dressed in pink and looking very like Snow White (who was alleged to have been modeled on the star). Holding laboratory glassware she is surrounded by an array of chemistry instruments, in the middle of which are placed a pink comb, vanity mirror, and powder compact. In the background are two bouquets of flowers, one labeled "Miss Lamarr." Of course, Lamarr was not a chemist, nor, to be fair, does the narrative suggest she was one. The front cover illustration does, however, render her an ideal role model for young women scientists — a woman who could remain feminine, while engaging

---

38. Ibid., 28
39. Ibid., 35
40. Uncredited newspaper cutting, Constance McCormick Collection USC Cinema-Television Library.

in practical research. Elsewhere, the narrative, as I have demonstrated, makes clear distinctions between the male sphere — insensitive, patriarchal, public — and feminine interiority, which is only matched by the mind of an eccentric composer, Antheil, who is almost uncharacterized.

Most of all, Ottaviani has enlisted Lamarr's melodramatic life story to render scientific discovery exciting. Her sexuality is hinted at throughout, while never being rendered as tawdry and excessive, as it was by the American popular press during her lifetime. She is, of course, only seen as young and beautiful, and exotically foreign. A very similar approach is taken by another comic book, *Hedy Lamarr and a Secret Communication System,* published in 2007 (see Figure 4.2). Its author is Trina Robbins, a highly regarded graphic novelist, who describes herself as "writer and herstorian."[41] Robbins' narrative, like Ottaviani's draws closely on *Ecstasy and Me*; her version opens with Mandl and Hitler discussing ways to control torpedoes at a dinner party (though, again, we have to remember that Lamarr never mentions the Secret Communication System in her autobiography). The episode with Colonel Righter and her escape, disguised as her maid, reappear. In this narrative, however, Lamarr is in greater control of events and, for instance, willingly accedes to Mayer's decision to change her name. She clearly articulates her position as an alien who wishes to help in the war effort and explains to Antheil that she listened in to Mandl's conversations and learned from them. She and Antheil are seen to work much more collaboratively, and we see the Navy stupidly misunderstand that the twosome planned to put a piano into a torpedo. Robbins follows the invention through the realization that it would be viable if transistors were placed in the remote control works, and details the use of the Secret Communication System in the blockade of Cuba. This allows her to conclude that:

> The leader of the Soviet Union, Nikita Khrushchev, knew that the United States had new foolproof torpedoes. On October 28, he announced that he would remove the missiles. The Cuban Missile Crisis ended without a shot being fired. Hedy and George's invention had helped save the world from disaster.[42]

The narrative ends with Tony Loder accepting the EFF award on his mother's behalf and a series of graphics explaining why "Hedy's invention" (again, no mention of Antheil) is now used in mobile phones, wireless internet and many more such devices.

It is remarkable how, in a few years, Lamarr moved from being an elderly recluse, best known for shoplifting charges and a tendency to sue, her film career now something of a joke, to saving Western democracy. In 2006,

41. See Trina Robbins. "Trina Robbins: Writer and Herstorian."
42. Trina Robbins, *Hedy Lamarr and a Secret Communication System* (Mankato, MN: Capstone Press, 2007), 22.

Figure 4.3   **Image from *Hedy Lamarr and a Secret Communication System* (reproduced with permission from Trina Robbins and Cynthia Martin).**

an Austrian prize for women in technology was initiated and named after Lamarr. Her birthday, November 9, is now celebrated as Inventors' Day in Europe. In early 2010, the Austrian Academy of Sciences named its series of public lectures the "Hedy Lamarr Lectures 2010."

Evidently, much of this activity can be ascribed to a pressing need to encourage women to engage with science. As a role model, Lamarr works well, if you take a selective approach to her career trajectory and know that she will not sully the project by suing. Very specifically, we can see the belated interest taken by Austria in Lamarr's narrative as being motivated by a need to redress a long history of anti-Semitism. Much of the coverage of her career in the Austrian press mentions her anti-fascist politics, so that she is at once returned to favor as a Jew and as an anti-fascist Austrian.

Researching the Antheil papers at Columbia University Archives, I found a reference to what seems to have been a suspicion by Lamarr that Antheil was benefiting financially from their invention. We will, of course, never know just to what extent, if at all, Lamarr was motivated by financial gain. Much of the latter part of the star's life was marked by her insistence on exploiting her name, her image and anything connected to both. All this was, of necessity, airbrushed from the "inventor" narrative as it was posthumously fashioned.

I do not want to make the case that Lamarr's reputation as inventor has eclipsed her previous persona, as a foreign beauty, with a limited acting range, a brief and relatively undistinguished career in pre-war Hollywood, and a penchant for nudity, as well as for shoplifting, excessive sexual activity and litigation. I am, however, certain that had the technology industry and the science community not so obviously needed to reach out to a non-tech public and to promote the notion of the beautiful but brilliant female inventor, Lamarr's posthumous celebrity would have been quite different and very much less engaging. Similarly, as I have argued, her corporeality, in particular when in decline, was at odds with technology's self-identification not just with youth and modernity, but also with a different kind of sexuality. With its shining surfaces, and its cold, hard brilliance, technology is perfect in a way that the female body, beautiful as it may be, cannot be imagined. Technology is born of the intellect not faulty, messy physicality.

As a case study, Lamarr offers us very specific insights into the nature of fame. I believe that we can draw wider conclusions, however, from her example to consider how posthumous celebrity alters a star persona. In her instance, we can see how successive generations re-invented Hedy Lamarr to suit their specific requirements. Her life story was re-edited, her achievements re-fashioned, her physicality re-imagined so that she could perform the new role identified for her in a technology-centered new millennium. Hers is surely not an isolated case, and by analyzing how the stars of the classic era are now discussed, we may reveal more about ourselves than we may ever know about them.

Bibliography

Antheil, George. *Bad Boy of Music*. London and New York: Hurst and Blackett, 1945.
—— *Every Man His Own Detective: A Study of Glandular Criminology*. New York City: Stackpole Sons, 1937.
Arnbom, Marie-Theres. *Friedmann, Gutmann, Lieben, Mandl und Strakosch*. Vienna: Böhlau, 2002.
Barton, Ruth. *Hedy Lamarr: The Most Beautiful Woman in Film*. Lexington, KY: University of Kentucky Press, 2010.
Braun, H-J. "Advanced Weaponry of the Stars," *Invention and Technology* (Spring 1997): 10–16.
Brem, Richard and Theo Ligthart (eds). *Hommage à Hedy Lamarr*. Vienna: Edition Selene, 1999. Festival catalogue entry available at: http://90.146.8.18/de/archives/festival_archive/festival_catalogs/festival_artikel.asp?iProjectID=8407 (accessed February 5, 2010).
Cook, Susan C. "George Antheil's Transatlantic: an American in the Weimar Republic," *The Journal of Musicology* 9(4), (1991): 498–520.
"Edison's Day is for Hedy, Dorothy, Lillian, Too," *Los Angeles Times*, February 7, 1974, 2.
Finkelstein, Alex. "Screen Siren Suing Software Manufacturer," *Orlando Business Journal*, April 24, 1998. Available at: http://orlando.bizjournals.com/orlando/stories/1998/04/27/story4.html (accessed February 8, 2010).
Fisher, Lucy. "*Ecstasy*: Female Sexual, Social, and Cinematic Scandal," in Adrienne L. McLean and David A. Cook (eds), *Headline Hollywood: A Century of Film Scandal*. New Brunswick, NJ: Rutgers University Press, 2001.
Garrett, Lou Ann. "Hedy's Secret Weapon," *Motion Picture Magazine*, November 1944. Unpaginated press cutting, author's private collection.
Grossman, Ron. "Brainy Beauty," *Chicago Tribune*, March 31, 1997, 1, 4.
"Hedy Invention Seen as Defense Aid," *Los Angeles Times*, October 11, 1941: 3.
Hertel, Howard. "But Calls it 'Filthy' and 'Nauseating,'" *Los Angeles Times*, September 27, 1966, 3.

Hill, Devra Z. *What Almost Happened to Hedy Lamarr 1940–1967*. Corona Books, 2008.

Horak, Jan-Christopher. "High Class Whore: Hedy Lamarr's Star Image in Hollywood," *CineAction* 55, (2001): 31–9.

"Labeled 'Old', 'Recluse', Hedy Lamarr Sues," *Los Angeles Times*, April 11, 1979, A1.

Lamarr, Hedy. *Ecstasy and Me*. Greenwich: Fawcett Publications, 1966.

McNeil, Carla Speed. "Hedy Lamarr," in Jim Ottaviani, *Dignifying Science: Stories about Women Scientists*. Ann Arbor, MI: G. T. Labs, 2003, 13–36.

—— "Re-Made for Television: Hedy Lamarr's Post-War Star Textuality," in Janet Thumin (ed.), *Small Screens, Big Ideas*. London and New York: I. B. Tauris, 2002, 105–17.

—— *Off-White Hollywood: American Culture and Ethnic Female Stardom*. New York and London: Routledge, 2001.

Negra, Diane. "Re-Made for Television: Hedy Lamarr's Post-War Textuality," in J. Thumin (ed.), *Small Screens, Big Ideas*. London and New York: I. B. Tauris, 2002, 103–35.

Newton, Ronald C. "The Neutralization of Fritz Mandl: Notes on Wartime Journalism, The Arms Trade, and Anglo-American Rivalry in Argentina During World War II," *Hispanic American Historical Review* 66(3), (1986): 541–79.

Ottaviani, Jim. *Dignifying Science*. Ann Arbor, MI: G. T. Labs, 2003.

Robbins, Trina. *Hedy Lamarr and a Secret Communication System*. Mankato, MN: Capstone Press, 2007.

—— "Trina Robbins: Writer and Herstorian." Available at: http://www.trinarobbins.com/ (accessed February 8, 2010)

Vidor, King. *King Vidor on Filmmaking*. New York: McKay, 1972.

Walters, Rob. *Spread Spectrum: Hedy Lamarr and the Mobile Phone*. [Great Britain]: BookSurge, 2005.

Weise, Elizabeth. "Hedy Lamarr: A Sultry Screen Star Who Didn't Just Act — She Invented," *Classic Images* 265, (1997): C14.

Whitesitt, Linda. *The Life and Music of George Antheil 1900–1959*. Epping: Bowker, 1983.

Documentaries

Hedy Lamarr: Secrets of a Hollywood Star. Directed by Donatello Dubini, Fosco Dubini and Barbara Obermaier, 2006. Germany, Canada, Switzerland: 3Sat, Dubini Filmproduktion, MI Films, Obermaier Film, Tre Valli Filmproduktion, Zweites Deutsches Fernsehen. DVD.

5

Grotesquerie as Marker of Success in Aging Female Stars

ANNE MOREY

WHILE THE CONCEPT OF THE GROTESQUE has been extensively studied by literary scholars such as Wolfgang Kayser and Mikhail Bakhtin, it has been of only intermittent interest to media scholars, usually in its comic manifestations as in Kathleen Rowe's thorough examination in *The Unruly Woman*.[1] Writing in 1978, shortly after Molly Haskell argued that contemporary film had become oriented entirely toward providing a showcase for "Godfather-like machismo" and the male bonding of the buddy film, M. C. Kolbenschlag observed:

> [T]he films of the seventies have been populated with the "grotesque" female: prostitutes, neurotic spinsters, schizos, nymphos, alcoholics, flakos, and other crazies. The best roles for a woman in this generation of films have been ones in which she is portrayed as eccentric or "sick," "under the influence" or even "possessed."[2]

While the case might be made that films in the 1950s and 1960s were also rife with female grotesques (some of whom, such as Mrs. Bates in *Psycho* [1960], weren't even played by women), Haskell and Kolbenschlag were writing at a moment when feminist critics realized that the end of the studio system and the rise of independent film production had not resulted in more sympathetic or progressive roles for women and that, in fact, the propensity toward misogynistic and radically unsympathetic representations of femininity had increased.

---

1. Kathleen Rowe, *The Unruly Woman: Gender and the Genres of Laughter* (Austin: University of Texas Press, 1995). See also Felicity Collins's "Brazen Brides, Grotesque Daughters, Treacherous Mothers: Women's Funny Business in Australian Cinema from *Sweetie* to *Holy Smoke*," *Senses of Cinema* 23 (November–December 2002), http://archive.sensesofcinema. com/contents/02/23/women_funny_oz.html.
2. Molly Haskell, *From Reverence to Rape: The Treatment of Women in the Movies* (New York: Holt, Rinehart and Winston, 1974), 323; M. C. Kolbenschlag, "The Female Grotesque: Gargoyles in the Cathedrals of Cinema," *Journal of Popular Film and Culture* 64(4), (1978): 328.

The implication of arguments such as Kolbenschlag's and Haskell's is that grotesque roles are demeaning to women — including, perhaps, the actresses who enact them. Yet, during the waning days of the studio era (and after), presentation as grotesque was often an acknowledgment of an actress's artistic effort and ability to perform at the margins of conventional femininity. The association frequently made between the grotesque role and the critically acclaimed actress suggests that grotesquerie may be a source of professional and even personal power, given the frequent overlap between the dramas played out on the screen and those associated with certain stars' personal lives. Significantly, as I will discuss below, the path to the female grotesque runs through the maternal melodrama, in which the actress who will later perform the grotesque takes on the role of the mother whose powers and capacities outstrip those of her daughter. I propose that in ignoring the grotesque, we ignore an important mechanism by which female performers move in public perception from a conception of female celebrity that focuses on their appearance to one that focuses on their abilities, a process during which the divide among star, celebrity, and role is troubled, even elided. Examination of the grotesque thus holds potential for a clearer understanding of the complex relationship between celebrity and aging femininity.

The female grotesque in the mid-twentieth century existed within a discourse in which celebrity, role, and star often appeared identical; gender, as Christine Geraghty notes, often undermines any discussion of the female performer's skill.[3] Karen Hollinger comments that

> the fame of stars as celebrities is based on the public dissemination of intimate revelations about their private lives in publicity, interviews, star biographies, and other sources of celebrity gossip. . . . stars as celebrities are famous for being themselves and not for the success of their films or their reputations as actors.[4]

Thus, while a number of major female stars of the studio era, such as Bette Davis and Joan Crawford, willingly embodied grotesques, the celebrity discourse that followed these roles often insisted that no "acting" was involved. For example, biographies by intimates in the 1970s asserted the unity of the onscreen role and the actress's private life, thereby illustrating Edgar Morin's contention that star and role exist in a reciprocally "infectious" relationship.[5] As Mary Desjardins puts it,

3. Christine Geraghty, "Re-Examining Stardom: Questions of Texts, Bodies and Performance," in Christine Gledhill and Linda Williams (eds), *Reinventing Film Studies* (London: Arnold, 2000), 187–8.
4. Karen Hollinger, *The Actress: Hollywood Acting and the Female Star* (New York: Routledge, 2006), 43.
5. Edgar Morin, *The Stars*, trans. Richard Howard (New York: Grove, 1960), 37.

Perhaps [child-of-the-star memoirs'] most important achievement is in how they reveal star making as an enunciation that is publicly — and perhaps collectively — performed, not only by studio publicists and star laborer, but also by those who have family ties to the star and the fans who consume their biographical narratives.[6]

I will return to child-of-the-star memoirs later in this chapter; for now let it suffice to note that the trajectory of the typical female performer of the grotesque during the studio era moves her from a youthful persona that emphasizes her physical attractions, to the role of the mother in one or more maternal melodramas, to a maturity in which her embrace of the grotesque acknowledges her prowess as an actress, and finally to a postmortem existence in which revelations by daughters or other intimates suggest that her enactments of the grotesque onscreen were not acting but a sort of cinema vérité — a faint reflection of an off-screen maternal melodrama in which the monstrous mother victimized her less powerful daughter. This process often revolves around female rivalries: between real-life mother and daughter, between older woman and rising beauty on screen, and even between the mature actress and her youthful self. The relationship between the actress and her potential devourers, I propose, is important not only because it seems to provide her with power as much as it undermines her, but also because it provides filmmakers with a metaphor for rivalries in which the industry itself is engaged. It is no coincidence that what I term the "elegiac grotesque," a role in which actresses play female stars at the end of their powers, emerged at the moment that Hollywood became conscious of the threat posed by television.

Nonetheless, even though the institutional impulses that gave rise to the elegiac grotesque have long since been assimilated, admired contemporary actresses such as Meryl Streep continue to find grotesque roles attractive, suggesting that the grotesque still tracks a kind of performative excellence. In order to avert the risk of celebrity discourse undermining recognition of skill, however, contemporary actresses such as Streep must uncouple the actress from the celebrity, in a process that, as Linda Mizejewski argues, attempts to keep the focus on performance by publicly disdaining stardom, and attempting to avoid presentation to the public as celebrities at all.[7] In so doing, I would contend, they emphasize the grotesque as a construction rather than as the natural product of aging femininity. As I argue below, the elegiac grotesque has always depended to some extent upon an

---

6. Mary R. Desjardins, "Dietrich Dearest: Family Memoir and the Fantasy of Origins," in Gerd Gemünden and Mary R. Desjardins (eds), *Dietrich Icon* (Durham: Duke University Press, 2007), 312.
7. Linda Mizejewski, "Meryl Streep: Feminism and Femininity in the Era of Backlash," in Robert Eberwein (ed.), *Acting for America: Movies Stars of the 1980s* (New Brunswick, NJ: Rutgers University Press, 2010): 203.

acknowledgment of femininity as construction; the contemporary grotesque similarly reveals age as, if not a construction, at least a performance.[8]

Sadie Wearing has productively suggested that the relationship between feminism and postfeminism might itself be read as both rivalry and maternal melodrama: "the feminist/postfeminist divide has often been represented as a familial affair, a struggle for autonomy between 'mothers' and 'daughters' often fought over the ground of culture and representation."[9] Wearing argues that in the Diane Keaton drama, *Something's Gotta Give* (2003), young women "appear to turn 'misogyny' to their own advantage" while older women "'merely' critique it,"[10] suggesting why postfeminist sensibilities might not demand misogyny's extinction. Indeed, at least from the point of view of the older woman (particularly in the years between the end of the Second World War and the apogee of second-wave feminism in the late 1970s), grotesquerie may embody not misogyny so much as misandry, an anger at male social power and its emphasis on youthful female beauty that engenders an answering and insistent performance of the power of the aging woman.

While certain patterns operate within the casting of the female grotesque, such as the common movement from playing the lovely young "daughter" of a grotesque to playing the grotesque "mother" (consider Elizabeth Taylor in *Suddenly Last Summer* [1959] and the subsequent *Who's Afraid of Virginia Woolf?* [1966], for instance, or Crawford first in *Mannequin* [1938] and later in *Queen Bee* [1955]), it was by no means inevitable that an ingénue of the studio era would "graduate" to crone roles if she stayed in Hollywood long enough, or that this progression would mark the end of her serious career. The issue here is more than what mid-twentieth-century Hollywood was to do with the aging female star. Indeed, not every major Hollywood star embraced grotesque roles at and after the midpoint of her career; although it is not possible here to draw up a comprehensive list, it could include figures such as Davis, Crawford, Katharine Hepburn, Gloria Swanson, Taylor and, more recently, Streep, but it would omit, say, Joan Fontaine, Claudette Colbert,[11] and Julie Andrews. In other words, what we have here is a specific strategy that leads, in a number of cases, to the augmentation rather than the diminishing of star reputation, rather than a chauvinistic sense on the part of sexist producers that the aging female actress

---

8. See Anne Davis Basting's *The Stages of Age: Performing Age in Contemporary American Culture* (Ann Arbor: University of Michigan Press, 1998) for a consideration of the performance of aging.

9. Sadie Wearing, "Subjects of Rejuvenation: Aging in Postfeminist Culture," in Yvonne Tasker and Diane Negra (eds), *Interrogating Postfeminism: Gender and the Politics of Popular Culture* (Durham, NC: Duke University Press, 2007), 281.

10. Wearing, "Subjects of Rejuvenation," 283.

11. Identifying Colbert as a non-grotesque, however, is complicated by the fact that the role of Margo Channing in *All About Eve* was written for her, although a back injury lost her the part.

should be grateful even for roles that emphasize her physical and psychic deterioration.

Although the female grotesque can be divided into a number of different modes, including the virginal grotesque associated with stars such as Katharine Hepburn and the comic grotesque explored by Rowe, I focus here on the elegiac grotesque because of its metafilmic dimension and its ongoing usefulness to the female performer, both of which make it particularly suitable for discussions of stardom and star power.[12] Both Kolbenschlag and Haskell glance only in passing at a set of grotesque roles that date from a moment two decades before they took notice of it. Writing of *What Ever Happened to Baby Jane?* (1962), Haskell notes that "Joan Crawford and Bette Davis were turned into complete travesties of themselves,"[13] while for Kolbenschlag, it would appear that relishing such roles is a form of feminist false consciousness with a mercenary aim, since "actresses who play this kind of role — like their predecessor Bette Davis, who excelled in playing grotesque females — are more likely to win awards and accolades."[14]

But the elegiac female grotesque is more complicated than the concept of self-travesty or feminist false consciousness would imply because the selection of these roles is not necessarily born of desperation. These parts permit female performers to dramatize the problems of female celebrity at the same time that they allow them to display their own talents as performers. In cases such as Crawford and Davis, false consciousness seems not to fit, since both stars were highly conscious and resentful of women's disadvantages in the mid-twentieth century relative to men.[15] Nor is the issue one of travesty imposed from without, but rather of the star's willing acceptance of a *self*-travesty so complete that it also embraces her personal life. I contend that self-travesty within the elegiac grotesque functioned simultaneously as an expression of rage against a system so totalizing that it took advantage of a star's personal life and an acknowledgment that this system was a source of power for the star. Meanwhile, the studios' own practices insisted on the commensurability of star and celebrity, especially as the studio system began to wane. These factors converge in the grotesque to trouble the boundary

---

12. To be sure, these modes of grotesque overlap and interpenetrate to some extent. Hepburn, as I will argue, appears once in an elegiac grotesque role (*Suddenly, Last Summer*), although the dominant mode of her later career is that of the virginal grotesque, which exploits a motherless androgyny that must affiliate with a man who resembles an admired father.

13. Haskell, *From Reverence to Rape*, 328.

14. Kolbenschlag, "The Female Grotesque," 334.

15. Davis's daughter recalls her mother telling her during her marriage to Merrill, "There's only one way for a female to be recognized in this man's world, as you'll all too soon discover, and that's to fight every inch of the way. You can *never* stop fighting. I fought and I'm still fighting and I'll go on fighting until my dying day." See B. D. Hyman, *My Mother's Keeper* (New York: William Morrow, 1985), 27. Somewhat similarly, Christina Crawford recalls her mother complaining, for instance, that Howard Hughes "wanted to own people," especially women, whom he "used for exploitation and she didn't want any part of that" (Christina Crawford, *Mommie Dearest* [New York: William Morrow, 1978], 90).

between star and celebrity, particularly since they appear to represent a place where the female performer actively demonstrates or even exaggerates the ravages of aging, rather than attempting to disguise them, for example, through the possibilities of cosmetic surgery.

As Vivian Sobchack provocatively observes, "the alternative to cosmetic surgery in what passes for the verisimilitude of cinematic realism is a change in genre, a transformation of sensibility that takes us from the 'real' world to the world of horror, science fiction, and fantasy."[16] One of the ramifications of this insight is that the grotesque is already latent in the maternal melodrama, and the refusal to disguise or elide aging (including the accumulation of power it can bring in its wake) mandates the movement of the performer from one genre to the other. This willingness to let the disguise of youth and beauty slip, to acknowledge difficulty and discomfort, suggests why these roles might appeal to performers with feminist impulses. The grotesque, in other words, recalls the vulnerability already latent even in women's most youthful roles, and thus demonstrates the omnipresence of effort in constructing femininity from youth to age, for the star and the celebrity.

The Narrative Arc of the Elegiac Grotesque

As I note above, the elegiac grotesque surfaced at the moment that the studio system reached its end, with *Sunset Boulevard* (1950), *All About Eve* (1950), *The Star* (1952), and *What Ever Happened to Baby Jane?* being obvious examples of the metafilm that dramatizes the personal costs of female stardom, one of which is evidently the transformation into something grotesque. This clutch of films uses the ruin of stardom to expose the fundamentally hostile relationship between the female star and a younger rival, and/or between the female star and the system that created her and that continues to create rivals. Consider *Sunset Boulevard*'s examination of the enmity between Norma Desmond and Betty Schaefer: Betty represents not only the threat of youth as seen from the vantage point of a woman in her fifties, but also the arrival of a more contemporary kind of story (her collaboration with Joe) that is at odds with Norma's impossible screenplay *Salome*. The mise-en-scène of the film makes much of different styles of female beauty, with Swanson's youthful but masklike face in *Queen Kelly* (1929), screened for Joe, contrasted with Betty's scrubbed, 1950s girl-next-door visage.

It initially appears that *Sunset Boulevard* emphasizes both the passage of time and the longevity of Hollywood's creations to suggest the rivalry between past and present modes of filmmaking. Figures such as Norma/Swanson or H. B. Warner and Buster Keaton, two of the male members of

---

16. Vivian Sobchack, "Scary Women: Cinema, Surgery, and Special Effects," in Kathleen Woodward (ed.), *Figuring Age: Women, Bodies, Generations* (Bloomington, IN: Indiana University Press, 1999), 202.

the "Waxworks," are not current, but neither have they disappeared from Hollywood in its off-screen form. The persistence of the forgotten and the culturally dead is the engine of the gothic in the film, with no element of Norma's home or person permitted to signal anything but a mortality that remains in plain sight: consider Max, the dismissed husband and director but current butler; the monkey whose corpse Joe encounters as he is mistaken for the undertaker;[17] the organ Max continues to play; the title of Noel Coward's 1932 "Mad About the Boy," engraved on Joe's cigarette case as if it were still a current song; the ancient car brought out of hibernation; and the reconditioned swimming pool that becomes Joe's final resting place. Norma's final close-up, as directed by Max and commented upon by Hedda Hopper, is the essence of Hollywood's unburied, unburiable past.

Despite Joe's and Betty's pretensions to contemporary creativity, however, it is a scene of Norma's *Salome* and not their screenplay that is "produced" at the film's conclusion, suggesting that Norma's imagination, while "dead," is nonetheless more powerful than their own. Moreover, the rivalries that *Sunset Boulevard* exploits are more complex than the rivalry between old and new as figured by Norma and Betty. Ultimately, Norma is Mikhail Bakhtin's pregnant crone, who represents the unity of life and death in a single figure.[18] Norma's films, as Lucy Fischer argues, constitute a permanent record of her youth, an ever-present contrast to her current decay. While Fischer sees this "doubling" as intensifying the trauma of aging for Norma,[19] it arguably also emphasizes her power, as Joe's belated realization of Norma's previous importance demonstrates. In contemplating this mixture of fecundity and decay, Bakhtin asserts that the grotesque body is never unique or isolated, as "it never presents an individual; the image consists of orifices and convexities that present another, newly conceived body. It is a point of transition in a life eternally renewed, the inexhaustible vessel of death and conception."[20]

All About Eve realizes this union of death and conception by concluding with a representation of theatrical rivalry in the form of a mise en abyme in which the devourer is already devoured. The rivalry between aging star and rising ingénue is even more overt than in *Sunset Boulevard*, with Margo's fear of being displaced by her young admirer amply justified, and the trope of death-in-life is captured in the exchange between Bill Sampson and Margo over the repetition of *Liebestraum* on the piano at the cocktail party. Bill asks, with reference to the lugubrious music, where the body can

17. Cameron Crowe reports that Billy Wilder delighted in describing the dead chimp to Gloria Swanson and William Holden as Norma's "lover" and thus Joe's predecessor in that role, although Joe Gillis also describes it as Norma's child. *Conversations with Wilder* (New York: Knopf, 1999), 304.

18. Mikhail Bakhtin, *Rabelais and His World*, trans. Hélène Iswolsky (Bloomington, IN: Indiana University Press, 1984), 25–6.

19. Lucy Fischer, "Sunset Boulevard: Fading Stars," in Janet Todd (ed.), *Women and Film*. New York: Holmes & Meier, 1988, 107.

20. Bakhtin, *Rabelais and His World*, 318.

be viewed, to which Margo replies that it cannot be seen because it is still being embalmed. Like *Sunset Boulevard*, *All About Eve* suggests that the aging star and the young rival each contain the other — if youth is pregnant with age, age is also pregnant with youth. At the Sarah Siddons Society Awards that open the film,[21] Eve is described as having young hands but a heart old in the theater; Addison DeWitt's voiceover informs the viewer that Margo made her debut at four as a fairy, while Bill later humorously claims to deny rumors that Margo was in *Our American Cousin* the night Lincoln was shot. DeWitt observes that Margo once played Peter Pan, the boy who never ages but who is conventionally played by a grown woman, and he urges her to return to this role.

This simultaneous rivalry and yet relationship between youth and age continues at the institutional level. Eve arrives on the scene as a conversation in Margo's dressing room invokes earlier theatrical forms such as flea circuses and vaudeville and compares them to mid-twentieth-century Broadway, just as Birdie, the vaudeville veteran, compares Eve's contemporary tale of woe and devotion to Little Eva's escape pursued by bloodhounds in *Uncle Tom's Cabin*, the most performed American drama. Notably, the title of the play on the marquee at the opening is "*Aged in Wood*," and the play is apparently set in the antebellum south, itself a marker of both all that is creaky and antique about American theater and all that was desirable to the Hollywood actress at the zenith of the studio system (recall Davis's role in Wyler's 1938 *Jezebel*, the consolation prize for failing to be cast as Scarlett O'Hara). Eve herself describes film as an upstart and an inferior form to theater, which is positioned as tested and enduring. Not only is the star under threat, then, but she also represents an industry that is itself undermined by newer rivals, just as Eve meets her nemesis in Phoebe, who is shown wearing Eve's cape before a set of mirrors that creates a mise en abyme of endless epigones ready to devour even the newest star. Yet it is the very power of theater (and by implication, cinema) and its grandes dames that makes them desirable targets. As Jodi Brooks notes, Davis is a "souvenir" of a previous mode of cinema, a fetish that simultaneously acknowledges and disavows a former power.[22]

While the film industry began to make films about the psychological or social costs of stardom almost as soon as there was a star system,[23] Susan Sontag's "Notes on 'Camp'" may explain the explosion of elegiac grotesque

---

21. Inspired by the film, the Sarah Siddons Society was founded in 1952 in Chicago and presents an annual award for an outstanding performance in a Chicago theater production. Davis was given an honorary Siddons Award in 1973 (a year in which she did not appear on stage in Chicago); Anne Baxter, who played Eve, was honored at the same time.

22. Jodi Brooks, "Performing Age/Performance Crisis," in Kathleen Woodward (ed.), *Figuring Age: Women, Bodies, Generations* (Bloomington, IN: Indiana University Press, 1999), 222.

23. For a treatment of the fading male star, see the iterations of the basic plot through *What Price Hollywood?* (1932) and *A Star Is Born* (1934, and 1954 and 1976 remakes).

roles for women commencing as the studio system was phased out as an economic institution. Sontag observes that "many of the objects prized by Camp taste are old-fashioned, out-of-date, *démodé*. It's not a love of the old as such. It's simply that the process of aging or deterioration provides the necessary detachment — or arouses a necessary sympathy."[24] The camp sensibility itself cherishes the grotesque, manifesting "a love of the exaggerated, the 'off,'" which is expressed partly, Sontag argues, in camp taste's sentimental relationship to the past.[25] While certain stars — such as Davis, focus of three of the elegiac films — are clearly key to the female grotesque as a form, the form does not merely target individual stars, since the studio system and its relationship to women is being fetishized and attacked as much as any one actress. To that end, we might note a certain fungibility in stars to whom roles are offered; for instance, Mae West was Wilder's first choice for Norma, while Crawford was Aldrich's first choice for Miriam in *Hush . . . Hush, Sweet Charlotte* (1964). Nonetheless, since Davis is one of the relics of the studio system that Sontag identifies in particular as receiving camp treatment, and because she figures so prominently in this genealogy as what Michel Mourlet might term an "axiom of the cinema," it is worth looking in detail at how her career illustrates the relationship between conspicuous excellence as a performer and an affinity for the grotesque.

Davis, Labor, and the Grotesque

Davis's career is framed by a contradiction that, in part due to studio publicity efforts and journalistic coverage, permeates the wider construction of stardom, namely the beliefs that on the one hand the star exposes her own life as it is actually lived, and that on the other that the star is a star because she is a chameleon who harnesses hard work and artifice to create something that is neither natural to her nor lived on a daily basis. Davis herself insisted on the latter interpretation of her rise to and maintenance of her success, one that, as Maria LaPlace observes, studio-sanctioned fan articles also used to contain some of Davis's eccentricities by subordinating the "mere movie star" discourse to the "great actress" discourse.[26] Davis began her career on stage, after a brief stint in a New York acting school. Her autobiography makes much of her early training, first as the daughter of a single mother and upright Yankee, and second as the product of a thorough and deliberate

---

24. Susan Sontag, "Notes on 'Camp'," in *Against Interpretation and Other Essays* (New York: Farrar, Straus & Giroux, 1966), 285.

25. Ibid., 279, 280. Thus when one of the drag queens in *Torch Song Trilogy* (1988) launches into a Bette Davis impersonation, the reference is to Davis at her most grotesque, refusing "din-din" to her wheelchair-bound sister in *What Ever Happened to Baby Jane?*

26. Maria LaPlace, "Producing and Consuming the Woman's Film: Discursive Struggle in *Now, Voyager*," in Christine Gledhill (ed.), *Home Is Where the Heart Is: Studies in Melodrama and the Woman's Film*, (London: British Film Institute, 2002 [1987]), 149.

education designed to efface the accidents of personality to create a reliable "instrument" for the performer. Thus, Davis recounts having taken elocution lessons to remove a marked Boston accent and modern dance lessons (with Martha Graham) to learn "how to use our bodies properly."[27]

Perhaps unexpectedly for female star discourse in Hollywood, Davis initially confronted the problem of insufficient femininity. Carl Laemmle Jr.'s response to Davis's first appearance in his office was apparently to exclaim in her hearing that she "has as much sex appeal as Slim Summerville!"[28] Davis remained a master manipulator of the extent to which femininity is on display in her performances throughout her career. Martin Shingler argues that Davis was particularly adept at playing androgynous roles that combine masculine attributes with "feminine qualities such as heightened emotion and vulnerability."[29] Yet he also notes her command of roles such as Fanny in *Mr. Skeffington* (1944), in which Davis appears to exaggerate the character's feminine qualities to the point of female impersonation, suggesting that that role in particular resists easy assimilation to what fans presumably know about the independent and vigorous Davis persona. In his consideration of possible motivations for her decision to perform Fanny in such an exaggeratedly feminine way, Shingler postulates that while Davis might be dissembling her power behind the camera through her apparent disavowal of it before the camera, we can still more safely assume that "Davis . . . was defining herself against the conventions of female gender identity — femininity — either because she herself could not conform to the model or because, in 1944, those conventions seemed out-dated within the social context of wartime."[30]

By 1950, however, *All About Eve* indicates that the wartime suspension of pre-war gender codes is over, and, indeed, that gender might now be more rigorously policed than before; the film relentlessly insists that career success means nothing to a woman without sexual fulfillment with a man, ideally within marriage. Davis speaks lines of dialogue that express Margo's preference for sexual fulfillment with Bill to continuing her career as permanent ingénue in Lloyd Richards's plays, a role that she cedes to Eve in order to retain her rights to Bill in the bedroom. Yet these lines are not coupled with a notably feminine performance, including as it does savagely witty drunkenness, knock-down drag-out fights with her director/suitor Bill, and other demonstrations that her powers as a star mean more to her than deference

27. Bette Davis, *The Lonely Life: An Autobiography* (New York: G. P. Putnam's Sons, 1962), 66. See also Martin Shingler, "Bette Davis: Malevolence in Motion," in Alan Lovell and Peter Krämer (eds), *Screen Acting* (London: Routledge, 1999), 49–50, which offers a nicely observed account of the specific movement techniques in *Of Human Bondage* that Davis may have acquired from Graham.
28. Davis, 133.
29. Martin Shingler, "Masquerade or Drag? Bette Davis and the Ambiguities of Gender," *Screen* 36(3), (Autumn 1995): 182.
30. Ibid., 189.

to male expectations. Shingler's observation of *Mr. Skeffington* that Davis is willing to perform contempt for femininity would appear to be correct, therefore, but what then are we to make of her marriage to *All About Eve* co-star Gary Merrill, which continued the most dysfunctional elements of their onscreen romance for the next decade? It would appear that Davis's personal life was in thrall to the ideological program of the film; B. D. Hyman reports that when she suggested that her mother leave Merrill, who physically abused them both, Davis retorted, "I won't face being alone again. I've been alone since my father walked out on me when I was a little girl like you."[31]

There is yet another way of reading Davis's impersonation, even "female" impersonation,[32] which is to emphasize its value as the marker of conspicuous acting ability, the extra value the good actress must deliver on top of whatever endowments nature gave her to start with. Davis is withering on the subject of the "star," observing that

> drive is considered aggression today; I knew it then as purpose. I looked at the glamorous stars of the day. . . . To me, they were not actresses, but personalities. I don't underestimate them to this day. But I wanted much more. The very quality that made goddesses of them was not what I wanted for myself. I wanted to be considered eventually a fine actress. I strove for reality.[33]

Davis permitted herself to be represented in the press as unattractive, or at least as unattractive to herself,[34] so that what she accomplished could be attributed to effort rather than to intrinsic beauty. This emphasis on power at the expense of beauty, or power that might remake the ugly into the beautiful, recalls Davis's tie to Graham, whose strategy for increasing the cultural standing of her choreography was to assert that "ugliness may be actually beautiful, if it cries out with the voice of power."[35]

Yet as Shingler and Christine Gledhill note, Davis was both star and great actress, a contradiction that had to be resolved in various ways, particularly since the great actress discourse required that Davis downplay the physical attractions associated with "mere" stardom. One of the consequences of the discourse of skill was to engender a certain nervousness about femininity, which is partly what is expressed in the elements of gender masquerade that structure these roles. Thus, Davis's first marriage to Ham Nelson, assuaged her and her mother's concerns that she might not be "functioning correctly

---

31. Hyman, *My Mother's Keeper*, 27.
32. *Sunset Boulevard* is no stranger to the prospect of gender impersonation; Mae West would have brought the prospect of female impersonation to the role had she taken it, while Norma tries to amuse Joe by performing Charlie Chaplin's Little Tramp routine.
33. Davis, *The Lonely Life*, 156.
34. See Gladys Hall, "Am I Homely!" *Modern Screen* 17(4), (1938): 30.
35. Quoted in Amy Koritz, "The Inner Self of Martha Graham: Versions of Authenticity," in *Culture Makers: Urban Performance and Literature in the 1920s* (Urbana, IL: University of Illinois Press, 2009), 95.

as a female."[36] As Hollinger observes in her excellent synthesis of views of the star/actress, the concept of performative skill on stage or in front of the camera is one associated in the main with actors and not actresses.[37] But the star/actress who, like Crawford, permits the studio to "make" her through the services of sympathetic designers, excellent make-up men, and/or cosmetic surgery, is no more natural than the star/actress who possesses exceptional technique. Even if the former may not be said to be "acting" in the sense of taking on, chameleon-like, another identity, she is nevertheless not being "herself." In both cases, something must be added to the "natural" woman to make her more eligible, and that addition threatens the genuineness of the product. Davis's rage at the varying sizes of Crawford's artificial breasts during the shooting of *What Ever Happened to Baby Jane?* reveals her contempt for the artifice associated with stardom (a state that Davis evidently considered more or less identical to celebrity);[38] the falsies also manifest the problem of unreal femininity that stardom itself created for stars such as Crawford.

Davis's autobiography signals that although she was as dependent as any "mere" star on the studios' provision of better costumes, better makeup, and more information about how to comport herself before the camera, she wanted to be seen as actress rather than as star/celebrity. The fragility of agency within perceptions of female performance suggests why "celebrity" and even "star" discourse is so poisonous to the ambitious actress. Andrew Britton has argued of Davis's foil and rival Katharine Hepburn that a similar discourse of anti-stardom appeared in her coverage in fan magazines.[39] Like Davis, Hepburn planned her own strategic withdrawal from the studio system in order to recoup some lost autonomy via the cultivation of Philip Barry, who, as Britton observes, developed with Hepburn's advice and consent in *The Philadelphia Story* a characterization that did not represent a feminist statement but rather its opposite, in the form of a woman to be tamed. This role permitted Hepburn's reinstatement in the movie business when she returned to Hollywood with the script,[40] having performed an avowal/disavowal of female power not unlike that to be found in *All About Eve* or Shingler's account of *Mr. Skeffington.*

The great actress as self-maker is such an important trope that it appears in accounts not only of her relationship to the studio (where, in Hepburn's and Davis's cases, access to Broadway or to English studios held the promise of serving as a counterweight to excessive studio power), but when it

36. Davis, *The Lonely Life*, 161.
37. Hollinger, *The Actress*, 55.
38. Hyman, *My Mother's Keeper*, 60.
39. Andrew Britton, *Katharine Hepburn: Star as Feminist* (New York: Continuum, 1995), 19–28. Britton quotes Davis describing Hepburn as "practically the only girl of my generation for whom I had admiration and envy" (169).
40. Britton, *Katharine Hepburn*, 72.

comes to her responsibility for shaping or reshaping her roles. So we have Hepburn's important collaboration with Barry, in which she directed him to create a more rebarbative character than he had originally planned to write for her in *The Philadelphia Story*,[41] and also the many stories of Davis's attempts to recharacterize her roles while under contract or on loan-out at various studios. As Shingler's account of *Mr. Skeffington* suggests, where Davis is given a freer hand in shaping a performance, she tends to drive it in the direction of the grotesque. Consider her execution of her own makeup for Mildred's decline, arguably her earliest grotesque, in John Cromwell's 1934 *Of Human Bondage*,[42] the shaved-back hairline for *Virgin Queen*, a role that, as Hyman comments, also involved a "specially made rubber cap with some bits of fuzzy gray hair stuck here and there. . . . absolutely awful-looking, which was precisely what Mother wanted";[43] and the "ugly, chalky mask of makeup" that she devised to Robert Aldrich's admiration for *What Ever Happened to Baby Jane?*[44]

Baby Jane affords the opportunity to consider how much the grotesque depends on a reputation for skill as a performer rather than on the notoriety of a star/celebrity. If Hepburn was Davis's one object of envy as a fellow stage performer, Davis dismissed Crawford, her co-star on *Baby Jane*, as no rival actress but rather a pure studio creation. Yet Crawford too emerges as

Figure 5.1   **Bette Davis in her makeup as Queen Elizabeth, from *The Virgin Queen* (20th Century Fox, 1955), from the Margaret Herrick Library, Core Collection.**

---

41. Ibid., 72.
42. Davis, *The Lonely Life*, 174.
43. Hyman, *My Mother's Keeper*, 28.
44. Edwin T. Arnold and Eugene L. Miller, *The Films and Career of Robert Aldrich* (Knoxville, TN: University of Tennessee Press, 1986), 102.

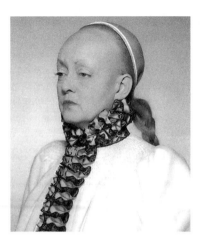

Figure 5.2 **Bette Davis as Mildred in *Of Human Bondage* (RKO Radio Pictures, 1934), from the Margaret Herrick Library, Core Collection.**

a grotesque in this film, as both Davis's victim and victimizer. In keeping with his other metafilms, such as *The Legend of Lylah Clare* (1968), Aldrich presents Hollywood and its hangers on as monsters of need, but always with a still more destructive parent lurking in the background to explain what goes wrong. In *Baby Jane*, Jane's successful career as child star, which causes her father to devote himself to her and ignore Blanche, is responsible for her monstrousness in later life; the early success is something she simply cannot survive as a personality. When success comes later to Blanche, she appears generously to have attempted to share some of her good fortune with her sister. Nonetheless, Blanche permits Jane to take the rap for an accident that was, in fact, Blanche's attempt to murder Jane. If that were not enough parental and sibling destructiveness, Jane's would-be accompanist is a mama's boy and a fraud, a failed composer who is reduced to encouraging Jane in her comeback hopes so that he may earn pocket money. His relationship to his mother displays the same mutual dependence and hostility that characterize the father/daughter and sister bonds in this film; each dysfunctional personality is the creature of another, as Blanche's confession that she made Jane what she is, namely "ugly," attests.

The Maternal Melodrama and Grotesquerie

In her analysis of films including *Sunset Boulevard* and *All About Eve*, Brooks argues that

> each of these films draws to a close with the aging actress staging (or restaging) her own disappearance in her very attempt to refuse it and carve or burn her

way into the present. As sole witnesses to their own disappearance, they have, it would seem, only one option — to reproduce that disappearance — now with an audience through performing an excessive visibility.[45]

This staging of her own disappearance, is, of course, what the mother in the maternal melodrama performs, which suggests why the maternal melodrama and the elegiac grotesque are related, and why the star of the former should become the star of the latter. So, for example, Stella must arrange her own casting off by her daughter in *Stella Dallas* (1937). In the somewhat more complex narrative of *Imitation of Life* (1934), the tragedy created by Peola's rejection of her mother results in Bea's decision to refuse Steve Archer's proposal in order to permit Jessie to work through her attachment to him. Similarly, in *Mildred Pierce* (1945) Veda condemns Mildred as vulgar; Veda even affects not to know who Mildred's "people" are, thus disavowing her own ancestors in her haste to sever herself from "my mother, a waitress." Nothing Mildred can do for her daughter, from showering Veda with piano and dance lessons in an effort to supply her with attainments that Mildred's own lower-class background lacked, to marrying Monte to afford Veda the class connections and even the sexual access to her own husband that Veda requires, can prevent Veda from dismissing her or using her. *Mildred Pierce* is particularly interesting inasmuch as it simultaneously represents Crawford's triumphant comeback from her dismissal from MGM (she won an Oscar for her performance) and hints at her first foray into the grotesque.[46] Similarly, Davis's character in *Now, Voyager* (1942) declares herself sexually unavailable by refusing Eliot Livingstone in order to assist the cure of Tina, even though her own mother's death has presumably left her free to marry whom she will.

The woman's film's ambivalence about the daughter is key to the rage contained in the figure of the elegiac grotesque; the daughter is simultaneously something fashioned by the mother as an offering to superior masculinity and a rival to her. The importance of rivalry as an element in grotesquerie is suggested by Britton's consideration of the different trajectories in later casting arising from Hepburn's and Davis's very different experiences in the maternal melodrama of the 1930s. In his comparison of the Hepburn vehicle *A Woman Rebels* (1936), in which there is no ultimate parting from the illegitimate daughter, and the Davis vehicle *The Old Maid* (1939), in which there is, Britton observes that "Davis is *incessantly* cast in narratives about relationships of more or less insatiable jealousy, animosity, loathing and resentment between women."[47] Hepburn, on the other hand, when "cast as another woman's romantic rival . . . invariably becomes friends

---

45. Brooks, "Performing Age/Performance Crisis," 238.
46. Davis was apparently considered for the role as well, which would support the proposition of the fungibility of stars to at least a limited extent in particular generic types.
47. Britton, *Katharine Hepburn*, 162.

with the woman and prefers to renounce the man rather than hurt her."[48] This distinction explains why, as Hepburn ages, the form of grotesquerie that overtakes her, or that she elects, with one significant exception, is that of the virginal or spinster grotesque, on display in films such as *The Rainmaker* (1956) and *Summertime* (1955). Notably, the first film in which she appears as a significant rival to a woman is her first appearance as an elegiac grotesque, as the monstrous matriarch in *Suddenly, Last Summer* who threatens a daughter figure whom she wants to have lobotomized in order to control the narrative about her son, Sebastian. Indeed, it is possible to argue that *Suddenly, Last Summer* is about dueling performances between the women, in which Violet and Cathy must compete to successfully embody sanity. In what is now a pattern in the elegiac grotesque, the generational struggle for the affections of a younger man is worked out between a woman and a successor young enough to be her daughter. Cathy threatens Violet's relationship with both Sebastian and Dr. Cukrowicz, who is said to resemble Sebastian.

As always, however, something more than the sexual desire and anxiety of the aging woman is at stake. Violet, like Margo, Blanche, and Norma, represents a system that has bestowed power on the aging woman. Dr. Hockstader and Cathy's mother, for example, are willing to accede to the lobotomy in return for the money that each of them hopes to receive from Violet. The victims of this power may be male or female, but the system that has created the grotesque is at least indirectly critiqued as excessively potent — as Haskell observes of the transition from the studio system to independent production, "the absence of the image-manufacturing apparatus gave the actresses greater freedom, but as non-stars they had less power."[49] The aging woman represents, therefore, an energy that needs to be refreshed and replaced precisely because she is so overwhelming as to leave insufficient space for the young.

Notably, there are rivalries within rivalries. For example, the studio style of performance that dominated acting from the 1920s to the 1940s itself confronted a rival in The Method at just the moment that the studio system was coming to a close. As Hollinger notes, The Method "distinctly became the province of male stars, such as Marlon Brando, James Dean, Rod Steiger, Montgomery Clift, Lee J. Cobb, and Karl Malden."[50] Importantly, Hollinger adds as a corollary Virginia Wright Wexman's observation that The Method "associated good acting with the expression of masculine emotion . . . and actresses in female-oriented genres like the 'woman's film' became increasingly connected with the emotionally excessive acting of the tearjerker,"[51] which was, of course, the previously highly valued form of performance

48. Ibid., 156.
49. Haskell, *From Reverence to Rape*, 326.
50. Hollinger, *The Actress*, 14.
51. Ibid., 15.

when Hollywood understood its audience and its most powerful exemplars as largely female.

This acknowledgment of female power as something that both waxes and wanes helps to explain the phenomenon, mentioned in the introductory section of this chapter, of the star biography written by the rejected, harassed, or "damaged" daughter of the star, a genre that subverts attempts to suggest that the star is doing anything but playing herself. This genre becomes multigenerational in the case of Davis, who suggests in her own autobiography that her mother was a sexual rival to her in her youth and who, Hyman claims, threatened to take away Hyman's fiancé.[52] Since Hyman's acting career was brief, her personal life became the target of her mother's interference. Christina Crawford, on the other hand, had to contend with her mother as rival also in the realm of her livelihood. When Christina was hospitalized with a Fallopian tumor, Joan took over her role on the soap opera *Secret Storm*. The role, appropriately enough, was that of "a neurotic young wife with a passion for mischief who developed a drinking problem when she suspected her husband of seeing other women."[53] According to Christina, this act of sabotage was presented in the guise of maternal kindness: "she said it was to save my part so they wouldn't replace me, but it was the absolute end of my character's credibility. I was playing a twenty-eight-year-old woman. My mother was well past sixty!"[54] Similarly, in an article headed "Living with Norma Desmond," Swanson's daughter is quoted as insisting on the identity of Gloria/Norma at the time of the shooting of *Sunset Boulevard*.[55]

That these accounts all assert the seamlessness between performer and role, at least as seen by intimates, encapsulates the problem of distinguishing between performance as impersonation, in which actors subordinate themselves to a role, and performance as personification, in which actors simply appear to play themselves. Even in those cases, such as Davis's, where the actor has staked her reputation on impersonation, the star biography merges her career and life into a personification amalgam, in which the declining years are spent playing herself — on occasion, as grotesque.

The Contemporary Grotesque

This confusion between impersonation and personification, stardom and celebrity, the actress and her roles, continues to animate the post-studio system fortunes of the grotesque. To some extent, the contemporary grotesque retains its connections to the woman's film and the maternal melodrama; for

---

52. Davis, *The Lonely Life*, 43; and Hyman, *My Mother's Keeper*, 102.
53. Crawford, *Mommie Dearest*, 249.
54. Ibid., 253.
55. Andrew Wilson, "Living with Norma Desmond," *The Observer* (March 9, 2003).

example, contemporary stars associated with such roles include Meryl Streep and Susan Sarandon. Often called the "best actress of her generation,"[56] Streep continues the Davis tradition of being a performer in command of "technique," acquired in this case at the Yale School of Drama. While Hollinger suggests that Streep, like many actors, either will not or cannot articulate just what it is that she does to prepare for and execute a role,[57] the great cliché of Streep's technical mastery, her command of accents, suggests that she is to be seen as the master of impersonation rather than personi-fication. Mizejewski observes, however, that Streep's very skill in mimicry tends to diminish the value of these performances for her harshest critics who expect, but do not find, her own personality on display.[58] Like Davis, Streep is famous for rewriting or recharacterizing roles as necessary, as in *Kramer vs. Kramer* (1979), where she is said to have risked the considerable anger of Dustin Hoffman in order to revise her role. Diana Maychick reports that Streep wanted to make Joanna Kramer a more believable character, while Hoffman guarded the original script jealously in order to fend off any upstaging by Streep, until she won him over.[59]

In other words, it is part of Streep's image that she has been able to exer-cise authority over her performances at a relatively early age, and she has since come to represent the powerful actress for a post-studio system gen-eration. Significantly, she has also modulated gradually into a performer of grotesques in roles such as Miranda Priestly in *The Devil Wears Prada* (2006). Moreover, like many of her predecessors she has arrived at the grotesque via the maternal melodrama, beginning with *Kramer vs. Kramer*, in which Joanna must ultimately relinquish her child to the superior claims of her husband,[60] and continuing with roles such as Lindy Chamberlain in *A Cry in the Dark* (1988) and Sophie in *Sophie's Choice* (1982). Streep's own carefully controlled press in the 1980s insisted on the primacy of her role as mother,[61] and this press often appeared, as Mizejewski observes, in general circulation women's magazines in preference to periodicals more directly associated with celebrity reportage.[62] Streep's avoidance of the glamour associated with stardom and her emphasis, in publicity materials, on the value that she places on her own maternity have the effect of avoiding the merger between star and role that overtake Swanson, Davis, and Crawford in their daughters' accounts. Streep both considers herself a feminist and is interested in roles

---

56. Hollinger, *The Actress*, 71.
57. Ibid., 86.
58. Mizejewski, 203.
59. Diana Maychick, *Meryl Streep: The Reluctant Superstar* (New York: St. Martin's Press, 1984), 86.
60. This family configuration represents an interesting, and presumably necessary, updating of the patterns of rivalry characteristic of the classical era maternal melodrama, in which older woman and younger woman are rivals for the affections of a man.
61. Mizejewski, 205.
62. Ibid., 205–6.

involving conflicted mothers; as Mizejewski observes, however, "while Streep was deeply implicated in the Superwoman narrative of 'having it all,' some of her most prominent choices of films reveal disturbing counter-narratives about guilt and motherhood circulating during [the 1980s]."[63]

Despite having her pick of such roles during a decade when there were notable roles available to women, in an echo of Haskell and Kolbenschlag, Streep has waxed nostalgic about the roles formerly available to female stars, listing Davis as one of her inspirations.[64] In her view, the scarcity of good roles for women (ones in which they are not reduced to playing "hookers," for example) is a feminist issue, but it is also an index of the waning aesthetic power of Hollywood itself. Streep quotes her 75-year-old mother, whose advice for the line to take in Streep's keynote speech to the first national women's conference of the Screen Actors Guild (subsequently published as "When Women Were in Movies") is, "Why don't you just tell them that when there were more women in the movies, the movies were better?"[65] Indeed, Tino Balio observes of the 1930s that "in the first half of the decade, the woman's film accounted for over a quarter of the pictures on *Film Daily*'s Ten Best,"[66] making almost inevitable the generic association between the woman's film and quality performance. Yet even in the absence of a studio system as such, the grotesque remains a marker of both performative ability and the quality film; the grotesque here again represents a simultaneous attack on and a cherishing, even fetishizing of, a previous system of film-making. Above all, the grotesque is a way of connecting important female performers, in an environment inimical to them since the 1950s, to a previous moment of female power that was itself the index of the success of the system that manufactured these powerful actresses.

Notably, Streep, unlike Davis and Crawford, has successfully uncoupled the grotesque on screen from the grotesque in private life. For example, the role shared between Streep and her daughter Mamie Gummer in *Evening* (2007), in which Gummer has much more screen time and is presented more attractively than Streep, suggests no damaging rivalry between mother and daughter, no maternal melodrama in real life. Similarly, actresses such as Streep and Sarandon, who are said to lead orderly private lives with little kiss-and-tell drama, are less celebrities now than are younger performers such as Lindsay Lohan (Streep's daughter in *A Prairie Home Companion* [2006]), whose endless trips in and out of substance-abuse programs guarantee celebrity without the professional power wielded by her "great actress" seniors in a stark illustration of the "Going Cheap" phenomenon discussed by the editors in the introduction to this volume. Thus one reason that the

---

63. Ibid., 211.
64. Meryl Streep, "When Women Were in The Movies," *Screen Actor* 29(2), (Fall 1990): 16.
65. Ibid., 17.
66. Tino Balio, *Grand Design: Hollywood as a Modern Business Enterprise, 1930–1939* (Berkeley, CA: University of California Press, 1995), 235.

grotesque remains a desirable role in popular culture is that it may now seem less threatening to women than was once the case; on the one hand, the aging woman may be the locus for moral authority (as in *Doubt* [2008], in which Streep plays an initially unsympathetic nun who faces down a more powerful priest), while on the other, young women may now have greater confidence that mature femininity offers no obstruction to their own aspirations, as the conclusion to *The Devil Wears Prada* suggests.

As a final contemporary example, we might consider Sarandon's recent role in a Disney film, *Enchanted* (2007), which returns the grotesque to its origins in the fairy tale. As Narissa, Sarandon may threaten the heroine both as evil queen and as dragon, but Giselle, while initially saccharine to the point of idiocy, is not intimidated. Rather, in a satisfying bit of role reversal, she vanquishes Narissa physically in order to save the inert hero, and her sunshiny understanding of the way the world works is triumphantly endorsed by the narrative. The film offers a sly examination of the costs of being the "good" wife (something, arguably, that all grotesque figures nod at by suggesting why women might want to wield power); Giselle's cleanup of Robert's apartment requires the services of rats, pigeons, and cockroaches, suggesting the sweated, unpaid, dirty labor required by the attractive middle-class façade, usually supplied, or supervised, by the woman of the house. The subplot of the henpecked Nathaniel, who becomes the darling of the book circuit with his bestseller *Vanquishing the Evil Queen Within,* is not only a nod at grotesque-as-gay-icon but also acknowledges male dependence on the dominating woman; in either case, the grotesque serves male interests as much as female interests.

That a film addressed to the preteen girl can afford to be so knowing suggests that the teeth have been drawn from the image of the grotesque, while at the same time, the presence of Giselle's grotesque older rival Narissa, like the Disney brand itself, is a kind of guarantor of quality. Embedded in a film that is simultaneously mocking and worshipful about the glories of a former fun factory, Narissa is costumed like the wicked stepmother in *Snow White* (1937); the forest creatures are Bambi's more fortunate siblings; Robert must be rescued from the top of a skyscraper like Fay Wray in *King Kong* (1933); even the classic Disney song-and-dance routines are both mocked and admired. Like the grotesque, these are gestures back at filmmaking as a more central, more dominant occupation than Disney can really practice in the era of fragmented attention, when its products may be as likely to be consumed on an iPod as in a theater and its homepage directs consumers to "theme parks, resorts, movies, *Disney* Channel programs, characters, games, videos, music, shopping, and more!"[67] Even if she must be vanquished at the end of the narrative, then, be it in the form of a film or a star biography, the grotesque continues to be admired, representing simultaneously an

---

67. www.disney.com

old-fashioned power and the promise of the fecundity of the studios that created her.

Bibliography

Arnold, Edwin T. and Eugene L. Miller. *The Films and Career of Robert Aldrich.* Knoxville, TN: University of Tennessee Press, 1986.

Bakhtin, Mikhail. *Rabelais and His World,* trans. Hélène Iswolsky. Bloomington, IN: Indiana University Press, 1984.

Balio, Tino. *Grand Design: Hollywood as a Modern Business Enterprise, 1930–1939.* Berkeley: University of California Press, 1995.

Basting, Anne Davis. *The Stages of Age: Performing Age in Contemporary American Culture.* Ann Arbor: University of Michigan Press, 1998.

Britton, Andrew. *Katharine Hepburn: Star as Feminist.* New York: Continuum, 1995.

Brooks, Jodi. "Performing Aging/Performance Crisis," in Kathleen Woodward (ed.), *Figuring Age: Women, Bodies, Generations.* Bloomington, IN: Indiana University Press, 1999, 232–46.

Collins, Felicity. "Brazen Brides, Grotesque Daughters, Treacherous Mothers: Women's Funny Business in Australian Cinema from *Sweetie* to *Holy Smoke*," *Senses of Cinema* 23 (November–December 2002). Available at: http://archive.sensesofcinema.com/contents/02/23/women_funny_oz.html (accessed November 10, 2010).

Crawford, Christina. *Mommie Dearest.* New York: William Morrow, 1978.

Crowe, Cameron. *Conversations with Wilder.* New York: Knopf, 1999.

Davis, Bette. *The Lonely Life: An Autobiography.* New York: G. P. Putnam's Sons, 1962.

Desjardins, Mary R. "Dietrich Dearest: Family Memoir and the Fantasy of Origins," in Gerd Gemünden and Mary R. Desjardins (eds), *Dietrich Icon.* Durham, NC: Duke University Press, 2007, 310–27.

Fischer, Lucy. "Sunset Boulevard: Fading Stars," in Janet Todd (ed.), *Women and Film.* New York: Holmes & Meier, 1988, 97–113.

Geraghty, Christine. "Re-examining Stardom: Questions of Texts, Bodies and Performance," in Christine Gledhill and Linda Williams (eds), *Reinventing Film Studies.* London: Arnold, 2000, 183–201.

Hall, Gladys. "Am I Homely!" *Modern Screen* 17(4), (1938): 30–1, 92–3.

Haskell, Molly. *From Reverence to Rape: The Treatment of Women in the Movies.* New York: Holt, Rinehart and Winston, 1974.

Hollinger, Karen. *The Actress: Hollywood Acting and the Female Star.* New York: Routledge, 2006.

Hyman, B. D. *My Mother's Keeper.* New York: William Morrow, 1984.

Kolbenschlag, M. C. "The Female Grotesque: Gargoyles in the Cathedrals of Cinema," *Journal of Popular Film and Culture* 64(4), (1978): 328–41.

Koritz, Amy. "The Inner Self of Martha Graham: Versions of Authenticity," in *Culture Makers: Urban Performance and Literature in the 1920s.* Urbana, IL: University of Illinois Press, 2009.

LaPlace, Maria. "Producing and Consuming the Woman's Film: Discursive Struggle in *Now, Voyager*," in Christine Gledhill (ed.), *Home Is Where the Heart Is: Studies in Melodrama and the Woman's Film* (2nd edn). London: British Film Institute, 2002, 138–66.

Maychick, Diana. *Meryl Streep: The Reluctant Superstar.* New York: St. Martin's Press, 1984.

Mizejewski, Linda. "Meryl Streep: Feminism and Femininity in the Era of Backlash," in Robert Eberwein (ed.), *Acting for America: Movie Stars of the 1980s.* New Brunswick: Rutgers University Press, 201–2.

Morin, Edgar. *The Stars,* trans. Richard Howard. New York: Grove, 1960.

Rowe, Kathleen. *The Unruly Woman: Gender and the Genres of Laughter.* Austin: University of Texas Press, 1995.

Shingler, Martin. "Bette Davis: Malevolence in Motion," in Alan Lovell and Peter Krämer (eds), *Screen Acting.* London: Routledge, 1999, 46–58.

——. "Masquerade or Drag? Bette Davis and the Ambiguities of Gender," *Screen* 36(3), (Autumn 1995): 179–92.

Shingler, Martin and Christine Gledhill. "Bette Davis: Actor/Star," *Screen* 49(1), (Spring 2008): 67–76.

Sobchack, Vivian. "Scary Women: Cinema, Surgery, and Special Effects," in Kathleen

Woodward (ed.), *Figuring Age: Women, Bodies, Generations*. Bloomington, IN: Indiana University Press, 1999, 200–11.

Sontag, Susan. "Notes on 'Camp'," in *Against Interpretation, and Other Essays*. New York: Farrar, Straus & Giroux, 1966, 275–92.

Streep, Meryl. "When Women Were in the Movies," *Screen Actor* 29(2), (Fall 1990): 15–17.

Wearing, Sadie. "Subjects of Rejuvenation: Aging in Postfeminist Culture," in Yvonne Tasker and Diane Negra (eds), *Interrogating Postfeminism: Gender and the Politics of Popular Culture*. Durham, NC: Duke University Press, 2007, 277–310.

Wilson, Andrew. "Living with Norma Desmond," *The Observer*, March 9, 2003. Available at: http://www.guardian.co.uk/film/2003/mar/09/features.review2 (accessed May 19, 2010).

Note

I am grateful to Claudia Nelson for her many helpful comments on this chapter and for having invited an earlier version of it as a talk in the Women's Studies lunch lecture series at Texas A&M, and to Jim Rosenheim for bringing *Who's Afraid of Virginia Woolf* to my attention in this context. Kristine Krueger kindly located illustrations.

6

"I'm Like a Kaleidoscope"

Mia Farrow and the Shifting Prismatics of Modern Femininity in the 1960s

LESLIE H. ABRAMSON

TO REGARD THE IMAGE OF MIA FARROW IN THE 1960S is to distinguish a figure who embodied the feminine, American culture, and Hollywood at the occasion of radical change. During a decade of profound social transformation mobilized, in significant part, by the rise of the women's movement, youth counterculture, and the sexual revolution, and accompanied by the film industry's struggles to reinvent itself amid the demise of the studio system, Farrow's stardom was located at the juncture of liberation from traditional gender roles, social codes, and cinema culture. Moreover, at a moment when Hollywood was mapping the rapidly shifting position of women onto the evolving images of female stars, Farrow's celebrity conspicuously epitomized something more abstract. In essence, Farrow became an icon of contemporary mutability itself, an incarnation of the feminine as site of metamorphosis.

In *The Feminine Mystique*, the 1963 book that inspired the decade's feminist movement, Betty Friedan wrote, "American women no longer know who they are. They are sorely in need of a new image to help them find their identity."[1] In the context of this critical historical period, Farrow surfaced as an emblem of the feminine unbound. In celebrity profiles, gossip columns, interviews, fashion shoots, and reviews, she was coded as a figure of free-spirited changeability, a captivating cipher. The remarkable nature of such mesmeric typecasting is that Farrow's famed indeterminacy and elusiveness was a shared illusion, a fantasy in which the performer, press, and public manifestly conspired. This exemplar of modern femininity was, ironically, a figure whose materialization as a star and continued notoriety was entirely indebted to her status as an individual firmly tethered to the industry and cultural milieu of the Hollywood Establishment by genealogical cords, as

---

1. Betty Friedan, *The Feminine Mystique* (New York: W. W. Norton & Company, 1997 [1963]), 72.

well as through the professional and personal attachments that she formed in the course of the decade.[2] At a time when contemporary womanhood and youth culture were defined by rebellion against the System, the young Farrow simultaneously represented feminine individualism and the patriarchal institution of American cinema.

In his canonical work on stardom, Richard Dyer explains that stars are figures of "structured polysemy, that is, the finite multiplicity of meanings and affects they embody . . ."[3] Accordingly, in the conjunction between her highly publicized off-screen life and on-screen performances, Farrow became a marker of the decade's tensions, a nexus of the competing rhetoric of classical stardom, Establishment values, and liberation discourses. Emerging as a celebrity in 1964 when, at age 19, she starred as a virginal, illegitimate teenager in *Peyton Place* (1964–1969) — a controversial television soap opera depicting small town licentiousness — Farrow was best known for her strong associations with Hollywood studio culture and moral conservatism as the Catholic school-educated daughter of 1930s movie star Maureen O'Sullivan and film director John Farrow. By the end of the decade, when her fifth feature film was released, Farrow had become a contract actress, wife and divorcée of middle-aged singer and veteran film star Frank Sinatra, celebrated nonconformist, established magazine cover image, modern fashion icon, devotee of Transcendental Meditation, temporary ashram resident, and paramour of conductor and film score composer Andre Previn, by whom the unwed Farrow was pregnant in 1969. Farrow's sphere of intimates and acquaintances — with whom her associations were followed by the media with considerably more interest than her screen work — included 1940s and 1950s studio stars, aged surrealist painter Salvador Dali, the Maharishi Yogi, and such contemporary performers as the Beatles. Taken together with her handful of film roles exploring untethered and delimited femininity — including the pregnant housewife in the horror film *Rosemary's Baby* (1968), her sole box office hit — Farrow's celebrity attracted intensely debated cultural divisions regarding the position of the feminine and shifting moral codes, the sexual revolution, and the opposition between baby boomers and their elders, popularly termed the generation gap.

At the same time, Farrow was a critical figure of suture, linking matrimony and liberated womanhood, the Establishment and youth culture, the studio system and New American Cinema, domestic and foreign film aesthetics, classical art and modern media, and traditional, folk, and contemporary spiritualism. In the process, Farrow arose as one of a handful of emergent

2. American society in the 1960s possessed an amplified sense of its own modernity as dramatic shifts from conservative 1950s culture were activated by new social, political, and aesthetic movements. "The Establishment" was a term widely used during the decade to refer to the dominant patriarchal institutions — and those who controlled them — constituting the repositories of power in American culture.
3. Richard Dyer, *Stars*, new edn. (London: British Film Institute, 1998), 3.

female stars in the 1960s who invigorated public fascination with celebrity in a fashion that both hearkened back to studio culture's longed-for Golden Age and celebrated the new.[4] During a decade of hemorrhaging box office returns, when the very industry of American cinema seemed to be at stake, within the realm of female stardom Mia Farrow's immense fame constituted one of the few affirmative ways of resolving the question, "Can Hollywood survive the 1960s?"

The velocity of Farrow's rise to fame and the dynamics of media fascination that propelled her immense popularity in the 1960s have been almost wholly forgotten in cultural memory and scholarship on stardom.[5] To recover Farrow for celebrity studies is to decipher how, according to Richard Dyer, "Stars articulate what it is to be a human being in contemporary society"[6] at a critical historical moment when the defining cultural condition of modernity was particularly at stake in her image. Further, in the archaeology of stardom's textual landscape, to revisit Farrow in the 1960s is to witness how, amid the dynamics of redefinition, the discursive operations of inquisition into female celebrity became self-consciously mobilized around this figure.

The dialectics between the fictional and nonfictive texts that established, aestheticized, and continually investigated her identity not only constructed Farrow as a unique juncture-figure integrating the magnetism and anxiety bound up with key cultural transitions as well as the condition of shift, but in critical respects seemed to call for female celebrity studies. Specifically, in the interplay between Farrow's image in the press and her performances, conspicuously at issue were the particular elusiveness of feminine identity, the position of stardom, woman's notoriety, and the association between private individual and public persona.

Delineating Farrow as conundrum in the pages of *Ladies' Home Journal*, for example, *Peyton Place* producer Paul Monash observed, "She has created a mystique about herself. Is she clever? Is this instinct? Is this vital truth? Is this assumed? I haven't the slightest clue."[7]

In fact, Farrow's celebrity constitutes a distinctly significant case in the

---

4. For example, celebrity discourse of the 1960s also allied Jane Fonda and Candice Bergen with the Hollywood establishment insofar as they, too, were daughters of famous performers, although the construction of their meanings widely diverged from that of Farrow. The stardom of such popular figures in the 1960s as Elizabeth Taylor and Audrey Hepburn also invoked the studio era, but these actresses were clearly of an older generation. Note that in this essay both the terms "celebrity" and "star" have been applied to Farrow because the media was fascinated with her private life yet at the same time she was perceived as a television and film star.

5. With the exception of my essay, "Mia Farrow: Categorically Intangible," in *New Constellations: Movie Stars of the 1960s* (New Brunswick, NJ: Rutgers University Press, 2010). Two small mass-market biographies of Farrow were published in the early 1990s and Farrow's autobiography, *What Falls Away*, was published in 1997.

6. Richard Dyer. *Heavenly Bodies: Film Stars and Society*, 2nd edn. (London: Routledge, 2004), 7.

7. Vernon Scott, "Mia Farrow's Swinging Life with Frank Sinatra," *Ladies' Home Journal*, May 1967, 168.

study of female stardom insofar as her image manifestly engaged the discursive interplay between the figure of woman as unknown Other and as eminently intelligible, contextualized in an era of pronounced gender slippage, during which the position of the feminine was in dramatic transition. Whereas Dyer stresses that it is the work of textual analysis to decipher the star's multiple facets of meaning, in the 1960s Farrow's fame was predicated on popular recognition of (and captivation with) her inherently "polysemic" nature. At the same time, Farrow's alluring multiplicity evoked a converse urge towards circumscription, engaging the fascination and problematics of feminine definition.

Though her image was mass distributed across no less than 60 magazine covers in the 1960s, issues of apprehension were foremost in media discourse dedicated to the representation of Mia Farrow as a star.[8] A figure whose existence within the celebrity sphere both predated and largely overshadowed her display of talent as a screen performer — one of a contemporary breed of star defined by historian Daniel Boorstin in 1961 as those "notorious for their notoriety" — the renowned Farrow seemed to both invite and elude definition.[9] From 1964 through to the end of the decade, Farrow's image in the popular press was that of the feminine as the inexplicable, unattached, and extramundane: a "waif," a "sprite," "almost unearthly," an "airborne colleen," a "merry little mystery, a misunderstood visitor from the future, or the occult past." This incarnation as the ineffable, as a shapeshifter, was evoked by Farrow herself who, in one of her earliest interviews, suggested to a *Look* reporter in 1964, "I'm like a kaleidoscope . . . I see a different person every time I look in a mirror."[10] Celebrating her transformative feminine nature, a *McCall's* writer observed in 1967, "She is Mia Superstar as the camera focuses on her, smiling, laughing, flirting, looking innocent, looking sexy. Completely in charge. She's everybody at once — a duke's daughter, Peter Pan, Joan of Arc, the Constant Nymph. Instant quicksilver."[11] By the end of the decade, Farrow's classification as the indeterminate incarnate remained a dominant trope in media texts. As late as 1969, *Time* magazine included among its compilation of quotes about the young star from fellow celebrities — an epistemological strategy frequently employed in what the press characterized as the difficult attempt to define Farrow — the observation by actor Roddy McDowell, "trying to describe Mia is like trying to describe dust in a shaft of sunlight. There are all those particles."[12]

As McDowell's remark indicated, in measuring the appeal of Farrow,

8. This number includes periodical covers on which Farrow's image appears singularly and those on which she appears with other celebrities.
9. Daniel Boorstin, *The Image: A Guide to Pseudo-Events in America* (New York: Harper Colophon Books, 1961), 60.
10. S. Gordon, "Mia Farrow: an Actress in Search of a Character," *Look*, December 1, 1964, 73.
11. Suzy Knickerbocker, "Mia," *McCall's*, May 1967, 144–5.
12. "The Moonchild and the Fifth Beatle," *Time*, February 7, 1969, 52.

female celebrity discourse became manifestly suffused with the problematics of knowing. Attempting to grasp her allure, *Newsweek* observed:

> Mia's uniqueness may yet make her into a movie star. People are interested in her, and it can't simply be because of the acting she's displayed up to now. . . . there is something about her — that lost sparrow look, her kooky comments in the columns, not to mention her marriage to, and estrangement from, Frank Sinatra, that makes her talked about.[13]

In effect, media texts interrogating Farrow's image converged issues of the epistemology of stardom with the study of woman as figure of difference.

Among the facets of her Otherness, Farrow's screen work was markedly Europeanized. Three of her five studio releases of the 1960s — *Guns at Batasi* (1964), *A Dandy in Aspic* (1968), and *Secret Ceremony* (1968) — were British-made and feature Farrow as English characters, while *Rosemary's Baby* was invested by its director, Polish émigré Roman Polanski, with a foreign art cinema aesthetic.[14] Taken together her Irish ethnicity, childhood in Beverly Hills, England, and Spain, ecumenical education, temporary residences in London for filming, much-publicized association with the Spaniard Dali, and her 1968 pilgrimage to India, Farrow's persona and work were inflected with tropes of geographic, psychic, and cultural dissociation.[15]

Amid the collective images of Farrow constructed in her literally and aesthetically foreign cinema, distinctly American work, and voluminous celebrity texts, "all those particles" assumed a particular shape. Farrow's aura was one of familiarity and estrangement, a figure of the feminine both affixed to and unmoored from the lineages of nationality, family, the Establishment, and conventional gender definition. Both as screen persona and media figure, Farrow was largely a cultural traveler, engaging the thematics of female investigation as both inquisitor and subject of inquisition through which the decade interrogated the nature and limits of its own social, industrial, and artistic metamorphoses.

Farrow's Otherness with regard to the institutions of studio and fan culture with which she was nonetheless closely allied constituted a distinct component of her gendered image in the 1960s. She was perceived as a new order of female star, a figure of sexuality who at the same time possessed a body and coiffure antithetical to such classically voluptuous Hollywood

---

13. "Faye Dunaway: Star, Symbol, Style," *Newsweek*, March 4, 1968, 43.
14. Farrow's single television film during the decade, *Johnny Belinda* (1967), contributed to the aura of foreignness insofar as she played a deaf and mute Nova Scotian girl.
15. In fact, Farrow's most prestigious awards and nominations were bestowed by the Hollywood Foreign Press Association. She received a 1965 Golden Globe as "New Star of the Year — Actress" and was nominated for Golden Globes for her performances in *Peyton Place* and *Rosemary's Baby*. In 1970, Farrow won the Golden Globes' Henrietta Award for "World Film Favorite."

Figure 6.1 **Mia Farrow in *Rosemary's Baby* (dir. Roman Polanski, 1968).**

figures of male fantasy as Rita Hayworth, Jane Russell, Marilyn Monroe, and Jayne Mansfield, who emerged during the 1940s and 1950s. *Time* noted that Farrow was endowed with "measurements . . . closely akin to a newel post's," and her hair was boyishly close-cropped, a style that was the subject of much press coverage as both the pinnacle of modern fashion and, as will be discussed, darkly significant.[16] Enthusiastically summing up her enigmatic appeal only two-and-a-half months after the debut of *Peyton Place, Look* noted, "Mia represents the new breed, the talented in-depth actress who has displaced, at least temporarily, the sexy starlets of yesteryear. This year [1964], say the Hollywood pros, 'those cute, round, bouncy, all-American girls can't even get arrested here anymore.'"[17]

In her essay, "Icons of Popular Fashion," Valerie Carnes observes, "our female icons were switching from *femme fatale* to nymphet. . . . The new Sixties girl was not only childlike; she was kinky, kooky, adventurous, spirited."[18] A central figure in ushering in this updated image of femininity, the wide-eyed and delicate boned Farrow cut a subtle alternate facet in the newly emerging surfaces of young femininity on screen. As opposed to the title characters in *Baby Doll* (1956) and *Lolita* (1962), Farrow — although romantically linked to older men on and off screen — defied the image of vulgarly sexualized nymphet (with the exception of passages in *Secret Ceremony*), instead embodying a more nuanced, paradoxical association with the erotic. Farrow's roles

---

16. "Moonchild," 52. Farrow claimed that her close-cropped hair — which sparked a new fashion trend — was inspired by Julie Harris' cut in *Member of the Wedding* (1952) (Emerson, 22), although her coiffure closely resembled that of Jean Seberg in *Breathless* (1960). In *Rosemary's Baby*, the style recalls the simple, self-abnegating cut worn by Maria Falconetti in *La Passion de Jeanne d'Arc* (1928) through thematic as well as graphic references insofar as Rosemary's body, too, is sacrificed in conjunction with heresy.

17. Gordon, "Mia Farrow," 76.

18. Valerie Carnes, "Icons of Popular Fashion," in Ray Browne and Marshall Fishwick (eds), *Icons of America* (Bowling Green, OH: Popular Press, 1978), 229.

and her popular persona combined innocence and juvenility with worldly sophistication; shelteredness and pure spirituality with exploration and experimentation; and desire with cool, almost matter-of-fact sexuality, repressing the erotic which played a significant part in her images on screen and in gossip culture.[19]

An ironically compelling figure of vulnerability at the inception of the feminist movement (as some have observed[20]), one of Farrow's central attractions was her precariously delicate physique and nature. Media texts characterized the actress on and off screen as "looking infinitely fragile," "hopelessly fragile," "enchanting in her fragility." Bearing resemblances to the image of Audrey Hepburn, whose delicate, gamine-like body, cooler sexuality, sophistication, and European Otherness were key to her appeal, Farrow was an updated figure whose image was that of a more liberated woman, unallied with the Cinderella narrative and the attendant imperative of masculine rescue. For example, in one of the numerous binary oppositions encompassed by her public persona, Farrow's celebrated delicacy was counterbalanced by reported toughness and manifest ambition. Pointing to this conjunction of qualities — quite unlike, for example, the unmitigatingly brazen Bette Davis of decades past — *Ladies' Home Journal* recognized Farrow as a "seemingly fragile but deceptively strong young woman," reporting that she had once informed gossip columnist Hedda Hopper, "'I want a big career . . . a big man and a big life. You have to think big — that's the only way to get it.'"[21]

In the course of the mid- to late 1960s, Farrow imported this captivating "fragility" to the cinema and celebrity discourse as a figure of purity and innocence in transition, a young woman informed, stained, or threatened by cultural, erotic, and psychic knowledge and violation. On screen, she permutated among daughter-figures in *Peyton Place,* the outset of *Dandy in Aspic, Johnny Belinda* (1967), and *Secret Ceremony* to seductive and worldly, often cosmopolitan, independent social and sexual adventurers — an alluring secretary in the British occupation drama *Guns at Batasi* (1964), a globetrotting photographer in the spy film *Dandy in Aspic,* and a Manhattan art gallery assistant and proponent of free love in *John and Mary* (1969) — to figures of the violated maternal, particularly in *Rosemary's Baby,* the apotheosis of the Farrow character as a woman at risk. Such representations of the feminine engaged in a constant dialectic with Farrow's off-screen life as her initial figuration as a daughter gave way to incarnations as a spouse and a liberated social, sexual, and spiritual quester who remained simultaneously

---

19. Dali observed that Farrow was "'a black moonchild, like Lilith. Her sex is not here,' he insists, pointing to his groin, 'but in the head, like a wound in the middle of the forehead.'" ("Moonchild," 52).
20. See, for example, Charles Derry, "Mia Farrow," *International Dictionary of Films and Filmmakers* (2001), http://www.encyclopedia.com/doc/1G2–3406801700.html.
21. Scott, 86.

attached to and disengaged from Establishment culture. In effect, Farrow's fragile physique became a screen onto which the tensions of the decade and fantasies of reconciliation were projected, embodying cultural contradictions and conjunctions key to the 1960s.

The attraction of Farrow's "particulate" image as a modern woman of ungraspable, constant shift was a central irony of her early career insofar as it belied an equally well-publicized, countervailing facet of her stardom: an absolute groundedness in traditional cinema culture. Integral to the construction and comprehension of the young Farrow as a celebrity was her status as a scion of Hollywood's Golden Age, evoking an aura of stardom, glamor, elite social circles, the studio system, and colonialism. It is nearly impossible to find an article on Farrow written in the mid-1960s that does not reference her ancestry as a second-generation cinema star, one in effect born into the industry and raised within the rarefied atmosphere of celebrity culture. This star, whom Pauline Kael and others referred to as a "waif,"[22] was invested with the heritages of the cinema Establishment and the British Empire as the daughter of often-described Hollywood "royalty": actress Maureen O'Sullivan and director and writer John Farrow, émigrés from Ireland and Australia. They appointed as her godparents fixtures of studio culture and its dissemination, MGM director George Cukor and Hearst newspapers gossip columnist Louella Parsons, a dual ancestry that anticipated Farrow's celebrity as a convergence of screen work and media fascination.

O'Sullivan's feminine screen persona and position of cultural notoriety as the plucky Jane Parker in the *Tarzan* series of the 1930s and early 1940s prefigured her daughter's first feature film appearance in the 1960s and her star image. In O'Sullivan's role as a young woman of "proper" English background who travels alone to Africa to become reunited with her father, an ivory trader, and ends up forsaking British culture for the lure of the wild, Jane bridges the Empire and the untamed. As a smitten Englishman observes in the second film of the series, *Tarzan and His Mate* (1934), "She's priceless. A woman who's learned the abandon of the savage, yet she'd be at home in Mayfair." The figure of the female as embodiment of both the Establishment and its relinquishment, a cultural adventurer who harbors the transformative agency to dually retain and shed an aura of colonialism — in Jane's case, by not only abdicating British life for the erotic and social freedoms of the jungle, but transporting English culture into treehouse living — informed Farrow's persona as a young woman conjoining both the known and exotic liberation, a nonconformist sustaining an approach-avoidance association with figures and structurations of patriarchy.

Farrow's first credited feature film appearance, in *Guns at Batasi*, echoed the Jane Parker role insofar as she was also cast as a young female Britisher in Africa who abandons English culture, albeit temporarily in this case, as

---

22. Pauline Kael, "Gloria, the Girl Without Hope," *New Yorker*, December 20, 1969, 62.

a secretary who has accompanied a team of UN observers to the continent and, after the mission, "stayed on for a little holiday."[23] In Farrow's minor role as a quiet woman caught in a British Army command post during a military coup by African rebels, she is a figure associated with diplomacy who, like Jane, coalesces innocence, eroticism, and liberation, bridging Establishment culture and the unbound in Africa. Attired in desexualized commonwealth khaki, Farrow — characterized by one of the English soldiers as an alluring "crumpet" — uninhibitedly acts upon her erotic desires, seducing a Private who readily reciprocates. Much like her costuming, some celebrity discourse in the wake of *Guns'* release attempted to cloak Farrow's display of female sensuality; a *Look* interview reported: "'I played a seductress,' [Farrow] giggles. 'It's marvelous playing a seductress.' But when she posed in sheer lingerie for a full-page picture in a fashion magazine, somebody said she looked exactly as if she were in church."[24] Again read as an embodiment of contradictions, Farrow's characterization in *Look* was one of numerous cases in which her ecumenical associations were foregrounded to neutralize suggestions of the young woman's waywardness.

Farrow was catapulted to celebrity as a daughter-figure incarnating cultural turmoil and abridgment upon her debut in the immensely popular new television series, *Peyton Place*, groundbreaking in its status as the first evening soap opera and, in accord with the sensationalist 1956 novel and 1957 film from which the program was adapted, in its forthright treatment of the lurid undercurrents of American communities.[25] In the series, which premiered on September 15, 1964 — nine days before the Warren Commission Report was issued in an attempt to quell the eruption of conspiracy theories that surfaced in the wake of the Kennedy assassination — the locus of rumors, assignations, scandals, and shock were displaced onto the circumscribed site of a small New England town. Farrow played a central role as a figure of notorious lineage and problematic innocence: Allison Mackenzie, the shy, illegitimate 17-year-old daughter of an unwed bookstore owner, "a romantic who believes in good [*sic*] and purity and is disturbed by anything contrary to that," according to the network's press release.[26]

In opposition to the widening generation gap of the mid-1960s, when youths increasingly rejected the parental, Farrow's character conducts a search for the progenitor. Likened by the *New York Times* to "some girl Oedipus . . . on the brink of discovery," Allison becomes a traveler through

23. Farrow appears in an uncredited role in *John Paul Jones* (1959), a film directed by her father. She first appeared on screen at the age of two in a documentary short involving Hollywood children, *Unusual Occupations: Film Tot Holiday* (1947). Farrow played her first credited role in *Age of Curiosity* (1963), a short promotional film about teenage girls produced for *Seventeen* magazine.

24. Gordon, 76.

25. *Guns at Batasi* was released in Great Britain one month prior to the October 1964 television debut of *Peyton Place*. The film opened in the US after Farrow emerged as a fledgling star.

26. Leo Litwak, "Visit to the Town of the Mind," *New York Times*, April 4, 1965, 46.

her own community, engaging in a journey to locate her father's identity.[27] At the same time, caught in another of the program's transgressive erotic and cultural entanglements, she must endure the consequences of a second illicit sexual coupling when her wealthy boyfriend is forced to marry the deviously alluring lower-class woman whom he has impregnated.

By the end of October, *Peyton Place* was ranked sixth in the Nielsen ratings and had caused its own scandal as a Kinsey-unleashed site of prurient interest and moral violation contested by forces of repression and clandestinism. As sexual liberation discourses of the 1960s were surging in the wake of such works as *Sex and the Single Girl* (1962), *Peyton Place* inspired a heated debate about contemporary sexuality, ethics, commercialism, and spectatorial desire. Specifically, the dialectic centered on whether the program stooped to new lows in sensationalism or, as its executive producer claimed, whether it "reflect[ed] the moral revolution in America."[28]

Farrow initially figured into this discourse as a celebrity whose off-screen life both mirrored and constituted an antidote to Allison's biography and *Peyton Place* culture. The actress who played the fictive daughter of an infamous soap opera coupling was introduced to the American public in 1964 as a child whose lineage was inscribed by "notoriety." Yet, given that her mother and father were prominent Hollywood figures, the "actual" Farrow was invested with familial and cultural legitimacy. Amplifying her character's innocence and purity in opposition to the lurid immorality of *Peyton Place*, the press foregrounded Farrow's devout spirituality. Numerous periodicals recounted her sheltered education in a series of foreign and domestic Catholic institutions, including a convent boarding school in England — in the wake of which, it was reported, she had briefly planned to become a nun. In this respect, as in many others, the Farrow who emerged from these early portraits was again a figure of oppositions. Embodying the decade's tensions between traditional and alternate spiritualism, she was often profiled as not only a strictly raised Catholic, but one with a polymorphic affinity for the Irish legends of her ancestry, palm readers, and the newly popularized Zen Buddhism. As Dyer notes, "stars frequently speak to dominant contradictions in social life — experienced as conflicting demands, contrary expectations, irreconcilable but equally held values — in such a way as to appear to reconcile them."[29] During a historical moment identified by youth culture as the "Age of Aquarius," a new era of exploratory spirituality (as well as social harmony), Farrow was constructed as a metaphysical quester who had relinquished her earlier beliefs yet nonetheless faithfully acknowledged a solid grounding in her Irish Catholic heritage.

---

27. Ibid., 47.
28. Gordon, 76.
29. Richard Dyer, "Four Films of Lana Turner," in Jeremy Butler (ed.), *Star Texts: Image and Performance in Film and Television* (Detroit, MI: Wayne State University Press, 1991), 225.

Cultivating Farrow's image as a figure of mass appeal, one who — again, in accords with Dyer's assertion — resolved rather than stirred cultural tensions, the media initially celebrated Farrow as a transitional emblem of alternative femininity negotiating the shift from ecumenically sheltered ingénue to free soul, without representing the threat of radical liberation. Shortly after the debut of *Peyton Place*, *TV Guide* described Farrow as a young woman fully cognizant of her kinship with the innocent Allison, "who lives in her own special world." In Farrow's case, this world was characterized as one in which the nonconformist, autonomous woman was self-contained. This actress with a "highly independent spirit" reportedly constructed her own site of circumscription: "I think of my life as a garden . . . I rarely go out of that garden."[30] The Victorian-inflected iconography of the once-sickly Farrow's life (at age 9, she suffered from polio) within a "protective garden," a figure of "girlish abstraction" was combined in her persona with a self-professed ambitious pursuit of stardom and masterful manipulation of the publicity machine's discursive levers. In another 1964 interview, she declared, "I can't stand being anonymous. I didn't want to be just 'one of the Farrows' . . ."[31] Yet Farrow's feminine ambition was formally delimited by the patriarchal institution of classical Hollywood cinema, even as it was declining. As the last vestiges of the studio era were disappearing with the elimination of long-term contracts for performers, Farrow committed herself to the cinema establishment through a five-film contract with 20th Century Fox, and a romance with a Hollywood star.[32]

Farrow's celebrity status was not only guaranteed, but launched into stratospheric heights shortly after her soap opera debut, when she embarked on a highly publicized love affair with the 49-year-old Frank Sinatra, who was 30 years her senior. In an actualization of what Molly Haskell has referred to as the decade's "Lolita cult,"[33] Farrow's image alchemized from ingénue to nymphet. In the process, the press transliterated her private life into the genre of real-life soap opera through accounts of a liaison so publicly riveting that it overshadowed the fictive scandals of *Peyton Place*.

In the course of the relationship — which began in secret in the fall of 1964 and extended through their two-year marriage from 1966–1968 — Farrow's association with Sinatra became a nexus of the decade's key tensions and fantasies of reconciliation, centering on the changing cultural position of women. The romance became an intensely controversial index

---

30. Marian Dern, "The Third of the Seven Little Farrows," *TV Guide*, October 9, 1964, 16–17.
31. Gordon, 75. This constitutes another similarity between Farrow and her *Peyton Place* character. As Moya Luckett points out, "Allison's fragility belied her desire to become a successful professional writer." Moya Luckett, "A Moral Crisis in Prime Time: *Peyton Place* and the Rise of the Single Girl," in Mary Beth Haralovich and Lauren Rabinovitz (eds), *Television, History, and Culture* (Durham, NC: Duke University Press, 1999), 80.
32. The film commitment was included in Farrow's television contract.
33. Molly Haskell, *From Reverence to Rape* (2nd edn.) (Chicago: University of Chicago Press, 1974, 1987), 345.

of the sexual revolution, cultural conservatism, normative moral and social codes, the generation gap, and the perception of female gender roles in the modern era. In response to gossip columnist Sheilah Graham's early reports of the relationship, "Irate women's groups, even the PTA, began petitioning the studio and the sponsors regarding Mia's behavior," according to a Farrow biography.[34] The romance became one of the mid-decade's most publicized scandals when mainstream media and fan texts fixated on a private cruise taken by the couple during the summer of 1965. With shocking velocity, reports of the vacation transformed her image from one of innocence to one of nubile eroticism, chronicling Farrow's literal embodiment of the cultural sea-changes represented by *Peyton Place.*

The cruise generated a spate of journey-narrative tropes attesting to the period's intense curiosity about the nature of its own transition and shifting social mores regarding gender relations.[35] According to *Time*, "The ensuing voyage was probably the most closely watched since Cleopatra floated down the Nile to meet Mark Antony," and *Photoplay* reported that the trip constituted "one of the world's most ballyhooed adventures since Homer's 'Odyssey.'"[36] The fictive infamy shading Allison Mackenzie's background became attached to Farrow insofar as the overriding preoccupation with the cruise centered around issues of sexual liberation and legitimacy. Cataloging the dramatic possibilities of the voyage, *Photoplay* positioned Farrow at a "plateau of prominence — and predominance in reflecting the moral revolution of America," suggested that the excursion "held infinite promises of relaxation, rounds of pleasure, romance and, conceivably, even marriage."[37]

As the controversy associated with *Peyton Place* was heightened (according to *Time*, the soap opera's executive producer "needed Mia Farrow's cruise like a hole in the hull,"[38]) Allison bore the marks of the off-screen scandal. As a victim of not only Farrow's infamy but of displaced anxiety about its consequences (the prospect of Farrow's marriage to Sinatra and, by extension, her potential withdrawal from the soap opera as she assumed a conventional spousal role), Allison solved the "problem" of Farrow's absence during the shooting schedule by lapsing into an indefinite coma. Through this symbolic

---

34. Edward Epstein and Joe Morella, *Mia: The Life of Mia Farrow* (New York: Dell Publishing, 1991), 83.

35. In this way — to adopt the point of view of scholarship on celebrity scandal — media discourse on the cruise foregrounded the still-extant power of American culture's conservative "dominant ideology" while signalling its breakdown. At the same time, insofar as, according to scandal studies, notoriety is responsible for keeping the performer in the public eye, the Farrow-Sinatra scandal was instrumental in producing Farrow's superstardom. (See Adrienne McLean and David Cook (eds), *Headline Hollywood: A Century of Film Scandal.* New Brunswick, NJ: Rutgers University Press, 2001.)

36. "Voyage of the Southern Breeze," *Time*, August 20, 1965, 64; George Carpozi, Jr., "The Shocking Voyage on the S.S. Southern Breeze," *Photoplay*, November 1965, 19.

37. Carpozi, 18.

38. "Triple Jeopardy," *Time*, August 20, 1965, 65.

co-option of Farrow's body — too unruly even for the producers of *Peyton Place* — fantasies of immobilizing the modern protean feminine surfaced at the site of sexual revolution.

One year before the founding of the National Organization for Women (NOW), traditional forces of cultural authorization remained crucial to rescuing Farrow for mass consumption from both daunting independence and one of the strongest remaining social taboos. As narrativized by celebrity discourse, members of the "old-time Hollywood establishment" who accompanied Farrow and Sinatra on the cruise (1940s studio legends Rosalind Russell, Claudette Colbert, and Merle Oberon and their husbands), represented classical female stardom's — and, accordingly, the industry's — endorsement and regulation of Farrow. Specifically, press accounts stressed that the stars from Hollywood's Golden Age both embraced the new television celebrity and acted as the Lolita-esque figure's "chaperones."[39] *Screen Stories*, among other magazines, worked just as hard to suture Farrow's troubling traversal of the generation gap as it had to scandalize the relationship, reporting, "His closest friends . . . had never seen the sea-going, going-on-50 Sinatra look younger" and "As for Mia . . . what could be better for her than the stabilizing influence of a man like The Leader." Repressing cultural anxieties through an excess of normalizing narratives, the article erroneously noted, "Mia's mother . . . had been practically a child bride herself," reporting that significant age gaps were both traditional in O'Sullivan's native Ireland and typical of Hollywood's numerous "May-September marriages."[40]

Most commonly, the theme of feminine loss of — and search for — the father central to Farrow's television character were projected on to the actress' off-screen romance, as it was to some of her other relationships, in a spate of pop Freudian diagnoses. Farrow was designated as the child of paternal absence insofar as her father had died in 1963, the year before her soap opera debut. Her relationship with Sinatra, subsequent association with Maharishi Yogi, also in his 50s, and oft-mentioned friendship with sexagenarian Salvador Dali, were typically interpreted as quests for a father figure in the wake of John Farrow's death. *Screen Stories*, for example, reported that one of Farrow's friends observed, "Mia has a built-in father complex."[41] Farrow herself tended to articulate such affiliations quite differently. During a decade when ageism was normative on the part of youth, Farrow fashioned her image as one of embracement: "I haven't been in touch with my own generation much. Most of my friends have been older people, like Salvador

---

39. T. Thompson, "Mia," *Life*, May 5, 1967, 79. Note that the collection of passengers and media accounts suggested an aesthetic abridgment and legitimation as well in the embracement of a television actress by classical Hollywood cinema stars.
40. Mike Connolly, "The Untold Story of Mia's Weird Love Cruise!" *Screen Stories*, November 1965, 47, 56.
41. Connolly, 57.

Dali."[42] Moreover, Farrow was commonly depicted as a figure who embodied both youth and old age. Bette Davis observed, "She was born with an old soul."[43] Shirley MacLaine described Farrow as "a child . . . from the neck up, she's 80."[44]

If Farrow was to be celebrated as an emblem of feminine contemporaneity, such oppositions would have to be reconciled for mainstream consumption. In *Vogue*'s 1966 "Who's a Breakaway?" photo spread, Farrow was described as a contemporary "It" girl: "They're the girls who look like the Generation [*sic*] as opposed to the Establishment." Yet, at the same time, struggling to accommodate her ties to the older generation, the magazine cited an unnamed source commenting, "she has the wonderful looks of the modern girl but not all the tiresome talk of youth."[45] Farrow's image was inflected by other problematizations of her modernity as well. The haircut that was key to her reputation as a fashion icon was represented as a mark not only of contemporaneity, freedom, and nonconformism, but of the wounds inflicted by classical masculinity. Dali famously characterized the cut as "a mythical suicide" insofar as — according to rumor — Farrow initially sheared her long hair in anger at not being invited to Sinatra's 50th birthday party.[46] With regard to her dramatic artistry, in an era when modern performance was allied with the Actors Studio, Farrow commented, "I hate starlets who spout off about the Method . . . Acting is simply telling the truth under different sets of circumstances," eschewing contemporary technique for classic naturalism.[47]

The media's most intense fascination centered on Farrow's embodiment of the hugely competing tensions between modern femininity and womanhood committed to the traditional ideals of domesticity, or what Betty Friedan termed the "feminine mystique."[48] Following her wedding in 1966, the media's interrogation of Farrow's metamorphic persona fixated on her inscrutably retrograde shift: that of matrimonial attachment to a figure of orthodox masculinity. A subject of particular inquisition was the degree to which Farrow's spousal status entailed the abandonment of a spate of liberation narratives (and, by implication, the eschewal of the burgeoning feminist movement) — including the temporary relinquishment of careerism. In a 1967 cover story subtitled, "The gifted, wide-eyed sprite who is Mrs. Sinatra," *Life* celebrated "her shapeless world — a place of surmise so fascinatingly complex and maddeningly naive that Sinatra could fathom it

---

42. Gordon, 73, 76.
43. Knickerbocker, 145.
44. "Moonchild," 52.
45. "Vogue's Eye View: Who's a Breakaway?" *Vogue*, April 15, 1966, 72.
46. Thompson, 79.
47. Knickerbocker, 145.
48. The "feminine mystique," as defined by Betty Friedan in her eponymous book, is the widespread, idealized notion that ultimate female fulfillment can only be achieved in the domestic role of housewife and mother.

only by marrying into it."[49] Yet, conversely, *Life,* among other publications, took Farrow's measure as a woman circumscribed by patriarchal culture. Cataloguing her new signs of domesticity, *Life* noted "there are evenings when Mia functions as the proud wife [watching Sinatra perform]," quoting Farrow's self-abnegating confession: "Nothing I could ever do in films would make me as proud as I am of him."[50]

Farrow's constitution as a modern woman nonetheless intimately attached to the Establishment — the elusive Other in both contexts — informed much of her screen work during the later 1960s. *A Dandy in Aspic, Rosemary's Baby,* and *Secret Ceremony* contain relationships between younger women and representatives of patriarchy, investigating through Farrow's roles the allure and acute dangers of containment insofar as her characters are both attracted to, and grapple with the monstrous flaws of, the masculine older generation. The imprimatur of her relationship with Sinatra — and the suggestion of personal risk — was central to Farrow's return to the screen after a post-marital hiatus, in her first 1968 release, *Dandy.* This spy film, starring 40-year-old Laurence Harvey as a world-weary Russian double agent who becomes romantically involved with the 23-year-old Farrow, reflexively references the latter's off-screen life, commodifying and interrogating her empirical condition. Not only are the leads figures of intergenerational ligature, but Sinatra's endorsement was implied by Farrow's appearance in a film starring his former cast-mate (from *The Manchurian Candidate* [1962]) and friend as the leading man, as well as by his graphic presence. In a clearly allusive shot, during one of Farrow's initial scenes, she picks up a camera next to a book titled *Frank Sinatra,* featuring a photograph of her real-life husband on the cover.

Dandy couples 1950s masculine Cold War subterfuge with contemporary feminine 1960s culture, represented in film by Farrow in the role of Caroline, a young, stylish, globe-trotting British photographer whose cosmopolitan presence foregrounds issues of gender, liberated sexuality, modern fashion, identity, and media notoriety. In her first starring film role, Farrow reenacts the narrative arc from daughter to the lover of an older man: she is introduced into the plot as the child of a socialite who alchemizes into a figure of eroticism and romantic attachment through relationship with a spy, Eberlin. In essence, Caroline encounters patriarchy at risk. Not only does Eberlin's status as a Russian double agent who works for British Intelligence threaten Western culture, but his midlife enervation and longing to extricate himself from his profession is a menace to the international spy establishment.

Counterbalancing the literal and figurative exhaustion of this middle-aged man tethered to the dated world of Cold War tensions and archaic

---

49. Thompson, 75.
50. Thompson, 81.

patriarchal establishments devoted to dramatic production in the form of spy plots, Farrow's character coalesces the magnetizing enigma of the new, untethered woman and contemporary aesthetics. Caroline offers the promise of youthful revitalization, erotic escapism, and the graphic invigoration of modern photography and fashion. At the same time, Caroline, like Farrow, constitutes a feminine figure of vulnerability and retrograde desire. In a world of disequilibrium represented by crumbling Cold War culture and modernity's constant shift — in the wake of which, referencing Farrow's persona, Caroline admits, "I just seem to drift endlessly half the time" — she is willing to forfeit her independence and free-spiritedness for the constancy of the older man's love and a stable attachment.

Amid *Dandy*'s numerous references to the biographical Farrow, most central is the film's meditation of issues of identity and notoriety, reflexively associated with celebrity. In its world of constant surveillance and infamy — cameras, photographs, film, slide shows, passport pictures, photo booths, stalking — one of the most acute dangers is the image. *Dandy* is preoccupied with the predicament of the fabricated persona: Eberlin not only longs to shed his public identity but is forced to take on an assignment to execute an elusive Russian agent — who is, in actuality, himself — in a mandate that amounts to the assassination of his true character. Through the figure of the female photographer — who embodies an unconventional feminine position of double agency, coalescing subject and object positions by continually shifting between the focus and bearer of the investigative and desiring gaze — the film repeatedly references Farrow's off-screen cultural status as both beneficiary and victim of the image. In an early exchange, after Caroline gazes at herself in a mirror, Eberlin advises, "Oh, I wouldn't be too unsettled about your reflection. . . . I haven't found one yet that has interpreted my image correctly." This counsel constitutes a manifest commentary on Farrow's stardom insofar as, by her own description, and in the wake of her romance and marriage, she was beleaguered by the press as an object of intrusive scrutiny.

According to the *New York Times* review of *Dandy*, "[Farrow] represents youth, mischief, innocence — everything that would draw Harvey into life again."[51] Yet, she is represented as a woman defined in part by lack. If the Farrow figure disengages herself from the familial at the outset of the film in order to become liberated, she quickly reconstitutes herself as one desirous of the security of masculine attachment. Whereas in *Dandy*, the older man ultimately rejects this commitment, protecting the young woman from imprisonment in dying male culture, in Farrow's next film, *Rosemary's Baby*,

---

51. Renata Adler and Vincent Canby, "Screen: Harvey Plays a Deadpan 'Dandy in Aspic': Tale of Double Agent Opens at Cinema 1; Burt Lancaster Stars in integrated Western," *New York Times*, April 3, 1968.

patriarchy seizes upon her as a figure whose presence is absolutely requisite for its continued reproduction.

The pinnacle of Farrow's film career in the 1960s, *Rosemary's Baby* constituted the actress' professional legitimation. As typified by a *Newsweek* reviewer's comment, Farrow was generally perceived, prior to the film's release, to be a star "whose achievements to date have been outstripped by her publicity."[52] Farrow's celebrated performance in this seventh top-grossing film of 1968 (which earned her a Golden Globe nomination for Best Actress), emerged in a work that not only problematized the feminine condition within Establishment culture, but also allied its dangers with the threat of classical Hollywood, implying the joint menace posed by her personal and professional associations.

A reply to *Dandy*'s representation of the Farrow figure as an untethered, yet attachment-seeking cultural traveler, *Rosemary* constructs multiple spheres of patriarchal containment for the actress' title character. Conferring upon Rosemary the conditions of Caroline's wish fulfillment, the Farrow character is not a female figure of drift, but a married child-bearer. Simultaneously, the film fully engages the thematics of the at-risk Farrow. In a commentary on what is at stake for the modern woman, released during a year in which feminist protestors threw their bras in a trash can outside the Miss America pageant, the consequences for one whose desire remains shaped by the feminine mystique of fulfillment in traditional domesticity is the horror of regulation, imprisonment, and violation by masculine culture.

In the film, Rosemary and her husband, Guy, a struggling actor, rent an apartment in the Bramford, a gothic Manhattan apartment building which, in decades past, has harbored practitioners of witchcraft and a series of strange fatalities. As Rosemary becomes pregnant and increasingly suffers, oddly monitored and controlled by her nosy elderly neighbors and an aged physician, she begins to suspect a conspiracy — but only when it is too late. Rosemary eventually discovers that the Bramford is inhabited by a satanic cult run by her neighbors, who have surreptitiously enlisted Guy in their scheme to impregnate her with the devil in exchange for professional success. Powerless against them, she ultimately, much to her horror, gives birth to Satan's offspring.

Typically considered a product of 1960s gender, familial, and social anxieties, *Rosemary's Baby* has been variously diagnosed as the "gynecological gothic," the "Maternal Macabre," and a "demon child film," born of the newly recognized traumas of pregnancy and domesticity undergone by women, and haunted by the specter of their progeny as juvenile delinquents.[53]

---

52. Paul Zimmerman, "Devil Child," *Newsweek*, June 17, 1968, 92.
53. Penelope Gilliatt, "Anguish Under the Skin," *New Yorker*, June 15, 1968, 87; Lucy Fischer, "Birth Traumas: Parturition and Horror in *Rosemary's Baby*," *Cinema Journal* 31(3), (Spring 1992), 3–18; Kevin Heffernan, *Ghouls, Gimmicks, Gold: Horror Films and the American Movie Business, 1953–1968* (Durham, NC: Duke University Press, 2004).

According to these pathologies, Rosemary occupies an intensely charged space in the warp of modernity, a chamber of procreative horrors in which contemporary feminine experience remains demonically institutionalized by patriarchal culture. Ratcheting up the menaces extant in *Peyton Place*, *Dandy*, and *Johnny Belinda*, the community surrounding Farrow's character in *Rosemary* constitutes an even more terrifying site of clandestine evil, threat to legitimacy, and endangerment.

Although Rosemary is a figure of traditional female desire insofar as she yearns for domesticity, in accordance with the actress' celebrity persona, Farrow (literally a shapeshifter in her role as mother-to-be) again emblematizes Otherness. As Lucy Fischer points out, "As Rosemary's pregnancy progresses, [the film's] baroque narrative constructs a distorted projection of quotidian experience."[54] Farrow's character becomes estranged from, and an inquisitor into, her own cultural context as she experiences child-bearing as victimization and increasing imprisonment by Establishment figures, who challenge her independent powers of perception: the elderly physician who counsels against reading contemporary books on pregnancy and taking vitamins; her husband, who tries to shield Rosemary from the advice of her female friends; the elderly couple next door — clandestine coven leaders — who take increasing charge of the young woman. Conversely, the Farrow figure's gendered difference is allied with modernity's contestation of classical patriarchal culture: the interest in reading new medical literature, the fashionably short-cropped hair which disturbs Guy, and the European aesthetic which the young woman imports into the film through a series of surreal, stream-of-consciousness subjective images, together violating the masculine Establishment's demonic plot and classic continuity editing.

As suggested by the above, another order of propagative struggle centers on the Farrow figure. *Rosemary* is haunted by the masculine lineage of institutionalized production that is classical cinema, engaging not only issues of aesthetics, but gender, celebrity, and the industry's power structure as well. In this work through which Polanski reconceived the horror genre for contemporary mainstream release — and which marked Farrow's apotheosis as a star — the demonic is no less than Hollywood itself. In a reflexively terrifying allegory, the studio system is encoded as a menacing enterprise whose habitués constitute a coven.

From the moment Rosemary enters the Bramford — a decades-old site of notoriety — she steps into a masculinized edifice of classical celebrity culture. Not only is the building introduced to the couple as a structure "very popular with actors," but the cast is rife with recognizable figures from the height of the studio era, including Ralph Bellamy, Elisha Cook, Jr., Ruth Gordon, and Sidney Blackmer. These apparitions of Hollywood's Golden Age, represented as Satanists, malevolently seize upon the bearers of contemporary culture

---

54. Fischer, 9.

(both Rosemary and her husband, the actor) to revive the operations of the star system, producing the ultimate figure of classical infamy through the antiquated genre plot. Most pointedly, through this aged patriarchy, aided by the archetypically ambitious Guy, classical cinema undertakes (via the young Farrow) to replicate an archaic production system amid the culture of contemporary performance within the landscape of the modern spectacle. As constructed by the new aestheticism of *Rosemary*, that which constitutes the most extreme horrific is not the struggling actor's sacrifice of his own (re)productivity for the promise of Hollywood stardom, but the harrowing appropriation of Farrow's body for the cinema establishment's revitalization.

Accompanying this film that burnished Farrow's image as an actress while problematizing the archaic context in which she had become firmly affixed, media texts were suffused with discourse on the peril to the young star posed by the specter of Old Hollywood. Foregrounding the tensions between homemaking and careerism, magazines rumored the off-screen Farrow to be a figure of troubled domesticity insofar as her film work was reportedly threatening her marriage. According to a *Ladies' Home Journal* article published during the year *Rosemary* was in production, "Most of her friends know that Mia does not want to give up her acting career. On the other hand, Sinatra once said that he would never again marry a career woman, especially an actress [after divorcing Ava Gardner]. . . . Sinatra might be happier if Mia became a full-time wife instead of making movies."[55]

If Farrow's screen character relinquishes herself to her husband's acting career in satanic domesticity — according to a *Newsweek* review, "sacrificed on the black altar of her husband's ambition" — the actress herself was of course not so self-renouncing.[56] She had recognized the crucial importance of taking on the role of Rosemary to advance her film career, initiating a marital struggle. In her autobiography, Farrow recounts how, upon reading the script, Sinatra's "only comment was that he couldn't picture me in the part." Suggesting her own dangerous proximity to Rosemary's condition — the perilous vulnerability of female spousal perception to a dominant masculine vision, Farrow recalls, "Suddenly, I couldn't picture myself in it either."[57] Paradoxically, although Farrow's independent discernment ultimately prevailed, her acceptance of the role of screen homemaker resulted in her disengagement from the sphere of domesticity. In the course of the film's production, it was widely reported that she was delivered divorce papers on the set, an act that marked both the power of patriarchy and her liberation from it.

As *Rosemary's Baby* entered its final stages of gestation, an alternative facet of Farrow's persona magnetized the public as the ecumenically raised actress,

---

55. Scott, 168.
56. "Devil Child," *Newsweek*, June 17, 1968, 92.
57. Mia Farrow, *What Falls Away* (London: Doubleday, 1997), 118.

who would soon become most celebrated for playing a violated Catholic, resurfaced in the headlines in conjunction with yet another metamorphosis: the spiritual journey. Months before the summer release of the film that would be the target of censorship efforts by the National Catholic Office of Motion Pictures, Farrow became a figure of renewed fascination, as a seeker of alternative spiritualism, when the press widely reported on her trip to India to meditate with the Maharishi Mahesh Yogi. Associated with yet another figure of older masculine guidance, ironically, Farrow's connection with the Maharishi constituted an explicit embracement of youth culture. Transformed into an emblem of the younger generation's psychic quest, Farrow was at last allied largely with contemporaries, including fellow ashram visitors, the Beatles. At the same time, her earlier obsession with celebrity shifted to a rejection of fame and those who, as she observed in an ashram interview, "got hung up with . . . their names in the paper."[58] Ironically, one of the primary offenders was the Maharishi himself, whose penchant for publicity and eroticization of Farrow (her autobiography recounts a sexual advance on his part) led to her flight from the ashram. A cover story in *Fate* magazine observed, "There is no doubt that the Beatles and Mia helped [the Maharishi's] ascension" as a star.[59] Mirroring her condition in *Rosemary*, again the spiritualized Farrow became a vessel for the production of classic celebrity.

Farrow's final release of 1968, *Secret Ceremony*, is an alternate version of the female gothic, reworking her persona as a fragile woman adrift in the archaic edifice, and again engaging issues of feminine perception — in this case to the extent that her character becomes almost fully delusional, in effect, a young madwoman in the attic. Concurrently, Farrow's character foregrounds the perversities of the woman-child stuck in time (as *Ladies' Home Journal* had pointed out, "there is a lot of Peter Pan in Mia Farrow")[60] initiating media discourse, as the decade came to a close, on insistent clinging to youth culture as a form of psychosis. In the film, Farrow plays another attachment-seeking figure, Cenci, an overgrown, orphaned child for whom liberation is the condition of being unmoored. Ensconced in a world of parental and sexual desire and violation, she latches onto a prostitute named Leonora (Elizabeth Taylor), who is grieving the loss of her daughter. Cenci hallucinates Leonora to be her longed-for, recently deceased mother, installing the older woman in her dark, empty London estate. Psychologically and genealogically unanchored and bereft, the shapeshifting Cenci metamorphoses, in her delusional state, from devoted daughter to nymphet to expectant mother, not only engaging in an unnaturally close relationship with Leonora — at times suggestive of lesbianism — but resuming an incestuous relationship

58. Lewis Lapham, "There Once Was a Guru From Rishikesh," Part II, *Saturday Evening Post,* May 4, 1968, 88.
59. James Crenshaw, "The Beatles' and Mia Farrow's Guru: What is His Power?" *Fate*, May 1968, 36.
60. Lena Tabori, "Mia Farrow Talks," *Ladies' Home Journal*, August 1968, 92.

with her mother's lover, in the wake of whose return, in an even more psychotic reconstruction of the events in *Rosemary's Baby*, she hallucinates her own pregnancy.

As part of a new order of discourse emerging just prior to *Ceremony's* release, in which Farrow's ethereal charm — located, in part, in her persona as a figure of girlish imagination — began to decay, Cenci's madness resonated with media reconsiderations of Farrow's empirical character in the wake of the star's widely reported breakdown before the filming began. In July 1968, *Movie Mirror* reported, "Mia . . . refuses to believe [in her forthcoming divorce], but seems anxious to make-believe instead. And, as long as her fantasy had at least a tiny bit of reality to it, she could keep her pretenses."[61] A *Ladies' Home Journal* reporter observed, "She struck me as one of those few extra-brilliant people walking a tightrope between madness and sanity, clinging to her fantasy life with one hand and the real world with the other."[62] Taking their cues from celebrity discourse surrounding the new release, writers began to detect strands of psychosis throughout Farrow's screen personae; according to a *Vogue* journalist, "There has always been a hint of the demented in Mia's performances, a feeling of imploding, careening panic: she seems simultaneously to be a strange child playing at being a woman, a woman playing a little girl."[63]

Only in her final feature of the decade, *John and Mary* (1969), did Farrow portray a stable figure of modern feminine liberation. Appearing on screen at last as an independent woman inhabiting young adult culture — the cosmopolitan, sexually liberated Manhattan bar scene (although the vestiges of her image as one affixed to the elder generation remain insofar as she is engaged in an affair with an older, married man) — Farrow emblematizes secure autonomy. Yet, Farrow nonetheless remained tethered to the classicism of her well-established image. According to the *New York Times* reviewer Vincent Canby, "What emerges is a character composed partly of the weird waif of 'Secret Ceremony,' partly of the haunted mother of 'Rosemary's Baby.'"[64]

As the decade ended, although Farrow had become in some ways more unmitigatingly allied with youth culture (in the wake of *John and Mary's* release, Farrow and her co-star, Dustin Hoffman, were seized upon by the press as spokespeople for the younger generation's perspectives on marriage and sex), celebrity texts conveyed a sense of the exhaustion, even decomposition with regard to her star image. *Vogue* noticed, "at twenty-four, the learning shows, her eyes are scarred. She looks grieved," commenting, "her unconventionality at times is tiresome."[65] According to *Vogue* and other

61. Fred Arthur, "Sinatra Ready to Marry Again!" *Movie Mirror*, July 1968, 50.
62. Tabori, 93.
63. Polly Devlin, "Mia Farrow: 'Her Thin-Skinned Courage,'" *Vogue*, May 1969, 92.
64. Vincent Canby, "Screen: 'John and Mary' at the Sutton," *New York Times*, December 15, 1969, 68.
65. Devlin, 80.

magazines, Farrow was becoming an aging imitation of herself: "Her look of helplessness is false — assumed, along with shrinking vulnerability, for the audiences and the camera. . . . she becomes in turn a shattered, fragile refugee . . . Mia-the-Imp, and the Cocotte, worldly-wise. . . . When the camera stops, so does the vulnerability."[66] Reviewing *John and Mary*, Pauline Kael noted:

> Everyone understood that the old fragile heroines — the Depression waifs like Loretta Young . . . needed to get well, and it's rather frightening that this little rabbit looking for a hutch is presented as a modern ideal. The waif who has done it to herself — made herself a sprite . . . Mia Farrow is beginning to strain her "delicious" mannerisms. Every tiny lick of the lips is just too vixenish; the childlike movements, and the odd little voice are getting rather creepy.[67]

By the close of the 1960s, Farrow had metamorphosed into a figure of haunting re-production — an uncanny recurring version of her earlier self, again combining notoriety and the prospect of domestic containment by an older man. Farrow had alchemized from portraying an illegitimate daughter to the condition of unwed pregnancy by married conductor and film music composer Andre Previn, 16 years her senior, who she would wed in 1970. Once appropriated by the film industry as a figure of revitalization suturing the Establishment to the modern, Farrow and Hollywood now seemed to reject one another. Representing, along with her *John and Mary* co-star Hoffman, according to *Time*, "the death of many myths — among them, the one of the movie star" insofar as they spurned the trappings and contractual commitments of the studio system, Farrow openly repudiated Hollywood, commenting, "The system is full of crap."[68] Such attitudes reportedly cost her an Oscar nomination for her role in *Rosemary's Baby*.[69]

Albeit newly scandalized and a figure associated with scandal decades later, Farrow was no longer quite such an object of epistemological inquiry — or contemporary womanhood — as she transitioned into a second marriage and motherhood, and a quieter career in the 1970s. An alternative tone of discourse now inflected her image: a distinct *ennui*, the vernacular of exhausted repetition. This altered textual body constituted not only a differently apprehended Farrow, but a new inscription in the narratology of female celebrity. Farrow's renown, which had rendered with exceeding

---

66. Devlin, 80.
67. Kael, 62.
68. "Moonchild," 50.
69. The *New York Times* quoted a Hollywood executive conjecturing, "'I think one reason [Farrow was not nominated for an Oscar] is that she is young and abrasive and very independent.'" (Steven Roberts, "Who (and What) Makes Oscar 'Possible'?" *New York Times*, April 14, 1969, 52.) *Time* reported, "The Reason: the Academicians Dislike Her Barefoot Hippie Attitudes." ("Grand Illusion," *Time*, April 25, 1969.)

legibility in celebrity discourse issues of modernity, womanhood, female stardom, and the transformative at a socially and culturally redefining moment, now suffered the repercussions of the terms of its own construction and allure. Initially appropriated and fetishized by the modern as a figure of captivating shift and indeterminacy, as the decade ended, Farrow was increasingly relinquished as a subject of public fascination.[70] In other words, with the ossification of Farrow's persona as the mutable feminine, her celebrity began to diminish.

At this new juncture, a historical moment of passage from the 1960s, when the ideals of revolutionary cultural change had ultimately proven unrealizable, concurrently it became distinctly explicit what was at stake for the female star too closely associated with modernity. In essence, Farrow had become an unsustainable abstraction, a figure so intimately allied with the metamorphic that the nature of her fame was impossible to indefinitely perpetuate. Further, the vicissitudes of Farrow's notoriety — in particular, the cracks that had formed in her image at the end of the decade — exposed the danger to female celebrity of the displacement of woman's classical Otherness onto the individual's ungraspability: the risk of the manifest invitation to determination. Once Farrow was discursively "solved," she was understood as facsimile, woman as performance of feminine images and nothing else; no longer was she wholly celebrated as original, but rather disclosed as a pure imitation.

Bibliography

Abrahamson, Leslie H. "Mia Farrow: Categorically Intangible." in New Constellations: Movie Stars of the 1960s. New Brunswick, NJ: Rutgers University Press, 2010.

Adler, Renata and Vincent Canby. "Screen: Harvey Plays a Deadpan 'Dandy in Aspic': Tale of Double Agent Opens at Cinema 1; Burt Lancaster Stars in Integrated Western," *New York Times*, April 3, 1968.

Arthur, Fred. "Sinatra Ready to Marry Again!" *Movie Mirror*, July 1968, 18, 48, 50–1.

"Cinema: At Bay in Africa," *Time*, November 6, 1964.

Battelle, Phyllis. "Mia Farrow and Dustin Hoffman Debate: Does Marriage Have a Future?" *Ladies' Home Journal*, April 1969, 80–1, 156, 158, 160.

Boorstin, Daniel. *The Image: A Guide to Pseudo-Events in America*. New York: Harper Colophon Books, 1961.

Canby, Vincent. "Screen: 'John and Mary' at the Sutton," *New York Times*, December 15, 1969, 68.

Carnes, Valerie. "Icons of Popular Fashion," in Ray Browne and Marshall Fishwick (eds), *Icons of America*. Bowling Green, OH: Popular Press, 1978, 228–39.

Carpozi, George, Jr. "The Shocking Voyage on the S.S. Southern Breeze," *Photoplay*, November 1965, 18–19, 78–80.

Chapman, Daniel. "Mia Farrow is a Trip," *Look*, August 1969, 46–50.

Connolly, Mike. "The Untold Story of Mia's Weird Love Cruise!" *Screen Stories*, November 1965, 47, 55–7.

---

70. However, the release of *The Great Gatsby* in 1974 garnered a spate of media coverage for Farrow, who played the role of Daisy Buchanan.

Crenshaw, James. "The Beatles' and Mia Farrow's Guru: What is His Power?" *Fate*, May 1968, 34–44.

Dern, Marian. "The Third of the Seven Little Farrows," *TV Guide*, October 9, 1964, 15–19.

Derry, Charles. "Mia Farrow," *International Dictionary of Films and Filmmakers*, 2001. Available at: http://www.encyclopedia.com/doc/1G2-3406801700.html (accessed November 26 2010).

Devlin, Polly. "Mia Farrow: 'Her Thin-Skinned Courage,'" *Vogue*, May 1969, 80, 92.

Dyer, Richard. "Four films of Lana Turner," in Jeremy Butler (ed.), *Star Texts: Image and Performance in Film and Television*. Detroit, MI: Wayne State University Press, 1991, 214–39.

——. *Heavenly Bodies: Film Stars and Society*. London: Routledge, 1986; 2nd edn, 2004.

——. *Stars*. London: British Film Institute, 1979; 2nd edn, 1998.

Emerson, Gloria. "Mia in Paris: 'I'm kind of 20–20–20,'" *New York Times*, February 15, 1967, 22.

Epstein, Edward and Joe Morella. *Mia: The Life of Mia Farrow*. New York: Dell Publishing, 1991.

Farrow, Mia. *What Falls Away*. London: Doubleday, 1997.

"Faye Dunaway: Star, Symbol, Style," *Newsweek*, March 4, 1968, 42–50.

Fischer, Lucy. "Birth Traumas: Parturition and Horror in *Rosemary's Baby*," *Cinema Journal* 31(3), (Spring 1992): 3–18.

Friedan, Betty. *The Feminine Mystique*. New York: W. W. Norton & Company, 1997.

Gilliatt, Penelope. "Anguish Under the Skin," *New Yorker*, June 15, 1968, 87.

Gordon, S. "Mia Farrow: an Actress in Search of a Character," *Look*, December 1, 1964, 72–6.

"Grand Illusion," *Time*, April 25, 1969.

Haskell, Molly. *From Reverence to Rape*. Chicago: University of Chicago Press, 1974; 2nd edn, 1987.

Heffernan, Kevin. *Ghouls, Gimmicks, Gold: Horror Films and the American Movie Business, 1953–1968*. Durham, NC: Duke University Press, 2004.

Kael, Pauline. "Gloria, the Girl Without Hope," *New Yorker*, December 20, 1969, 62.

Knickerbocker, Suzy. "Mia," *McCall's*, May 1967, 70–1, 144–6.

Lapham, Lewis. "There Once Was a Guru from Rishikesh," Part II, *Saturday Evening Post*, May 4, 1968, 28–33, 88.

Litwak, Leo. "Visit to the Town of the Mind: Peyton Place," *New York Times Magazine*, April 4, 1965, 46–7, 50–64.

Luckett, Moya. "A Moral Crisis in Prime Time: *Peyton Place* and the Rise of the Single Girl," in Mary Beth Haralovich and Lauren Rabinovitz (eds), *Television, History, and Culture*. Durham, NC: Duke University Press, 1999, 75–97.

McLean, Adrienne and David Cook (eds). *Headline Hollywood: A Century of Film Scandal*. New Brunswick, NJ: Rutgers University Press, 2001.

"The Moonchild and the Fifth Beatle," *Time*, February 7, 1969, 50–4.

"New Pillow Talk," *Time*, December 19, 1969.

Roberts, Steven. "Who (and What) Makes Oscar 'Possible'?" *New York Times*, April 14, 1969, 52.

Scott, Vernon. "Mia Farrow's Swinging Life with Frank Sinatra," *Ladies' Home Journal*, May 1967, 84–6, 168.

Tabori, Lena. "Mia Farrow Talks," *Ladies' Home Journal*, August 1968, 59, 92, 94.

Thompson, T. "Mia," *Life*, May 5, 1967, 75–81.

"Triple Jeopardy," *Time*, August 20, 1965, 65.

"Vogue's Eye View: Who's a Breakaway?" *Vogue*, April 15, 1966, 72.

"Voyage of the Southern Breeze," *Time*, August 20, 1965, 64–5.

York, Alice. "What Mia Farrow Does For Love that Barbara Parkins Doesn't Have to," *Photoplay*, November 1965, 52–7, 73.

Zimmerman, Paul. "Devil Child," *Newsweek*, June 17, 1968, 90, 92.

Note

This is a revised and expanded version of an essay that appears in *New Constellations: Movie Stars of the 1960s*, edited by Pamela Robertson Wojcik (Rutgers University Press, 2010).

7

Girls Imagining Careers in the Limelight
Social Class, Gender and Fantasies of "Success"

KIM ALLEN

OVER THE PAST DECADE, the UK has witnessed mounting public debates around young people's desires to become celebrities. These debates have been most keenly focused on the "inappropriate" aspirations of teenage girls. In 2008, Culture Minister Barbara Follett stated that "kids nowadays just want to be famous . . . If you ask little girls, they either want to be footballers' wives[1] or win *The X-Factor*.[2] Our society is in danger of being Barbie-dolled".[3] Such concerns have been mobilized by politicians as well as educational organizations, and within a range of media forms including both the broadsheet and tabloid press. Numerous surveys have been referenced as evidence of teenage girls' "unhealthy appetite" for fame, suggesting that they are more interested in becoming actors, singers, and glamour models[4] than in pursuing careers as teachers, lawyers, doctors, politicians, or scientists.[5]

1. Footballers' wives (and girlfriends) have emerged as a recent and distinctive category of celebrity in the UK where they are also referred to as WAGS. They are often seen as "free-loaders" who are not famous in their own right. See Diane Negra and Su Holmes, "Editors' Introduction" in Diane Negra and Su Holmes (eds), "Going Cheap? Female Celebrity in the Reality, Tabloid and Scandal Genres," *Genders* 48 (Fall 2008).
2. *The X-Factor* (ITV) is a British reality TV show and singing contest, launched in 2004 to replace *Pop Idol* (ITV) and *Pop Stars* (ITV). Aspiring singers are selected from national auditions and compete in live shows to win a recording contract. *The X-Factor* has also been launched in several other countries.
3. Cited in James Chapman "'Barbie Doll': Girls Only Want to Be WAGs or Win the X Factor, Complains Culture Minister", *Daily Mail*, October 15, 2008.
4. "Glamour model" is a term used in the UK to refer to female models who are generally photographed topless and feature in tabloid papers, such as *The Sun*'s page 3, and "lads mags" (British magazines, such as *Zoo, Nuts* and *Loaded* which are aimed at young men). High-profile celebrity glamour models in the UK include Jordan (Katie Price), Jodie Marsh, Danielle Lloyd and Keeley Hazell.
5. See Martin Beckford "Teenage Girls Would Rather Be WAGs than Politicians or Campaigners." *The Telegraph*, November 18, 2008; Laura Clark "High Heels, Low IQs: 'Dazzled' Girls Want to Be WAGs Instead of Having Careers, Warn Headmistresses," *Daily Mail*, January 9, 2009; Mark Gould "Girls Choosing Camera Lenses Over Microscopes," *The Guardian*, October 3, 2008; "Naked Ambition Rubs Off on Teen Girls," *Manchester Evening*

Meanwhile, research commissioned by the UK government suggests that young people who look up to celebrities as their role models are more likely to be disengaged from education.[6]

These debates confirm Catherine Lumby's observation that "popular concerns about young women's relationship to fame have been gradually shifting away from concerns about their irrational idealization of predominantly male idols to concerns that they are obsessively fantasizing about *becoming* famous themselves" (original emphasis).[7] Yet it is immediately clear that there are value judgments present within such debates. First, they reinforce classed hierarchies of young people's career aspirations, whereby hopes to enter middle-class professions are deemed more valuable and "legitimate" than wanting to become a model or singer. What is neglected here is how *becoming* a celebrity may be seen as a more attainable aspiration for working-class girls who have been traditionally excluded from accessing "high-status" professional careers. Second, the suggestion that young women are rejecting education and hard work in preference for "easy fame" neglects the ways in which celebrity can play an integral and productive role in the construction of young people's educational and future work identities. Finally, the image of the young female "wannabe" has psycho-pathological undertones, where girls' desires to *become* celebrities are read as deluded fantasies in need of correction. These debates do not capture the complexity of young women's relationship with contemporary celebrity.

Against this backdrop of wider public concerns, this chapter aims to illuminate the cultural significance of young women's relationship with celebrity and the complex ways in which it functions within their everyday lives. While there has been minimal empirical work on young women's relationship to celebrity, this chapter draws upon recent research carried out with teenage girls in the UK. Aged between 16 and 19 years, and from mixed social and ethnic backgrounds, these girls were enrolled in performing arts courses in state-funded institutions in Greater London. In particular, this chapter is concerned with how this specific group of girls navigated the discourses of celebrity in their everyday lives as they constructed their identities and imagined futures as "potential celebrities" within the performing arts industry (namely careers in music, acting and dance).

Two central themes are discussed in turn: First, the chapter examines how the girls assessed the desirability of fame and the legitimacy of different routes to "success" within the industry. Social class is identified as a key informant of how young women situate fame in relation to their future identities. The next part of the chapter explores the perilous terrain of the

News, June 6, 2005.

6. Sherbert Research. *Aspirations and the Children and Young People Segmentation*: Research Report No. DCSF-RR150. (London: DCSF, 2009).

7. Catharine Lumby. "Doing it For Themselves? Teenage Girls, Sexuality and Fame," in Sean Redmond and Su Holmes (eds), *Stardom and Celebrity: A Reader* (London: Sage, 2007), 342.

female celebrity body as a site of punitive surveillance and as central to the construction of "authentic" selfhood. It illuminates how the concept of "staying true to yourself" is significant to the girls' perceptions of success, but how the performance of femininity complicates the performance of "authentic" celebrity selfhood.

Understanding Celebrity: Young Women, Celebrity and "Identity Work"

Recent feminist theorizations of celebrity have sought to illustrate its role within the wider neoliberal project, where popular culture has been identified as a key site in which the "successful girl" discourse of neoliberalism[8] is reproduced. Celebrity culture, alongside other popular media, is understood to articulate new ideals attached to "have it all" femininity oriented around social mobility and compulsory success, and self-reinvention and transformation through consumption.[9] It is also seen to encompass new forms of (self-)regulation through its increasingly punitive surveillance of women's bodies and the reproduction of the "post-feminist" ethic of sexual subjectification.[10]

Diane Negra and Su Holmes have illuminated how cultural hierarchies, established to distinguish between different typologies of celebrity, are highly gendered. They suggest that female celebrities in particular have come to represent a perceived divorce of "hard work," "merit", and "talent" from contemporary fame.[11] The classed nature of what Richard Dyer calls celebrity's "ideological function"[12] has also been explored. Imogen Tyler and Bruce Bennett, for example, suggest that celebrity culture operates to establish "social hierarchies and processes of social abjection" which include both gendered and classed distinctions between "proper" and "improper"

---

8. Jessica Ringrose, "Successful Girls? Complicating Post-feminist, Neo-liberal Discourses of Educational Achievement and Gender Equality," *Gender and Education* 19(4) (2007): 471–89.

9. See for example: Angela McRobbie, "Post-feminism and Popular Culture," *Feminist Media Studies* 4(3), (2004): 255–64; Angela McRobbie, "Top Girls? Young Women and the Post-Feminist Sexual Contract," *Cultural Studies* 21(4), (2007): 718–37; Sarah Projansky, "Mass Magazine Cover Girls: Some Reflections on Postfeminist Girls and Postfeminism's Daughters," in Diane Negra and Yvonne Tasker (eds), *Interrogating Postfeminism: Gender and the Politics of Popular Culture*. (Durham, NC: Duke University Press, 2007), 40–72; Jessica Ringrose and Valerie Walkerdine. "The TV Make-over as Site of Neo-liberal Reinvention Toward Bourgeois Femininity," *Feminist Media Studies* 8(3), (2008): 227–46.

10. Ros Gill, "Postfeminist Media Culture: Elements of a Sensibility," *European Journal of Cultural Studies* 10(2), (2004): 147–66; Diane Negra and Su Holmes, "Editors Introduction" in Diane Negra and Su Holmes (eds), "Going Cheap? Female Celebrity in the Reality, Tabloid and Scandal Genres," *Genders* 48 (Fall 2008); Natasha Walters, *Living Dolls: The Return of Sexism*. (London: Virago Press, 2010).

11. Ibid., 2. See also Su Holmes and Sean Redmond (eds), *Framing Celebrity: New Directions in Celebrity Culture* (New York: Routledge, 2006).

12. Richard Dyer, *Stars*. (London: British Film Institute, 1979).

personhood.[13] Vilified as "illegitimate" and "undesirable," the (typically female) working-class "celebrity chav" (or "white trash" celebrity), comes to articulate concerns around the nature of contemporary celebrity: the working-class reality TV contestant or glamour models represent "improper" fame and the antithesis of "authentic" stardom, understood to be achieved through "hard work" and talent. Imogen Tyler and Bruce Bennett argue that these "improper" celebrities function to "generate celebrity capital for 'real' stars, providing them with opportunities to differentiate themselves as comparatively skilled". Celebrity can therefore be understood to contain highly classed and gendered discourses which operate to mark out "proper" and "improper" success.

However, these classed and gendered discourses do not fix the meanings of celebrity. Rather, as Graeme Turner reminds us, the meanings of celebrity are highly contingent and unfixed, negotiated, and remade as celebrity culture is "put to work" by individuals in their everyday social practices.[14] This chapter contributes to a small but growing body of empirical work which attends to the particular ways in which young women and girls make use of celebrity within their everyday lives and processes of identity construction.[15] Empirical studies on young women's relationship to celebrity illuminate how young women negotiate, rework, and resist the images and narratives of femininity, class, sexuality, morality, work, and success that celebrity appears to offer.

However, while it is important to locate to the instances in which young women resist and rework regressive and normative discourses contained within popular culture, as Catherine Lumby warns, it is also crucial to attend to the wider structural context within which these relationships are located.[16] Thus, understanding celebrity as a social practice and central to young women's "identity work" means attending to the social, cultural, and economic contexts in which it occurs and to the classed and gendered discourses it contains which operate to regulate contemporary selfhood. In this chapter, identity is understood not as the subject of a voluntary project

13. Imogen Tyler and Bruce Bennett, "Celebrity Chav: Fame, Femininity and Social class," *European Journal of Cultural Studies* 13(3), (2010): 375–93; see also Kim Allen and Jayne Osgood, "Young Women Negotiating Maternal Subjectivities: The Significance of Social Class," *Studies in the Maternal* 1(2), (2010) online journal; Bev Skeggs and Helen Wood, "The Labour of Transformation and Circuits of Value 'Around' Reality Television," *Continuum: Journal of Media and Cultural Studies* 22(4), (2008): 559–72.

14. Graeme Turner, *Understanding Celebrity*. (Sage, London: 2004), 102.

15. This empirical work includes: Linda Duits and Pauline van Romondt Vis, "Girls Make Sense: Girls, Celebrities and Identities," *European Journal of Cultural Studies* 12(1), (2009): 41–58; Mary Jane Kehily, "More Sugar? Teenage Magazines, Gender Displays and Sexual Learning," *European Journal of Cultural Studies* 2(1), (1999): 65–89; Catharine Lumby, "Doing it For Themselves? Teenage Girls, Sexuality and Fame;" Rebecca Feasey, "Reading *heat*: the Meanings and Pleasures of Star Fashions and Celebrity Gossip," *Continuum: Journal of Media & Cultural Studies* 22(5), (2008): 687–99.

16. Catharine Lumby, "Doing it For Themselves? Teenage Girls, Sexuality and Fame."

of DIY self-making, free from structural constraints, but rather is "discursively produced . . . within contexts of multi-layered structural inequalities".[17] The ways in which young people engage with celebrity within processes of identity construction is thus understood to be informed by their social positioning: their gender, class, race/ethnicity, sexuality, and so on. The next section of this chapter provides greater detail on the unique social positioning of the young women discussed here.

Young Girls in the Performing Arts

The research was conducted between 2006 and 2007 with 20 young women aged between 16 and 19 years old who were studying vocational courses in music, drama, and dance in two state-funded (free) educational institutions[18] in urban areas in Greater London, areas within close proximity to the performing arts industry which is predominantly located in London. The girls were from a variety of ethnic backgrounds, including white, Black African and Black Caribbean, Asian and mixed ethnicity, and were from working-class and lower-middle-class families[19]. Pseudonyms were given to the interviewees and are used throughout this chapter.

Alongside observations of the daily practices of the specific educational institutions which they attended,[20] one to one interviews and small focus groups were conducted with the girls. Ethnographic interviewing practices were used to elicit their self-narratives. Interviews and focus groups were highly informal and loosely structured but based around a number of discussion themes including: their extracurricular interests in the arts; their educational histories and trajectories; their perceptions of their course and enjoyment of learning; and their career aspirations and hopes for the future

---

17. Louise Archer, "The Neoliberal Subject? Young/er Academics' Constructions of Professional Identity," *Journal of Education Policy* 23(3), (2008): 269.
18. The girls were all enrolled on a BTEC national diploma course. In the English education system, the BTEC qualification is a more practical and vocationally oriented equivalent to academic qualifications (A-Levels). The two institutions were state-funded. In England there are other independent performing arts schools in the private education sector which charge between £2,000 and £3,000 per term in fees. All the girls discussed the financial impossibility of attending such schools.
19. Social class was assigned and analyzed using a "culturalist" framework, informed by Bourdieu (1984). Social class indicators used in this study included parental occupation, family history of participation in education, data collected about the schools' socio-economic profile, as well as the girls' self-identified social class when it was given. Participants with parents in lower professional and intermediate occupations, who had experienced recent upward social mobility, were designated lower-middle-class; and those with parents in lower-supervisory, technical, semi-routine, and routine occupations were designated working class. Few of the girls in either group had any family history of higher education. Both institutions defined their intake as "socio-economically mixed," incorporating pupils from disadvantaged areas.
20. This included observations of lessons, rehearsals and workshops, discussions with staff, and collection of institutional promotional materials.

more generally. Fame and celebrity entered their self-narratives at various points.

Linda Duits and Pauline van Romondt Vis have suggested that where it does occur, empirical work on celebrity tends to focus on fandom rather than the practices of a more "oblique and accidental audience."[21] The young women in this research cannot be characterized as such an audience. They had a unique and direct relationship with celebrity due to their location in education and training for the performing arts. Celebrity is not only intrinsic to the types of selfhood associated with work in the performing arts and creative industries more generally.[22] Narratives of achieving fame are also central to the popular imagery of young performers and performing arts schools, as represented in films such as *Fame* (1980, and its 2009 remake), *Flashdance* (1983), *Step Up* (2006) and in the *High School Musical* franchise (2006, 2007, 2008). The young women in this study were therefore very directly encountering discourses of celebrity as they negotiated what a career in the performing arts may be like. For them celebrity functioned not simply as a general site of everyday consumption. Neither could it be understood as a form of what Jackie Stacey[23] calls "stargazing" associated with female spectatorship of 1950s cinema, where "stars" were much more remote and far less pervasive than in contemporary celebrity culture. Rather, for these girls, celebrity represented a possible outcome or by-product of their future careers — a more realizable and attainable "way of being." In this sense, these young women were undertaking deeply felt identity work as *potential* celebrities. Furthermore, their experiences mark a departure from those described in earlier cultural studies scholarship of the 1970s and 1980s, such as that by Angela McRobbie and Jenny Garber[24] where girls were restricted to the realm of the bedroom and the consumption of teenage magazines (1976). No longer "private consumers," "teenyboppers," or "groupies," idealizing (male) singers and musicians, the young women in this study were quite literally taking center stage as performers themselves. This shift towards active *participation in* rather than *consumption of* popular culture provides unique insights and adds a new and important dimension to understanding girls' relationship with celebrity.

21. Linda Duits and Pauline van Romondt Vis, "Girls Make Sense: Girls, Celebrities and Identities," 41–58.
22. Mark Banks and David Hesmondhalgh, "Looking For Work in Creative Industries Policy," *International Journal of Cultural Policy* 15(4), (2009): 415–30; Angela McRobbie, *British Fashion Design*. (London: Routledge, 1998).
23. Jackie Stacey, *Stargazing: Hollywood Cinema and Female Spectatorship*. (London: Routledge, 1994).
24. Angela McRobbie and Jenny Garber, "Girls in Subcultures," in Tony Jefferson and Stuart Hall (eds), *Resistance through Rituals: Youth Subcultures in Post-war Britain* (London: Hutchinson, 1976): 209–22.

Routes to Success: Cultural Hierarchies, Social Class, and the Desirability of Fame

The girls discussed aspirations for a range of careers in the performing arts. Becoming a singer, television presenter, or film or theatre actress were the most frequently mentioned aspirations. Some of the girls discussed "being open" to careers "behind the scenes," for example working in television production or film direction. The girls thus constructed a "successful career" variously. However, fame as a possible reward or by-product of a career in the performing arts was a consistent feature of their discussions. But the ways in which fame was situated in relation to their future career identities were not straightforward, as fame, and its desirability, provoked a complex array of responses.

The wider cultural hierarchies, which attribute different types of celebrity with value, played a significant role in structuring the girls' understandings of "legitimate" aspirations and routes to success in the performing arts. However, it was in the accounts of the lower-middle-class girls that these cultural hierarchies were most clearly felt. The girls appeared to be self-regulating the future identities they were constructing according to these cultural hierarchies, displaying an acute awareness of the aforementioned debates which dismiss young people's aspirations for fame as inappropriate.

> Reece: When you say you want to be famous people think you're shallow and you're not doing it for the right reasons.

This concern that desires for fame would be seen as shallow and inappropriate appeared to be reinforced by the practices of the school in which some of these girls were located. In the school, aspirations for fame were deemed undesirable and interest in more esoteric careers, and careers behind the scenes rather than on the stage or screen, were encouraged by staff. Thus, while the girls' desires for fame were strong, these had to be hidden to some degree. Declaring aspirations for following the careers of more "obscure" and lesser-known performers was perceived to show dedication and commitment to a career in the industry rather than just wanting fame in and of itself.

> Vicky: Everyone want[s] to make it. They want to say "I've made it, I'm on telly and I've got a fan base and a steady career" . . . But, you can't really say that. Before I came here, when I'd get asked whose career I'd like to achieve, I'd want to say some big Hollywood actress like Julia Roberts or Cameron Diaz . . . but now 'cos I know they [the teachers] don't like that I'm more inclined to think "what theatre actress can I say?" . . . "What answer will they like?" . . . [T]hey've [the school] brainwashed us . . . they've told us that people who say they admire big TV or film actresses look like all they want is to be a celebrity . . . So saying you like some obscure theatre actress is better 'cos it shows you're more dedicated.

For some of the girls then, the pedagogic practices of their school worked alongside wider public discourses to reinforce cultural hierarchies and distinctions around fame and success within the celebrity system. Fearing that they would be seen as "shallow," they felt compelled to fiercely defend or reframe desires for fame. This regulation of aspirations contributed to the girls drawing distinctions between "recognition" and "fame" as they discussed what they wanted to achieve in their future careers. Achieving a career where you are recognized and respected for your talents was constructed as more valuable than simply achieving fame. The lower-middle-class girls frequently discussed the careers of lesser-known theatre and film actresses, who they thought had a lower public profile but were "highly respected" in the industry, and who they thought had achieved their success through hard work, the possession of "raw talent" and dedication.

> Jodie: I wouldn't mind fame but I don't think you need to be famous to have a rewarding career. There are loads of people in theatre and music who are fantastic but you don't necessarily hear about them, they're recognized in their own way.
> Amy: I don't think my aim is to be famous or rich just more to have someone appreciate and respect what I do.

Most often the performers the girls identified as having a "successful career" were associated with theatre or independent film, "high legitimacy" cultural forms which are organized along the lines of social class.[25] Furthermore, as Bev Skeggs has illustrated, "respect" and "respectability" provide key mechanisms for displaying moral value among the middle classes.[26] Thus, in constructing a "successful career" as one that is "highly respected," and in aligning their career aspirations with particular cultural genres, the girls were mobilizing middle-class strategies of distinction.[27] They were displaying middle-class cultural capital, and expressing tastes, preferences and cultural knowledge congruent with those legitimized by their school.

The "successful career" was not always constructed in this way by the lower-middle-class girls. Some discussed the worthiness of careers of television celebrities such as popular television presenter Davina McCall. McCall started her career as a dancer and presenter of the cult television dating show *Streetmate* (Channel 4, 1998–2001), and went on to present *Big Brother* in the UK, as well as many other prime-time television shows. As the following quote from Vicky shows, aspirations for careers that involved celebrity necessitated the deployment of particular caveats: it was not Davina's celebrity status that was highlighted by Vicky as making her career desirable, but

25. Tony Bennett, "Postscript: Cultural Capital and Inequality: Refining the Policy Calculus," *Cultural Trends* 15(2), (2006): 242.
26. Bev Skeggs, *Formations of Class and Gender: Becoming Respectable*. (London: Sage, 1997).
27. Pierre Bourdieu, *Distinction*. (London: Routledge, 1984).

Figure 7.1 **Davina McCall, presenter of the UK *Big Brother*.**

rather the hard work and dedication through which Davina went from being "an unknown girl" to a famous TV presenter.

> Vicky: If I did TV presenting, I'd love a career like Davina. She's done so well for herself. She started off on that little TV show as an unknown girl with a small camera crew on some high street doing *Streetmate*. And now look at her. To think she's gone from that to something massive, presenting the biggest show on TV [*Big Brother*]. She worked hard to get there. I'd love to be up there doing what she does.

The prioritization of success based on hard work, talent, and dedication over fame in and of itself was also clear in the lower-middle-class girls' rejection of celebrity careers associated with "fame by proxy," for example, becoming a wife or girlfriend of a footballer (WAG) or being the child of a celebrity. Others discussed the "injustice" of a system which rewards "talentless" and "ordinary" people such as reality TV contestant Jade Goody. A working-class girl from South London, Goody rose to fame through her appearance on *Big Brother* (Channel 4, 2002) and subsequent appearances on *Celebrity Big Brother* (Channel 4, 2007) as well as her own reality TV shows. This type of template for contemporary celebrity was seen to bypass the necessity of hard work and talent.

> Reece: You have to be famous in the right way . . . You have to make a name for yourself based on your own virtues and talents . . . because you're good, because people enjoy watching you, because people enjoy working with you. That's how you become recognized, that's the right way. It's important that you get fame for having talent.

Jodie: You think to yourself . . . you're only famous 'cos your dad was famous or you slept with some footballer . . . I'd hate to get fame off someone else's back . . . I want it from standing on my own two feet and working hard and being talented.

Carly: It's very shallow . . . people who aren't famous for anything . . . [like] Jade Goody . . . people who don't work hard.

Such accounts illustrate a middle-class defense against what Anita Biressi and Heather Nunn call the "media-driven social mobility"[28] through which people without talent gain status and economic power. Being famous in the acting or music industry was only constructed as acceptable and desirable when it was achieved through "working hard and standing on your own two feet," rather than achieving fame "off someone else's back." Diane Negra and Su Holmes have argued that the "famous for nothing" celebrity label is highly gendered,[29] and thus it is striking but not surprising that it is typically women who are both implicitly ("sleeping with footballers") and explicitly (Jade Goody) identified by these young women when discussing "improper" success.

Big Brother was not the only reality TV show identified by the lower-middle-class girls as representing "improper" celebrity. Other shows which were premised on contestants' musical talent, such as *The X-Factor* (ITV), were also used by the girls to illustrate "easy" and thus illegitimate pathways into the industry. These discussions replicated the wider negative responses to "manufactured" music shows as signalling a *"regrettable democratization of fame."*[30]

Emma: Getting fame [by going on *The X-Factor*] is different from you working so hard at it and actually creating it yourself . . . I'd rather have something I've built myself, on my talent and my hard work. That's proper success.

However, as Su Holmes reveals, reality TV talent shows like The *X-Factor* mobilize highly contradictory discourses: while they acknowledge and overtly display a discourse of celebrity as a manufactured product, they also mobilize very traditional discourses of fame oriented around hard work, authenticity, "specialness" and dedication.[31] Indeed, they are strongly aligned with Dyer's notion of the "success myth", the idea that one's lucky break can happen at any time, as long as you work hard.[32] This complex layering of old and new

---

28. Anita Biressi and Heather Nunn, "The Especially Remarkable: Celebrity and Social Mobility in Reality TV," *Mediactive* 2(1), (2004): 44–58.
29. Diane Negra and Su Holmes (eds). "Going Cheap? Female Celebrity in the Reality, Tabloid and Scandal Genres."
30. Su Holmes, "'Reality Goes Pop!' Reality TV, Popular Music and Narratives of Stardom in Pop Idol," *Television and New Media* 5(2), (2004): 147–72.
31. Ibid.
32. Richard Dyer, *Stars*. (London: British Film Institute, 1979).

discourses of fame within The *X-Factor* can perhaps be seen to contribute to the very different responses to these reality TV talent shows among the working-class girls in this study. For the working-class girls, such shows were identified as a valuable opportunity to gain success as a performer. Unlike the lower-middle-class girls in the study, the working-class girls constructed the contestants on these shows as "stars," displaying talent and dedication. One of these girls, Anusha, had auditioned for the show herself and saw it as "a great way to break into the business."

While discourses of ambition, talent, and hard work were central to the working-class girls' constructions of a "successful career" in the performing arts, they were much less cynical than their lower-middle-class peers in relation to the "worthiness" of certain types of celebrity, and less critical of the means by which fame is achieved. Furthermore, these girls attributed value and status to those celebrities who were perceived to have gained their success through exploiting the celebrity machine, using it to break into other sectors. For example, ex-Spice Girl Victoria Beckham and Latina singer and actress Jennifer Lopez were respected by the girls for their entrepreneurship. Victoria Beckham, also known as "Posh Spice" from her early career in the 1990s girl group the Spice Girls, is married to footballer David Beckham. No longer a singer, she is now frequently referred to as a celebrity "fashion icon," has her own fashion label and has released a range of perfumes (with her husband). She has also appeared on numerous television shows, including documentaries and reality TV shows. Lopez (also known as J-Lo) began her career as a dancer, famously appearing as a backing dancer in the music video for Janet Jackson's 1993 single "That's the Way Love Goes." She then became a singer and Hollywood actress and now has her own fashion line and a range of perfumes. For the working-class girls in this study, the perceived lack of singing or acting ability displayed by Posh Spice and J-Lo was not important. Rather they tended to praise the determination and hard work that these celebrities put into rebranding themselves as fashion icons and business women.

> Denise: Posh Spice. She has not got talent. She's really only still famous 'cos she's married to a successful footballer, she don't sing no more and she never could sing anyway. But whether we like it or not the girl can dress, and she can do whatever she wants now 'cos she has that money [. . .] So good on her for doing what she did. She knew exactly what she wanted and went for it.

> Ruth: I love J-Lo. I think she's an excellent role model because she's done so much. It doesn't matter she can't really sing, she has her own empire, she's a business woman — she was a dancer but has achieved in so many areas . . . It just shows you that if you can get just *somewhere* in the industry [then] it opens other doors . . . even if you're a girl in a music video like J-Lo was, you can get noticed then you can end up being a singer in your own right or star in a film.

The girls' investment in the image of the "celebrity entrepreneur" that is embodied within the discursive construction of these celebrities reveals the ways in which celebrity discourses work alongside wider neoliberal discourses of self-reinvention, and what Linda Duits and Pauline van Romondt Vis call "makeability",[33] within girls' identity work. It also indicates a strong belief in the capacity for upward social mobility through the celebrity machine.[34]

Indeed, social mobility is central to the discursive construction of the image of both of these female celebrities. Alongside J-Lo's ambiguous ethnic identity, the narrative of her working-class struggle to stardom has tended to be incessantly conveyed in press coverage as well as in her music lyrics and videos, while signifiers of her relatively comfortable upbringing have been disguised[35]. Her earlier life in the New York neighbourhood, the Bronx, is recalled in songs like *Jenny from the Block* and in the music video for pop single *I'm Glad*, in which she recreates scenes from *Flashdance* (1983), a film about a working-class woman whose dream is to become a dancer. While the realities of J-Lo's trajectory to fame are far less dramatic, having featured in several minor films and television shows prior to her roles in major Hollywood films, for girls like Ruth, J-Lo represents the possibility of being catapulted from relative anonymity (as an unknown, working-class dancer in a pop video) to Hollywood stardom.

Despite Posh Spice's moniker and early image as the "sophisticated" Spice Girl, her image has always been underlined by irony and complicated by alternative discourses which deny her middle-class status. Media discussions of her upbringing have constituted her as coming from the upwardly mobile working class or "nouveau riche." Meanwhile, as Joanne Lacey has illustrated, Posh Spice's lavish and "vulgar" wedding to Beckham was seen by the press to "expose" her lack of middle-class credentials.[36]

The working-class girls' investment in the celebrity "Cinderella story" was also evident in a discussion with Anusha, who shared her plans to open a club in London called "The Dream Factory." She described a future self who, having achieved fame and wealth, would then give other young people from deprived inner-city boroughs (people "like her") the opportunity to "make it." Young, undiscovered "talent" would be given a chance to perform at "The Dream Factory" and be discovered by invited celebrity guests like African-American pop singer Beyonce Knowles.

33. Linda Duits and Pauline van Romondt Vis, "Girls Make Sense: Girls, Celebrities and Identities," 41–58.
34. See Anita Biressi and Heather Nunn, "The Especially Remarkable: Celebrity and Social Mobility in Reality TV," 44–58.
35. For a further analysis of this, see Jo Littler, "Making Fame Ordinary: Intimacy, Reflexivity and 'Keeping it Real,'" *Mediactive* 2(1), (2004): 8–25; Priscilla Ovalle, 'Urban *Sensualidad*: Jennifer Lopez, *Flashdance* and the MTV Hip-Hop Re-generation," *Women and Performance: A Journal of Feminist Theory* 18(3), (2008): 253–68.
36. Joanne Lacey, "Identifying Characteristics of Class in Media Texts," in Adam Briggs and Paul Cobley (eds), *The Media: An Introduction* (2nd edn), (Harlow: Longman, 2002), 340–56.

Anusha: Imagine, you'd have 15-year-old girls, amazing singers, and they'd be able to go to this club and sing to a massive crowd. And I'd invite all the biggest stars along like Beyonce . . .'cos I'll have made loads of contacts in the industry by then — and these young girls would get signed up to Beyonce's record label. It would be amazing.

These imagined selves cannot be written off as representing delusion or mere fantasy. Rather, they are constructed through very powerful and pervasive discourses of celebrity which offer the possibilities and promise of upward social mobility. Just over a year after this interview was conducted, Knowles appeared on *The X-Factor* in the UK, and sang a duet with finalist (and eventual winner) Alexandra Burke, a young black singer from North London.

As Bev Skeggs and Helen Wood argue, fame can operate as an important "opportunity structure" for those who have been denied success, recognition and social mobility.[37] Across the narrative accounts of the working-class girls, fame was constructed both as a highly valued and desired reward of a career in the performing arts and as the ultimate validation of their achievements: a sign to others that they had "gone far" and "become someone."

Anusha: I won't give up 'cos there are a lot of people who hope that I don't succeed . . . so it will be nice to know that when I'm successful, when I'm famous and I'm performing somewhere, or on TV, those girls will be watching at home and think "damn, the bitch made it" . . . It would just be nice to say to people, "I know you thought I was just a girl who weren't gonna go far but, actually, ha! Look at me"!

For Nadine, below, achieving fame ("seeing my name in lights") is equivalent to graduating from university. Higher education can be a strange and alienating space for women from working-class backgrounds.[38] Achieving success through celebrity may thus appear a safer and more realizable aspiration than that achieved within the formal education system.

Nadine: Ever since I was little I wanted to see my name in lights. I always wanted to be famous. With fame everyone knows that you have achieved in life . . . I wanna share my achievements with the world. Like when you get your grade and tell your parents, or when people graduate in front of everyone. It's like that. I want everyone to see that I'm successful . . . I want the whole world to know, what's wrong with that?

The working-class girls' investment in particular routes into the industry

---

37. Bev Skeggs and Helen Wood, "The Labour of Transformation and Circuits of Value 'Around' Reality Television," 559–72.
38. Sarah Evans, "In a Different Place: Working-class Girls and Higher Education," *Sociology* 43(2), (2009): 340–55.

that explicitly entail fame can be seen as a means for generating symbolic capital, where fame is equated with status and power. Valerie Walkerdine argues that fame offers working-class girls the "possibility of a talent from which they have not automatically been excluded by virtue of their supposed lack of intelligence or culture".[39] For Kelly, becoming a famous actress would "prove wrong" those who had written her off.

> Kelly: I used to get bullied and I'd love to prove those people wrong . . . and my dad, he told me I'd end up working in [supermarket chain] Tesco. So I was like "right I'm gonna show you now: I'm gonna get into the school, do theatre, be famous . . . I'll show you."

While Kelly is talking here about her father and school bullies, her reference to a job at a supermarket checkout provides an important reminder of the ways in which working-class girls are "written off" more generally in society. Her words, like those of Anusha, tell of the inequalities that working-class girls must negotiate in the education system and the labor market, and the ways in which working-class femininity is positioned as Other to the "successful girl" of neoliberalism.[40] Celebrity thus operates as a powerful symbol of the possibilities for escaping the trajectory expected of working-class girls. For these girls, the rewards of fame — recognition, autonomy, and economic security — were so desirable that wider cultural hierarchies and distinctions did not regulate their identities in the same way that it did for the lower-middle-class girls.

Social class is therefore central to the ways in which wider discourses of celebrity are encountered and negotiated. In particular, it is integral to the ways in which young women understand and construct notions of "success" within celebrity culture and it informs their own attachments to aspirations for celebrity.

The "Problem" of the Female Body: Popularity, Authenticity and the Double Standard

Catherine Lumby talks of a "knowing and ambivalent relationship" to celebrity that was displayed by the teenage girls in her study. She explains how, while they talked about the "potentially damaging effects of women packaging themselves as an image [. . . they were also] very aware that fame offers a potential escape from other kinds of surveillance and repression they encounter in their everyday lives".[41] This conflicting relationship was

---

39. Valerie Walkerdine, *Schoolgirl Fictions.* (London: Verso, 1990), 50.
40. See Valerie Walkerdine, Helen Lucey, and June Melody, *Growing Up Girl: Psychosocial Explorations of Gender and Class.* (London: Palgrave, 2001).
41. Catharine Lumby, "Doing it For Themselves? Teenage Girls, Sexuality and Fame," 346.

similarly present in the narrative accounts provided by the girls in this study. However, because of celebrity's central position within their imagined future selves as *potential* celebrities, these girls were caught in an even greater bind between an investment in the more transformative potential of the celebrity lifestyle and a critical distancing from the "negative" aspects of fame.

Many of the girls expressed interest in the "glamour" of fame and a pleasure in constructing and investing in their appearance. In this way, imagining the self as a female celebrity was closely associated with the performance of "desirable" hyper-feminine subject positions.[42] For example, Carly discussed a number of British female television presenters whose careers she associated with not just fun and entry to new social networks but also "glamour," namely access to make-up artists and designer fashions.

> Jo: I'd love to do TV presenting — it's my main passion. I've wanted to do it since I was about six. I just loved watching people like Cat Deely, Davina McCall, or Tess Daley, and thinking "wow I'd love that job so much" . . . It seems like such a fun job, you get to meet loads of people, being invited to lots of events. And it's really glamorous, getting all your clothes paid for, dressing up in sexy, glam[orous] clothes all day, having your hair and makeup done so you look amazing . . . It would be incredible.

While many of the girls invested in celebrity's potential for the transformation of the self through stylization of the body, this was not straightforward. The girls were acutely aware of the punitive body surveillance on female stars and were critical of the "double standard" they felt they would encounter in the industry, whereby the female celebrity body is more harshly judged than the male celebrity body. Just as Rebecca Feasey's research[43] shows that readers of celebrity magazines are offended by the attention given to female celebrities' bodily "transgressions," the women in this study were similarly critical of the ways in which female celebrities are publicly scrutinized for their appearance.

> Jade: Men get acting jobs easier than women. You can be an amazing actress but if you aren't good-looking they don't want you. It shouldn't be like that — it should be based on your talents.

> Emily: There's definitely a major pressure on women. Magazines swing from slating a celebrity for being overweight then saying that size zero isn't good . . . and if Sharon Stone has a wrinkle, she's got to have Botox. But when a man has

42. Louise Archer, Anna Halsall, and Sumi Hollingworth, "Class, Gender, (Hetero)sexuality and Schooling: Paradoxes Within Working-class Girls' Engagement With Education and Post-16 Aspirations," *British Journal of Sociology of Education* 28(2), (2007): 165–80.
43. Feasey, "Reading *heat*", 687–99.

a wrinkle they're seen as distinguished. I don't want to have a boob job to get noticed in the industry. I want people to recognize me for my talents, not just looking *at* me, not just saying "oh she's put on weight" or "her dress is too frilly" or "she's too old". But I don't think that kind of recognition for your talent happens much for women. It does for men.

Christine Geraghty has identified the ways in which female performers are judged on their appearance and private relationships rather than their public "work",[44] and this gendered "double standard" had implications for the girls' processes of self-construction. The girls perceived the prioritizing of looks above talent as a barrier to achieving a successful career. As Emily says, she doesn't want to just be "looked at" for her body or clothes but recognized for her talent as an actress. For many of the girls, there was a fear that they were unable to fit the current beauty ideal of young, thin, and blonde (and white).

> Vicky: There is that Hollywood image that you have to fit as a woman. Like Kate Winslet is pretty but she's had problems 'cos of her weight and hasn't got jobs ... I think with guys, they can just say "we're just here to act and it doesn't matter what I look like," but most women think "I can act but I have to look pretty too" ... And that's not fair. I don't want to lose parts 'cos I don't fit that image.

Concerns about negotiating the industry's beauty norms in order to find "success" were acutely felt by a number of the young black girls in the study, like Reece.

> Reece: I do worry about appearance. Not everyone can be stick thin and meet that mold. As a black girl, I'm bigger than the other girls in my class. Not big but bigger, curvy. And white girls are slimmer and smaller ... I don't fit that type so it's hard to be yourself when there is all this pressure to look a particular way.

In discussing how they might negotiate this pressure, the notion of authenticity — the importance of "being yourself" — was central. Within celebrity discourses there is a "persistent cultural attachment to authenticity."[45] The girls in this study all discussed how far they would be willing to change or adapt in order to gain success in the industry. This discussion included whether they would appear in violent films or do a topless glamour shoot, but was most commonly oriented around whether, and how much, they

---

44. Christine Geraghty, "Re-examining Stardom: Questions of Texts, Bodies and Performance," in Christine Gledhill and Linda Williams (eds) *Reinventing Film Studies*. (London: Arnold, 2000), 183–201.
45. William Tregoning, "Very Solo: Anecdotes of Authentic Identity," *M/C Journal* 7(5), (2004); see also: Jo Littler, "Making Fame Ordinary: Intimacy, Reflexivity and 'Keeping it Real'", 8–25.

would alter their appearance. The girls suggested that a willingness to change one's "self" was required for success. More specifically, they argued that flexibility was fundamental when starting out in the industry, but that once you achieve fame, you can "be yourself" again.

> Jade: I wouldn't change my values or what I think. But I'd change my appearance — 'cos at the end of the day you have to change a bit at the start of your career to get where you want but then when you've got to the place you want to be you can be who you want, look how you want, it doesn't matter.

The notion of being *just* flexible or malleable enough — adapting only so much in order to get ahead — was consistent across the girls' accounts. However, changing oneself in order to "make it" in the industry was fiercely regulated by the girls. Indeed, as Linda Duits and Pauline Van Romondt Vis found in their discussions with teenage girls, "changing too much means distancing yourself from your essence which makes it unnatural and therefore can be seen as selling out."[46] For Vicky, the perceived necessity to adapt to the latest industry demands provoked a great deal of anxiety as she questioned how much she could change without losing a sense of an "authentic," essential self.

> Vicky: I know that I shouldn't have to change myself to be famous but you have to be open to everything until you get that break . . . Even if there are times where you think "that's not me," you just have to do it until you get to that point where you're so good that you can do what you want . . . But it's hard. If you say you'll do anything you can probably get to the top easier than if you say, "I won't do nudity" or "I won't get plastic surgery." I do question myself and think "do I really want to do this as a job?" . . . I'm worried about becoming superficial and losing who I am from doing stuff I don't want to or thinking I have to look pretty all the time just because I want to get to the top.

Vicky's discussion of the potential sacrifices she may have to undergo in order to "get to the top," and the associated risks of "losing herself," can be read in the context of the wider neoliberal project of the self as "individual." Indeed, as Dyer reminds us, stars do not offer "straightforward affirmations of individualism. On the contrary, they articulate both the promise and the difficulty that the notion of the individual presents for all of us who live by it."[47] The difficulties and dilemmas of becoming the successful girl of neoliberalism are illuminated in the girls' constructions of their identities

46. Linda Duits and Pauline van Romondt Vis, "Girls Make Sense: Girls, Celebrities and Identities," 54.
47. Richard Dyer, *Heavenly Bodies: Film Stars and Society*, (2nd edn), (London: British Film Institute, 2004), 86.

Figure 7.2 **Pop music star "Pink."**

as potential celebrities, where they are impelled to invest in practices of self-reinvention and self-improvement while at the same time staying true to some inner and "authentic" self.[48]

Many of the girls, however, did identify celebrities who they felt had successfully navigated the dilemma of being malleable enough to achieve success while staying true to oneself. American singer Pink was frequently cited by the girls to demonstrate that changing oneself while maintaining authenticity *was* possible for celebrities. Pink began her career as an urban R&B singer before taking on a more alternative rock sound and aesthetic with her second album *Missundaztood*. Her "resistance" to the music industry's desire to mold her has been central to the construction of her media image as the "husky voice of authenticity."[49] Pink's song "Don't Let Me Get Me," includes the lyrics:

> LA told me, "You'll be a pop star,
> All you have to change is everything you are."
> Tired of being compared to damn Britney Spears
> She's so pretty, that just ain't me.

48. Jessica Ringrose and Valerie Walkerdine. "The TV Make-over as Site of Neo-liberal Reinvention Toward Bourgeois Femininity," 227–46. For a more detailed discussion of young people's engagement with questions of "authenticity" in relation to celebrity, see Kim Allen and Heather Mendick (forthcoming) "Making it and Faking it? Social Class, Young People and Authenticity in Reality TV" in Bev Skeggs and Helen Wood (eds), *Real Class: Ordinary People and Reality Television Across National Spaces.* (London: BFI).
49. Kate Spicer, "Shocking Pink," *The Observer,* November 9 2003.

For the girls in this study, authenticity was located in the continuity between the public persona and the private self.[50] For Emma, Pink's transition to an "edgy" image and sound represented her return to authentic selfhood: Pink stopped "living a lie" (represented by her R&B sound and soft pink hair) and became true to herself again.

> Emma: It's hard being yourself in this industry. You have to be true to yourself otherwise you're living a lie — you're just living like an actor . . . But it's hard. You can change but you have to be careful not to sacrifice too much of yourself just to get a role otherwise you can lose part of you . . . Maybe at the beginning there might be a few things you have to change to get somewhere. Like Pink. In the beginning she was all R&B and pretty with her soft pink hair but now she's so successful she can be who she wants to be, which is more edgy and punkish. So it's important to be true to yourself. Maybe you have to start with a lie but, with Pink, you can see you don't have to live that lie forever, finally you can become who you really are.

"Being yourself" and being willing to change was understood to be a careful balancing act for these girls. The perceived industry pressure to meet the current beauty ideal was complicated not only by their own desires for authentic selfhood but also by a concern with how their authenticity would be (mis)read off their female bodies. For example, Carly, a petite blonde and self-defined "girlie-girl," discussed at length the challenges she may face in her dream to become a TV presenter. Carly was unsure how she would navigate the industry pressure to look beautiful and still be popular with the audience, claiming that female celebrities who are "too pretty" are never liked. Indeed, "making an image too conspicuously is seen as inauthentic."[51] Carly's words reflect the fine balancing act that must be achieved in order to perform femininity and be seen as "real."

> Carly: I think there is pressure to change yourself to be successful. . . . There are things I feel I'd have to change . . . like I have bad skin and I know I'd have to sort that out to get anywhere, and have nicer clothes and I'd have to lose weight. Things like that I think you have to do — you see Cat Deely and Tess Daley and they look gorgeous and you'd wanna look like that . . . but it's a lot harder to be liked as a woman, especially by other females. I think Davina is an exception . . . maybe 'cos she's not a very girlie-girl, she's more natural-looking and she's really down to earth and does stupid things . . . she doesn't dress up and wear loads of make up . . . she's more real. Whereas people like Jessica Simpson get slated. People say "she's so fake" 'cos she's blonde and [has] big boobs so she gets a

---

50. Dyer, *Stars*.
51. Linda Duits and Pauline van Romondt Vis, "Girls Make Sense: Girls, Celebrities and Identities," 53.

harder time . . . I worry what I'll do 'cos I'm a really girlie girl so people might not like me.

What emerges from Carly's dilemma is a sense not only that authenticity is central to her construction of a successful celebrity career, but furthermore that for women, authenticity and "ordinariness" are always located in the body: the natural-looking, goofy, unpretentious, Davina McCall will always be read as "more real" than hyper-feminine celebrities like "blonde and big-boobed" American singer and actress Jessica Simpson. The performance of authenticity is thus constrained by the performance of "girlie-girl" hyper-heterosexualized femininities. This presented a difficult dilemma for Carly as she wondered whether she would be liked by audiences or simply written off as "fake." Popularity, authenticity, and femininity were thus complexly intertwined in the girls' constructions of their future selves as potential celebrities.

Social class is also a central mediator of authenticity within celebrity discourse, where celebrities are both scorned for getting "above their station" and celebrated for maintaining their working-class values.[52] Remembering where you've came from, both geographically and socially, was central to the construction of celebrity selfhood among the British working-class girls in this study. Below, Anusha, a working-class girl originally from Leeds in the North of England, discusses the difference between ex-Spice Girls Mel B and Posh Spice as she talks about the importance of "keeping it real":

> Anusha: I hate those celebrities who get too big for their own good. You have to stay true to yourself — remember where you have come from. Remember the people who helped you on your way. Especially 'cos, at any minute, your fame can end. Then you're screwed. Mel B she's a good person — she keeps it real. She's proud of coming from Leeds. Not like Posh Spice who thinks she's above everyone now, moving to LA and everything. She needs to be herself. I hope that if I make it famous I'm not like that. I wanna be able to keep it real and for people to treat me the same way.

Thus, while Posh Spice is read negatively as inauthentic, Mel B is attributed with positive value for remembering her "roots." Discourses of authenticity were central to Anusha's identity work as she imagined her future self as a celebrity (*"I wanna be able to keep it real"*). I want to go further to suggest that in emphasizing the importance of authenticity in this way, these working-class girls were contemplating, and attempting to negotiate, the potential risks attached to gaining upward social mobility through the celebrity machine. While celebrity was equated with recognition and a "better life," for

---

52. Su Holmes, "'Off-guard, Unkempt, Unready'?: Deconstructing Contemporary Celebrity in *heat* Magazine," *Continuum: Journal of Media & Cultural Studies* 19(1), (2005): 21–38. Jo Littler, "Making Fame Ordinary: Intimacy, Reflexivity and 'Keeping it Real,'" 8–25.

working-class girls, the promise of social mobility can provoke difficult emotions of guilt, betrayal and loss.[53] Aspirations for fame for the working-class girls thus involved contemplating how they would reconcile the distance travelled from working-class girl to celebrity. While becoming a celebrity was far from guaranteed, investing in the discourses of authenticity can be seen as one of the ways in which they sought to build *a bridge between* who they are now and who they may become.

Conclusion

The study discussed in this chapter has focused on a unique group of girls who were neither "fans" nor the "oblique and accidental" audience[54] of previous research on the topic. The insights this chapter provides into the cultural function of celebrity must be read within the context of their specific social positioning and their relationship to celebrity as performing arts students. For these girls, celebrity was a central and inescapable part of their identity work as they contemplated their careers in the performing arts. They were actively negotiating discourses of celebrity as they made assessments and judgments about the kinds of careers they wanted to achieve and what "success" would look and feel like.

Throughout this chapter social class has been shown to inform the ways in which young women situate celebrity within the construction of their future selves. I have argued that while celebrity operates as an important symbol of recognition for all young women in the study, aspirations for fame were framed differently by lower-middle-class girls and working-class girls. Lower-middle-class girls carefully self-regulated their aspirations by mobilizing middle-class strategies of distinction and drawing upon wider cultural hierarchies of fame. They emphasized the importance of hard work, local recognition, and respect over fame in and of itself as they constructed the "successful career." In contrast, for working-class girls, while hard work and talent were central to their constructions of a "successful career," they frequently rejected, and indeed inverted, cultural hierarchies of "proper" and "improper" fame. They attributed positive value to those celebrities who had found success regardless of whether they perceived them to be talented. For these working-class girls celebrity operated as a powerful opportunity structure, a way in which to overcome disadvantage and gain the recognition that they are denied under neoliberalism. They invested in the possibilities for upward social mobility through the celebrity machine. It was later suggested that for these young women, the attachment to authenticity occupied

---

53. Helen Lucey, June Melody, and Valerie Walkerdine, "Uneasy Hybrids: Psychosocial Aspects of Becoming Educationally Successful for Working-Class Young Women," *Gender and Education* 15(3), (2003): 285–99.

54. Linda Duits and Pauline van Romondt Vis, "Girls Make Sense: Girls, Celebrities and Identities," 41–58.

a central place in their negotiation of the possibilities of upward social mobility via celebrity. I have also discussed how the performance of femininity informed the girls' construction of celebrity selfhood. In particular I have suggested that the project of authenticity was central to their understandings of what was required for a "successful career" in the industry: keeping it real was highly valued by all the girls. However, the female body presented a series of dilemmas for how authenticity could be performed and maintained. The girls were caught between the perceived pressure to change in order to "get ahead" and a desire to maintain a sense of their authentic, essential self. The girls' anxiety at being read as too feminine and thus "fake" was also discussed, where the performance of femininity was complexly interlinked with perceptions of popularity and authenticity. For these girls, to live in a female body *and* be famous is to occupy a precarious position.

There are various implications which emerge from the analysis in this chapter. First, it attests to the importance of empirical work on celebrity and audience. Celebrity cannot be understood only through looking at its texts and images. It is a social practice and its meanings are never fixed but always negotiated. Specifically, empirical work illustrates the ways that women's relationships with celebrity are differentially structured and experienced across the social locations of class and gender. The analysis presented here has illuminated how social class produces very different readings of, and investments in, celebrity. While the ways in which ethnicity and culture inform young women's relationships with celebrity are subjects beyond the scope of this chapter, these are areas which warrant greater attention. Additionally, it would be interesting to explore the ways in which male performing arts students engage with celebrity in their identity work.

Second, this chapter illustrates that it is not just worthwhile but essential that empirical work looks not only to the active and resistant readings of the celebrity audience, but attends equally to the regulatory and disciplinary nature of celebrity discourses. While celebrity provided an important site of pleasure, fantasy, and meaning-making for the girls in this study, it also operated to regulate their aspirations. The inscriptions of gendered and classed value judgments of personhood within celebrity discourses had consequences for the kinds of choices these young women made about their future careers and, no doubt, how these choices are read, given or perhaps denied value by others.

Finally, this chapter suggests that celebrity plays a much more complex and significant role in young women's lives than is reflected in the mounting public debates around girls' "inappropriate" aspirations to become famous. Rather than being antithetical to ambition, for these girls, celebrity was closely aligned to their constructions of a "successful career" in the performing arts. This chapter thus makes a case for disrupting taken-for-granted assumptions about young women's relationship with celebrity and for the urgent need for further empirical explorations into the complex ways in which contemporary celebrity is lived and negotiated by young women today.

Bibliography

Allen, Kim and Heather Mendick (forthcoming). "Making it and Faking it? Social Class, Young People and Authenticity in Reality TV" in Bev Skeggs and Helen Wood (eds), *Real Class: Ordinary People and Reality Television Across National Spaces*. (London: BFI).

Allen, Kim and Jayne Osgood. "Young Women Negotiating Maternal Subjectivities: The Significance of Social Class," *Studies in the Maternal*, 1(2), (2009) online journal.

Archer, Louise. "The Neoliberal Subject? Young/er Academics' Constructions of Professional Identity," Journal of Education Policy 23(3), (2008): 265–85.

Archer, Louise, Anna Halsall, and Sumi Hollingworth. "Class, Gender, (Hetero)sexuality and Schooling: Paradoxes Within Working-class Girls' Engagement With Education and Post-16 Aspirations," *British Journal of Sociology of Education* 28(2), (2007): 165–80.

Banks, Mark and David Hesmondhalgh. "Looking For Work in Creative Industries Policy," *International Journal of Cultural Policy* 15(4), (2009): 415–30.

Beckford, Martin. "Teenage Girls Would Rather Be WAGs than Politicians or Campaigners." *The Telegraph*, November 18, 2008; Available at: http://www.telegraph.co.uk/sport/football/wagshire/3479322/Teenage-girls-would-rather-be-WAGs-than-politicians-or-campaigners.html (accessed November 12, 2010).

Bennett, Tony. "Postscript: Cultural Capital and Inequality: Refining the Policy Calculus," *Cultural Trends* 15(2), (2006): 239–44.

Biressi, Anita and Heather Nunn. "The Especially Remarkable: Celebrity and Social Mobility in Reality TV," *Mediactive* 2(1), (2004): 44–58.

Bourdieu, Pierre. *Distinction*. London: Routledge, 1984.

Chapman, James. "'Barbie Doll': Girls Only Want to Be WAGs or Win the X Factor, Complains Culture Minister," *Daily Mail*, October 15, 2008.

Clark, Laura. "High Heels, Low IQs: 'Dazzled' Girls Want to Be WAGs Instead of Having Careers, Warn Headmistresses," *Daily Mail*, January 9, 2009. Available at: http://www.dailymail.co.uk/femail/article-1110045/High-heels-low-IQs-Dazzled-girls-want-WAGs-instead-having-careers-warn-headmistresses.html#ixzz0Z0RV42Mm (accessed November 12, 2010).

Duits, Linda and Pauline van Romondt Vis. "Girls Make Sense: Girls, Celebrities and Identities," *European Journal of Cultural Studies* 12(1), (2009): 41–58.

Dyer, Richard. *Stars*. London: British Film Institute, 1979.

——. *Heavenly Bodies: Film Stars and Society* (2nd edn). London: British Film Institute, 2004.

Evans, Sarah. 'In a Different Place: Working-class Girls and Higher Education," *Sociology* 43(2), (2009): 340–55.

Feasey, Rebecca. "Reading *heat*: the Meanings and Pleasures of Star Fashions and Celebrity Gossip," *Continuum: Journal of Media & Cultural Studies* 22(5), (2008): 687–99.

Geraghty, Christine. "Re-examining Stardom: Questions of Texts, Bodies and Performance," in Christine Gledhill and Linda Williams (eds), *Reinventing Film Studies*, London: Arnold, 2000: 183–201.

Gill, Ros. "Postfeminist Media Culture: Elements of a Sensibility," *European Journal of Cultural Studies* 10(2), (2004): 147–66. Available at: http://eprints.lse.ac.uk/2449/1/Postfeminist_media_culture_%28LSERO%29.pdf (accessed February 15, 2009).

Gould, Mark. "Girls Choosing Camera Lenses over Microscopes," *The Guardian*, October 3, 2008. Available at: http://www.guardian.co.uk/education/2008/oct/03/science.choosingadegree (accessed November 12, 2010).

Holmes, Su. "'Reality Goes Pop!' Reality TV, Popular Music and Narratives of Stardom in Pop Idol," *Television and New Media* 5(2), (2004): 147–72.

——. "'Off-guard, Unkempt, Unready'?: Deconstructing Contemporary Celebrity in *heat* Magazine," *Continuum: Journal of Media & Cultural Studies* 19(1), (2005): 21–38.

Holmes, Su and Sean Redmond (eds). *Stardom and Celebrity: A Reader*. London: Sage, 2007.

Kehily, Mary Jane. "More Sugar? Teenage Magazines, Gender Displays and Sexual Learning," *European Journal of Cultural Studies* 2(1), (1999): 65–89.

Lacey, Joanne. "Identifying Characteristics of Class in Media Texts," in Adam Briggs and Paul Cobley (eds), *The Media: An Introduction* (2nd edn), Harlow: Longman, 2002: 340–56.

Littler, Jo. "Making Fame Ordinary: Intimacy, Reflexivity and 'Keeping it Real,'" *Mediactive* 2(1), (2004): 8–25.

Lucey, Helen, June Melody, and Valerie Walkerdine. "Uneasy Hybrids: Psychosocial Aspects of Becoming Educationally Successful for Working-class Young Women," *Gender and Education* 15(3), (2003): 285–99.

Lumby, Catharine. "Doing it For Themselves? Teenage Girls, Sexuality and Fame," in Sean Redmond and Su Holmes (eds), *Stardom and Celebrity: A Reader.* London: Sage, 2007:341–52.

Manchester Evening News. "Naked Ambition Rubs Off on Teen Girls," *Manchester Evening News,* June 6, 2005. Available at: http://www.manchestereveningnews.co.uk/news/s/161/161338_naked_ambition_rubs_off_on_teen_girls.html (accessed November 12, 2010).

McRobbie, Angela. *British Fashion Design.* London: Routledge, 1998.

——. "Post-feminism and Popular Culture," *Feminist Media Studies* 4(3), (2004): 255–64.

——. "Top Girls? Young Women and the Post-feminist Sexual Contract," *Cultural Studies* 21(4), (2007): 718–37.

McRobbie, Angela and Jenny Garber. "Girls in Subcultures," in Tony Jefferson and Stuart Hall (eds), *Resistance through Rituals: Youth Subcultures in Post-war Britain.* London: Hutchinson, 1976: 209–22.

"Naked Ambition Rubs Off on Teen Girls," *Manchester Evening News,* June 6, 2005.

Negra, Diane and Su Holmes. Editors Introduction, "Going Cheap? Female Celebrity in Reality, Tabloid and Scandal Genres," *Genders* 48 (Fall 2008). Available at: http://www.genders.org/g48/g48_negraholmes.html (accessed June 29, 2010).

Ovalle, Priscilla. 'Urban *Sensualidad*: Jennifer Lopez, *Flashdance* and the MTV Hip-Hop Re-generation," *Women and Performance: A Journal of Feminist Theory* 18(3), (2008): 253–68.

Projansky, Sarah. "Mass Magazine Cover Girls: Some Reflections on Postfeminist Girls and Postfeminism's Daughters," in Diane Negra and Yvonne Tasker (eds), *Interrogating Postfeminism: Gender and the Politics of Popular Culture.* Durham, NC: Duke University Press, 2007, 40–72.

Ringrose, Jessica. 'Successful Girls? Complicating Post-feminist, Neo-liberal Discourses of Educational Achievement and Gender Equality," *Gender and Education* 19(4), (2007), 471–89.

Ringrose, Jessica and Valerie Walkerdine. "The TV Make-over as Site of Neo-liberal Reinvention Toward Bourgeois Femininity," *Feminist Media Studies* 8(3), (2008): 227–46.

Sherbert Research. *Aspirations and the Children and Young People Segmentation.* Research Report No. DCSF-RR150. London: DCSF, 2009.

Skeggs, Bev. *Formations of Class and Gender: Becoming Respectable.* London: Sage, 1997.

Skeggs, Bev and Helen Wood. "The Labour of Transformation and Circuits of Value 'Around' Reality Television," *Continuum: Journal of Media and Cultural Studies* 22(4), (2008): 559–72.

Spicer, Kate. "Shocking Pink," *The Observer,* November 9, 2003. Available at: http://www.guardian.co.uk/music/2003/nov/09/popandrock (accessed November 12, 2010).

Stacey, Jackie. *Stargazing: Hollywood Cinema and Female Spectatorship.* London: Routledge, 1994.

Tregoning, William. "Very Solo: Anecdotes of Authentic Identity," *M/C Journal* 7(5), (2004).

Turner, Graeme. *Understanding Celebrity.* Sage, London, 2004.

Tyler, Imogen and Bruce Bennett. "Celebrity Chav: Fame, Femininity and Social Class," *European Journal of Cultural Studies* 13(3), (2010): 375–93.

Walkerdine, Valerie. *Schoolgirl Fictions.* London: Verso, 1990.

——. *Daddy's Girl: Young Girls and Popular Culture.* Basingstoke: Macmillan, 1997.

Walkerdine, Valerie, Helen Lucey, and June Melody. *Growing up Girl: Psychosocial Explorations of Gender and Class.* London: Palgrave, 2001.

Walters, Natasha. *Living Dolls: The Return of Sexism.* London: Virago Press, 2010.

Films

Fame. (1980). Directed by Alan Parker. Century City, CA: United Artists.
Fame. (2009). Directed by Kevin Tancheroen. Century City, CA: MGM.

Flashdance. (1983). Directed by Adrian Lyne. Hollywood, CA: Paramount Pictures.
Step Up. (2006). Directed by Anne Fletcher. Burbank, CA: Touchstone Pictures.
High School Musical. (2006). Directed by Kenny Ortega. Burbank, CA: Walt Disney Pictures.
High School Musical 2. (2007). Directed by Kenny Ortega. Burbank, CA: Walt Disney Pictures.
High School Musical 3: Senior Year. (2008). Directed by Kenny Ortega. Burbank, CA: Walt Disney Pictures.

8

Cool Postfeminism
The Stardom of Sofia Coppola

CAITLIN YUNUEN LEWIS

Sofia Coppola, director of the bewitchingly ethereal Lost in Translation
and, now, the airy, dreamlike Marie Antoinette, *swaggers into the room
and slaps me heartily on the back. She is wearing a pair of greasy cargo
pants and, only occasionally visible through clouds of rancid cigar smoke, a
black patch over her heavily bruised right eye. After extracting the cork from
a bottle of cheap whiskey with her jagged teeth, she swills some of the pungent
liquid into a dirty glass, knocks back an inch or two and begins shouting
about politics and baseball.
I'm joking of course. You will never, I suspect, have encountered anybody
quite as vague and psychologically diffuse as Sofia.*

— DONALD CLARKE[1]

In 1975 Molly Haskell wrote, "Although the area of independent filmmaking
has attracted women in numbers equal to men, as have most of the other
arts, commercial filmmaking remains a last stronghold — a stag nation of
male supremacy."[2] Unfortunately, over thirty years later, this still remains the
case. However, as one of the few high-profile female directors in contemporary Hollywood, Sofia Coppola is an exception to this rule, having directed
three successful feature films, *The Virgin Suicides* (1999), *Lost in Translation*
(2003), and *Marie Antoinette* (2006), with another, *Somewhere* (2010), forthcoming[3] Coppola is both commercially successful and largely admired as
a filmmaker of quality and artistic merit. In 2004, she became the first
American woman, and the third female filmmaker, ever to be nominated

---

1. Donald Clarke. "Girl Interrupted/Ancien Regime," *The Irish Times*, October 13, 2006.
2. Molly Haskell, "Are Women Directors Different?" in Karyn Kay and Gerald Peary (eds),
   Women and the Cinema: A Critical Anthology, (New York: Dutton, 1977), 429.
3. Coppola's debut film was the short *Lick the Star* (1998), which tells the story of a group of
   preteen girls who devise a plan to kill the boys in their school. Though this short would be
   very interesting to consider, my focus is on Coppola's feature-length, commercial releases.

for an Academy Award in Directing, after Lena Wertmuller for *Seven Beauties* (1975) and Jane Campion for *The Piano* (1993).[4] She has only recently been succeeded by the fourth such nominee and first female winner of this award, American director Kathryn Bigelow for *The Hurt Locker* (2009).

Despite her commerciality, Coppola has retained covetable "indie" and art house connotations. Just as her father Francis Ford Coppola's "movie brat" directorial success is associated with the simultaneously commercial and countercultural "New Hollywood" era, Coppola is one of the few female directors who maintains a position in what Geoff King calls "Indiewood" and Jeffrey Sconce calls the "smart film" category: "an area in which Hollywood and the independent sector merge or overlap," blending qualities "associated with dominant, mainstream convention and markers of 'distinction' designed to appeal to more particular, niche-audience constituencies."[5] As Indiewood is generationally the successor of New Hollywood's mainstream cinematic "coolness," Coppola can be understood as the heir to Francis Ford's mildly countercultural legacy. Both father and daughter are commercial directors yet are respected artistically, appearing slightly at odds with mainstream Hollywood while being part of it.

According to Pam Cook, Coppola's association with the hip "play group" of contemporary American filmmaking "has helped to consolidate her identity as a cool style icon," and her persona is that of "an artist/auteur unafraid to take risks with style and subject matter."[6] Held up as innovative and avant-garde, her films have been described as "sublimely romantic," "visually sumptuous," and "stylish and assured."[7] Coppola is widely credited as being the creator of "zeitgeist-defining films" that epitomize the contemporary cultural climate for young, middle-class Westerners, and *The New York Times* has called her "the most original and promising young female filmmaker in America."[8]

However, Coppola is unique as a director not only for being successful and female; she is also a star. Richard Dyer writes that stars are "embodiments of the social categories in which people are placed and through which they have to make sense of their lives," categories like "class, gender, ethnicity, religion, sexual orientation, and so on."[9] I seek to analyze Coppola's high-profile

---

4. Coppola received an Academy Award for Best Original Screenplay for *Lost in Translation*.
5. Geoff King, *Indiewood, USA: Where Hollywood Meets Independent Cinema* (London: I. B. Tauris, 2009), 1–2; and Jeffrey Sconce, "Irony, Nihilism and the New American 'Smart' Film," *Screen* 43(4), (2002): 349–69.
6. Pam Cook, *The Cinema Book* (3rd edn). (London: British Film Institute, 2007), 480–1.
7. Lou Lumineck, "'Lost in Translation': The Fall's First Essential Movie," *New York Post*, n.d.; Padraic McKiernan, "A Man Overbored? Not This Time," *Irish Independent*, October 22, 2006; Edward Guthmann, "The Message is Loud and Clear in 'Lost in Translation': Director Sofia Coppola Knows What She's Doing, and Bill Murray's Performance is a Subtle Miracle," *San Francisco Chronicle*, September 12, 2003.
8. Ibid., 2006; and Lynn Hirschberg, "The Coppola Smart Mob," *The New York Times*, August 31, 2003.
9. Richard Dyer, *Heavenly Bodies: Film Stars and Society* (London: Macmillan Education, 1987), 18.

persona as director-as-star, considering the particular social categories that she is perceived to embody. Focusing on her "branded" intertextuality across various forms of media, I will consider how her stardom is constructed through the marketable class, gender, and ethnic social categories she occupies, showing how her brand is created from contemporary notions of whiteness, postfeminism, and counterculturalism, and proposing that her stardom is best understood through the concept of "cool postfeminism."

In so doing, I consider coolness as "a kind of passive resistance to the work ethic through personal style," characterized by "narcissism, ironic detachment and hedonism."[10] As such, coolness can be explicitly linked to the constructions of pleasure, leisure, attraction, and allusiveness which characterize contemporary stardom. Furthermore, as Daniel Harris writes, "the basic credo of coolness is nihilism"; coolness is always conceptualized as at odds with the status quo, though this is often one of the very things it upholds.[11] As a key figure in the Indiewood school of filmmaking and one of Sconce's "smart" directors, "whose use of irony and focus on surface style" disguise a "melancholy nihilism," Coppola's postfeminist authorship, and stardom, are intrinsically constructed around the concept of coolness.[12] Identifying and theorizing what Coppola's stardom is, and means, will be this article's aim.

Collapsing Boundaries: A Postfeminist Director-as-Star

Directors are rarely analyzed as stars, but more often as auteurs, largely and customarily understood through the collective meanings of their work. While a small number of directors are "famous," few possess the charisma, propensity for mythology, and visibility of stardom, which seems at once evanescent and timeless. Of those directors who are stars, many are actors turned filmmakers, who remain predominantly identified as the former (such as Tom Hanks, Mel Gibson, George Clooney, Jodie Foster, and Barbra Streisand); of those who are equally or better known for their directing — Orson Welles, Quentin Tarantino, Dennis Hopper, Clint Eastwood — all are male, with the exception of Sofia Coppola.

Dyer writes that star images are "a complex configuration of visual, verbal and aural signs," which "function crucially in relation to contradictions within and between ideologies, which they seek variously to 'manage' or 'resolve.'"[13] Although authorship has become a contested theoretical arena in film studies, it is often reinforced in the director-as-star's persona; as it

10. Dick Pountain and David Robins, *Cool Rules: Anatomy of an Attitude* (London: Reaktion, 2000), 41 and 26.
11. Daniel Harris, *Cute, Quaint, Hungry and Romantic: The Aesthetics of Consumerism* (New York: Basic Books, 2000), 62.
12. Cook, 480.
13. Richard Dyer, *Stars* (London: British Film Institute, 1979), 38.

is an organizing principle around which to manage and resolve the signs that constitute a star, it thus contributes in creating the illusion of a singular, authoritative persona. Additionally, as Cook observes, in contemporary cinema "auteur status can be seen as a strategic necessity" which endows filmmakers with "creative capital," "enabling them to establish themselves as a brand" in the context of highly competitive and globalized markets, with possibilities of extending this brand outside the cinematic market.[14] Timothy Corrigan sees this commercial "branding" of the auteur as originating in "the cult of personality that defined the film artist of the seventies," and reads the contemporary auteur as having become "increasingly situated along an extratextual path in which their commercial status as auteurs is their chief function as auteurs: the auteur-star is meaningful primarily as a promotion or recovery of a movie or group of movies, frequently regardless of the text itself."[15] The director-as-star is often strategically separated from actual film production to increase their market appeal. In the words of Yvonne Tasker, "the director, as overdetermined symbol of 'authority' in the cinema, is as much framed by marketing (and the work of signification) as the performer."[16]

Always carrying the connotational baggage of their films into their star persona, a director maintains a stardom filtered through their authorship; their stardom is not only constructed through their public/private persona, but also through their filmic work. Hence they perhaps have the ability to shape their own star image to a greater extent than most stars can, for they are the makers of the cinematic images and ideologies that define stardom, even if it is their own. The director-as-star functions not only as the symbolic bearer of Dyer's "visual, verbal and aural signs," but also as the supposed creator of these signs; as inscriber, as well as inscribed. Thus, contradictorily, the director-as-star can be read as almost a potential inversion of stardom, in that they blur the lines between being producer and (produced) star, being behind and in front of the camera, and being the bearer and the subject of the look. This inversion is further complicated in the case of the female director-as-star; as Tasker writes, there is "a negotiation of visibility" at work in her production and performance of films and identities.[17]

Sofia Coppola's stardom can be read from such a perspective. Coppola has manufactured and managed her own image, appropriating stardom to inscribe not only others, but herself, with meanings. And yet, her stardom is more complex than this. As Christine Gledhill writes,

14. Cook, 479.
15. Timothy Corrigan, *A Cinema Without Walls: Movies and Culture After Vietnam* (New Jersey: Rutgers University Press, 1991), 105.
16. Yvonne Tasker, *Working Girls: Gender and Sexuality in Popular Cinema* (London: Routledge, 1998), 204.
17. Ibid.

The star challenges analysis in the way it crosses disciplinary boundaries: a product
of mass culture, but retaining theatrical concerns with acting, performance and
art; an industrial marketing device, but a signifying element in films; a social sign,
carrying cultural meanings and ideological values, which expresses the intimacies
of individual personality, inviting desire and identification; an emblem of national
celebrity, founded on the body, fashion and personal style; a product of capitalism
and the ideology of individualism, yet a site of contest by marginalized groups; a
figure consumed for his or her personal life, who competes for allegiance with
statesmen and politicians.[18]

Sofia Coppola's stardom is so complex because she interacts with Gledhill's
"disciplinary boundaries" in more ways than most directors-as-stars. Her stardom is not only shaped by the films she has directed and acted in, but also
by her social connections and her non-filmic ventures. Her family is one of
the foremost Hollywood dynasties, whose most famous members include not
only her father, but her grandfather, the late composer Carmine Coppola,
her brother, director Roman Coppola, her aunt, actress Talia Shire, and her
cousins, actors Jason Schwartzman and Nicolas Cage; she and her family continually collaborate in their filmic work. As member of the "play group" Cook
describes, she is both personally and professionally based in a social network
of filmmaking professionals, who interlink beyond the filmmaking scene and
into the other arts, at varying degrees of the countercultural: Coppola was
married to Spike Jonze, director of *Being John Malkovich* (1999), *Adaptation*
(2002), and *Where the Wild Things Are* (2009), is currently dating Thomas
Mars of the French band Phoenix (who are also characterized by their bourgeois coolness), and is best friends with filmmaker Zoë Cassavetes (another
of Hollywood's dynastic inheritors); she has acted in music videos for the
Chemical Brothers and Madonna, hosted the underground music show *Hi
Octane* with Cassavetes, and modeled in the work of art photographers Paul
Jasmin, Oliver Roller, and the late Shawn Mortensen.

As a self-styled fashion and lifestyle icon, Coppola is a regular in the front
row of catwalk shows and is featured in glossy women's magazines; she is
celebrated for her taste, and is a respected figure in the fashion industry,
having appeared in as well as made advertisements for luxury fashion labels
(she directed a Miss Cherie Dior commercial, was the face of Marc Jacobs
perfume, and modelled in an advertisement for Louis Vuitton's "Core
Values" campaign with her father), and has designed her own collection of
bags and shoes for Louis Vuitton, as worn by celebrities such as Kate Moss
and Sienna Miller. Coppola also manufactures her own wide-ranging series
of products, including the clothing label Milk Fed, which is only sold in
Japan, in sizes small and extra-small, and a "mini" pink-canned sparkling
wine, called "Sofia Blanc de Blancs," the ads for which she both directed

---

18. Christine Gledhill, *Stardom: Industry of Desire* (London: Routledge, 1991), xiii.

and starred in, and whose website includes a "Style" section where you can "Explore Sofia style in words, pictures, sound and motion."

Moreover, Coppola's films are allegedly inspired by her personal life, and are thus constructed around the private persona of their director, her authorship described as "a kind of ongoing metaphorical autobiography."[19] There seems to be an especially palpable crossover between the characterization of the director and her films, in their exploration of the interior life of an auspicious young woman who is largely misunderstood. Similarly, there are striking parallels between Coppola and her female protagonists, who are depicted as amorphous and contemplative, both plagued and blessed by a chic romantic ennui, similar to how Coppola is herself depicted in interviews, publicity photographs and other popular cultural representations.[20]

As Amy Woodworth notes, Coppola's "careful decisions for visually presenting her female characters . . . trademark slow pacing, privileging of impression over plot, and development of emotional texture and mood constitute a kind of feminine aesthetic."[21] This "feminine aesthetic" extends beyond her filmic texts (along the "extratextual path" Corrigan identifies) and clearly, all of Coppola's work is intensely feminized: her narratives explore women's experiences of the private sphere, her aesthetic and taste is hyper-feminine, the commodities she promotes — designer fashion, pink champagne, perfume, handbags — are predominantly geared toward the female consumer. She has made a career out of publicly interacting with the feminized private sphere; in this way, Coppola has found success in the male public sphere specifically through her femininity.

Due to her position as a female filmmaker, her status as a feminine style and fashion icon, and her professional "publicing" of the private sphere, Coppola's femininity is the dominant feature of her stardom. Thus, Coppola is associated with the "woman's film" and to some extent feminist filmmaking, as Sean Dwyer's description demonstrates: "She seems acutely aware that she is one of the few women in a male-dominated industry, and even from her very first film, *The Virgin Suicides*, she has taken it upon herself to tell stories about female characters confronting feminist issues."[22]

At the same time, however, Coppola is often subjected to critiques that seem based on stereotypical assumptions about her gender. She has

19. Elvis Mitchell, "An American in Japan, Making a Connection," *The New York Times*, 2003.
20. *Lost in Translation* (the only one of Coppola's feature films that was not an adaptation) most explicitly references these similarities. The characterization of Charlotte was based on the characteristics and sartorial style of the director herself, Charlotte's husband John (Giovanni Ribisi) is rumored to have been loosely based on Jonze, and the film's depiction of Charlotte and Bob's experience of Tokyo was inspired by Coppola's prior visit to the city.
21. Amy Woodworth, "A Feminist Theorization of Coppola's Postfeminist Trilogy," in Marcelline Block (ed.), *Situating the Feminist Gaze and Spectatorship in Postwar Cinema* (Newcastle Upon Tyne: Cambridge Scholars Publishing, 2008), 151.
22. Sean Dwyer, "Sofia Coppola's Next Film: Victorian-era Lesbianism in *Tipping the Velvet*," *Film Junk*, November 13, 2006.

frequently been accused of creating films that are shallow and materialistic, victims of style over substance. Critic Lesley Chow wonders if *Marie Antoinette* is the work of "a director with vision, or a good stylist?" and continues with a rhetorical question: "Coppola has made a career out of mix-ups that sound interesting conceptually — Japan and ennui, royalty and pop — but is there anything beyond the excitement of the initial disconnect?"[23] This shallowness has been connected to her membership in the elite Coppola family; as Cook writes, "[T]he aura of privilege surrounding the Coppola name has sometimes aroused disproportionate envy and malice in critics."[24] Matthew Bond derides Coppola for not being able to manage her money and trivializing her subject matter, turning "Marie Antoinette, a high-born Austrian princess, into a Californian valley girl," and hints that she has frivolously blown her film budget on clothes: "it is only the undeniably fabulous costumes that give Coppola any sort of decent return on her money."[25]

The clearly contrasting views of Coppola's film practice — one that she is an innovative feminist filmmaker articulating important issues of contemporary womanhood, the other that she is a shallow, spoiled daughter of privilege who spends excessive amounts of her father's money on frivolous girlishness — highlight a contrast that reflects the contemporary dilemmas of femininity that are at work in all aspects of her stardom. Rather than being feminist, anti-feminist, or even quasi-feminist, Sofia Coppola is strongly located in the current climate of postfeminism.

Postfeminism is a social, cultural and commercial discourse that has become a dominant way of representing and understanding women, feminism and femininity in contemporary Western culture and society. As a discourse of "diverse manifestations" and a multiplicity of interpretations, postfeminism is characterized by its ambiguity.[26] The ambiguity of "post"-ing feminism is indicative of an uncertainty surrounding womanhood in the contemporary Western world. The dispersal of the women's movement, a strongly anti-feminist, patriarchal discourse, and the disintegration of traditional female roles and lack of definite alternatives to replace them, exist alongside the continued achievements of feminism and a drastic improvement in the lives of many Western women. These ambiguous factors have led to a postfeminist climate that is fraught with contradiction, conflict, and uncertainty, resulting in a contemporary state which seems to be continuously in flux while at the same time maintaining very fixed ideas and traditions.

23. Lesley Chow, "Fashion and Dunst: The Substance of *Marie Antoinette*," *Bright Lights Film Journal* 56, (2007).
24. Cook, 480.
25. Matthew Bond, "Valley Girl of Versailles," *Irish Mail on Sunday*, October 22, 2006, Review: Film section.
26. Stéphanie Genz and Benjamin A. Brabon, *Postfeminism: Cultural Texts and Theories* (Edinburgh: Edinburgh University Press, 2009), 2.

Postfeminism is partially based on the assumption that feminism is over, "that it is no longer needed," and as Angela McRobbie writes, feminism is consequently evoked and undermined "as that which can be taken into account, to suggest that equality is achieved."[27] However, postfeminism is more multifaceted than its literal definition implies. While it does presume an "after" feminism, it also presumes a continuation of feminism: it is where the tensions, disputes, and outcomes of these presumptions are realized, debated, enacted, played out. Postfeminism is the depository for the unresolved struggles of feminism, and of the wider social, cultural, political, and economic factors which affect women and the concept of gender. As Stéphanie Genz and Benjamin A. Brabon write, "Rather than being tied to a specific contextual and epistemological framework, postfeminism emerges in the intersections and hybridization of modern media, consumer culture, neoliberal politics, postmodern theory and, significantly, feminism."[28] Complicatedly and contradictorily, feminism and postfeminism co-exist and continue to progress simultaneously. In this way, postfeminism is perhaps best understood as a concept of consilience: where several "apparently irreconcilable concerns evolve, if not together, at least in parallel."[29]

Coppola's stardom can be understood as deeply postfeminist, as it exemplifies the conflicted nature of contemporary womanhood. She is a woman who has made a successful career in a male-dominated industry, and the ambiguity of this position is apparent in the gender-biased criticism and praise she receives; she is both challenging and complicit to the status quo. Having formed her career through exploring the postfeminist ambiguities and contradictions of contemporary womanhood, Coppola embodies a romantic, dreamy aesthetic in her persona and her work, which references her own white femininity and traditional notions of the private sphere, which she simultaneously critiques and upholds.

As the various elements out of which her postfeminist stardom and authorship are assembled are so overlapping and ambiguous, Coppola's stardom not only crosses Gledhill's "disciplinary boundaries," but collapses these boundaries, interlinking her professional and personal life, her self and her productions, her public and her private personas. Coppola's stardom is founded on this collapse: she is "a figure consumed" for her filmic work as well as for her "body, fashion and personal style"; her own interpretation of her "personal life" is "a signifying element" in her commercial success,

---

27. Angela McRobbie, "Postfeminism and Popular Culture," *Feminist Media Studies* 4(3), (2004): 254.
28. Genz and Brabon, 5.
29. The term "consilience" is borrowed from James Lovelock, *The Revenge of Gaia* (London: Penguin, 2006). The term was formulated by evolutionary biologist E. O. Wilson, in his book *Consilience* (1998). Wilson, Lovelock writes, "when writing on the incompatibility of twentieth-century science and religion, was mindful of the unconscious need in most of us for something transcendental, something more than could come from cold analysis" (161).

and hence is "an industrial marketing device" and "a product of capitalism"; the supposed "intimacies" of her "individual personality" contribute to the "cultural meanings and ideological values" of her work, both "inviting desire and identification," but also functioning as a marginalized "site of contest," as this article will show.

Generational Italian Ethnicity and Glamour

As a star who has always been framed by the generation that came before her, Sofia Coppola first became known through her father's iconic adaptation of Mario Puzo's *The Godfather* trilogy, "the single most significant work in the history of Hollywood Italians."[30] According to Thomas J. Ferraro, *The Godfather* "referred less to a book or a film than to a modern secular mythology of Romanesque proportions and ancestry," "reimagining the place of Italians in America."[31]

The Godfather's "reimagining' occurred as part of the late twentieth-century resurgence of interest in (and resulting commodification of) nostalgic "ethnic" hyphenated American identities, particularly those of white European origin. As "ethnicity offers tangible markers and potent symbols of ascribed commonality," this ethnic revival was perhaps "a response to the fragmentation, ambiguities, and rapid pace of change inherent in the postmodern world"; however, it also functioned as a way to distinguish the Euro-American self in the context of a deeply racialized melting-pot society, in which whiteness remains the most powerful and normative racial category, yet has also been undermined by the sense of homogeneity and even *lack* of identity that has resulted from its very claims to normality and its historic assimilation.[32] The ethnic revival functioned to ideologically counter the "undesirable" or banal aspects of quintessential (white) American life, while also appropriating some of the perceived vivacity, exoticism, and "color" of ethnicity, and reinvigorating the aspiration to individualism so typical of both classic American "self-reliance" and contemporary neoliberalism.

The reassertion of white European ethnic identities has resulted in a hierarchy in which some ethnicities become more desirable and "American" than others. As Diane Negra observes, "white Americans of mixed European ancestry have been almost uniquely positioned to claim or disclaim aspects of their heritage at will, often electing one ethnicity based on social definitions of what it implies."[33] Thus, as Richard D. Alba writes, "No longer, then, need

30. Peter Bondanella, *Hollywood Italians: Dagos, Palookas, Romeos, Wise Guys and Sopranos* (London: Continuum, 2004), 235.
31. Thomas J. Ferraro, *Feeling Italian: The Art of Ethnicity in America* (New York: New York University Press, 2005), 107 and 110.
32. Marilyn Halter, *Shopping for Identity: The Marketing of Ethnicity* (New York: Schocken Books, 2000), 83 and 81.
33. Diane Negra, *Off-White Hollywood: American Culture and Ethnic Female Stardom* (London:

there be any contradiction between being American and asserting an ethnic identity. Increasingly, they are accepted as the same thing."[34]

The ethnic revival's influence on Hollywood was apparent from the late 1960's onwards, with many "ethnic" films utilizing de-assimilation narratives that promoted the ideal of hyphenated ethnic identities as distinct from "normal" American ones, constructing them as desirable, essentialist, and even in need of violent protection. Negra observes that *The Godfather*

> invokes a nostalgic conception of ethnicity which can be traced to the historical specificities of its production and an increasing cultural desire to return to an ethnic past . . . *The Godfather* marks a cinematic shift in thinking about ethnicity, where assimilation is now linked to sterile bureaucratization and the preservation of an ethnic past to vitality.[35]

Vera Dika reads a fantasy of "Italianicity" at work in the *Godfather* trilogy, as it utilizes an ethnic nostalgia to simultaneously glorify, attempt to revive, and mourn the passing of the "old Sicilian ways."[36]

Having become associated with the iconic "Italianicity" of *The Godfather* trilogy and the Corleones, the Coppolas are perhaps the most prominent Italian-American family in Hollywood. Allen L. Woll and Randall M. Miller write that Italians possess a certain "bankability," a "commercial appeal as symbols of emotional liberation and sexuality in an age when Americans are struggling to get in touch with their true feelings," granting them an association with deep-rooted family values and authenticity (which is often depicted as working class).[37] The Italian is constructed as "a creature of passion, an emotional being given to excess in love or hatred, whose religion, culture, and condition seemingly explained his exaggerated behaviour."[38] Accordingly, an Italian-American ethnic identity is stereotypically associated with uncontrollable and unruly excesses of emotion, noise, violence, food, religion, sexuality, and temper, and hence many of the archetypal traits of the dark, exotic Other (darkness being an "excess" beyond whiteness). Thus, while Italian Americans benefit from possessing a valued white European ethnicity, at the same time they occupy an ambiguous position between the categories of whiteness and off-whiteness, for "ethnicity within whiteness threatens to erase the comfortable distance between whiteness and color"; if "orderliness, civilization, rationality, modernity and industry are all figured

---

Routledge, 2001), 3.

34. Richard D. Alba, *Ethnic Identity: The Transformation of White America* (New Haven: Yale University Press, 1990), 318–19.

35. Negra, 141.

36. Vera Dika, "The Representation of Ethnicity in *The Godfather*," in Nick Browne (ed.), *Francis Ford Coppola's The Godfather Trilogy* (Cambridge: Cambridge University Press, 2000), 97.

37. Allen L. Woll and Randall M. Miller, "Italians," in *Ethnic and Racial Images in American Film and Television* (New York: Garland, 1987), 296.

38. Ibid., 275.

as white, then color signifies the oppositional attributes of disorder, primitivism, and recidivism."[39]

However, Italians are also historically associated with style, high fashion, art, romance, and culture, their alleged appreciation of "the finer things in life" making them exemplars of the class, taste, and quality often equated with Europeanness. Thus, if glamour is widely understood to be an alluring attribute that seems more exhilarating, romantic, desirable, or stylish than the ordinary, glamour is often equated with Italianness as a national characteristic. This glamorousness can be tied to Italians' supposed excess; as Stephen Gundle writes, "glamour is often about excess," "always more than average: more showy, more visible, more beautiful, more sexy, more rich."[40] Stereotypically characterized by both "low" and "high" cultures of excess, Italians possess a contradictory cultural identity; likewise, glamour is similarly contradictory, epitomized by "oxymoronic qualities," "always a fusion . . . of class and sleaze, of high style and lowly appeals."[41] If Italians possess glamorous contradictions, these have proven particularly adaptable to the context of both the ethnic revival and the American Dream, for glamour has contained "the dreams" and "the promise of a mobile and commercial society that anyone could be transformed into a better, more attractive, and wealthier version of themselves."[42]

The Coppolas are strongly associated with glamorous Italianness, straddling the border between high style and the hinted "lowly" qualities that Gundle identifies, and thus slightly destabilize notions of celebrity decorum. While Francis Ford is a restaurateur and owns a vineyard, he is rumored to have an unruly directorial approach and volatile temper; Nicolas Cage is widely known for his accumulation of vintage cars and property, yet is notorious for his questionable and risky financial affairs, namely overspending and tax evasion; and the Coppola family originally came from one of the then-poorest regions of Italy, Basilicata. In fact, Francis Ford and Sofia's occupation of a directorial space between the countercultural and the commercial epitomizes this connection between glamorous high and low culture.

Glamorous Italianness is a trait the Coppolas share with the fictional Corleones. As Dika observes, the *Godfather* films have served to glamorize the Italian-American gangster, depicting the Corleones as "aristocracy" with lower-class roots.[43] The Coppola name embodies a similar connotation of a prosperous, generational "family business" to that of the Corleones, and the Coppolas can be understood as Hollywood aristocracy (their wealth associated with the glamorous excess of the arts, wine-making, and over-spending,

---

39. Negra, 5.
40. Stephen Gundle, *Glamour: A History* (Oxford: Oxford University Press, 2008), 15.
41. Ibid., 12 and 390.
42. Ibid., 7.
43. Dika, 99.

rather than of crime). Diane Negra has asked, "how does the 'natural' way in which so many stars' children become stars themselves interact ideologically with the strengthened sense of belief . . . that one's family capital is more reliable than any other form of social or political capital?"[44] In this context it is surely significant that the Coppolas possess a high-class Italian heritage with "family capital," which equates their celebrity nepotism to the "family values" so mythologized in contemporary American culture.

The Coppolas' glamorous family capital is exemplified in an advertisement for luxury fashion designer Louis Vuitton's "Core Values" campaign, which features Sofia and Francis Ford. In this ad, the Coppolas are dressed in classic, designer clothing, but wear it with an everyday casualness that seems to disregard its expense. Sofia lounges in the grass on a balmy evening, half-dreaming, half-concentrating as her father appears to impart his wisdom, in what we can presume to be filmmaking. While Francis Ford is relaxed yet upright, instructional, and authoritative in his "director's chair," Sofia's loose, child-like/intimate body posture suggests that she is unthreatened by the viewer, and does not need to be self-aware or self-guarded. Rather, she is comfortable enough with us to lose herself in a reverie, "forgetting" about her body, her designer clothes, and her audience, oblivious to our presence. Impeccable elegance and style appear to come "naturally" to Sofia, as a daily and normal state of being, which is effortless and which she seems unaware of. It is clear that the scene of generational exchange between father and daughter we are witnessing is a construction, framed by Louis Vuitton's white border and the name of photographer Annie Leibovitz, who specializes in constructing hyperreal, fantasy star images. Despite this, it feels as if we are intruding on a private personal moment, but the intrusion is welcome, expected. Both father and daughter, it seems, are in their element. The Coppola family business is being handed down, and Sofia is heir, yet this family business is represented in highly gendered ways. Sofia is depicted as a novice, her father as an expert; while he has intellectual tools in the form of his books, director's chair, and papers, Sofia has none of these, and instead is portrayed as at one with nature, her romanticized pose recalling those of her female protagonists and the aesthetics of her films more broadly. The ad highlights how Coppola has always been framed by the generation that came before her in a particularly *gendered* way, and here, as elsewhere, she is depicted as being in a perpetual state of girlhood.

As indicated by this ad, Sofia Coppola's familial capital and glamorized Italian ethnicity have significantly shaped her stardom. Coppola visibly "grew up" through the *Godfather* trilogy, playing characters that symbolized both the hope of birth and the tragedy of death in the films. As an infant, she played the baby (boy) in the iconic baptism scene that concluded the first film, she was a child on a steamship in the second, and finally, in *Part III*,

---

44. Diane Negra, "Celebrity Nepotism, Family Values and E! Television," *Flow TV* 3(1), (2005).

LOUIS VUITTON

Figure 8.1   **Francis Ford and Sofia Coppola (photographed by Annie Leibovitz, for Louis Vuitton's "Core Values" campaign, 2009).**

she controversially played Mary Corleone, who dies on the steps of an opera house, shot by an assassin trying to kill her father.

If the *Godfather* trilogy works to deconstruct the melting-pot ideal in favor of a glorified ethnicity, Mary can be read as representing the death of an assimilated, hyphenated ethnic innocence in American culture. Thus the trilogy ends by symbolically severing the family's main female tie to America; by the conclusion of *Part III*, only ethnicity survives, and Michael returns to the Italian homeland to die. As Woll and Miller note, Michael's "great crime was his Americanization"; in succumbing to the American Dream, the family had lost its roots, and the film is ultimately suggesting that "the old ways are the best ways."[45] This failure is embodied in the figure of the daughter, who represents familial (and hence national) hope of continuation, regeneration and new life. Even Mary's name bears this message ("Mary, the mother, the symbolic center of the family, and especially of young and future families").[46] The staged, symbolic "death of ethnic assimilation" that Sofia performed in the *Godfather* trilogy has registered as a (submerged) rhetoric of her star persona. While on the one hand Sofia embodies the glamorous ethnic identity that the Coppolas/Corleones are associated with, there is a sense that her Italian ethnicity is in the past, left behind and belonging to a different time, along with her father's trilogy and Mary.

Disclaimed Ethnicity, Classic Whiteness

As her fictional "ethnic death" symbolizes, Coppola has managed to negotiate a star persona that is influenced, but not predominantly defined, by her Italian ethnicity; this is a unique position for an "off-white" female star, as Hollywood has a "tendency to absorb and commodify female ethnicity."[47]

---

45. Woll and Miller, 286, 296 and 284.
46. Dika, 102.
47. Negra, 1.

Coppola distances herself from archetypal constructions of feminine Italianicity, which vary from what Mary Ann McDonald Carolan describes as the unprofessional and sentimental Italian American woman, with her "big hair, pantsuits, lots of gold jewellery, a Brooklyn accent, and stiletto heels," to an off-white fantasy figure like actress Marisa Tomei, whose "vivacious style enables her to be positioned as an ethnic antidote to contemporary cultural exhaustion," as Negra writes.[48]

However, Coppola does retain a sense of Italianicity's glamour, in its associations with high fashion, art, culture, and taste, although her glamour is constructed through tropes of classic, idealized, and normative white, rather than Italian, femininity. In fact, Coppola epitomizes a quintessentially American contemporary glamour, which Gundle describes as "a mix of ideas and themes drawn from the past and rendered contemporary by some skilful blending and fashioning."[49]

Coppola's persona embodies the archetypal ideals of "classic" white femininity; she is dressed, positioned, and constructed to connote elegance, managed sexuality, demureness, self-control, emotional etiquette, and an ethereal denial of the abject, the bodily, and the earthly. She is known for her soft-spoken and relaxed directorial style (contrasting with her father's alleged dictatorial approach), and, almost in the mode of a Victorian "angel of the house" or a stereotypical 1950s housewife, seems to avoid scandal, appears to be the epitome of serenity, and is rumored never to lose her temper or raise her voice. In this way, Coppola's glamour draws upon past aesthetics of stardom and recalls something of the quintessential figures of American glamour (such as Audrey Hepburn and Jackie Onassis) rather than those of glamorous Italian femininity, as embodied by the voluptuous and earthy Sophia Loren. As Rachel Moseley writes, "the whiteness of 'Audrey Hepburn' is key to the hegemonic status of her femininity," but, like Coppola's, goes largely unnoticed: "Hepburn's whiteness is unmarked in the same way that the middle-classness of her 'look' remains unmarked and appears 'classic.'"[50]

The publicity surrounding Coppola promotes this idealized white image of her, especially through visual representations. According to Dyer, any visual medium "not only assumes and privileges whiteness but also constructs it."[51] He writes that light is used "in constructing an image of the ideal white woman within heterosexuality," who "glows," appearing to be both bathed

48. Mary Ann McDonald Carolan, "Italian American Women as Comic Foils Exploding the Stereotype: *My Cousin Vinny, Moonstruck* and *Married to the Mob,*" *Literature Interpretation Theory* 13(2), (2002): 155; and Negra, 139.
49. Gundle, 383.
50. Rachel Moseley, *Growing Up with Audrey Hepburn: Text, Audience, Resonance* (Manchester: Manchester University Press, 2002), 14 and 15.
51. Richard Dyer, *White* (London: Routledge, 1997), 122.

in and the source of radiating white light.[52] Echoing these conventions, Coppola is usually lit to look as if she is glowing, as she is in the Louis Vuitton ad, which works in contrast to her father, who is noticeably darker (Figure 8.1). However, as contemporary glamour mixes "ideas and themes . . . drawn from the past," her white skin is often emphasized to contrast strongly with her hair, eyes and eyebrows, connoting, perhaps, a compliment-ary distinction between the present-day desirability of her Italianness and that of her classic whiteness.[53]

In distancing herself from an identity defined by ethnicity and instead embracing archetypal, classic white femininity and glamour, Coppola's stardom explores the "female embodiments of national fantasies" not through ethnicity, but rather through a white femininity that is rendered contemporary.[54] Thus Coppola utilizes the social definitions of her ethnicity to her advantage not so much by claiming it, but by somewhat *disclaiming* it. In disclaiming ethnicity, perhaps Coppola is responding to the enduring appeal of whiteness, to the ethnic revival's potential to alienate white America, and to the Otherness which always surrounds off-white immigrant and ethnic groups, no matter how "desirable." However, while on the one hand she invokes an idealized white femininity, she also retains a tinge of desirable ethnicity that differentiates her from the ordinary. Thus, her whiteness grants her not an uncertain or homogeneous lack of identity, but an advantageous adaptability.

In a utilization of this adaptability, Coppola's associations with high-class glamour, quality, and taste, interpreted through her classically inspired white femininity, are constructed as almost pan-European, and particularly associated with France. For example, a 2006 *New York Times* travel feature entitled "Sofia Coppola's Paris" accompanied Coppola while she ran errands round the city, depicting her as a high-class flâneuse: "we shopped as if we were engaged in a kind of sociological study of French customs and style," the author attests.[55] The article offered a multimedia slideshow of the journey, and provided readers with "Sofia's Address Book," which included details of specialty shops, patisseries and bars that one could visit in order to emulate the director's experience of Paris. The article not only promoted these establishments and her "new film" *Marie Antoinette*, but also served to remind readers of Sofia's privileged class status, the feminine aesthetic of her filmic style (as replicated in the slideshow), and her previous film *Lost in Translation*, in which Scarlett Johansson played a similarly idle flâneuse, wandering the streets of Tokyo.

Another example of Coppola's adaptable glamorousness positioned her

---

52. Ibid.
53. Gundle, 383.
54. Negra, 3.
55. Lynn Hirschberg, "Sofia Coppola's Paris," *The New York Times*, September 24, 2006, T Style Magazine: Travel section.

as guest editor of *Paris Vogue* in 2005, in an issue that blended images of her films, personal life, and lifestyle in a manner similar to "Sofia Coppola's Paris." Her magazine spread "Vogue par Sofia Coppola" was a collection of various images — objects, characters, and memorabilia from her films, photographs of her family (Francis Ford is labelled "Mon Père") and friends, with a color and textural palette echoing her aesthetic — which were blended with fashion products, including details of where to purchase them and their prices. While "Sofia Coppola's Paris" emphasized Coppola's sophistication, class and womanliness, "Vogue par Sofia Coppola" highlighted her girlishness and "creativity" in its scrapbook/collage layout; both articles drew upon her classic white femininity as the strongest feature of her persona, substituting her Italian-American roots for a French "chicness." Through popular cultural representations such as these, coupled with her international filmmaking practice, Coppola has become a subtle ethnic mediator of sorts, a commodified ambassador who is associated with a high-class European sphere of culture and can represent a tinge of glamorous foreignness and cosmopolitanism for an American audience, without it being threatening or Other. Dina M. Smith describes contemporary Hollywood films which use French actors, settings, or storylines as functioning to "resolidify Hollywood's hegemony over the European film market while 'looking' more European."[56] Coppola's position can be understood in a similar way; in an era of ambivalence surrounding globalization, the mixture of praise and criticism she receives perhaps stems from these associations.

Amorphousness, Postfeminism and Coolness

Coppola's stardom is characterized by the adaptability of her white femininity, formed through the intersection between her disclaimed ethnicity and contemporary glamour. As authorship can be understood as a feature of the director-as-star's persona, Coppola's films also contribute to her brand of white femininity. However, they explore another feature of whiteness in addition to the "classic" aspects of her persona.

Centered upon narratives of white femininity, *The Virgin Suicides*, *Lost in Translation* and *Marie Antoinette* explore the confusion and amorphousness not only of whiteness and the absence of ethnic identity, but also of contemporary womanhood. Using female stars whose appeal lies in their hyperfeminine whiteness (and who are often cast in roles that depict their white femininity as tragic and/or romantic), Coppola positions Kirsten Dunst and Scarlett Johansson as the narrative and visual centerpieces of her films. Like Coppola's publicity photos, which echo Dyer's assertion that light can be used in constructing the image of the ideal white woman, Coppola

56. Dina M. Smith, "Global Cinderella: *Sabrina* (1954), Hollywood, and Postwar Internationalism," *Cinema Journal* 41(4), (2002): 48.

uses light to exemplify her protagonists' beauty, desirability, and whiteness. But while Coppola appears grounded in her images, with soft, subdued lighting that brings out the strong color contrasts of her hair and her white skin, her film protagonists are lit somewhat differently, especially those played by Dunst. The lighting enhances their fair hair, pallor and delicate femininity, but their characterization is also determined by how bright or dim the light is; they exist by the light, thriving only when bathed in it.

Dyer contends that whiteness can descend into blankness if pushed to its extremities, which also draws upon common stereotypes surrounding femininity. That women are blank, or "lacking," has been a long-held idea in Western culture (perhaps expressed most explicitly in Sigmund Freud's theory of penis envy). One of the ramifications of this perceived "lack" is the proliferation of representations of women who are constructed as blank or deficient in some way, and lack is one of the many negative female stereotypes that feminism has struggled to revise.

Lack is a defining feature of Coppola's female protagonists, and constitutes their version of white femininity. Lux, Charlotte, and Marie Antoinette do not work or have strong interests, and are unsure of their place in the world, always "missing something"; their characterizations are not predominantly constructed through dialogue or action. Rather, the viewer gains information about them mostly through visual observation, absorbing the music and colors that accompany and inform images of them. Long sequences of watching these dreamy and beautiful fair-haired women, lounging in sunny grass or white cotton bedding, are dispersed throughout Coppola's films; pastel-hued and highly textured cinematography, accompanied by an emotive soundtrack, fill the ambiguous, unsatisfactory space of female life, work, and social relations. While Coppola's films, like her stardom, draw upon white femininity as their defining feature, the latter is characterized by a simultaneous celebration and anxiety about this space, which draws upon female lack and blankness. Coppola's protagonists are defined by amorphousness rather than their director's adaptability; this amorphousness is derived not only from whiteness but also from postfeminism. Coppola's characters are struck by a melancholy that mourns the limits of their roles, exemplifying the ambiguity of postfeminist womanhood. At the same time, the traditional roles Coppola depicts (wife, mother, daughter, object of male lust) can be stultifying, suffocating, and perhaps only escapable through death, as in *Marie Antoinette* and *The Virgin Suicides*.

However, the white female amorphousness that Coppola explores in her authorship and the white female adaptability of her stardom intersect through coolness; coolness is the fantasy of escape, its "passive resistance" functioning to mitigate the anxieties of contemporary youth. While the ethnic revival worked to counter the ordinariness of assimilated whiteness for Francis Ford's generation of Americans, perhaps the younger generation finds a solution to banality through coolness. Peter N. Stearns interprets coolness as a "distinctly American" cultural "style" of middle-class emotional restraint, a "preoccupation with dispassion" and "an emotional mantle, sheltering the whole personality from embarrassing excess," which originated in Victorianism and was reinvigorated by a translation of "the apparent needs of an increasingly managerial, health-conscious society into the emotional realm" of mid-twentieth-century American society.[57] Thus, in its bourgeois restraint, dispassion, and rejection of emotion and excess, coolness shares similarities with archetypal whiteness. Offering "the disaffected middle class an enticing fantasy," coolness works to provide relief for "privileged youth desperate to rid themselves of what they perceive as the taint of inauthenticity" in a similar way to the ethnic revival.[58] By utilizing the very traits the ethnic revival deems undesirable — the nothingness of nihilism, the detachment from place and family, the dispassion of restraint, the shallowness of hedonism — coolness can be understood as countering the anxieties surrounding whiteness by making a feature of them; the anxieties of whiteness are rendered desirable, "cool."

The concept of coolness can also be linked to postfeminism, although it has been theoretically ascribed to masculinity rather than femininity. Susan Fraiman defines coolness as "a 'male' individualism," "a construction of left/ bohemian rebellion that presumes masculinity and actually requires distance from the feminine" and is "defined above all" by a "strenuous alienation from the maternal."[59] However, although it is perhaps a more common defining feature of masculinity, many of the stereotypes surrounding femininity share traits with coolness. In its emotional restraint, demureness, and ethereality, idealized classic white femininity shares characteristics with coolness, and the nihilism and dispassion of coolness can be linked to postfeminist blankness and lack. In their unavailability and aloofness, both past and present archetypes of the idealized white woman lend easily to coolness: she is effortlessly detached from normality, her style is one of resistance to mortal humanity, her beauty implies narcissism, she is a creature who exists for hedonism. In cinematic terms, this is expressed famously by Alfred Hitchcock's "cool blondes," a category that included actresses Grace Kelly, Tippi Hedren, and Janet Leigh.

However, the most significant way that postfeminism grants opportunities for feminine coolness is through its commercialization. Where postfeminism is the struggle and ambiguity surrounding women's roles and feminism, neoliberal consumer culture has capitalized on this struggle and ambiguity, and the neoliberal market logic that Jeremy Gilbert describes as seeping into

---

57. Peter N. Stearns, *American Cool: Constructing a Twentieth-Century Emotional Style* (London: New York University Press, 1994), 1 and 310.
58. Harris, 55 and 54.
59. Susan Fraiman, *Cool Men and the Second Sex* (New York: Columbia University Press, 2003), xii and 157.

"many kinds of social relations" occurs within postfeminism.[60] A globalized, neoliberal, female lifestyle economy in which gender is highly commodified has emerged as a dominant feature of Western women's cultural life. Contradictorily, discourses within this economy draw on feminist ideals (women should have equal access to happiness, freedom, and choice as men), but find solutions to women's dilemmas through female purchase power, seeking to convince women of the legitimacy and desirability of a neoliberal, capitalist value system. These discourses exert severe pressure to establish female identity through consumption, positing the successful woman as possessing power, freedom, beauty, love, or happiness through being an avid (but not a critical) consumer. This neoliberal lifestyle economy commodifies female struggles as resolvable through the use of consumer products (e.g. self-help books, household products, the "power" that supposedly comes with sexiness, prettiness, stylishness), as well as an emancipatory female individualism that is realized in market terms (e.g. personal style, subcultures like indie or goth, fan cultures, and cool postfeminism).

Coppola's "cool" stardom demonstrates the commodification of postfeminism's ambiguity. While her films might be read as critiques of contemporary female lifestyles, options, and consumerism (and perhaps even of postfeminism itself) in the limited (and often morbid) options for women she portrays through her female protagonists, they also find solutions to women's dilemmas through female purchase power, reinstating that which they critique. This is most apparent in Coppola's reliance on fashion, beauty, taste, and style (i.e. the very consumerism that alienates her protagonists) for the sumptuous visual effects of her films, and also in her own high-profile, covetable position as a self-styled lifestyle icon, who has achieved this status through her consumer choices. Coppola's stardom — as Tasker and Negra describe of postfeminism as a whole — is "anchored in consumption as a strategy (and leisure as a site) for the production of the self."[61] The films, along with their visual and narrative links to their director, portray the protagonists' typically postfeminist "selves as projects" and, in their heavy autobiographical aspect, almost function as Coppola's own "self project."[62] Femininity in Coppola's films is not only based on the postfeminist assumptions of middle-class status and a heavy rhetoricizing of "lifestyle," but in its postfeminism critiques these elements as well as simultaneously undermining any feminist qualms about them.

Within postfeminist popular culture, white femininity has become increasingly imbued with certain features of commodified coolness. Narratives surrounding cool female protagonists who outsmart others with witty

---

60. Jeremy Gilbert, *Anticapitalism and Culture: Radical Theory and Popular Politics* (Oxford: Berg, 2008), 30.

61. Yvonne Tasker and Diane Negra, *Interrogating Postfeminism: Gender and the Politics of Popular Culture* (Durham, NC: Duke University Press, 2008), 2.

62. Ibid., 28.

Figure 8.2 **Sofia Coppola in the Marc Jacobs Perfume Advertising Campaign (photographed by Juergen Teller).**

dialogue, construct their worlds out of countercultural references, and have an ironic and nihilistic attitude to contemporary life have proliferated in Indiewood (*American Beauty* [1999], *Ghost World* [2001], *Juno* [2007], *Nick and Norah's Infinite Playlist* [2008], *500 Days of Summer* [2009]). Super-heroine fantasy figures, who display masculine traits of tough coolness, replace "damsels-in-distress" as objects of contemporary desire (*Sin City* [2005], the *Transformers* saga [2007 and 2009]). Fashion campaigns make a feature of feminine dispassion and nihilism (the decimated yet desirable "heroin chic" model aesthetic; the anti-pose of the skinny and scowling girls who feature in the ads for clothing brand American Apparel). The star personae of a number of Hollywood actresses are constructed around an ironic countercultural sensibility and a pseudo-rejection of the mainstream (Zooey Deschanel, Chloë Sevigny, Thora Birch), drawing on the legacy of the many generations of female musicians who have defined cool feminin-ity, from Nico to Debbie Harry to Beth Ditto. Through cool postfeminism, white femininity's ideals have become ironic and marketable, as have its "darker" opposites, the sexual and moral transgressions that were once most threatening to it (exemplified by the commodified appeal of contemporary burlesque star Dita von Teese, and the pseudo-subversive *Juno* scriptwriter and former stripper Diablo Cody). Through constructions such as these, cool postfeminism functions to broaden concepts of womanhood; yet as it is so commercially viable it is ultimately absorbed by the status quo, serving rather than resisting the needs of a capitalist value system.

"She Is the Epitome of This Girl I Fantasize of": Coppola's Cool Postfeminism

Coppola's cool postfeminism functions in a similar way to the examples described above. In addition to connoting an adaptable and classically white femininity, Coppola's image is also "alternative," combining styles and tastes that might have once signified resistance (punk, indie, hippie, grunge, avant-garde), but which now are highly commercialized, while still retaining their countercultural connotations (albeit in a diluted version). In her essay on Parker Posey's middle-class bohemianism, Negra writes that there is a "privileged class of taste-makers" in contemporary American culture that functions to reconcile "bohemian and bourgeois sensibilities."[63] Coppola functions as just such a bourgeois bohemian "taste-maker," and is held up as a lifestyle icon not only through the chic aesthetics of her films but also through her ironic association with luxury brands and style choices.

The cool postfeminism of Coppola's persona is particularly exemplified in her role as the face of fashion designer Marc Jacobs' perfume (Figure 8.2). Jacobs is associated with a grunge-inspired yet highly feminized design style, and has a reputation for bucking trends.[64] According to Angela Partington, perfume "has the ability to engage even those who feel excluded from contemporary fashion," its "status as a gift, and its more private/intimate uses and connotations mean that it can acquire additional meanings distinct from those of fashionable dress."[65] Most women's perfume design is highly feminized, inviting "emotional identification" and even "a celebration of narcissism" through the elaborateness of its design.[66] It often utilizes "incorporated organic or illustrative forms, pastel or bright colours and tones, decorative, textural, sculptural, or sensual surfaces, and symbolic references to birds, flowers, eggs, shells, fossils, landscapes, sensuous materials, and precious stones."[67] The design and advertising of men's fragrances, by contrast, tends to be minimalistic, avoiding excessive decoration or imagery to imply "a detached, 'objective' rational/functionalist relationship with the object."[68] Perfumes that make use of this knowledge and produce "androgynous" fragrances (like Chanel, Armani, and Calvin Klein) give the consumer the impression they are transcending gender stereotypes and divisions. As Partington writes, "'Androgynous' packaging is part of a lifestyle image in which traditional gender roles have been challenged but it only appeals to very specific consumer groups who are self-consciously 'progressive,' however, 'any style which minimizes/reduces gender distinction can be seen as an idealistic denial of it,'" and androgyny in fact "intensifies the boundaries as it claims to transcend them."[69]

---

63. Diane Negra, "'Queen of the Indies': Parker Posey's Niche Stardom and the Taste Cultures of Independent Film," in Chris Holmlund and Justin Wyatt (eds), *Contemporary American Independent Film: From the Margins to the Mainstream* (New York: Routledge, 2005), 71.
64. In his 2004/2005 Spring Collection, Marc Jacobs countered other designers' seasonal themes in making his collection ultra-feminine, lining the runway with archways made of 450,000 roses.
65. Angela Partington, "Perfume: Pleasure, Packaging and Postmodernity," in Pat Kirkham (ed.), *The Gendered Object* (Manchester: Manchester University Press, 1996), 205.
66. Ibid., 210.
67. Ibid., 209.
68. Ibid.
69. Ibid., 210.

As is evident from the advertisement in Figure 8.2, Jacobs employs a somewhat androgynous design aesthetic. This aesthetic, along with his reputation as being countercultural and the very male brand name "Marc Jacobs," serves to somewhat masculinize his products, evoking the message that the woman who wears, carries, or spritzes Marc Jacobs will be a rational, intelligent, and countercultural individual herself. However, in order to avoid alienating the female consumer and preserve the product's association with femininity, he uses Sofia Coppola, who signifies classic white femininity. This balances the product's masculine connotations and design, while also retaining some of the masculine/cool qualities of the original message, namely emotional control, detachment and intelligence (Coppola is often depicted as a "thinker," her expression repeatedly portrayed as one of contemplation). Therefore, as Partington writes, supposedly "androgynous" packaging "can signify a *certain kind* of femininity, understated and elegant."[70] Sofia Coppola is the poster-girl for Marc Jacobs' pseudo-androgynous perfume, because she connotes that "certain kind" of "understated and elegant" femininity, yet also challenges it in her coolness, and thus ironically alludes to Jacobs' countercultural sensibilities.[71]

In her publicity images, Coppola is often depicted as idle, inactive and enjoying leisure time, which portrays her as laidback while palpably referencing her upper-class and "artistic" status, but also rids her classic white femininity of its uptightness, properness, and repression, replacing it with a hedonistic, cool nonchalance. This is evident in both the ads for Vuitton and Jacobs. In the majority of her publicity images Coppola is looking away from the camera, seemingly caught in moments of distraction, daydream or deep thought, both classically demure and coolly aloof, and always "classically" rather than provocatively clothed. While she is portrayed this way in the Vuitton ad, in the Jacobs ad she is uncharacteristically topless and looking straight at the viewer, in a position that should be overtly confrontational or sexual, but is instead rendered unthreatening and intimate.

When asked why he chose Coppola as his perfume poster-girl, Marc Jacobs replied "She is young and sweet and beautiful . . . the epitome of this girl I fantasize of."[72] In her cool postfeminism, Coppola is associated with youth, and thus her "girlishness" is a prominent feature of her persona, despite her

---

70. Ibid., 213.
71. Coppola has very different connotations to other celebrities who endorse or have their own fragrances, for example Elizabeth Taylor ("White Diamonds"), Jennifer Lopez ("Glow") or Britney Spears ("Curious" and "Fantasy"). All of these perfume brands are associated, to one degree or another, with "trashy" and lower-class popular culture. Even a highly admired actress like Catherine Zeta-Jones — who promotes Elizabeth Arden's "Mediterranean" and was reportedly picked by the company because they saw her as "the epitome of personal style, elegance, and sophistication" — does not embody the same high fashion connotations and cultural capital that Coppola does.
72. Amy Larocca, "Lost and Found," *New York Magazine*.

being in her late thirties (it is also a prominent feature of Jacobs' advertising, especially in his 2006 campaign featuring the then 12-year-old child actress Dakota Fanning, whose sister Elle is the female star of Coppola's film *Somewhere*). Through her girlishness Coppola defuses any potential threat that might emerge from her powerful female position in Hollywood. Discourses of girlishness are a prominent feature of postfeminism, with Negra and Tasker writing that in many postfeminist texts, "girlhood offers a fantasy of transcendence and evasion, a respite from other areas of experience."[73]

Conclusion

Coppola's "unthreatening" girlishness demonstrates how, more broadly, her stardom's cool postfeminism dismantles and diffuses the potential threat of her status as a female director-as-star. As this essay's epigraph demonstrates, it seems unthinkable, almost comic, that Coppola could swagger, spit, slap, shout, bruise, smoke cigars, drink cheap whiskey, get dirty or greasy, be vexed by common things like politics or sports; it is inconceivable that she could be anything but ethereal, vague, or diffuse, which are, as we have seen, defining features of cool postfeminism. Collapsing Gledhill's "disciplinary boundaries," Coppola has constructed a branded authorship defined by cool postfeminism, not only through her films, but as a consistent aesthetic across all elements of her stardom.

In the context of Dyer's assertion that stardom is "a complex configuration of visual, verbal, and aural signs," functioning to "manage" or "resolve" "contradictions within and between ideologies," the reasons that Coppola has achieved stardom become clear. The complex meanings she embodies result from an interplay between the ideologies surrounding social categories of whiteness, ethnicity, and femininity, which her stardom seeks to resolve. Most of all, however, Coppola has achieved the rare position of director-as-star because her stardom manages the tensions between upholding and challenging the status quo, be they between mainstream/indie filmmaking, progressive/regressive female representations, male/female authorship, or within postfeminism itself. The tensions between these contradictory positions fuel Coppola's stardom, and the ambiguity of these debates is the crux of her persona.

Bibliography

Alba, Richard D. *Ethnic Identity: The Transformation of White America*. New Haven, CT: Yale University Press, 1990.
Bond, Matthew. "Valley Girl of Versailles." *Irish Mail on Sunday*, October 22, 2006, Review: Film section.

---

73. Tasker and Negra, 24.

Bondanella, Peter. *Hollywood Italians: Dagos, Palookas, Romeos, Wise Guys and Sopranos.* London: Continuum, 2004.

Carolan, Mary Ann McDonald. "Italian American Women as Comic Foils: Exploding the Stereotype in *My Cousin Vinny, Moonstruck* and *Married to the Mob.*" *Literature Interpretation Theory* 13(2), (2002): 155–66.

Chow, Lesley. "Fashion and Dunst: the Substance of *Marie Antoinette.*" *Bright Lights Film Journal* 56, (2007). Available at: http://www.brightlightsfilm.com/56/fashion.htm (accessed July 26, 2007).

Clarke, Donald. "Girl Interrupted/Ancien Regime." *The Irish Times,* October 13, 2006, The Ticket: The Irish Times Weekly Guide to Entertainment section.

Cook, Pam. *The Cinema Book* (3rd edn). London: British Film Institute, 2007.

Corrigan, Timothy. *A Cinema Without Walls: Movies and Culture After Vietnam.* New Brunswick, NJ: Rutgers University Press, 1991.

Dika, Vera. "The Representation of Ethnicity in *The Godfather*," in Nick Browne (ed.), *Francis Ford Coppola's The Godfather Trilogy.* Cambridge: Cambridge University Press, 2000.

Dwyer, Sean. "Sofia Coppola's Next Film: Victorian-era Lesbianism in *Tipping the Velvet.*" *Film Junk,* November 13, 2006. Available at: http://www.filmjunk.com/2006/11/13/sofia-coppolas-next-film-victorian-era-lesbianism-in-tipping-the-velvet/ (accessed June 9, 2007).

Dyer, Richard. *Stars.* London: British Film Institute, 1979.

——. *Heavenly Bodies: Film Stars and Society.* London: Macmillan Education, 1987.

——. *White.* London: Routledge, 1997.

Ferraro, Thomas J. *Feeling Italian: The Art of Ethnicity in America.* New York: New York University Press, 2005.

Fraiman, Susan. *Cool Men and the Second Sex.* New York: Columbia University Press, 2003.

Genz, Stéphanie and Benjamin A. Brabon. *Postfeminism: Cultural Texts and Theories.* Edinburgh: Edinburgh University Press, 2009.

Gilbert, Jeremy. *Anticapitalism and Culture: Radical Theory and Popular Politics.* Oxford: Berg, 2008.

Gledhill, Christine. *Stardom: Industry of Desire.* London: Routledge, 1991.

Gundle, Stephen. *Glamour: A History.* Oxford: Oxford University Press, 2008.

Guthmann, Edward. "The Message is Loud and Clear in 'Lost in Translation': Director Sofia Coppola Knows What She's Doing, and Bill Murray's Performance is a Subtle Miracle." *San Francisco Chronicle,* September 12, 2003.

Halter, Marilyn. *Shopping for Identity: The Marketing of Ethnicity.* New York: Schocken Books, 2000.

Harris, Daniel. *Cute, Quaint, Hungry and Romantic: The Aesthetics of Consumerism.* New York: Basic Books, 2000.

Haskell, Molly. "Are Women Directors Different?" in Karyn Kay and Gerald Peary (eds), *Women and the Cinema: A Critical Anthology.* New York: Dutton, 1977.

Hirschberg, Lynn. "The Coppola Smart Mob." *The New York Times,* August 31, 2003.

——. "Sofia Coppola's Paris." *The New York Times,* September 24, 2006, T Style Magazine: Travel section.

King, Geoff. *Indiewood, USA: Where Hollywood Meets Independent Cinema.* London: I. B. Tauris, 2009.

Larocca, Amy. "Lost and Found." *New York Magazine,* August 21, 2005. Available at: http://nymag.com/nymetro/shopping/fashion/12544/ (accessed August 21, 2007).

Lovelock, James. *The Revenge of Gaia.* London: Penguin, 2006.

Lumineck, Lou. "'Lost in Translation': The Fall's First Essential Movie." *New York Post,* n.d.

McKiernan, Padraic. "A Man Overbored? Not This Time." *Irish Independent,* October 22, 2006.

McRobbie, Angela. "Postfeminism and Popular Culture." *Feminist Media Studies* 4(3), (2004): 255–64.

Mitchell, Elvis. "An American in Japan, Making a Connection." *The New York Times,* 2003.

Moseley, Rachel. *Growing Up with Audrey Hepburn: Text, Audience, Resonance.* Manchester: Manchester University Press, 2002.

Negra, Diane. *Off-White Hollywood: American Culture and Ethnic Female Stardom.* London: Routledge, 2001.

——. "Celebrity Nepotism, Family Values and E! Television." *Flow TV* 3(1), (2005). Available at: http://flowtv.org/?p=287 (accessed August 20, 2007).

———. "'Queen of the Indies': Parker Posey's Niche Stardom and the Taste Cultures of Independent Film," in Chris Holmlund and Justin Wyatt (eds), *Contemporary American Independent Film: From the Margins to the Mainstream*. New York: Routledge, 2005.

Partington, Angela. "Perfume: Pleasure, Packaging and Postmodernity," in Pat Kirkham (ed.), *The Gendered Object*. Manchester: Manchester University Press, 1996.

Pountain, Dick and David Robins. *Cool Rules: Anatomy of an Attitude*. London: Reaktion, 2000.

Sconce, Jeffrey. "Irony, Nihilism and the New American 'Smart' Film." *Screen* 43(4), (2002): 349–69.

Smith, Dina M. "Global Cinderella: *Sabrina* (1954), Hollywood, and Postwar Internationalism." *Cinema Journal* 41(4), (2002): 27–51.

Stearns, Peter N. *American Cool: Constructing a Twentieth-Century Emotional Style*. London: New York University Press, 1994.

Tasker, Yvonne. *Working Girls: Gender and Sexuality in Popular Cinema*. London: Routledge, 1998.

Tasker, Yvonne and Diane Negra. *Interrogating Postfeminism: Gender and the Politics of Popular Culture*. Durham, NC: Duke University Press, 2008.

Woll, Allen L. and Randall M. Miller. "Italians," in *Ethnic and Racial Images in American Film and Television*. New York: Garland, 1987.

Woodworth, Amy. "A Feminist Theorization of Coppola's Postfeminist Trilogy," in Marcelline Block (ed.), *Situating the Feminist Gaze and Spectatorship in Postwar Cinema*. Newcastle Upon Tyne: Cambridge Scholars Publishing, 2008.

9

The Insanity Plea

Female Celebrities, Reality Media and the Psychopathology of British Pop-Feminism

EMMA BELL

I N CONTEMPORARY CONSTRUCTIONS OF FEMALE CELEBRITIES, apparent transgressions of "accept-able" femininity that are represented as "bad girl" excesses are increasingly being reframed as symptoms of "mad girl" mental distress. This particular discourse surrounding female celebrity in the UK context is articulated through the complex textual and market relations between tabloids, scandal media, and reality and autobiographical products. After a period of media antagonism (and subsequent cultural and market devaluation), "bad girl" celebrities can re-gain public attention and cultural value through revelations of mental illness. What is more, they often do so through what can be termed "reality and life products" — including autobiographies, documentaries, reality TV series, self-help books, diet, makeover and lifestyle products, magazine columns and internet blogs. This media articulation of, and consumer market for, mental health distress signifies a problematic trend in contemporary culture whereby the bad girl/mad girl-redeemed forms part of a postfeminist backlash against both culturally "acceptable" forms of femininity and female celebrity agency.

To understand this discourse, it is effective to explore the ways in which revelations of mental health problems have been of particular, yet ambiguous, usefulness for celebrity women who were strongly associated with a 1990s/early 2000s cultural moment of "pop-feminism," marked by a high-profile, culturally pervasive, quasi-feminist rhetoric. This rhetoric relied heavily on female celebrities who embraced the "bad girl" stereotype and who were both derided and revered in the media for that reason. In its British context, pop-feminism took the form of self-proclaimed feminist "ladette" and "Girl Power" cultures. "Girl Power" was primarily a promotional device for girl bands, most notably the Spice Girls and Atomic Kitten, to describe a new kind of liberated and empowered femininity marked by assertiveness, provoca-tion, and success. The term "ladette" was applied to, and embraced by, the wolf-whistling-beer-drinking-independent-wild-girls epitomized by female media presenters, such as radio DJs and actors including Gail Porter, Denise Van Outen, Zoë Ball, Sara Cox, and Billie Piper. Both labels were also media constructs to describe an apparently new generation of apparently boisterous, immoderate, and scandalizing young females led by such media celebrities.

The interrelatedness of "pop-feminism" and "postfeminism" is complex and instructive. If postfeminism involves a cultural undermining of the trajectories of feminism, 1990s pop-feminism marked a significant moment in the popularization and commodification of seemingly feminist sentiments regarding the empowerment, self-expression, and cultural agency of young women in the West. As Angela McRobbie has shown, "elements of contemporary popular culture are perniciously effective in regard to this [postfeminist] undoing of feminism, while simultaneously appearing to be engaging in a well-informed and even well-intended response to feminism."[1] Both "Girl Power" and "ladette" culture mobilized the rhetoric of feminism, yet they simultaneously undermined the feminism of the 1970s and 1980s by reframing female equality through a conflation of the hyper-feminine and the masculine. Simultaneously, as McRobbie points out, during the 1990s, feminist academics began to pay more particular attention to "the concept of popular feminism" and its contemporary expression.[2] For all its seemingly feminist rhetoric, "Girl Power" was both praised and vilified by feminist critics. Kathy Acker, for example, praised "Girl Power" as "Being who you wanna" and "not taking any shit";[3] Rosalind Coward, however, denounced it as "a good label to use in any situation in which girls might put themselves forward in new, brash, 'unfeminine' ways,"[4] complaining that "Girl Power" was a declawed and market driven caricature of the more earnestly feminist and political Riot Grrrl movement.[5]

Spice Girl Geri Halliwell herself clearly differentiated the playful sexuality of "Girl Power" from negative images of feminism, rejecting traditional feminists as "bra-burning lesbians." She bemoaned that "[feminism is] very unglamorous. I'd like to see it rebranded. We need to see a celebration of our femininity and softness."[6] Despite Halliwell's call for a new kind of "feminine-feminism," like many women in postfeminist culture, the most vociferous and high-profile celebrity advocates of pop-feminism now

1. Angela McRobbie, "Post-Feminism and Popular Culture," *Feminist Media Studies* 4(3), (2004): 255.
2. Ibid., 256.
3. Kathy Acker, quoted in Germaine Greer, *The Whole Woman* (London: Doubleday, 1999), 331.
4. Coward, Rosalind. *Sacred Cows* (London: HarperCollins, 1999), 122.
5. See Anna Feigenbaum, "Remapping the Resonances of Riot Grrrl: Feminisms, Postfeminisms, and the 'Processes' of Punk," in Yvonne Tasker and Diane Negra (eds), *Interrogating Postfeminism* (Durham, NC: Duke University Press, 2007), 132–52.
6. Geri Halliwell, quoted in Joanna Moorehead, "Girl Power Comes of Age," *The Guardian*, October 24, 2007, G2 14.

"stake a distance from [pop-feminism], for the sake of social and sexual recognition";[7] this distancing is very often attempted through candid disclosures about their sense of self-alienation and mental ill health in celebrity media forms. The subjects of 1990s popular-feminism were "expected to embody more emboldened (though also of course 'failed') identities."[8] In the context of their biographical products, these women's revelations of mental ill health articulate this sense of personality "failure" through pop-feminism, and simultaneously express a belief in the unprofitability and alienation of feminism as such; their assertions of the redundancy of feminism parallels their own "redundancy" as commercially viable personnel in postfeminist mass culture.

In *The Whole Woman*, Germaine Greer notes, "the cultural phenomenon [of the "bad girl"] is depressingly durable."[9] She then invites us to question the enduring cultural construct of the "bad girl," not as a courageous rebel, but as an ill-fated casualty. Far from being empowered or radical, the bad girl's career is both tragic and transitory: she is, from the outset, fated to an unhappy end. Greer's invitation also begs the question as to what process of transformation — of self-making — might becoming "good" involve? What if the girl turns out not to have been bad, but *mad*? What if her rebelliousness, excesses, provocativeness, and belligerence are reframed as pathological, as symptomatic not of a frustrated and ostensibly feminist refusal to conform, but of mental illness? Doesn't self-pathologization conceal and reinforce the repressive gender structures the bad girl once transgressed?

Three superlative examples of this representational process in the British context — Spice Girl Geri Halliwell, "ladette" Gail Porter, and "wild child" Kerry Katona — reveal that the "bad-to-mad-girl" transformation trope is indicative of a complicated postfeminist backlash against 1990s pop-feminism. As these women entered their late twenties and early thirties, their celebrity personas became surplus to the popular cultural market, being both incompatible with, and unmarketable within, the shift in the early 2000s from "girl-power" to "girlie" culture.[10] These womens' comeback strategies frequently take the form of "brand-enhancer" reality and life products that are used to fashion penitent apologies for un-feminine behavior and overt involvement in pop-feminism. Reality, life, and gossip products, as Jo Littler points out, foreground celebrities' "emotional responses (and 'real') behavior" and they "generate interest in 'other' sides of their characters, to present us with new ways of getting intimate with them."[11]

---

7. Ibid., 255.
8. Ibid., 256.
9. Germaine Greer, *The Whole Woman* (London: Doubleday, 1999), 310.
10. For an insightful discussion of "girlie" culture, see Ewan Kirkland, "The Politics of Powerpuff: Putting the 'Girl' into 'Girl Power,'" *Animation* 5, (2010): 9–24.
11. Jo Littler, "Making Fame Ordinary: Intimacy, Reflexivity, and Keeping it Real," *Mediactive* 2, (2004): 20.

In Halliwell's autobiographies *If Only* (1999) and *Just for the Record* (2002), and the TV documentary *Geri* (1999), she talks candidly about her struggle with eating disorders and depression; in the memoir *Laid Bare: Love, Survival, and Fame* (2007) and numerous interviews and reality shows, Gail Porter discusses her public breakdown and mental illnesses ranging from bipolar disorder to stress-related alopecia; in *Too Much, Too Soon* (2007) and the MTV reality shows Katona discloses her struggle with anorexia, depression, drug addiction, and bipolar disorder, and in her self-help book, *Survive the Worst, Aim for the Best* (2007), and in her the MTV reality series, *What's The Problem?*, she explains her experience of, and recovery from, these illnesses while imparting wellness advice.

Yet repackaged bad girls habitually reassert their sanity — and seek social acceptability and cultural worth — by engaging with, and invoking deeply problematic discourses about, the relationship between femininity, fame, and mental health, and reactionary stereotypes derived from the tabloid press. The women's autobiographical reality and life products evidence the ways in which perceived female transgression in celebrity culture is intertwined with discourses of pathology and mental instability. These products are indicative of the ways in which female celebrities now seek to intervene in a media culture primed and impatient to pathologize female celebrity. What is more, these women describe mental illness as being a consequence of an ostensibly unruly, "fame-hungry" female body — documenting etiologies between fame and symptoms of eating disorders, self-harm, sexual promiscuity, and post-partum depression.

The three women under discussion here produce autobiographical reality and life products that construct a continual process of self-making that is interwoven with their representation in the tabloid media as "unstable." They remake and rebrand their selves in noticeably similar forms, making revelations of mental ill health through reality and life products and dramatic physical makeovers, displaying commitment to public service and charity, and claiming redemption through motherhood. They seek public roles as charity ambassadors, psychological and diet gurus, and producers of products for children. Setting the record straight, then, often means asserting, "I'm not bad, I'm mad . . . !"

Halliwell, Porter, and Katona's autobiographical products pathologize their pop-feminism as both a cause of and escape from mental health problems. Their autobiographies follow a set format: they re-narrate the breakdown of fame, discuss early childhood trauma, explain "bad girl" behavior as symptomatic of mental illness caused by trauma, explain their fame as a pathological lack of sense of self and reframe fame-seeking as a symptom, explain how the celebrity false-self collapses under the pressures of fame, and delineate the processes of, and motivation for, recovery, before finally asserting their redemption though motherhood. However, this latter discourse can also be problematic in that it most often invokes moral panics over the "instability" attributed in the tabloid media to single mothers. Their reality and life products are attempts to re-emerge into the celebrity mainstream; to assert their control over their personas, they repudiate the "bad girl" behaviors they once proudly promoted as "feminist."

Reality and life products can be used to counteract negative media constructs, in this case those based on seemingly unacceptable images of femininity and discourses of mental instability, which then invite public judgment and prompt outrage and derision. Repackaged as "mad girls," celebrity women use such products to reassert their sanity, seek social acceptability and regain cultural worth. In the final analysis, these discourses are unreconstructed from the very tabloid and scandal media they seek to both engage with and resist.

For male celebrities such as Stuart Goddard (Adam Ant), Russell Brand and Johnny Depp, the hedonism they attribute to expressions of mental distress can function to re-consolidate and actually increase their "cultural power."[12] This is because a "bad boy" image of hedonistic excess and mental wildness — drug and alcohol addiction, promiscuity, sex-addiction, violence, mania, and melancholia — stands in many ways as a culturally acceptable expression of "essential" masculinity as well as the masculinized rhetoric of artistic genius. Stephen Harper notes how revelations of mental illness and excess by male stars are often constructed as courageously therapeutic acts of survival and "self-fashioning" — actively made by autonomous men. Thus, mental distress is reframed as indicative of essentially male attributes of creativity, uniqueness and the power to overcome life's challenges. In contrast, female celebrities' revelations of mental illness are tragedies, melodramas, and narratives of "failure" that undermine their creative agency and diminish their cultural power. If "bad girl" hedonism is "unfeminine," then rebellious and uncontained female celebrities are often constructed as somehow insane. And popular media reporting of psychopathologies and mental illnesses are habitually structured according to deeply problematic notions of acceptable gender roles. Media reporting of the "sex addiction" of Tiger Woods and Russell Brand, for example, frame narratives of moral and patriarchal redemption and contrast sharply with the salacious reporting of female hedonism. The "unruly" and sexual behavior of women such as Amy Winehouse or Britney Spears is absorbed by an unrelenting discourse on female celebrity per se as pathologically narcissistic and out of control. As such, the need for famous women to re-brand their psyches and reveal mental ill health is paradoxically both self-creating and self-defeating; the work of being a commodifiable "self" is intrinsic to the gendered structures

---

12. Stephen Harper, "Madly Famous: Narratives of Mental Illness in Celebrity Culture," in Su Holmes and Sean Redmond (eds), *Framing Celebrity: New Directions in Celebrity Culture* (London: Routledge, 2006), 316.

of Western consumer capitalism, celebrity culture, and the culture of compulsory self-articulation and expression.

To explore mental distress and celebrity in its British context allows us to realize more fully the gendered structures of postfeminist backlash. Kerry Katona offers an ideal example through which to begin to explore the interrelationship between female celebrity breakdown and reality media. A high-profile British celebrity who appeared in tabloid and reality media after a brief career as a pop star in the teen girl band, Atomic Kitten, Katona was represented early in her career as an ex-lap-dancing "bad girl" from a deprived and abusive background who transitioned to more "respectable" fame as a pop star. Katona was seen as the hard-faced little sister of the British power-girl pop-feminists of the 1990s, such as the Spice Girls and the "ladettes." Katona left the Kittens in 2001 after becoming pregnant, but also because she had suffered a mental breakdown. Katona was diagnosed with bipolar disorder in 2004, and tabloid scandals about her mental health proliferated.

Since leaving Atomic Kitten, Katona has carved out a career for herself as a media celebrity through a steady stream of reality products and ancillary media, including autobiographies, reality TV shows, a column in celebrity gossip magazine *OK!*, self-help literature and internet blogs. Through such media, Katona's image is conveniently portable in that the perceived instability of her personality makes her adaptable to almost limitless narratives and scenarios. She is constructed as a profitably mercurial personality engaged in an ongoing process of managing, repudiating, and creating the tabloid scandals that simultaneously afford her media attention. Her most high-profile appearances have been in the MTV series *Crazy in Love* (2008), which portrayed her tempestuous marriage; *Whole Again?* (2009), which charted her "recovery" from pregnancy through a mind and body makeover; and *Kerry Katona: What's the Problem?* (2010), which purports to give viewers unrestricted access to Katona's therapeutic transformation.[13] The show follows Katona as she "embarks on an emotional journey into her troubled past, in an attempt to fully understand bipolar disorder and how it affects both herself and the people closest to her."[14] MTV acknowledges that Katona's mental health is intertwined with her negative celebrity persona, and it is explained how "Katona's name is now synonymous with sensational tabloid headlines featuring bankruptcy, depression, marital bust-ups — to name a few," with the program promising to "address the question that's on everyone's lips: Kerry Katona: What's the problem?"[15]

Katona attracts conflicting media attention. Locked into a vicious and

13. *Kerry Katona: Crazy in Love* (MTV, 2008); *Kerry Katona: Whole Again* (MTV, 2009); *Kerry Katona: What's the Problem?* (MTV, 2010). Television series.
14. *Kerry Katona: What's the Problem?*
15. Ibid.

contradictory bond with the British tabloid and celebrity media, she is hailed as a survivor, but most pervasively as "Crazy Kerry." The British media consistently represent her as a "car-crash" celebrity: a lower-class, disorderly, physically uncontained and morally bankrupt substance addict with a complex array of psychological defects.

Katona's mental health was brought to the very center of her media profile when in 2008 on an ITV daytime show, *This Morning*, she appeared to be drunk during an interview designed to promote her comeback MTV reality show, *Whole Again?* Katona already had a reputation for alcoholism and drug use and had been through a very public stay in a rehabilitation clinic. *This Morning* presenter, Philip Schofield, asked her if she was abusing drink or drugs again, asserting that concerned viewers were contacting the show to ask what was wrong with her as she performed live on air. Katona explained at the time that she was experiencing side-effects of chlorpromazine — an antipsychotic drug used to treat bipolar disorder — that made her slur her words. Katona's PR team issued explanatory press releases and set up tabloid interviews and another *This Morning* interview to counteract negative press about "mad Kerry."

What's the Problem? is Katona's most direct attempt to construct a media role around her mental health by directly intervening in her negative tabloid construction. In one of the establishing statements in the show, Katona's husband, Mark Croft, asserts, "[Kerry's] got her confidence back, the body's back, but she's still nuts. She's on new medication [and] doesn't do any of that slurring anymore" (MTV 2010). In the MTV reality format, the ostensibly therapeutic process involves candid biographical revelation, interpersonal confrontation and emotional upheaval; the show's "big reveal" promises personal psychological transformation, as well as renewed celebrity status and cultural value.

Narratives of mental illness are profuse in contemporary popular culture from psychologized reality television shows such as *Big Brother,* and confessional and chat TV, to weblogs and documentaries. Similarly, celebrity autobiographical products are self-reflexive texts predicated on a perceived need to continually remake the self within popular culture. As Su Holmes and Sean Redmond observe, tabloids, celebrity autobiographies, and gossip magazines "would now seem strangely empty without celebrity disclosures ranging from the horrors of plastic surgery to eating disorders, and drug and alcohol abuse, not to mention 'confessions' about depression." But as they point out, "to observe this is not to trivialize the experience of any of these matters (whether associated with celebrities or not) but only to point out their increasing conventionalization within celebrity discourse."[16] It is the gendered structures of this popular discourse of mental ill health by which female celebrities such as Katona have to construct their media selves,

---

16. Su Holmes and Sean Redmond (eds), *Framing Celebrity* (London: Routledge, 2006), 289.

appealing to culturally acceptable gender roles as indicators of mental illness and mental health.

Moreover, the use of reality media to articulate mental distress brings ethical issues about the representation of mental health into sharp focus. The relationship between reality and tabloid media raises important questions about the motivations of, and consequences for, the people they depict, as well as an increasingly fascinated — and potentially empathic — audience. Given the extent to which mental health has become an urgently topical issue in contemporary society more generally, media images help to shape public attitudes toward, and knowledge about, mental illness. Many studies have established that most people in the West receive their basic information about mental health from the mass media. As reality media allege to portray individuals that audiences can identify with, the opportunity to positively represent mental distress becomes both timely and potentially lucrative.

Harper points out that we should examine "positive" representations of mental distress and recovery in the media because they can be vehicles for consumer capitalist ideologies in that they emphasize personal, but not social, disorders. In doing so, they simultaneously exert problematic discourses about gender, class, and race.[17] At the same time, we should not dismiss the positive and consolatory role that celebrities can play in stigma reduction by offering intimate, potentially empathic, and edifying representations of mental health survival and recovery. Through reality media, the representation of mental illness in popular culture may shift from predominantly negative and stigmatizing images to more socially inclusive first-person representations. As Harper notes, scandals about celebrities' mental health may function by "reassuring audiences that, far from being a barrier, mental distress may in some sense constitute a rite of passage leading, ultimately, to social and/or professional success."[18] However, there is a strong case to be made that the new images of mental illness are no more helpful or "realistic" in that they repackage personal problems as entertaining spectacles.

Harper's work emphasizes the importance of paying very close attention to the social and media contexts through which popular media images of mental distress are produced. In terms of famous women's revelations of mental distress, it is therefore imperative to contextualize them within post-feminist culture and the emergence of reality media and celebrity culture.

Reality media forms trade on provoking the compulsory emotionality, confrontation, and apparent personality transformation that comprise contemporary celebrity culture. Foundational reality shows such as *Big Brother*, for example, construct personalities through formulaic narratives

17. Stephen Harper, *Madness, Power and the Media: Class, Gender and Race in Media Representations of Mental Distress* (Basingstoke: Palgrave, 2009).
18. Stephen Harper, "Madly Famous," 314.

and quasi-scientific psychological observation. Removed from their every-day lives, the subjects often exhibit extreme behavior, which is prompted by bizarre tests and trials. Simultaneously, emotional and interpersonal problems are dramatically exacerbated by confrontational production strat-egies, then seemingly resolved by the program's compulsory intimacy and psychologized format. In the UK, reality TV shows such as Channel 4's *House of Obsessive Compulsives* (2005) and drug detox series *Going Cold Turkey*, and the BBC's *Teenage Tourette's Camp* (2005) firmly moved the issue of mental illness away from the traditionally earnest documentary and repackaged it within the scandalized genre of reality television — often condemned for its willingness to stimulate the public's appetite for spectacles of perceived difference. Competitive reality shows such as ITV's *I'm a Celebrity: Get Me Out of Here!* (2002-pres) use extended periods of surveillance in isolated locations in the hope that celebrity personas will dissipate, allowing "real" personalities to emerge. Yet such shows simultaneously endorse the idea that participation in documentary and reality media is a "therapeutic encounter," a valid socio-psychological experiment and positive public intervention. In reality television, for example, the participant's inner lives are central to the generic formula that alleges "the restoration of psychic health for speakers, studio and home audiences."[19]

As Jon Dovey points out, reality media and confessional television can exploit its subjects as "freaks,"[20] and this was certainly a liberal press response to the tabloid media's treatment of Katona's mental health scandals. As Julia Raeside put it: "[W]e've all read the [broadsheet] opinion columns likening reality TV to the open-house policy at Bedlam hospital in the darker days of British psychiatric care. But Katona's interview [on *This Morning*] was the closet I've ever come to peering through the bars and staring at a howling unfortunate who is unable to shut the curtains and hide."[21]

While celebrity interviews and reality media appearances can be edited and misappropriated, the autobiographical product is more controllable. Furthermore, there is a clear market for these products. In the UK, celebrity memoirs of mental ill health are a regular product line for publishers such as Ebury Press and Hodder & Stoughton. They are categorized in bookstores under "mind-body-spirit" and "self-help" sections, as well as "autobiography." In terms of categorization, they overlap with "misery-lit," as well as "true-life" first-person accounts of trauma and survival by everyday people.

Spice Girl Geri Halliwell's autobiographical products expose the ways in which female celebrity becomes pathologized through correlative dis-courses of femininity and mental ill health. Simultaneously, they chart the

19. Jon Dovey, *Freakshow: First Person Media and Factual Television* (New York: Pluto Press, 2000) 109.
20. Ibid.
21. Julia Raeside, "Kerry Katona's *This Morning* Appearance was a New TV Low," *Guardian TV and Radio Blog*, October 22, 2008.

postfeminist backlash against "Girl Power" and pop-feminism. In this regard, it is problematic that the un-conforming female is defined as a "girl" in the pejorative sense of being diminutive and immature. Yet "girl" is also being used to convey a sexualized precociousness, a provocative, Lolita-like sensibility.

"Girl Power" was primarily aimed at adolescents, but the "bad girl" stereotype is all-pervasive, and even participants in female political and cultural movements can unhelpfully self-identify as "girls." Whereas "Riot Grrrl" framed feminism as defiance against social power through an essentially female strength, "Girl Power" offered a playful individualism, confrontational attitude, and material success. Halliwell — "Ginger Spice" — was "serious about 'Girl Power'" and felt that the band was "on a mission to save girls and lift their self-esteem."[22] "Girl Power" also espoused sexual forthrightness and "girls on top" hedonism, which often took the form of sexualized exhibitionism. In this way, Halliwell enjoyed media affection for provocative behavior; in 1996, for example, at the height of Spice-mania, soft-core photos of Halliwell emerged and were republished in *Teazer* porn magazine. Rather than threatening her career, the photos played into and were recuperable by sexualized "Girl Power" rhetoric. In fact, Halliwell went on to pose for *Playboy* in May 1998 in her Ginger Spice costume.

By the late 1990s, Ginger Spice became derided for her seeming brashness. As the Spice Girls' teenage fan base matured, the group's mischievousness came to look like clichéd adolescent rebellion and their cultural value diminished. Halliwell left the Spice Girls in 1998, effectively ending the band altogether, and immediately produced *If Only*,[23] her first autobiography. The book narrates her early life, her "wannabe" desire for fame, and her decision to leave the band.

Although they are produced in reaction to a relentlessly prying media, autobiographical products are an almost uniquely controllable means of trying to reconstruct a media persona. While press and media interviews afford opportunities for emotional intimacy and self-expression, they can be undermined by the dialogical nature of their form and the complex media contexts in which they are positioned. The monologue format of the memoir, however, can be more controlled and a substantive vehicle for intimacy and disclosure, for disputing or creating media scandals, and for asserting authenticity.

Halliwell immediately began to talk about mental health in her post–Spice Girls autobiographical work, for example in a video diary and Molly Dineen's 1999 candid television documentary, *Geri*.[24] Halliwell explains her motivation for making the film as an attempt at a process of personal discovery and self-making through media reflection: an effort "to understand me and what

---

22. Geri Halliwell, *Just for the Record* (London: Ebury, 2002), 93.
23. Geri Halliwell, *If Only* (London: Bantam Books, 1999).
24. *Geri*. Directed by Molly Dineen. RTO Pictures, UK, 1999.

happened to me."[25] Yet using the media to find a sense of self is extremely risky, and the film profitably depicted Halliwell as a newly vulnerable persona: "I probably revealed more than I should about my loneliness and low self-esteem, but I was feeling lost [and] looked to the film for help." She used the film to "work through" her depression and identity confusion "very publicly and very loudly."[26] She seems to have been acutely aware of the popularity this new kind of openness and narrative uncertainty would attract in a burgeoning culture of obligatory self-examination.

As key texts in a growing market for celebrity reality and life products, Halliwell's late 1990s book and films offered the compulsory and candid authenticity and intimacy that Littler describes as fundamental to contemporary celebrity media. As Halliwell put it:

> People [now] want aspirational figures who are also accessible. Even during the making of [*Geri*], I realized that I couldn't give people a one-dimensional character any more because that's not what they wanted. The public want to see you, feel you, and touch you enough to know that you are real. That's exactly what they got!"[27]

Geri enjoyed huge ratings, and viewers were mostly sympathetic to the "real woman" behind the cartoonish Spice Girl façade. As she explained: "people realized that I was a real person with real feelings who gets lonely and unhappy just like they do."[28]

Halliwell attempted to rebrand herself by replacing "Ginger Spice" with "Geri Halliwell," and this clearly involved a pathologizing of "Girl Power." Along with an un-ironically titled first single *Look at Me* and album *Schizophonic*, Halliwell's second autobiography, *Just for the Record*, dealt more overtly with her ongoing struggle with mental illness.[29] In the book, Halliwell apologizes for her wild behavior, claiming that "Girl Power" was a displacement of depression because: "you don't have to think, you don't have to deal with being a human being." Being in the band and being a celebrity "was perfect for a vulnerable young woman who didn't want to feel anything."[30] She rejects pop-feminism and laddishness as symptoms of mental instability and self-alienation. She wanted to drop "Ginger" and become "Geri" in both the media and in her sense of self. Both acts of transformation became focused on pathologizing "Girl Power" pop-feminism.

As a Spice Girl, Halliwell had sometimes been dubbed "Podge [chubby] Spice" in the media, and *Just* promoted her dramatic physical makeover. Yet

---

25. Geri Halliwell, *If Only*, 105.
26. Ibid.
27. Ibid
28. Ibid., 126.
29. Halliwell, *Just for the Record*.
30. Ibid., 94.

Figure 9.1   **Body-as-self on the front cover of Geri Halliwell's autobiography, *Just for the Record* (2002).**

Halliwell's transformation was the subject of tabloid scandals that potentially jeopardized her solo career. In *Just* she confronted this by affirming that she had suffered from anorexia and bulimia since adolescence, and that her eating disorders intensified after she joined the Spice Girls. Over 50 percent of the book comprises pictures of the newly (and extremely) thin Halliwell and are framed as evidence of her new psychological stability and authenticity. After leaving the group, she claims, she was able to gain control of her body and cure her depression through yoga. She released "mind-body-spirit" yoga DVDs, which remain one of her most lucrative products. The products exploited tabloid speculation about how everyday women could "get Geri's body." However, tabloid speculations about her radically thin body soon recuperated her attempts at agency by trading on gossipy revelations of anorexia and bulimia.

While Halliwell used her makeover products to assert her recovery from eating disorders, they also showcased a modishly size-zero — and therefore potentially very unhealthy — female body ideal. Media reporting of her makeover sought out signs of the unruly and fame-hungry female body, constructing the celebrity body as both pathologically and essentially remarkable. In the media, Halliwell's body became an immediately available signifier of her perceived stability and, therefore, prompted gossip stories about an eating disorder. Any and all changes in her body — perceived, or real — were (as is the case for all contemporary female celebrities) central preoccupations in media discourse when it came to interpreting her emotional well-being and value.

By the early 2000s, the dramatic makeovers of other ex-Spice Girls also attracted accusations of mental illness and eating disorders. Victoria Beckham — Posh Spice — endures vigorous speculation about her own dramatic weight loss, low weight, and general physical appearance. Tabloid coverage of her miraculous "recovery from pregnancy" scrutinized the female celebrity body for signs of post-partum ugliness, sexual unavailability, undesirability and mental and emotional instability. In her 2001 autobiography, *Learning to Fly*,[31] Beckham revealed that she too had suffered from anorexia as a psychopathological reaction to fame. As *Learning* was published, Beckham was trying to launch a solo career with the perhaps unfortunately titled single *Out of My Mind*. According to her publisher, Michael Joseph Limited, the book was an attempt to "set the record straight on the controversies that surround her especially regarding her new appearance." Beckham revealed that she had suffered from anorexia and binge eating caused by capitulating to the "pressures of [the Spice Girls'] management team to lose weight."[32] Despite the media speculation about her extremely thin post–Spice Girls body, Beckham's publicity team asserted that she had recovered from her eating disorder and was, like Halliwell, "sanely thin." Melanie Chisholm — "Sporty Spice" — also revealed that she had suffered from anorexia and bulimia during her pop career. Through autobiographies and documentaries, "Girl Power" was being reconstructed as mentally and physically disempowering.

Female celebrities who confess to eating disorders can be accused of being negative role models that other girls or women may seek to emulate. Yet male celebrities can be applauded for facing up to the stigma which men with eating disorders may suffer, precisely because of the assumption that the disorder is "feminine." As an example of this gendering of mental distress, it is worth noting the ways in which John Prescott, ex-New Labour Deputy Prime Minister, used his 2009 autobiography *Prezza* to admit to his own long battle with bulimia nervosa.[33] Psychiatrist Dr. Ty Glover, for example, applauded Prescott's "bravery" in confessing to an ostensibly girlish madness, adding "for a high profile male politician approaching 70 it is especially impressive."[34] Prescott explained his illness in terms of the stresses of public office, but due to his political unpopularity, it was reported in the media as an immoderately "feminine" obsession — "feminine" overindulgence underscoring the perceived irrationality of his political decisions, and thus proving him "unfit" for public office.

This notion of "fitness" and mental stability similarly influences female celebrities' attempts to forge more socially constructive and politicized roles for themselves. Halliwell, for example, works as a UN Ambassador for women's health and for breast cancer awareness charities, yet her role is undermined by cynicism about her sincerity and motivations. In a *Guardian* newspaper article entitled "We're all for Girl Power, we just don't want this

---

31. Victoria Beckham, *Learning to Fly* (London: Michael Joseph, 2001).
32. "Posh Admits Eating Disorder," BBC News, September 2, 2001, Entertainment section.
33. John Prescott with Hunter Davies, *Prezza: My Story: Pulling No Punches* (London: Headline Review, 2008).
34. Collin Brown, "Prescott Confesses to Battle with Eating Disorder," *The Independent*, April 21, 2008.

girl to have any," feminist commentator Marina Hyde acerbically assesses Halliwell's celebrity charity work:

> Pay attention, apocalypse-forecasters: Geri Halliwell has held talks in Washington in her role as UN ambassador [and] one of these Washington power players describes Geri as "a shining example of how one woman can make a difference for the health and dignity of women everywhere." Um . . . is it OK to say, "Not in my name"?[35]

Hyde's comment is predicated on the assumption that it is acceptable for Halliwell to comment on "private" feminine matters, but not on "public" masculine spheres.

TV presenter Gail Porter is another post-pop-feminist celebrity who uses her autobiographical work and life products to ostensibly provide some form of public service. Porter was the pin-up of the "lad" and "ladette" cultures that appeared simultaneous with the rise of "Girl Power" in Britain. In the reappraisal of gender roles inherent in 1990s British culture, "laddism" was framed as a rejection of the emotionally open "new man" which involved rebelling against social "feminization" and "emasculation." "Laddism" reclaimed an ostensibly essential, unreconstructed masculinity to compete with the new "Power Girls." It found expression not so much through specific celebrities but through male-oriented magazines such as *FHM*, *GQ*, and *Loaded*, which trade on soft-pornography representations and broad themes of male willful immaturity and compulsory hedonism. First coined in 1995 by advertising agency Collett Dickenson, the term "ladette" referred to a growing market of young women and female celebrities engaged in traditionally male-oriented activities including drinking and sport. Ladettism was postfeminist in that it was predicated on assertions about female power constructed through rhetoric, practices and imagery that affirmed the self-determination, supremacy, and cultural dominance attributed "masculine" subject positions and male-oriented cultural forms.

Gail Porter was an essential figure in both the "lad" and "ladette" scenes, being a female and a pin-up of lads' magazines. She was feted for her supposed hedonism and sexual promiscuity in media scandals that appealed to both male and female "lads." Increasingly represented as a wild-child sex symbol, Porter's notoriety came into conflict with her media role as a wholesome children's television presenter and she rebranded herself within adult popular media and became established as a celebrity in her own right.

Yet ladettism always involved a kind of hyper-femininity aimed at soliciting the male gaze through direct participation in lad culture. Ladettes supplemented their ostensibly laddish hedonism by assuming a sexually provocative

---

35. Marina Hyde. "We're All for Girl Power — We Just Don't Want This Girl to Have Any," *The Guardian*, April 4, 2008, 12.

position in compliance with the sexual and gender dynamics of lad culture. Ladettes legitimized the sexism inherent in lad culture by taking an active role in the sexual objectification of women through what they saw as an ironic and playful self-reflexivity about sexual power. The women frequently posed nude in lads' magazines, asserting that participating in mass-media soft-pornography is an empowering exploitation of male sexuality and an expression of female sexual power. Porter, for example, attracted scandal by appearing naked in soft-core shoots for *FHM, GQ,* and *Loaded* around the time that Halliwell's nude photos appeared in *Teazer* and *Playboy.* Lads' magazines were keen to exploit this new kind of quasi-feminist, sexually compliant pin-up. For example, in May 1999, naked photographs of Porter were projected onto the Houses of Parliament as a marketing stunt for *FHM* magazine, which Porter claimed to know nothing about. Porter is now at pains to distance herself from "ladette" culture and assert what she understands to be her "feminine" self:

> We were all called "ladettes." [After] the Spice Girls and "Girl Power" in the mid-90s there's been all this stuff about "sisters doin' it for themselves," challenging men at their own game [but] I've never had the slightest inclination to be a man or, rather, a lad.[36]

Yet Porter's career and positive media image came to an abrupt halt in 2005 due to a mental breakdown that was initially made visible by her sudden hair loss. After a much reported suicide attempt, "Ladette-Gail" became known as "Mad-Gail" and became a target for aggressive mockery in the tabloid media. After a period of recovery, she was approached in 2006 by Ebury to write an autobiography to counteract negative press about her mental illness. The title of the book, *Laid Bare,* plays on her previous soft-porn shoots for lads' magazines, as well as her candid attitude to her life story and mental ill health. In the book, Porter describes being a ladette in terms of a lack of self and loss of agency that became defining symptoms of her mental illness. Like Halliwell, she claims she was acting out and playing a role cultivated through, and encouraged by, the media. Porter clearly understands that she is in a battle with the popular media over her persona and her cultural value, stating in the book that that she would not have agreed to write it, nor make documentaries, had stories about her mental health not prompted media derision in the first place.

Porter now mostly appears publicly in contexts that focus on mental health. In a high-profile 2006 BBC documentary *One Life: Gail Porter Laid Bare,* she talks about living with bipolar illness and alopecia to reassure sufferers and to educate the public about these conditions. Attitudes to alopecia are, of course, highly gendered, and one can compare Porter's

---

36. Gail Porter, *Laid Bare: My Story of Love, Fame, and Survival* (London: Ebury, 2007), 150.

public appearance with media reactions to Britney Spears shaving off her hair in 2007 (which was read as a sign of her mental instability). Yet Porter has asserted that, not only does she feel that she should not have to conform to idealized images of femininity, but that doing so can be disempowering. Her decision to appear in public without hair is framed as a post-pop, more maturely feminist act. Now that she is no longer seen as conventionally attractive, she is liberated to do "serious" work:

> With big eyes and blonde hair I was going to get fluffy jobs. [Then] your hair falls out and you get invited to go to Cambodia to do a documentary on inter-country adoption. [I'm] . . . probably going to have a longer career now than I might have — because how long can you be blonde and pretty for? I keep seeing in the papers, "Oh, poor Gail's gone mad!" Everyone wants to feel sorry for you, but I'm fine, I'm great.[37]

Thus, Porter's transition to heroic survivor stages a sense of renewed cultural and personal value as well as purpose. She shuns the "heroic survivor" label, yet exerts an ambiguous kind of agency by encouraging media interest in her mental ill health: "I refuse to be called brave or a victim. I urged charities to capitalize on my novelty value."[38]

Like Halliwell, Porter regularly appears in public to raise awareness of mental illness, global poverty, and women's health. Porter's autobiographies are sold in the "social and health issues" and "mental heath" sections of online booksellers such as Amazon.co.uk, and her documentaries about bipolar disorder and stress-alopecia are presented as serious attempts to edify the viewer and reduce mental health stigma. Like Halliwell, she shares her life story as a positive intervention in the public sphere whereby she might use her celebrity notoriety to speak openly about mental illness and to reach out to other people — especially women. She sees her role as de-stigmatizing mental ill health, and is attractive to organizations that are "keen to garner celebrity support as they raise news profile of an issue and engender affective identifications."[39]

Nonetheless, Porter's apparent altruism is routinely undermined and pathologized by the media as the desperate fame seeking of another burnt-out pop-feminist. When she made a candid documentary about her mental illness, tabloids such as the *Daily Mail* suggested that she was paying the price for her "unfeminine" misbehavior, going so far as to ask, "did she deserve it?"[40] Even more liberal broadsheet commentary undermined her assertions of autonomy because of assumptions about her inauthenticity

---

37. Gail Porter, quoted in Phil Hogan, "The Interview: Gail Porter," *The Observer: Review*, September 9, 2007, 14.
38. Ibid.
39. Jo Littler, "Making Fame Ordinary," 17.
40. Porter, quoted in Phil Hogan, "The Interview," 14.

due to her mental ill health. Appearing without her hair was reframed as a tragically defiant refusal to recover, because recovery would effectively end her newfound career as a celebrity expert on mental health survival. In this way, public knowledge about her mental illnesses challenges her attempts to assert agency. In an indicative interview with Porter in the broadsheet newspaper *The Observer*, psychologist Phil Hogan adopts a negatively analytical stance that is surreptitiously shared with the reader through his "expert" readings of her body language: "I ask [Porter] whether she would have written [*Laid Bare*] if she'd still had her hair. 'No' she says, twiddling with one of her false eyelashes which has become unhinged."[41] The fake, synthetic hair that has "become unhinged" signals to Hogan that Porter's decision to go public is an unhealthy psychopathology only vaguely concealed by her bright forthrightness. He pathologizes her willingness to speak about mental illness in the public sphere and to be seen with no hair, but he does not share this (potentially helpful) analytical information with Porter herself. Such media commentaries betray an urge to devalue the credibility of the female celebrity by approaching her assertions with a condescending skepticism. Needless to say, this stance does not reflect critically on attitudes toward women's mental illness, nor the postfeminist culture, which shapes this apparently marketable yet devalued subject position for female celebrities.

The interdependency of Porter's physical attractiveness and her media credibility represents the kind of deeply problematic construct that continues to subjugate female celebrities, including other post-pop-feminists. By the late 1990s, pop-feminism became synonymous with the idea that liberated, independent, and progressive, females participate in, consume and exploit sexual products. Young wannabes like Katona, who cut their teeth on "Girl Power," were embracing its message of liberation and empowerment through notoriety and provocation. Selling the female body became not a barrier to, but a quasi-feminist vehicle for fame. In the 1990s, at aged 16, Katona paid for her own soft-pornography portfolio for the "Page Three" topless pin-up section of tabloid newspaper, *The Sun*. She wanted the photos to start a career, not in pornography but in mainstream popular culture. As bodies are valuable commodities in consumer capitalist culture, soft-porn can be seen to offer a "feminist" means of transcending poverty and fame-lessness. As Ariel Levy explains, the mainstreaming of pornography engenders the rise of "raunch culture" — a kind of female misogyny whereby women attempt to achieve parity with men by sexually objectifying themselves, as well as other women. In "raunch culture," the "artificial schism reinvents itself: the Good Girls who exhibit fear and repulsion [and] the Bad Girls who get a kick out of being politically out of line."[42]

---

41. Hogan, 14.
42. Ariel Levy, *Female Chauvinist Pigs: Women and the Rise of Raunch Culture* (New York: Free Press, 2005), 115

Likewise, pop-feminist ideals of sexual freedom and pleasure seeking have been quickly recuperated by a postfeminist culture in which participation in the sex industry is a lucrative, acceptable career choice. Katona started working as a lap dancer until being discovered by music band The Porn Kings who were looking for dancers to accompany them on tour. Sex work was seen as no barrier to mainstream success or acceptability. She was then approached by producer Andy McCluskey to be in a new "Girl Power" band called Atomic Kitten — the band's name playing on images of empowered and volatile "sex-kittens." The Kittens imitated their big-sister power girls and were "sold as the new-Spice Girls."[43]

Yet during her time in the Kittens, Katona was widely represented as "white trash." She has always been associated with notions of lower-class intemperance, and went on to be dubbed by the tabloids as a "Bingeing Hellcat" and "Drunken Slapper [slut]."[44] She quickly became a scapegoat for a moral panic in Britain surrounding drinking and its impact on young women. With striking similarity to Halliwell, Katona is now at pains to state that joining the band was an attempt to avoid the reality of her deteriorating mental state: "Being one of the Kittens was like acting [so] I wasn't being myself."[45] She explains her behavior as nascent bipolar disorder brought about by childhood abuse and the pressures of fame. Katona felt she had recovered by leaving the Kittens and devoting herself to motherhood and family life.

Katona returned to the screen in the early 2000s to co-present ITV's daytime celebrity magazine show called *Loose Women* which plays lightly on notions of "bad girl" promiscuity and candid, gossipy "loose talk."[46] She also appeared as both judge and contestant on talent-contest reality shows *You're a Star* and *Stars in Their Eyes*.[47] Her real comeback came in 2004, when she won the public vote on the reality show *I'm a Celebrity, Get Me out of Here!*,[48] being crowned in the media as "Queen of the Jungle." Yet tabloid stories about drug addiction quickly re-focused media attention on her as an at-risk and unfit mother. She soon checked into "rehab" at the London Priory clinic where innumerable celebrities in Britain go for private treatment.

After this, Katona appeared as the remorseful pathological "ladette" in a Pygmalion reality show entitled *My Fair Kerry*.[49] In the show, she was subject to therapeutic behavioral correction by learning how to be "the perfect lady"

---

43. Kerry Katona, *Too Much, Too Young: My Story of Love, Survival, and Celebrity* (London: Ebury, 2006), 179
44. Matthew Acton, "Drunken Slapper: Kerry's Mum-in-law Tells all About Booze, Drugs & Violence," *News of the World*, January 6, 2008.
45. Kerry Katona, *Too Much, Too Young*, 120
46. *Loose Women* (Granada Television, 1999 – present)
47. *You're a Star* (Radio Telefís Éireann/Screentime ShinAwil, 2002–2003); *Stars in Their Eyes* (Granada Television 1990 – present)
48. *I'm a Celebrity, Get Me Out of Here!* (Granada Television, 2002 – present)
49. *My Fair Kerry* (Granada Television, 2005)

and thereby prove to the public that she could change. The show followed the format of an ongoing reality show called *Ladette to Lady*[50] that was pivotal in a broader cultural backlash against pop-feminism. In the show, predominantly working-class women are chastised, tamed, and trained in traditionally "lady-like" skills. The show's producers frame this spectacle as a quasi-public-service intervention into Britain's unruly, "ladette" female youth culture. Both shows draw on discourses of psychological therapy, moral reform and punitive behavioral correction to "cure" ostensibly un-feminine behavior.

In 2006, with her public image at an all-time low, Katona released the autobiography *Too Much, Too Young: My Story of Love, Fame, And Survival,*[51] a rags-to-riches story of brutal childhood neglect, addiction, and domestic abuse. It details the wild "excesses" of her early fame, her mental breakdown and recovery, her experience of single motherhood and her ongoing struggle with bipolar illness. In the book, she tries to exert agency over her public image by pathologizing her urge for fame, her inability to deal with fame, and presenting her wild-child persona as a symptom of bipolar illness. "Star agency" is, as David Marshall points out, increasingly reduced to such "privatized, psychologized representation of activity and transformation."[52] Accordingly, Katona's transformation involved explaining how chronic mental illness contributed to her urge for fame. And as Rebecca Williams explains, the exchange of power and privileges between celebrities and the media gives only the impression of 'star agency.'[53] So, Katona works within the limitations of the "Crazy Kerry" media construct to reframe her self and her media image as a self-controlled woman who is psychologically self-actualized and likeable, and who has matured beyond the self-harming excesses of pop-feminism.

As previously mentioned, the market for celebrity memoirs of mental illness intersects with that of an increasingly pervasive culture of psychological transformation, self-help, and makeover products. Katona's 2007 self-help book, *Survive the Worst, Aim for the Best,*[54] is also classified under the "self-help" and "mind-body-spirit" sections of bookstores, marketed as an expert guide to survival and recovery. Micki McGee persuasively argues that self-help books serve to reinforce traditional moral values and gender roles in a consumer capitalist culture in which emotional and psychological health is equated with material success: one's sense of self, and one's ability to be a successful self, is a commodity that operates according to market

50. *Ladette to Lady* (RDF Media, 2005–present)
51. Kerry Katona, *Too Much, Too Young.*
52. David Marshall, quoted in Rebecca Williams, "From Beyond Control to In Control: Investigating Drew Barrymore's Feminist Agency/Authorship," in: Su Holmes and Sean Redmond (eds), *Stardom and Celebrity: A Reader* (London: Sage, 2007), 118.
53. Williams, "From Beyond Control to in Control," 112.
54. Kerry Katona, *Survive the Worst and Aim for the Best* (London: Ebury, 2007).

forces.[55] On the gendering of self-help literature, McGee points out that the mythic narrative of the "self-made man" is juxtaposed to the tragic narrative of the "self-salvaged" woman. This gendering is also apparent in celebrity life-products in which being a self — "being somebody" — is the fundamental substance of both identity and career success. Unlike most self-help literature, these celebrity books emphasize that fame is a consolation for unhappiness and a means of measuring success, worth, and recovery. Katona wrote her self-help book in part to show that even "trash" like her can make it: "I want people to say 'If she can do it, so can I.'"[56] Paradoxically, the women's autobiographical books explain the urge for fame as pathological and the experience of being famous as exacerbating mental illness. Cynicism about the financial or careerist motivations for celebrity self-help products veils a sad irony; these women who talk about having had little or no sense of self are habitually being "ghost written" for the celebrity market. Media constructions of female celebrity may often appear more real than the women themselves.

In the final stages of transformation, the credibility of the ex-"bad girl" depends on her accessing an ideological safe-space for rebranding and media exposure. Most often, this is achieved by promoting an image of a good, sane, mother who has successfully achieved female heterosexual normality — and therefore sanity and renewed cultural value. McGee notes how lifestyle makeover gurus, such as Oprah Winfrey, mobilize the rhetoric of maternal and domestic "female" qualities such as nurturing, support, and emotionality, to achieve material success and encourage the female consumer to self-actualize. Stars such as Madonna exploit a classic "femme fatale turned mother" archetype whose ongoing profitability now seems to depend to a large part upon embracing an essential maternalism.[57] Likewise, Katona's cultural value can be charted through the UK's Best Celebrity

Figure 9.2 **Madness and motherhood in brand imagery for MTV UK's 2008 docusoap, Kerry Katona: Crazy in Love.**

---

55. Micki McGee, *Self-Help Inc.: Makeover Culture in American Life* (Oxford: Oxford University Press, 2005), passim.
56. Kerry Katona, *Survive the Worst and Aim for the Best*, 15
57. Micki McGee, *Self-Help Inc.*, 203n19

Mother polls — she won in 2002 and 2005, but was voted worst mother in 2008 when tabloids called for her to have her children removed by Social Services after another mental health scandal. Katona became a media scapegoat for moral panics about single mothers to the extent that she was voted "Most Hated Woman in Britain 2008."[58]

With the MTV show *Crazy*, Katona believed that being frank about her mental illness in the very context of her role as a mother could help her reclaim public affection. In the trailer, she tells viewers: "I'm pregnant, as you can see, very pregnant, and I'm even going to give birth on TV. So watch the show, you never know, you might even like me!"[59] But *Crazy* integrates Katona's negative personas — "bad girl," mad woman, and (un)fit mother — in brand imagery portraying Katona and husband Mark Croft bound together in matching straitjackets with the restraints pulled tight over her heavily pregnant belly. Her attempts to establish herself as a survivor were again undermined because of a perceived need to focus media attention on her mental health and fitness to mother.

Crazy also demonstrates the ways in which celebrity culture is intractably fixated on domestic intimacy and on the vacillations of the fame-hungry female body. During the show, Katona undergoes a breast reduction and liposuction to "cure" her of post-partum "deformities," having failed to reclaim her size-zero body after having four children. Rather than seeking healthfulness, or promoting diet and exercise regimes, Katona undertook a rapidly constructed reality-genre makeover to culminate in the show's "big reveal."

As they grow older, female celebrities are even more subject to reconstructed Madonna/whore archetypes. They negotiate the self-salvaging transition from "bad girl' to "good woman" by trying to break down the negative public persona through the "mad-girl" script. Increasingly, female celebrities' cultural value is predicated on an ambiguous discourse of redemption through essential maternalism. Transitioning to the more culturally valuable archetype depends on this fitness to mother or, better still, the ability to be seen to be the beautiful, healthful, and culturally domesticated "yummy mummy." This cult of maternalism offers celebrity women an opportunity to challenge negativity about their appearance and personalities, and connect with the contemporaneous life-experiences of their original female fan-base. Yet this role is extremely precarious in that women have to be seen to epitomize a particular kind of motherhood. The glamorous "yummy-mummy" reclaims her sexual and cultural value by overcoming and surviving the "deformities" such as weight gain that are culturally associated with pregnancy. She performs, and is under media pressure to perform, radical post-partum makeovers that reinforce idealized images of the female body and is rewarded with positive media attention. The "yummy-mummy"

58. Gordon Smart, "Kerry is Most Hated Woman," *The Sun: Gordon Smart's Bizarre,* July 7, 2008.
59. Trailer: *Kerry Katona: Crazy in Love* (MTV, 2008).

image mirrors the life trajectory, gender aspirations, and generational nostalgia of some of these women's fans, and is marketable in the kinds of television programs, magazines, and consumer products that that market consumes. Hence, perhaps, why Halliwell's next career step after the auto-biographies was to produce children's books about a character called *Eugenia Lavender*, promoted as the re-launch of "Girl Power" for the next generation. The books are marketed to original Spice Girl fans with young children in their lives. Commentators such as Hyde dismissed Halliwell's maternalism as both insincere and as contrived as "Girl Power": "Geri has totally bought into this [yummy-mummy] version of herself [and] she's about to start on your daughter with her forthcoming range of empowering children's books about a thinly disguised Geri Halliwell character."[60] Porter, also, is involved with numerous children's charities, yet is still represented as "mad Gail." These women's assertions of maternalism dissipate the perceived threat of pop-feminism by appealing to essentialist gender stereotypes. But neither the bad girl nor the good mother is acceptably authentic to the media. This is because the women are no longer in talent-based careers, but in self-selling roles that demand a personality narrative that is continually in a process of making and remaking.

In their attempts to assert agency and rebrand their media personae, the "bad girl" pop-feminists of the 1990s have not fared well. The rhetoric of pop-feminism was fated insofar as it constructed female power as a form of girlish, rebellious, and pathologically excessive identity that disappears with maturation to adulthood — in this case heterosexual maternalism. Halliwell, Porter, and Katona claim not to have been the agents of pop-feminism, stating emphatically that that person "wasn't me." As McRobbie puts it, such "utterances of forceful non-identity with feminism have consolidated into something closer to repudiation rather than ambivalence" and typify the broader "cultural space of post-feminism."[61] Theirs are stories of lost identities; the "bad girl" is newly made vulnerable and repentantly feminized. Their sense of identity confusion is framed as a symptom of latent mental problems that are only resolved by a redemptive construct of essential female maternalism. In this way, the very women who were once its pin-ups now pathologize pop-feminism. Their reality and life products in which they self-pathologize and assert redemption raise important issues about the relationship between authenticity and femininity in popular culture. To trade on the celebrity persona, the reality and gossip media demand access to, while also constructing, identities that must be somehow unstable. That is, to stay in the limelight of media celebrity women must be continually in flux and process. Mental illness and negative constructs of "bad girl" femininity afford lucratively ongoing episodes of "excessive" emotionality, drama, and psychological

---

60. Marina Hyde, "We're All for Girl Power."
61. Angela McRobbie, "Post-Feminism and Popular Culture," 257.

change. Mental illness becomes a functional element of postfeminist female celebrity culture; psychologically (re)branding runs the risk of replicating and reinforcing an already pathologized image of female celebrity.

Halliwell, Porter, and Katona have been able to partly rebrand their personalities and career trajectories via their willingness to talk about their mental ill health. Yet they have played hostage to fortune. Many other ex-bad-girl female celebrities have produced autobiographical products about mental illness to counteract bad press. For example, one-time "ladette" actress Billy Piper's *Growing Pains* (2006), reveals her struggle with eating disorders, soap opera star Danielle Westbrook's *The Other Side of Nowhere* (2006) details her battle with anorexia and the very public cocaine addiction that famously destroyed her nose, and soft-core model and celebrity Jordan/Katie Price's *Pushed to the Limit* (2008) contains revelations about post-natal depression, stress, and anxiety.[62] All of these women found fame at a very early age, were known as bad girls and/or pop-feminists, and were the subjects of innumerable scandals about drink, drugs, sex, and generally being "out of control." The cultural interest in these women depends on their being simultaneously in and out of control with regard to the circulation and contours of their public images. They speak about mental distress as an attempt to assert agency and redeem a culturally devalued pop-feminist persona, but at what cost? As they confront media derision and a postfeminist backlash, these women pay a discounted price for a "cheapened" celebrity persona, and their penitent tales of "unfeminine" sin and "feminine" regret often end up in the bookstore "bargain bin."

Bibliography

Acton, Matthew. "Drunken Slapper: Kerry's Mum- in-law Tells all about Booze, Drugs and Violence," *News of the World*, January 6, 2008. Available at: http://www.newsoftheworld. co.uk/showbiz/4691/Kerrys-mum<mom>-in-law-tells-all-about-booze-drugs-amp-violence. html (accessed November 22, 2010).

Ashby, Justine. "Postfeminism in the British Frame," *Cinema Journal* 44(2), (2005): 127–33.

Beckham, Victoria. *Learning to Fly*. London: Michael Joseph, 2001.

Brand, Russell. *My Booky Wook*. London: Hodder & Stoughton, 2009.

Brown, Collin. "Prescott Confesses to Battle with Eating Disorder," *The Independent*, April 21, 2008.

Cochrane, Kira. "Now, the Backlash," *The Guardian*, January 7, 2008, G2 6.

Coward, Rosalind. *Sacred Cows: Is Feminism Relevant to the New Millennium?* London: HarperCollins, 1999.

Diefenbach, Donald L. and Mark D. West, "Television and Attitudes Toward Mental Health Issues: Cultivation Analysis and the Third-Person Effect," *Journal of Community Psychology* 35(2), (2007): 181–95.

Douglas, Susan. "Girls 'n' Spice: All Things Nice?" *Nation* 265(6), (1997): 21–4.

Dovey, Jon. *Freakshow: First Person Media and Factual Television*. New York: Pluto Press, 2000.

Feigenbaum, Anna. "Remapping the Resonances of Riot Grrrl: Feminisms, Postfeminisms,

---

62. Billie Piper, *Growing Pains* (London: Hodder & Stoughton, 2006); Daniella Westbrook, *The Other Side of Nowhere* (London: Hodder & Stoughton, 2007); Jordan, *Pushed to the Limit* (London: Century, 2008)

and the 'Processes' of Punk," in Yvonne Tasker and Diane Negra (eds), *Interrogating Postfeminism*, Durham, NC: Duke University Press, 2007, 132–52.

Furedi, Frank. *Therapy Culture: Cultivating Vulnerability in an Uncertain Age*. London: Routledge, 2004.

Geri. Directed by Molly Dineen. RTO Pictures, UK, 1999. Television documentary.

Greer, Germaine. *The Whole Woman*. London: Doubleday, 1999.

Halliwell, Geri. *If Only*. London: Bantam Books, 1999.

——. *Just for the Record*. London: Ebury, 2002.

Hatloy, Inger. *Statistics 1: How common is mental distress?* Mind, March 2008. Available at: http://www.mind.org.uk/help/research_and_policy/statistics_1_how_common_is_ mental_distress (accessed November 22, 2010).

Hardy, Rebecca. "Sara Cox: How I went From Ladette to Lady via Binge-Drinking, Drugs, and Open Air Sex." *Daily Mail*, May 2, 2008

Harper, Heaton, Jeanne Albronda, and Nona Leigh Wilson. *Tuning in Trouble: Talk TV's Destructive Impact on Mental Health*. San Francisco, CA: Jossey-Bass, 1995.

Harper, Stephen. "Madly Famous: Narratives of Mental Illness in Celebrity Culture," in Su Holmes and Sean Redmond (eds), *Framing Celebrity: New Directions in Celebrity Culture*. London: Routledge, 2006, 311–27.

——. *Madness, Power and the Media: Class, Gender and Race in Media Representations of Mental Distress*. Basingstoke: Palgrave, 2009.

Hogan, Phil. "The Interview: Gail Porter," *The Observer: Review*, September 9, 2007.

Holmes, Su and Sean Redmond (eds). *Framing Celebrity: New Directions in Celebrity Culture*. London: Routledge, 2006.

——. *Stardom and Celebrity: a Reader*. London: Sage, 2007

Hyde, Marina. "We're all for 'Girl Power' — We Just Don't Want this Girl to Have Any," *The Guardian*, April 4, 2008, G2 12.

I'm a Celebrity, Get Me Out of Here! Granada Television, 2002 – present. Television series.

"Interview with Geri Halliwell," *Glamour*, June 2008, 12.

Jordan. *Pushed to the Limit*. London: Century, 2008.

Katona, Kerry. *Too Much, Too Young: My Story of Love, Survival, and Celebrity*. London: Ebury, 2006.

——. *Survive the Worst and Aim for the Best*. London: Ebury, 2007.

Kerry Katona: Crazy in Love. MTV, 2008. Television series.

Kerry Katona: Whole Again. MTV, 2009. Television series.

Kerry Katona: What's the Problem? MTV, 2010. Television series. View online at: http://www.mtv. co.uk/artists/kerry-katona/news/120376-watch-mtv-kerry-katona-show.

Kirkland, Ewan. "The Politics of Powerpuff: Putting the 'Girl' into 'Girl Power,'" *Animation* 5, (2010): 9–24.

Ladette to Lady. RDF Media, UK, 2005–present. Television series.

Levy, Ariel. *Female Chauvinist Pigs: Women and the Rise of Raunch Culture*. New York: Free Press, 2005.

Littler, Jo. "Making Fame Ordinary: Intimacy, Reflexivity, and Keeping it Real," *Mediactive* 2, (2004): 8–25.

Loose Women. Granada Television, 2005 – present. Television series.

Lumby, Catharine. *Bad Girls: The Media, Sex, and Feminism in the 1990s*. London: Allen & Unwin, 1997.

McGee, Micki. *Self-Help, Inc.: Makeover Culture in American Life*. Oxford: Oxford University Press, 2005.

McRobbie, Angela. "Post-Feminism and Popular Culture," *Feminist Media Studies* 4(3), 2004: 255–64.

Moorehead, Joanna. "Girl Power Comes of Age," *The Guardian*, October 24, 2007, G2 14.

Murray, C. J. L. and A. D. Lopez (eds). *The Global Burden of Disease: A Comprehensive Assessment of Mortality and Disability for Diseases, Injuries, and Risk Factors in 1990 and Projected to 2020*. Cambridge, MA: Harvard School of Public Health, 1996.

My Fair Kerry. Granada Television, 2005. Television series.

Negra, Diane and Yvonne Tasker. *Interrogating Postfeminism: Gender and the Politics of Popular Culture*. Durham, NC: Duke University Press, 2007.

One Life: Gail Porter Laid Bare [Part of the BBC's ONE Life documentary strand]. Directed by Hannah Berryman. Maverick Television, 2006. Television documentary.

Philo, Greg (ed.). *Media and Mental Distress.* London: Longman, 1996.

Piper, Billie. *Growing Pains.* London: Hodder & Stoughton, 2006.

Porter, Gail. *Laid Bare: My Story of Love, Fame, and Survival.* London: Ebury, 2007.

"Posh Admits Eating Disorder," BBC News, September 2, 2001, Entertainment section. Available at: http://news.bbc.co.uk/2/hi/entertainment/1521479.stm (accessed November 15, 2010).

"Posh Admits Weight Worries," BBC News, January 28, 2000, Entertainment section. Available at: http://news.bbc.co.uk/2/hi/entertainment/621944.stm (accessed November 15, 2010).

"Posh Denies 'Anorexia' Claims," BBC News, December 1, 1999, Entertainment section. Available at: http://news.bbc.co.uk/2/hi/entertainment/544766.stm (accessed November 15, 2010).

Prescott, John with Hunter Davies. *Prezza: My Story: Pulling No Punches.* London: Headline Review, 2008.

Raeside, Julia. "Kerry Katona's *This Morning* Appearance was a New TV Low," *Guardian TV and Radio Blog,* October 22, 2008. Available at: http://www.guardian.co.uk/culture/tvandradioblog/2008/oct/22/kerry-katona-this-morning (accessed November 15, 2010).

Smart, Gordon. "Kerry is Most Hated Woman," *The Sun: Gordon Smart's Bizarre,* July 7, 2008. Available at: http://www.thesun.co.uk/sol/homepage/showbiz/bizarre/1258854/Kerry-Katona-most-hated-by-women.html (accessed November 22 2010).

Stars in Their Eyes. Granada Television, 1990 – present. Television series.

Stewart, George. *Men's Mental Health,* Mind, updated by Rachael Twomey, 2007 [February 2000]. Available at: http://www.mind.org.uk/help/people_groups_and_communities/mens_mental_health (accessed November 22, 2010).

Wahl, Otto. *Media Madness.* New Brunswick, NJ: Rutgers University Press, 1995.

Westbrook, Daniella. *The Other Side of Nowhere.* London: Hodder & Stoughton, 2007.

World Health Organization (WHO). *International Report on Mental Health 1997.* Available at http://www.who.int/whr/2007/en/index.html (accessed April 14, 2010).

Williams, Rebecca. "From Beyond Control to in Control: Investigating Drew Barrymore's Feminist Agency/Authorship," in Su Holmes and Sean Redmond (eds), *Stardom and Celebrity: A Reader.* London: Sage, 2007, 111–25.

You're a Star. Radio Telefís Éireann/Screentime ShinAwil, 2002–2003. Television series.

Diane Negra and Yvonne Tasker, *Interrogating Postfeminism: Gender and the Politics of Popular Culture* (Durham, NC: Duke University Press, 2007).

10

The Horror of Something to See
Celebrity "Vaginas" as Prostheses

MARGARET SCHWARTZ

THE WORD "VAGINA" (and its sassy cousin, "vajayjay") has so penetrated popular discourse in the twenty-first century that it is hard to remember it was once viewed as either coldly clinical or uncomfortably explicit. The shock value of a title like *The Vagina Monologues* has almost evaporated, as a contemporary theater-goer might well expect to see a light farce rather than a feminist manifesto. To say "vagina" these days is to mark oneself as hip and modern but certainly not — perhaps even *particularly* not — a feminist in the politicized sense of the term. It is, as Sarah East of the online *Popcrunch Show* quips, "commonplace in the forty-something soccer mom's vocabulary."[1]

"Vagina" emerged as a postfeminist buzzword in part thanks to the 2007 "flashing" fad among young female celebrities in Hollywood. In that year, Paris Hilton, Lindsay Lohan, Kim Stewart, Kim Kardashian, and Britney Spears were all photographed without their underwear. These seemingly accidental exhibitions happened when the women, exiting cars or climbing stairs in short skirts, gave the paparazzi a brief but clear shot of their naked privates. The most infamous (and thus the most valuable monetarily) of all these images shows Britney Spears — whose career as a pop star had only recently been eclipsed by her role as a tabloid queen — exiting a car so that her legs and torso are exposed all the way up to the lower abdomen, where in addition to her completely hairless privates, the shiny swatch of a cesarean scar is clearly visible.

For a time in 2007–2008 it seemed like a "crotch shot" was a requisite publicity stunt for a particular subset of young female celebrities: reality TV stars, socialites and tabloid regulars. These women are mostly famous for being famous — i.e. famous for being famous for nothing, or what Jeffrey

---

1. Sarah East, Jay Bowman, and Kevin Palmer, "Year of the Vajajay," PopCrunch.com, March 19, 2009.

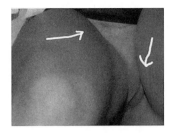

Figure 10.1   **An extreme close-up of Britney Spears' most famous crotch shot. The arrows were added by celebrity blogger Perez Hilton. (Photo sourced from WENN [World Entertainment News Network].)**

Sconce calls "meta/meta-famous."[2] Yet despite such dismissal, they can be seen as canny exploiters of an increasingly visual celebrity culture where visibility is equated with access, as expressed in so-called "celebreality" TV and in the proliferation of gossip in both print and online media.

At first, people wondered: Did these celebrities mean to go out without underwear? Didn't they realize that their skirts were too short? This shock value soon faded, however, as the perpetrators/victims mounted. The crotch shot became merely the most explicit — even literal — apotheosis of this visual celebrity culture: like paparazzi shots and reality TV, it was doubtlessly staged, but staged-as-candid, and always, it would seem, sinfully fun to watch.

Britney Spears was by far the biggest star thus photographed, so it may be tempting to assume this is the only reason that her crotch shot is so iconic. For a time in 2008–2009, you could buy a doll figurine of the crotch shot. The site, which has since disappeared, also sold figurines of Michael Jackson dangling his baby son over a balcony. The re-circulation of the Spears crotch shot here indicates that the event/image was chosen not simply because it was shocking or pornographic, but because it was also seen as iconic. Second, artist Jonathan Horowitz used the image in his 2008 piece *CBS Evening News/www.Britneycrotch.org*, which showed at MoMA PS1 from February 22 to September 14, 2009, as part of Horowitz's *And/Or* solo exhibition. The image combines the lower half of Spears' photograph with an upper-torso image of CBS News anchor Katie Couric, creating the unsettling effect that the vulva looms under Couric's anchor desk or that, conversely, Spears' vulva has grown Couric's head.[3] Though there are several Spears crotch shots, it is always this particular image — the one that shows her c-section scar — that is reappropriated in examples such as those cited above, and which comes up most frequently in online searching.

---

2. Jeffrey Sconce, "A Vacancy at the Paris Hilton," in Jonathan Gray, Cornell Sandvoss, and C. Lee Harrington (eds), *Fandom: Identities and Communities in a Mediated World* (New York: New York University Press, 2007), 331.

3. Jonathan Horowitz, CBS Evening News/www.britneycrotch.org (New York: New Museum, 2009).

While other female celebrities' crotch shots only enhanced their visibility and notoriety, the photographs of Spears were read as signs of her increasing derangement. That year, Spears would be hospitalized for mental illness and lose custody of her two small sons. Other celebrities had used the crotch shot to get exposure, with minimal negative effects. In Spears' case, however, the image was read as a sign of her instability: the tabloids dubbed her "Unfitney" and "Princess of Pop and Poon."[4] Suddenly, antiquated sexual standards were invoked: she was immodest, inappropriate, desperate, and an unfit mother.

Why did Britney Spears get such treatment when other celebrities got off with only a slap on the wrist for their "famewhoring"? Why did she arguably suffer legal consequences for her crotch shot (loss of custody of her children), while other female celebrities feared only that theirs would be ignored? Certainly, the fact that Spears is a mother changed how her body and behavior were viewed, but the increasing pressure on mothers and pregnant women to project sexiness[5] suggests that a finer boundary is being policed here.

What is at stake is not so much whether or not Spears was *too* sexy, but the fact that she (inadvertently) hinted that her body had a function beyond being sexy. Her transgression was to display her body in such a way that it undermined the hegemony of sexualized visual display. The c-section scar is the key to this undermining, because it points to the maternal functions of Spears' body. The use, or rather prosthetic *misuse*, of the word "vagina" to describe what is on display is the key to understanding the way female celebrity is kept within the strict confines of male visual pleasure.

Misrecognizing the Vagina: A Discursive Prosthesis

Why say "vagina," when, as any woman who has visited the gynecologist knows, the vagina is in fact an internal organ? You can't "flash" your vagina any more than you can flash your kidneys. In fact, the word vagina comes from the Latin word for "scabbard" or "sheath," thus underscoring its (culturally inflected) anatomical position as enclosure.

Yet the word is used *precisely* to describe and highlight these images' explicitness. Moreover, it is used to mark a certain — i.e. very mainstream — flaunting of conventional sexual mores. Women who "flash" their vaginas are at best famewhores and at worst sluts or unfit mothers; women who *use* the word "vagina," however, are bold, sassy, and liberated. They are also increasingly commonplace with the mainstreaming of postfeminism.

I suppose that the word "vulva" would appear too clinical (not to speak of

---

4. www.perezhilton.com
5. Diane Negra, *What a Girl Wants? Fantasizing the Reclamation of Self in Postfeminism* (New York and London: Routledge, 2008), 63.

"labia majora"), but such discursive tics are never accidental. They operate as sutures, stitching together moments of cultural contradiction — like, for example, that photographs of women's naked privates may circulate without being considered pornography and yet still work — as they did in the case of Britney Spears — to maintain prefeminist standards for women's sexuality.

Using "vagina" or "vajayjay" to describe what these explicit photographs reveal is what I will call a discursive *prosthesis*: a suturing, as I said, but also a kind of substitution that is structured much like a fetish, that is, as a replacement that also memorializes a loss. The nature of the prosthesis is ambiguous: as both supplement and substitute, extension and replacement, it constitutes a relation rather than a repression.[6] In this sense, the prosthesis may always be said to be supplementary, in excess, while simultaneously acting as an extension or a support.

David Wills points to this supplementarity in its embodied context: the prosthesis both replaces an absent limb and exceeds it.[7] Like Freud's fetish, which both substitutes for and forever marks the mother's fantasized castration, in the very act of replacing a missing limb, a prosthesis always points out its absence. It shows that something is missing by compensating for what is missing. Moreover, the prosthetic limb has a life of its own: it is more durable than flesh, impervious to pain and articulated, literally and figuratively, to technological and communicative structures that exceed the purely physical. Rather than a more static suture or stitch, the prosthesis is an articulation, a relation between the body and technology that because of its connective function maintains the ambiguity between the two. In other words, it represents an unresolved binary. The prosthesis thus "treats of whatever arises out of that relation [between the body and technology], and of the relation itself, of the sense and functioning of articulations between matters of two putatively distinct orders."[8]

A discursive prosthesis, then, links or articulates different orders of signif-ication. "Vagina" thus extends and supports patriarchal, prefeminist sexual roles while simultaneously substituting for strategies that a postfeminist society has since rejected. The relation out of which it arises is the contra-diction between a postfeminist cover story in which women's sexuality is no longer repressed, is in fact celebrated — and a reality wherein this sexuality may only be celebrated, or even acknowledged, when it remains within the confines of patriarchy.

Specifically, these patriarchal confines work to keep women's sexuality male-oriented by keeping it *specular*, that is, on a two-dimensional, visual scale that does not admit the inner-directed pleasure of touch. I take this for-mulation from Luce Irigaray's notions of *phallocentrism* (a phallic orientation

---

6. Craig Dworkin, "Textual Prostheses," *Comparative Literature* 57(1), (2005): 1–25.

7. David Wills, *Prosthesis* (Stanford, CA: Stanford University Press, 1995).

8. Ibid., 10.

to culture and language) and its privileging of the visual, which Irigaray calls the "scoptophilic order."[9] I explain below the relevance of Irigaray's work to show the deeply patriarchal and exploitative workings of this seemingly postfeminist term. For now, however, suffice it to say that "vagina" makes sense of the contradiction between a very-visible *something* and the patriarchal need to retain it as a certain kind of *nothing*. As long as women's bodies are kept within the realm of male visual pleasure — as long as their function is to be visually penetrated by the male gaze — then this excess of vision is tolerable. What is threatening is the suggestion that a woman's body might experience a function, pleasurable, sexual, or otherwise, that does not fit within this erotic economy.

In exposing both her privates and the scar from her c-section, Britney Spears thus showed *too much*: she showed us that her "vagina" was actually her vulva. As an indexical sign pointing to the existence of the *actual* vagina — i.e. the *birth canal*, the cesarean scar makes it obvious that the vagina is not what is on display here, but that it is somewhere under the skin. If the scar is a sign that says "Here lies Britney Spears' vagina," we are left with the uncomfortable question of what, exactly, this photograph reveals.

The reaction to Spears' crotch shot is thus a postfeminist expression of essentially conservative ideas about women's sexuality. Spears' exposed scar marks her body as maternal as well as sexual. Thus, what was taboo here was not so much explicit sexuality — in whose display postfeminism revels — but an explicit reference to the female body in a role *outside* the economy of visuality and male spectatorship that underwrites celebrity culture. According to Irigaray's theory of phallocentrism and the scoptophilic order, all crotch shots, in showing the tactile and self-touching vulva, have the potential to make this kind of reference. I argue that this is the reason why they are insistently captioned as *vaginas*, that is, as scabbards. Because Spears' c-section scar points towards her role as mother and the vagina's function as birth canal, it thus troubles the prosthetic work done by "vagina," making necessary the resort to a more obviously conservative notion such as the "unfit mother."

The scar photograph thus lays bare the prosthetic workings of the popular use of "vagina" or "vajayjay" as a substitution for more vulgar words like "twat" or "cunt." "Vajayjay" substitutes for the basely sexual, the violence of the "slit" or the bizarre zoomorphism of "beaver" or "pussy." As such, it appears to be more progressive, more pro-woman, than these derogatory terms that only work in a feminist context if they have been extensively rehabilitated.

In its apparently clinical precision, "vagina" both passes and defines borders between the pornographic and the anatomical. It is perfectly positioned, then, to work as a pop-feminist gesture — a funny, ironic, hip

---

9. Luce Irigaray, *This Sex Which Is Not One*, trans. Catherine Burke and Carolyn Porter (Ithaca, NY: Cornell University Press, 1985).

word that marks a woman's comfort with her own body AND her sense of fun about its freighted history.

In what follows I discuss Luce Irigaray's theory of phallocentrism and its visual bias (or "scoptophilic order"), in order to apply it to the popular (mis)use of "vagina" to caption these explicit images. "Vagina" only appears as prosthetic with an understanding of phallocentrism in place, because it is the particular contradiction between the extreme visual register of the crotch shots and the phallocentric investment in the *vulva* as "nothing" that appears here as a contradiction in need of prosthetic articulation. I then turn to a discussion of paparazzi culture and the intensely visual nature of modern celebrity. I end by returning to the popular use of the terms "vagina" and "vajayjay" both to caption the crotch shots and to distinguish liberated women from "tabloid trash," thus arguing for an essentially patriarchal, conservative, and misogynist character for this seemingly postfeminist term.

Luce Irigaray, Phallocentrism, and the "Scoptophilic Order"

The association of the female sex organs with emptiness has a long and well-known history in feminist critiques of psychoanalysis. I invoke this history here to give substance to my claims about the prosthetic functioning of "vagina/vajayajay" for several reasons. First, although I think the claim that "anatomy is destiny" is going a bit far, I do think that the psychoanalytic grounding in the human body provides a detailed vocabulary for describing embodied and engendered cultural formations. Here, I make use of this vocabulary to do what postfeminism — particularly in its popular circulation — has been unable to do: address issues of exploitation of the female body.[10] In the end, we are talking about pornographic images of (celebrity) female genitalia, and the ways in which such images are produced and distributed in the service of a particular kind of celebrity.

Moreover, the "captioning" of these images with the word "vagina" or "vajayjay" indicates a policing of the line between "trashy" or "slutty" and a certain kind of postfeminist liberation, playfulness, or boldness. Postfeminism seeks to deprive us of any analytical vantage point with regard to such rhetorical phenomena, excepting to limit our response to an unproblemetized "embracing of female sexuality" or pleasure. Not every kind of exhibitionism or sexualized behavior "counts" as acceptable. In other words, postfeminism cannot account for the opposite pole of this embracing of sexuality — the "trashy," trainwreck woman deemed a slut. Second-wave feminist Luce Irigaray provides an account of the logic behind this polarization, because her theory of feminine pleasure and subjectivity distinguishes meaningfully between self pleasure and pleasure for the consumption of others.

---

10. For a more detailed version of this critique, see Yvonne Tasker and Diane Negra, "Postfeminism and The Archive For the Future," *Camera Obscura* 21, (2006): 170–76.

In *This Sex Which Is Not One,* Luce Irigaray defines phallocentricism as a discursive, historical, and philosophical suppression of sexual difference. Freud and later Lacan, with whom Irigaray studied but whose work she heavily critiques — stipulate anatomical sexual difference as the foundation of subjectivity. Lacan further analyzes the development of subjectivity as an entrance into the symbolic, that is, into language.[11] For Irigaray, women's bodies and hence their subjectivities are already defined in relation to the phallus, making them strangers to their own pleasure and ventriloquists of a discourse that is not their own. That is, she accepts the Freudian emphasis on anatomy as the foundation of subjectivity, and the Lacanian development of the relationship of that subjectivity to language, but she radicalizes these concepts' application to a particularly feminine subjectivity.

For Irigaray, the suppression of sexual difference is the key to understanding phallocentrism. Thus sexual difference (here defined as having or not having a penis) is the root of human subjectivity, which in turn plays itself out in the discursive realm. As the name suggests, this suppression of difference happens via a privileging of all things phallic, starting with the famous Freudian definition of the female genitalia as lack or even "mutilation." This suppression, for Irigaray, is principally discursive. That is, language is itself the tool by which phallocentrism asserts itself.

Thus, the use of the term "vagina" or "vajayjay" in popular discourse carries the mark of phallocentrism insofar as it "captions" what is essentially an external and *dual* organ, the labia, as an internal, invisible, and *singular* organ, the vagina. To see *something* (i.e. the labia) where, in terms of a patriarchal psychology, there should be *nothing*, is what motivates the prosthetic use of "vagina." What is visible — the vulva — is an organ that has little to do with male pleasure and much to do with female pleasure and self-touching. The labia are the origin of a subjectivity whose principle logic is sensual: because the double lips are continually in contact, they provide the woman with the experience of *touching herself* without any intervention. The prosthetic links it to the invisible vagina, whose primary sexual function is to be a conduit for the phallus and its pleasure, thus restoring things to their properly phallocentric place.

Irigaray also identifies an optical logic in phallocentric discourse: the discourse of knowledge, analysis, philosophy, and reason, its principle sense is sight, its concern the visible or the invisible. Phallocentric discourse suppresses the sensual experience of the labia's touching lips: touch is not intelligible to a logic based solely on seeing or not seeing. The key psychoanalytic example of this logic is Freud's Oedipal drama, which begins with the little boy *seeing* female genitals for the first time and realizing that *something is missing.* It is this experience of knowledge and understanding

11. Jacques Lacan, *Écrits*, trans. Bruce Fink, Héloïse Fink, and Russell Grigg (New York and London: W. W. Norton and Company, 2006).

based on sight that forms his assumptions about masculine power, the fear of castration, and the taboo of incest.

This visual primacy extends to entire cultural systems of representation. In his analysis of Hoffmann's "The Sandman," Freud asserts that the fear of having one's eyes put out is linked by a logic of substitution to castration.[12] For Irigaray, "within this logic . . . [woman's] sexual organ represents *the horror of nothing to see*. A defect in this systematics of representation and desire. A 'hole' in its scoptophilic lens. It is already evident in Greek statuary that this horror of nothing to see has to be excluded, rejected, from such a scene of representation."[13] Here she is referring to statuary in which the vulva are represented as a smooth plane, undivided by what in anatomical reality are the two lips of the vulva. Thus, what Freud calls the "uncanny" quality of the female genitals stems from their understanding, within the economy of subjectivity formation established by psychoanalysis, as a "lack" or a castration. There exists no positive representation of what *is* there to see. The exclusion of the statuary closes over the "hole in the scoptophilic lens" — that is, by returning the appearance of the vulva to singularity, it is restored to a particular kind of intelligibility here understood as representability.

For Irigaray, the labia elude a visual logic of signification because their primary sense is touch — as lips, they are always touching each other. As such, they represent "the horror of nothing to see," not because they are invisible, but because they disrupt what she calls the "scoptophilic" order. Crotch shots, therefore, punch hole after hole after hole in the scoptophilic order.

A vagina, on the other hand, is simply not visible from the outside. As passage, communicating corridor, or conduit, the vagina is defined by negative space — by what it opens on to, or allows in. It upholds visual logic because as invisible, it still invokes a binary between what can and cannot be seen. Within this logic, the unseen is nonexistent or at best secondary. Touch, the primary sense of the labia for Irigaray, is disavowed because it cannot be seen, and thus cannot be visually represented. This is why the vagina is a phallocentric organ: defined as sheath or receptacle, itself properly singular and decorously out of sight, the vagina is made visible only by the probings of "scoptophilic" science: the speculum, the mirror, the pelvic exam.

When people say that Spears flashed her vagina, they are therefore participating in this disavowal, by calling the touching lips by the name of the unseen but phallic organ, the vagina. Yet what was represented in the photographs was precisely something that upsets and confounds visuality: an organ of touch, where appearance tells us very little about its function as an organ of pleasure. Thus, the use of the word "vagina" or "vajayjay" to caption the images serves in part to contain this excess of representations

12. Phillip Rieff (ed.), *Sexuality and the Psychology of Love: The Collected Papers of Sigmund Freud.* (New York: Collier Books, 1993).
13. Irigaray, *This Sex Which Is Not One*, 26.

of the unrepresentable. By calling the labia a vagina, therefore, I argue that a displacement is effected that moves the very visible *but not visually coded* labia into the sphere of invisibility, turning "the horror of nothing to see" into "there's nothing to see here."

Stars Just Like Us: The New Paparazzi

Thus, divested of its horror, the crotch shot could only emerge as a so-called "famewhoring" maneuver in today's increasingly specular celebrity culture. Paparazzi coverage and the online gossip sites that are its primary market made possible an explicit display — nay, barrage — of images of this most intimate and elusive private part, heralding its entry into discourse as "vagina" and "vajayjay."

The *Atlantic Monthly*'s April 2008 cover article, "The Britney Show: Days and Nights With the New Paparazzi,"[14] is an ethnography by journalist David Samuels documenting several days with a team of Brazilian paparazzi who work for X17, one of the largest photo agencies in Los Angeles. It was an X17 photographer who captured the now iconic images of Britney Spears shaving her head, and later attacking a car with an umbrella. X17 employs teams of photographers with cars and a variety of digital cameras to camp outside of a celebrity's house or outside a popular nightclub, waiting for shots of the hopelessly mundane or the tantalizingly shameful. While the paparazzi have always been a force in modern celebrity, the distinctive element of what Samuels calls the "new" paparazzi is that it operates in a pop culture environment in which even the most mundane shots are in demand. That is why an agency like X17 can afford to employ hundreds of photographers to take countless shots: there's a little profit in almost all of them, and tremendous profit in those that actually capture something taboo, scandalous, or secret.

A quick glance at the most popular gossip sites (dlisted.com.com, perezhilton.com, tmz.com) reveals mostly photographs of stars shopping, drinking a Starbucks, or even pumping gas — not exclusive shots from premieres or other glamorous events, nor even scandalous shots taken with telephoto of secluded vacation spots or trysts. Tabloid gossip's mainly consists of photographs of celebrities shopping or posing at red carpet events in designer clothes — while the tabloid copy supplies the narrative, largely by pitting "bad" characters against "good" ones. Of course, the shots that are the most valuable do portray some kind of scandal, like the photographs of Spears exposing her cesarean scar. The new paparazzi economy holds that a thousand shots of Spears buying frappuccinos or getting out of a limo will eventually yield one crotch shot.[15]

---

14. David Samuels, "The Britney Show: Days and Nights With the New Paparazzi," *The Atlantic Monthly* April 2008: 36–51.

15. It is interesting to note here that even the "vagina" shots of Spears carried a certain

Samuels attributes the rise of the "new" paparazzi to *Us Weekly*'s popular segment "Stars — They're Just Like US!" This segment created a new market for the Hollywood paparazzi, allowing this kind of photography to evolve "from a marginal nuisance to one of the most powerful and lucrative forces driving the American news-gathering industry."[16] The segment focuses precisely on the sorts of banal, un-fabulous activities that celebrities "like us" also engage in. An average issue might feature Jennifer Garner going to Whole Foods, or Jennifer Aniston curbing her dog. And, the segment also favors moments of everyday embarrassment: a piece of gum stuck to Paris Hilton's Juicy Couture sweats, Eva Longoria without makeup, Mischa Barton with perspiration staining her underarms. Stars: they're just like us!

Of course, the blatant falsehood of this statement helps to fuel much less playful, more spiteful commentary in other realms. Paris Hilton is obviously not "like US!" because she is extraordinarily wealthy. That makes it fair game to call her "Wonky McValtrex," as Michael K of dlisted.com does, in a reference to her reputed promiscuity (Valtrex is a herpes medication) and the fact that one of her eyes often looks a bit off-center.

The "like us" conceit also fuels the consumption of celebrities in a variety of different contexts, maintaining the long-standing notion that there is a "real" person behind the public image.[17] The crotch shot serves, then, as a kind of limit case to what "overexposure" can mean. It appears as emblematic of a culture of visibility, where the most ordinary and off-screen moments are the most coveted. Here, women are both the perpetrators and the victims, both the "attention whores" we love to hate, like Paris Hilton, and the "trainwrecks" who become the targets of more serious approbation, like Spears.

In the examples cited above, almost all are also women: online commentators snigger over cellulite and sweat stains, problems for which men are rarely called to task. During the flashing fad, public commentary even turned to such specialized topics as pubic hair grooming and the size and shape of the labia. This is objectification at its most intimately cruel, yet, much in the spirit of the new openness about pubic hair waxing ushered in a few years earlier by *Sex and the City*, the tone of the comments often suggested that this was hip, modern, liberated behavior. Nevertheless, the effect is to identify the "bad" girls and lay out for everyone else the standards of "proper" female behavior.

The feminization of being "famous for nothing" crystallizes in the

---

banality: she flashed so often and in the span of such a short time that there was nothing exclusive about most of the shots, which is what made the cesarean scar image so iconic.

16. Samuels, "The Britney Show," 38.
17. See Richard Dyer, *Heavenly Bodies: Film Stars and Society* (London: Routledge, 1986); Joshua Gamson, *Claims to Fame: Celebrity in Contemporary America* (Berkeley, CA: University of California Press, 1994); and Kevin Esch and Vicki Mayer, "How Unprofessional: the Profitable Partnership of Amateur Porn and Celebrity Culture," in Susanna Paasonen, Kaarina Nikunen, and Laura Saarenmaa (eds), *Pornification: Sex and Sexuality in Media Culture*, (Oxford: Berg, 2007): 99–111.

paparazzi expression "to give it up." A star who "gives it up" is someone who "work[s] with the paparazzi to create memorable shots."[18] This transparently sexual metaphor not only feminizes those who are photographed, but also subjects them to a prefeminist dichotomization contrasting those who "give it up" and those who don't — i.e. good girls and bad girls. There is no masculine position on the other side of the paparazzi lens — one is either a slut who lets herself be photographed, or a virgin who doesn't.

Britney Spears' story over the past several years has made her one of the most photographed and visible celebrities of our time. According to Samuels, sales of Spears photos account for a full 25 percent of X17's gross profit.[19] Her "trainwreck" story — and, later her "comeback" — is therefore a kind of avatar of the genre. Not only that, but Spears "gave it up" in the most literal sense of the term, providing so many crotch shots in so short a span of time that they were undeniably staged.

Gender therefore matters in this instance, and quite specifically. Gender is impossible to ignore when one is talking sex scandal — and sex scandal has long since accompanied celebrity.[20] Moreover, we are talking sex and *values*: whether it is "good" or "bad" to be photographed without underwear; whether a celebrity "gives it up" or not. Yet in postfeminist culture, certain kinds of "bad girl" behavior are celebrated. Moreover, postfeminist culture requires careful boundary work to distinguish between acceptable and unacceptable kinds of bad behavior — work in which the word "vagina," I am arguing, is deeply implicated. Postfeminists embrace all the trappings of textbook female exploitation from catfights to stripping with only the thinnest veneer of irony.[21] In this cultural climate, it is hard to find a tenable

Figure 10.2 **Paris Hilton "gives it up." (Photo from WENN [World Entertainment News Network].)**

18. Samuels, "The Britney Show," 42.
19. Ibid., 38.
20. David A. Cook and Adrianne L. McLean (eds), *Headline Hollywood: A Century of Film Scandal* (New Brunswick, NJ: Rutgers University Press, 2001).
21. Susan A. Owen, Sarah R. Stein, and Leah R. Vande Berg, *Bad Girls: Cultural Politics and Media Representations of Transgressive Women* (New York: Peter Lang, 2007).

position from which to critique the feminization of celebrity "trashiness," for example. This celebrity culture's reliance on the most obvious equations between vacuousness, stupidity, femininity, and sexual exploitation therefore seem ambiguous, possibly ironic reappropriations of a less-enlightened era's vices. The crotch shot phenomenon thus operates in a cultural climate that is unwilling or unable to distinguish between exploitation and empowerment in the wake of the popular uptake of postfeminism.

Vajapocalypse: Policing the Border between "Trainwrecks" and "Famewhores"

The work that the words "vagina" and "vajayjay" do is twofold. First, they contain the tactile labia's disruption of the phallocentric, "scoptophilic" order of paparazzi celebrity culture by operating as discursive prostheses. Second, the circulation of "vagina" and "vajayjay" polices this ambiguity between exploitation and empowerment, but not by speaking up for the exploited. Rather, it works to distinguish the "trashy" women from the modern, liberated women, and in so doing relies on essentially conservative gender standards.

If being "famous for nothing" or "meta/meta-famous" and modern celebrity in general are collapsing into equivalency, the "vagina" is the banner of these terms' solidarity and synonymousness. The words "vagina" and "vajayjay" are used in two different contexts in early twenty-first-century popular culture. On the one hand, the ability to "say that word" has become a badge of a certain hip, postfeminist sexual liberation. On the other hand, it is often deployed to label someone as "trashy" or "slutty." Those who can say it are hip; those who show it are "trash."

Comedian Sarah Silverman took advantage of the changed value of the term during her opening monologue at the 2007 MTV Movie Awards, commenting that there were "a lot of famous vaginas in the house tonight"[22] — meaning that Paris Hilton and Britney Spears were there. Here the joke is established by a metonymy with the genitals, and the dig pivots on the ambiguity between the anatomical term and its pornographic connotations. Moreover, although Silverman was broadcast live, her use of "vagina" would not incur the censorship bleep-out that something like "cunt" or "pussy" would have done. Thus she was able to pretend that she was merely stating an obvious, even clinical fact, while essentially calling these women (fame) whores.

Elsewhere, "vagina" and its cruder counterparts was also shorthand for "famous-for-nothing." This March 28, 2008, post from the celebrity gossip blog dlisted.com is a particularly brutal example (Hilton's quote is taken from *OK Weekly*, another celebrity tabloid of the *Us Weekly* variety). It leads off: "Parasite Hilton held a press conference in Turkey to talk about what a

---

22. *MTV Movie Awards*, MTV, June 3, 2007.

skank slut she is. Paris defended herself against the 'media lies' and thinks she's a good role model to little girls" (K). The post continues:

> She said, "I don't pay attention to lies because I am a good person. I work very hard and I've built this empire on my own. I think this is an inspiration for a lot of girls out there."
>
> Hold up! Who answered this question? Paris or her vagina? Paris' vagina is the only thing that's working hard for the money. Come on Paris! Give your pussy a little credit.[23]

Michael K, the writer and editor of dlisted.com, sets the tone by dubbing his subject "Parasite" Hilton. The name establishes her as a leech with nothing of her own to contribute. The only thing she *does* have to contribute is her "vagina," that is, her sex, her nothing. The fact is that Hilton is here referring to her "legitimate" career — forging "Paris Hilton" into a brand that sells perfumes, clothes, and books worldwide. Despite these easily verifiable facts, the post takes it as obvious and undeniable that Hilton has no right to her millions, and that her only working part is her "vagina." Of course, Michael K starts off by calling Hilton a "skank slut," but the force of the post derives from the way this name-calling plays out in the image of her personified "vagina," the "only thing that's working hard for the money." It confers an odd, postmodern dignity upon that organ, thus elevating the post beyond simple slander — taking calling Hilton a "whore" to a whole new level.

Around the same time as the flashing fad, the words "vagina" and "vajay-jay" also began to circulate as a kind of badge of postfeminist liberation, providing an interesting counterpoint to the metonymy of "vagina" and "famous for nothing." Here, postfeminism and celebrity gossip share a taste for the catfight. Pitting "Team Aniston" against "Team Jolie," (as tabloids do years after Angelina Jolie became the "other woman" in Jennifer Aniston and Brad Pitt's divorce) is read as merely the right of women to compete as equals — never mind that they are always competing for attention, either the literal attention of a particular man or the masculinized gaze of public exposure. It can also be read as an ironic redeployment of pre-feminist relations.[24]

The slang term "vajayajay" first appeared in episode 17, season 2 (2006) of ABC's hit medical soap *Grey's Anatomy*. Miranda Bailey, an African-American physician, yells at her intern to "stop looking at my va-jay-jay" — while she is in the throes of labor.[25] Series writers, looking for a way around censored words like "beaver" on the one hand and the clinical, non-conversational

---

23. Michael K, "An Inspiration To Us All," dlisted.com, March 28, 2008.
24. Helene A. Shugart, Catherine Egley Waggoner, and D. Lynn O'Brien Hallstein, "Mediating Third-Wave Feminism: Appropriation as Postmodern Media Practice," *Critical Studies in Media Communication* 18(2), (2001): 194–210.
25. *Grey's Anatomy*, "(As We Know It)" Season 2, Episode 17. Touchstone, February 12, 2006.

"vagina" on the other, used this somewhat obscure slang term to enhance the ongoing presentation of Miranda Bailey as a woman of verve and self-respect. Moreover, the fact that the character who used the term was a sassy black woman gave it a certain underground hipness so typical of mainstream appropriations of black culture.

Tee shirts emblazoned with the phrase became popular items in the *Grey's Anatomy* online store. Oprah Winfrey — another sassy black woman — then popularized the term, saying "I think vajayjay's a nice word, don't you?"[26] while the ladies on *The View* discussed the word at length in what the satiric clip show *The Soup* termed the "Vajapocalypse."[27]

Oprah and the members of *The View* panel were discussing the word as a sign of liberation: that is, as a word that is often taboo or uncomfortable for people, particularly men, to say. They underlined their own use of the words "vagina" and "vajayjay" as marks of a feminism understood as sexual liberation, as comfort in talking about their bodies. On *The View*, Barbara Walters, a woman of the Betty Friedan generation, complained that the viewing public seemed shocked by her use of the term and objected that she certainly was not the prude they thought she was.

The slang term vajayjay, then, carries the veneer of a certain liberation: still raunchy, but stripped of the feminist shock value it carried when *The Vagina Monologues* debuted in 1996.[28] The *Monologues* was originally a one-woman show where, much in the spirit of the book *Cunt*,[29] the word operates as a reclamation on feminist grounds of a body part either cloaked in euphemism or stained with shame.

In *The Vagina Monologues* Eve Ensler wrote, "I say the word vagina because I want people to respond." In 2007, "vagina" and "va-jay-jay" were no longer the province of feminist provocateurs operating on the fringes. In what is perhaps the ultimate mainstream quasi-feminist gesture, the March 2008 *Cosmopolitan* previewed an article titled: "Your Va-jay-jay: Fascinating New Facts About Your Lovely Lady Parts." That pop singer Rhianna, the issue's cover girl, is lifting her short skirt over her parted legs in an apparent invitation to examine her lovely lady parts, underlines the unresolved tension of the word: somewhere between liberation and exhibitionism is that mythical organ, the vajayjay.

These competing connotations of "vagina/vajayajay" echo the polarization of the current celebrity landscape with regard to feminine sexuality. On the "bad" or "transgressive" end of the spectrum, women's "vaginas" are the basis of their fame — that is, nothing. On the "good" or "appropriate" end, "vagina" is, crucially, *not* a body part, but a bit of discourse: a word that

---

26. *The Oprah Winfrey Show*, in syndication, 1986 – present.
27. Rosenbloom, Stephanie. "What Did You Call It?" *New York Times*, October 28, 2007.
28. Eve Ensler, *The Vagina Monologues* (New York: Villiard, 1998).
29. Inga Muscio, *Cunt: A Declaration of Independence* (Seattle, WA: Seal Press, 1998).

is used to indicate what I am arguing is a patriarchal, even misogynistic view of the female body and feminine sexuality.

Conclusion: The Horror of Something To See

In reading Spears' scar as an index, I am arguing for a connection between its designation of her uterus and vagina as *internal* organs and the entire economy of paparazzi, online gossip sites, and the association of female celebrity with emptiness and superficiality. The scar reveals a different kind of "reality." The scar *marks the effacement* of the female body as anything other than sexual object of consumption. It is a monument to the "something" lost in the process whereby the photographs were captioned as "nothing." One might think of the scar like Magritte's famous painting, *Ceci n'est pas une pipe*. The scar is the painting that comments on a nonverbal, unconsciously negotiated moment of cognitive dissonance.

The scar points to both the action of intercourse *as* procreation and the function of the vagina as birth canal. The scar cannot but indicate the *internal* location of the vagina: if it weren't inside, there would be no need to cut into the flesh to get at it. The scar thus lays bare a more or less unconscious misrecognition, and forces the recognition of the labia as something *other than* the birth canal or phallic sheath. It exposes the labia as *something to see*.

Because this reality evades the phallocentrism of visual culture, only a remarkable reversion to a very old gender politics can contain it. In this context of behavioral boundaries, the word "vagina" operates as a discursive prosthesis, a supplement whose invisibility depends on the phallocentric fear of the female genitals. To name what is *seen* in the photographs is to give symbolic power to the uncanny referent, the anatomical "dark continent," the lips that defy the subject/object split so necessary for phallocentric reasoning to function. In order to maintain its hegemony, therefore, the word "vagina" was grafted onto the images and proudly circulated as a badge of new liberation — after the women's movement gave us the clitoris, Oprah, the ladies at *The View*, and Sarah Silverman are returning us to the vaginal.

With the flashing fad, what the Greeks had tidily "sewn back back up inside its crack" is on full, inescapable display. Celebrity crotch shots are precisely not tidily corralled in the pornographic enclosure, they are not "hard core," as lewd as they are. Rather, they are moments of carelessness so intense that they generate their own system of value.[30] The obvious question — who

---

30. Crotch shots do seem to be part of a general "pornification" of mainstream culture — for more, see Pamela Paul, *Pornified: How Pornography Is Damaging Our Lives, Our Relationships, and Our Families* (New York: Henry Holt, 2006); and Ariel Levy, *Female Chauvinist Pigs: Women and the Rise of Raunch Culture* (New York: Simon & Schuster, 2005). Importantly, the collection *Everyday Pornography*, edited by Karen Boyle (Routledge, 2010), details the specifically heterosexual, *male* audience towards which this "pornification" is inevitably directed.

leaves the house without underwear in a miniskirt? — is itself in on the fun, as its answer is the intentional exhibitionism of the women, made manifest in the photograph as document. Thus these images, unfettered by social norms restricting the consumption of pornography, made it impossible to turn away from the horror of nothing to see — they constituted, rather, the horror of *something* to see.

In the absence of a visual curative, a discursive prosthesis developed instead to render invisible what was so unsettlingly apparent: the vagina, the willing counterpart of the phallus, the invisible "hole" whose appearance in public is not only impossible but unthinkable. Here, where the images were nearly unavoidable and certainly undeniable, the "nothingness" that the vagina connotes grafted absence and invisibility onto the spectacularly visual. It also served to police the boundary between acceptable and unacceptable feminine sexuality in the postfeminist era.

What relation is implied by the tension between anatomical correctness (the actual organ being the labia) and sexual fantasy (the dream of penetration exceeding the literal anatomy of the photograph)? And in what ways does this relation arise from the intensely spectacular nature of the images — that is, from the excess of vision produced by their ubiquity and explicitness? I would argue that the relation is between a (famous) woman's body as the source of her subjectivity and the way that body is consumed as an object. Where it is not possible to purely objectify — that is, where a non-visual economy such as the labia threatens to disrupt the visual — words step in as prostheses to re-objectify this body, reinsert it into a visual and moral economy that is essentially patriarchal. In the world of female celebrity, a ubiquitous catchphrase has served to mark important behavioral boundaries in a culture seemingly bereft of such standards.

Sarah Silverman's crack about "famous vaginas," for example, obviously drew its humor from the vulgar synecdoche, however clinical, while *Cosmopolitan*'s cover metonymically connects the words to "lovely lady parts." Using vagina in this way references phallic penetration insofar as it reinforces the notion of the vagina as sheath and receptacle for the penis, and thus the primary sexual organ in terms of male pleasure (as opposed, for example, to the polymorphous clitoris). That, for example, porn star Jenna Jameson sells a plastic mold of her own vagina as a sex toy only underlines the prosthetic nature of the word in this context: as a detachable hole, the vagina indexes male pleasure alone. Jenna Jameson may be a celebrity, but her power as such stems not from her talent and not even from her allure, but from the availability of her anatomy, (separate from her subjectivity) to masculine desire. Because they operate much like this detachable object, the words "vagina" and "vajayjay" thus become powerful weapons in the policing of feminine behavior: Silverman's use of the term designates the whore, *Cosmopolitan*'s use designates the virgin, lovely and intact, but also modern and (seemingly) self-aware.

"Vagina" and "vajayjay" give postfeminist women license to call other women "sluts" and "whores" — all the more so if they are in the public eye. When Oprah says that it is a "nice" word, she's implying that by extension "nice" women may use it. This implication pays for the empowerment of some with the condemnation of others, measuring women's strides in terms of who we eagerly prohibit from making the same progress.

What Spears' scar shows is that the vagina is not the labia. It exposes the prosthesis and the cultural work that it does to maintain sexist distinctions between women who have gotten postfeminist liberation "right" and those who have gotten it "wrong." It unveils a prosthetic relation between celebrity visibility and feminine sexuality, converting the horror of something to see into the old, familiar nothing.

Bibliography

Boyle, Karen (ed.). *Everyday Pornography*. London: Routledge, forthcoming September 2010.

Cook, David A. and Adrianne L. McLean (eds). *Headline Hollywood: A Century of Film Scandal*. New Brunswick, NJ: Rutgers University Press, 2001.

Cosmopolitan. "Your Va-jay-jay: Fascinating New Facts About Your Lovely Lady Parts," *Cosmopolitan* March 2008.

Dworkin, Craig. "Textual Prostheses," *Comparative Literature* 57(1), (2005): 1–25.

Dyer, Richard. *Heavenly Bodies: Film Stars and Society*. London: Routledge, 1986.

East, Sarah, Jay Bowman, and Kevin Palmer. "Year of the Vajayjay," PopCrunch, March 19, 2009. Available at: http://www.popcrunch.com/the-year-of-the-vajayjay/.

Ensler, Eve. *The Vagina Monologues*. New York: Villiard, 1998.

Esch, Kevin and Vicki Mayer. "How Unprofessional: The Profitable Partnership of Amateur Porn and Celebrity Culture," in Susanna Paasonen, Kaarina Nikunen, and Laura Saarenmaa (eds), *Pornification: Sex and Sexuality in Media Culture*. Oxford: Berg, 2007: 99–111.

Gamson, Joshua. *Claims to Fame: Celebrity in Contemporary America*. Berkeley, CA: University of California Press, 1994.

Grey's Anatomy. Touchstone. February 12, 2006. Season 2, Episode 17.

Hilton, Perez. perezhilton.com. http://www.perezhilton.com, 2007.

Horowitz, Jonathan. *CBS Evening News/www.britneycrotch.org*. 2008, New York. Artwork.

Irigaray, Luce. *This Sex Which Is Not One*, translated by Catherine Burke and Carolyn Porter. Ithaca, NY: Cornell University Press, 1985.

Lacan, Jacques. *Écrits*, translated by Bruce Fink, Héloïse Fink, and Russell Grigg. New York and London: W. W. Norton and Company, 2006.

Levy, Ariel. *Female Chauvinist Pigs: Women and the Rise of Raunch Culture*. New York: Simon & Schuster, 2005.

Michael K. "An Inspiration To Us All," dlisted.com, March 28, 2008. Blog post. Available at: http://www.dlisted.com.com/node/24868 (accessed November 29 2010).

MTV Movie Awards. MTV, June 3, 2007.

Muscio, Inga. *Cunt: A Declaration of Independence*. Seattle, WA: Seal Press, 1998.

Negra, Diane. *What a Girl Wants? Fantasizing the Reclamation of Self in Postfeminism*. New York and London: Routledge, 2008.

Owen, Susan A., Sarah R. Stein, and Leah R. Vande Berg. *Bad Girls: Cultural Politics and Media Representations of Transgressive Women*. New York: Peter Lang, 2007.

Paul, Pamela. *Pornified: How Pornography Is Damaging Our Lives, Our Relationships, and Our Families*. New York: Henry Holt, 2006.

Rieff, Phillip (ed.). *Sexuality and the Psychology of Love: The Collected Papers of Sigmund Freud*. New York: Collier Books, 1993.

Rosenbloom, Stephanie. "What Did You Call It?" *New York Times*, October 28, 2007.

Samuels, David. "The Britney Show: Days and Nights With the New Paparazzi," *The Atlantic Monthly* April 2008: 36–51.

Sconce, Jeffrey. "A Vacancy at the Paris Hilton," in Jonathan Gray, Cornel Sandvoss, and C. Lee Harrington (eds), *Fandom: Identities and Communities in a Mediated World.* New York: New York University Press, 2007, 328–43.

Sex and the City. HBO, 1998–2004. Television series.

Shugart, Helene A., Catherine Egley Waggoner, and D. Lynn O'Brien Hallstein. "Mediating Third-wave Feminism: Appropriation as Postmodern Media Practice," *Critical Studies in Media Communication* 18(2), (2001): 194–210.

Tasker, Yvonne and Diane Negra. "Postfeminism and the Archive For the Future," *Camera Obscura* 21, (2006): 170–76.

The Oprah Winfrey Show. In syndication, 1986 – present.

The Soup. E! Network Studios, 2004 – present. Television series.

The View. ABC, 1997 – present. Television series.

Wills, David. *Prosthesis.* Stanford, CA: Stanford University Press, 1995.

11

Strengthening as They Undermine
Rachel Maddow and Suze Orman's Homonormative Lesbian Identities

JOSELYN LEIMBACH

S CENE 1: American television host and financial advisor Suze Orman faces the camera, addresses her audience, and makes a Valentine's Day argument for gay marriage:

> We are taking away a birthright, if you ask me, for people to get the most out of the money they have spent their lives working [*sic*]. Those people are making money, they pay taxes on the money, every single one of us deserves to have the same financial benefits, whether we are gay, or whether we are straight. And therefore we have got to do everything we can to turn that around. Every single one of us deserves to be loved. Every single one of us deserves to love. And every single one of us deserves to make the most out of the money that we have. That's my Valentine's Day wish for every single one of us.[1]

Scene 2: A celebrity profile in *People* discusses American television host and political commentator Rachel Maddow's relationship with her partner:

> While [Susan] Mikula [Rachel Maddow's romantic partner] loves indulging in girlie accessories like purses, Maddow frankly points out: "I look like a dude."[2]

The Rachel Maddow Show premiered September 8, 2008, on MSNBC, a news outlet that targets younger and left-leaning viewers. According to Jonanna Widner, its host "almost single-handedly made MSNBC — for years the loser third wheel of the cable-news party — a player."[3] Maddow is known for her

---

1. *The Suze Orman Show*, CNBC, February 16, 2009, Television.
2. Michelle Tan, "MSNBC's Rachel Maddow: At Home & Unplugged," *People*, April 12, 2010, 106.
3. Jonanna Widner, "The Rachel Papers: What a Hot, Smart, Lesbian Pundit Means For an Uneasy America," *Bitch: Feminist Response to Pop Culture*, Spring 2009, 37.

"intelligence, wit, and fresh take on politics."[4] *The Suze Orman Show* began March 9, 2002, on CNBC. Orman is the author of eight *New York Times* best-sellers which, along with her television show, provide her audience with a "no nonsense" approach to personal finance. She has ties to Oprah Winfrey, serving as the star's go-to financial advisor and as a contributor to *O: Oprah Magazine.*

Both Maddow and Orman have made their lesbianism known to their audiences. However, as seen in the rhetoric they employ in the epigraphs, both attempt to temper their potentially threatening sexuality by articulating conciliatory and conservative rhetorics relying upon homonormativity, postfeminism, and neoliberalism in their purchase of mainstream success. While advocating for same-sex marriage, Orman uses obtuse language that refuses to clearly state her intent, focusing instead upon notions of individual rights, fiscal equality, and love. Maddow describes her female masculinity and its ties to lesbianism as immature and unconventional, while her relationship to her romantic partner is discussed in highly gendered and heterosexualized terms. Both Orman and Maddow rely upon principles of individualism, normative sexual practices, and capitalism to reinforce their conformity to dominant social norms and reject potential reading of their star texts as "queer." Their female bodies, lesbian sexuality, and approaches to their subject matter, politics, and finance respectively, distinguish them from their predominantly male and presumably heterosexual counterparts. Yet, their differences are also potential disadvantages. Maddow and Orman must reconcile their identities as women and lesbians, two potential disqualifying elements with regard to their authoritative positions, with their mainstream success. Whereas in the past outing oneself as a lesbian would have meant career suicide or ghettoization, *The Advocate*, the most recognizable US magazine focusing on lesbian, gay, bisexual, and trans (LGBT) issues, claims that the success and skill displayed by Maddow and Orman overshadow potential discrimination based on their sexuality.[5] By invoking credos of homonormativity, postfeminism, and neoliberalism, both walk a fine line between remaining accessible to the masses while being open, in their own distinct ways, about their lesbianism.

The success of Orman and Maddow increases lesbian visibility and complicates early millennial media representation, which has previously relied upon simplistic tropes to depict lesbians, but marked the gay male as a high profile lifestyle expert. It is clear that both women deploy mollifying tactics to construct their markedly different gender performance, their position as experts, discussions of their romantic partners, and their engagement with lesbian, gay, and bisexual (LGB) political concerns in the maintenance of

---

4. Suzan Colon, "The New American Classic," *The Advocate*, December 2, 2008, para. 5.
5. Colon, "The New American Classic," para. 4; "Suze Orman," *The Advocate.* January 13, 2009, para. 1.

their mainstream appeal.[6] Their purchase of success is dependent upon their ability to construct their sexuality as a lifestyle that does not challenge hegemonic power structures and to create a space where their lesbianism is perceived as non-threatening to the heterosexual status quo. Thus, their difference is subverted by their conformity to other social codes.

Theoretical Foundations: Homonormativity, Postfeminism, and Neoliberalism

In *The Trouble with Normal*, Michael Warner discusses homonormativity as a trend that promotes the evolution of LGB activism from the recognition and celebration of the unique aspects of queer life ("We're here, we're queer, get used to it" and Gay Pride), to a focus upon the LGB community existing within a "post-gay" space, including a move away from urban spaces towards the suburban. Working to downplay homosexuality as a form of significant difference, homonormative conventions mark individuals within LGB communities as indistinguishable from heterosexuals.[7] The articulation of the legalization of same-sex marriage as the primary concern of most LGB activist groups exemplifies homonormative rhetoric. In prioritizing marriage, LGB relationships are marked as "just like" those of heterosexuals in privileging legally sanctioned long-term monogamous relationships. Republican lawyer Theodore B. Olsen, arguing for the legalization of same-sex marriage, contends, "[w]hat better way to make this national aspiration [equality] complete than to apply the same protections to men and women who differ from others only on the basis of their sexual orientation?"[8] Olson relies upon constructions of LGB individuals as distinct from heterosexuals only in the sex of their romantic partner while making other forms of systemic oppression invisible. Warner problematizes the precedence of marriage in LGB activism as an attempt to "implicitly desexualize the movement and depoliticize queer sex."[9] LGB communities' concession to the prioritization of conformity to conventional (hetero)sexual expectations rejects the privileging of difference previously seen in the activism of ACT UP and Queer Nation, the gay/queer movements of the 1980s and 1990s. Expressions of homonormativity can also be seen via high-profile lesbian icon Rosie O'Donnell's publicized battle to adopt children and her emphasis upon the gay family in promotions for cruise ship vacation packages. Homonormativity provides a relevant lens through which to examine the ways Maddow and Orman perform

---

6. Although transgender and transsexuality are often included, I have chosen to specifically address lesbians, gays, and bisexuals due in part to Maddow and Orman's engagement with activism around marriage and military service that renders transgender and transsexual individuals invisible.

7. Michael Warner, *The Trouble with Normal: Sex, Politics, and the Ethics of Queer Life* (Cambridge, MA: Harvard University Press, 2000), 61–2.

8. Theodore B. Olson, "The Conservative Case for Gay Marriage: Why Same-Sex Marriage is an American Value," *Newsweek*, January 18, 2010, 49.

9. Warner, *Trouble with Normal*, 66.

celebrity in relation to their sexuality, particularly as it affects their gender performances, representations of their relationships with their romantic partners, and their engagement with LGB politics. Maddow and Orman "mainstream" their images in an attempt to reach a broader heterosexual audience by marginalizing the difference associated with their lesbianism.[10]

The prioritization of conventionality also applies to postfeminist rhetoric. Diane Negra, in *What a Girl Wants*, contends, "the overwhelming ideological impact that is made by an accumulation of postfeminist cultural material is the reinforcement of conservative norms as the ultimate 'best choices' in women's lives."[11] Ties to homonormativity and consumerism no longer mark lesbian relationships as abject other to the concept of "best choice," which relates to the presumed "ideal" relationships associated with monogamy and companionate marriage, as well as extremes of femininized gender performance both in appearance and behavior. Postfeminist principles work to reimagine conventions of gender and sexuality as the ultimate form of progress leading to privilege. In promoting these ideals, postfeminism relies upon the power of consumption and the fantasy of achieving perfection and satisfaction through the purchase of the correct products. This proves particularly relevant to the ways that Maddow and Orman negotiate issues of appearance, convey their expert status, and construct public perceptions of their relationships with their romantic partners.

The power of the consumer is also paralleled in neoliberalism. As with postfeminism, the influence of the individual is derived from economic status, emphasizing the centrality and correctness of the marketplace, while simultaneously rejecting state involvement, and removing any social safety net that may cushion those unable to achieve economic sustainability on their own. The focus upon consumerism presupposes society as a level playing field, disregarding other identity-based hierarchies that contribute to broader oppressions. Because neoliberalism is based upon the privileging of the individual, group membership, as a source of support and discrimination, is ignored. For Maddow and Orman, the centering of the individual as the primary subject of analysis, allows for mainstream acceptance that would otherwise be undermined by the politics of and their membership in LGB communities.[12]

---

10. For more on homonormativity, see Kath Browne, Jason Lim, and Gavin Brown, *Geographies of Sexualities: Theory, Practices, and Politics* (Burlington, VT: Ashgate, 2007); Jasbir K. Puar, *Terrorist Assemblages: Homonationalism in Queer Times* (Durham, NC: Duke University Press, 2007); and Roderick A. Ferguson, "Race-ing Homonormativity: Citizenship, Sociology and Gay Identity," in *Black Queer Studies: A Critical Anthology*, edited by E. Patrick Johnson and Mae G. Henderson, (Durham, NC: Duke University Press, 2005).

11. Diane Negra, *What a Girl Wants? Fantasizing the Reclamation of Self in Postfeminism* (New York: Routledge, 2009), 4.

12. For an expanded discussion of neoliberalism in the media see Laurie Ouellette and James Hay, *Better Living Through Reality TV: Television and Post-Welfare Citizenship* (Malden, MA: Blackwell, 2008); Toby Miller, *Cultural Citizenship: Comopolitanism, Consumerism, and*

Homonormativity, postfeminism, and neoliberalism privilege whiteness as a means of undermining the recognition of oppression related to other marginalized identities. In allowing race to remain an unmarked signifier of advantage, they remain blind to societal power structures that disproportionately oppress individuals marginalized by racial and ethnic identities. The class privilege tied to these hegemonic formations is a source of power that relies upon the ability of the individual to perform influence through consumerism. Other forms of cultural oppression are made invisible because prevailing logic dictates that discrimination can be overcome through the enactment of individualized consumer choices and the "purchase" of privilege.

Gendered Scripts

On their eponymous television programs, Orman and Maddow perform gender in ways that comply with the codes of normative professional femininity, ensuring their legibility as experts in fields traditionally dominated by men. Orman presents a consistent femininity that promotes readings of her as a financial expert, yet Maddow imparts a femininity that is complicated by the butch aesthetic displayed in secondary mediation (publicity interviews, photo shoots, magazine profiles, etc.). Orman's particular gender performance relies upon highly professional modes of hegemonic femininity. Appearing with a stylized blond bob, impeccable makeup, a constant smile that displays her perfectly white teeth, and designer clothing, Orman physically epitomizes the success she encourages her viewers to obtain. She invokes conventional femininity and her appearance both on-screen and off projects its associated values. Because of this her femininity is made invisible and construed as "real."[13] Sustaining her position as a financial authority in all public appearances, Orman conveys the expertise she has cultivated over the course of her career. She maintains an image of confidence and competence and the main topic of conversation is always personal finance. According to Richard Dyer in *Heavenly Bodies*, "Stars are involved in making themselves into commodities; they are both labour and the thing that labour produces."[14] Orman's consistency creates publicity for herself as an individual and for the products produced by and associated with her brand.

In an interview with Ben Tracy for CBS News, a caption placed under her picture acknowledges this management of her celebrity persona, "Suze Orman Isn't Afraid to Think of Herself as a Brand — or Call Herself 'The

Television in a Neoliberal Age (Philadelphia, PA: Temple University Press, 2007); and Aihwa Ong, *Neoliberalism as Exception: Mutations in Citizenship and Sovereignty* (Durham, NC: Duke University Press, 2006).

13. For more on performativity, see Judith Butler, *Gender Trouble: Feminism and the Subversion of Identity* (New York: Routledge, 1990).

14. Richard Dyer, *Heavenly Bodies: Film Stars and Society* (New York: Routledge, 2004), 5.

Money Lady.'"[15] Because of this, Orman's performance of "self" must be held to the standards set by the brand. For Orman work is life, thus fiscal concerns permeate every interaction made privy to the public. Consistent gender performance conveys her homonormativity, undermining the "difference" associated with her sexuality because of her conformity to expectations of femininity. In this, she may remind her (seemingly straight) viewers of their mother, sister, wife, or even themselves. Orman depends upon postfeminist constructions of female presentation, which, as we have seen, privilege conventional and idealized notions of femininity. In her work and appearance, Orman displays neoliberal ideologies which conflate success with her power as a consumer. Her gender consistency allows her to engage in behavior that is often associated with masculinity, such as her constant involvement with work and her "no nonsense" attitude. Ironically, Orman's conventionally feminine appearance creates a space in which her masculine behavior becomes marketable. She relies upon "common sense" as the foundation of her financial advice and staunchly rejects "feminine" characteristics, such as impulsivity and emotion, in making fiscal decisions. In maintaining a feminine appearance she is able to enact the characteristics that have been coded as necessary for success, without undermining the construction of her image as personable, accessible, and, above all, feminine. Orman's consistency of appearance is sharply contrasted by the gender shifting performed by Maddow.

For Maddow, "work" is marked by her performance of a professional femininity, and is distinguishable from publicity appearances that emphasize a gender performance coded as masculine. However, the potential threat of her female masculinity is undermined through her failure to successfully perform masculine tasks. Her femininity is reinforced through displays of self-deprecation and passivity in the face of "real" (male) masculinity. Maddow's performance of butch chic in publicity appearances has garnered much attention, but equally significant to this analysis is the homonormativity and postfeminism she relies upon in the construction of her on-program personality. Appearing in coiffed hair, makeup, and wearing form-fitting blazers, Maddow's gender performance does not detract from the importance of her message and the display of a conservative femininity places her on par with her professional peers. When questioned about the significance of her feminized on-screen appearance, she states "It wasn't at anybody else's encouraging. I wanted my appearance to not be the only thing people would pay attention to. So essentially I was seeking genericness."[16] Maddow suggests that the decision to construct a femininized appearance on her self-titled show is an act of agency consciously assumed to avoid standing out.

---

15. Ben Tracy, "Meet 'The Money Lady': Suze Orman Talks about Her Life, Her Philosophy and Financial Mistakes Everyone Makes," *CBS News*, February 17, 2008.
16. Clara Jeffery, "The Maddow Knows," *Mother Jones*, January 2009, 13.

Yet, when questioned about her appearance in an interview on a morning talk show, *The View*, she asserts, "In terms of, like, wearing makeup to be on television [. . .] I go into the makeup room, I sit down and I close my eyes, and then when they are done, I get up and I walk onto the set."[17] Maddow's response to questions concerning her appearance conveys a passivity, which further emphasizes the performativity of her femininity, and falls into post-feminist constructions of idealized womanhood that rely upon traditional norms of feminine appearance and behavior. In this interview her female masculinity is visible, yet is mitigated by behavior that conforms to feminine expectations. Her willingness to undergo a "makeover" mirrors postfeminist principles that rely upon the prioritization of a hegemonic feminine appearance as a means of obtaining success. Her performance of femininity, unlike Orman's, is perceptible because it is clearly distinguishable from her gender display in other arenas.

Whereas Maddow's gender performance on *The Rachel Maddow Show* conforms to dominant expectations of feminized professionalism, the butch gender she performs in mainstream publicity interviews draws ties between her gender and her lesbian identity. Sporting her signature horn-rimmed glasses, loose-fitting button-down shirts or sweaters, and "natural" hair and makeup, Maddow appears to enact her lesbian identity via her appearance.[18] Her lesbianism is invoked by her role as consumer, through her style, rather than her politics. Unlike Orman who relies upon the consistency of her feminine appearance in the construction of a brand, and the maintenance of her homonormativity, Maddow cannot, or will not, enact the gendered conventions of appearance associated with her female body. Her inconsistent gender marks her feminized on-air appearance as an aspect of her professional performance that rejects ties to "realness." Her femininity becomes part of a costume or "drag" that she can remove once work is complete.[19]

Maddow's marketability is further enhanced by the "benign" masculine behavior she displays in these interviews. In publicity appearances Maddow is often shown engaging in her hobby of mixology, a throwback to 1950s

---

17. *The View*, ABC, March 5, 2009, Television.
18. The appearances I am specifically referring to include, but are not limited to, *The Daily Show* (January 7, 2009); *Late Night with Conan O'Brian* (November 21, 2008); and *The Tonight Show with Jay Leno* (October 9, 2008). It is important to note that the majority of the appearances to which I refer occurred in the first half of 2009. In recent publicity interviews Maddow's gender performance increasingly resembles her appearance on her program. This may be due to time constraints, as the interviews often occur directly after she appears on her own show, or to her desire to, as expressed earlier, to make her appearance less noteworthy, or to increased pressure/advice by outside agents (the network, her own publicity agent/manager) to maintain a consistent gender performance which will allow her to develop the Maddow "brand" much like Orman has done.
19. My reading of Maddow and Orman is limited by the performance of their lesbianism as it is made accessible to the public. Therefore, my analysis of the performance of their lesbianism is dependent upon mainstream "common sense" definitions of lesbianism and the means by which it is conveyed to audiences who are outsiders to the LGB cognoscenti.

masculinity, and a subject less controversial than politics, her area of expertise. When asked about her hobby Maddow states, "I'm a hobbyist, but I'm kind of intense about it. [. . .] I'm a bit of a bully. I don't cook and I don't have any other useful skills. [. . .] I'm like a mean dork about it."[20] It is significant that Maddow compares her mixology skills with her lack of talent in the markedly feminine realm of cooking; as in the interview in *People* referenced in the epigraph, this rejection of conventional femininity undermines the feminine presentation she displays on her show, marking it as performance. In an interview with late night talk-show host Jimmy Fallon, Maddow critiques Fallon's drink of choice, gin and tonic, stating "I think you can drink a more manly drink."[21] Maddow becomes the enforcer of social norms when she teaches Fallon to mix and drink an appropriately masculine drink. However, her "expert" status in this realm is contested by the difficulty she has in creating it, evidenced in copious spilling of the alcohol. Maddow's display of failed female masculinity undermines what might be seen as a challenge to male power.[22] Her self-deprecation is seen in her willingness to laugh along with the audience at her clumsiness. Following postfeminist logic, the undermining of Maddow's authority acts as punishment for the seriousness with which she takes both her career and this particular hobby. Her ineptitude works to reposition her within the appropriately feminine sphere of unsuccessful masculinity and diminishes the potential disruption of the gender hierarchy that would be associated with a successful display. In sum, Maddow's appearances on *The View* and *Late Night with Jimmy Fallon* convey a masculinity tempered by her feminine personality. Even when presenting characteristics associated with lesbianism, specifically female masculinity, Maddow's engagement with postfeminist rhetoric destabilizes her lesbianism through her reliance upon other conventions of femininity.

Performing the Role of Expert

A professional and feminized appearance contributes to Orman and Maddow's authority as experts, is reinforced through their personal histories and legitimizes their claim to professional authority. In publicity interviews both are marked by their professional trajectories as uniquely qualified to act as experts in their respective fields, which emphasizes neoliberal concerns and presents them as role models for their audiences. Their reliance upon a balance of the common and the spectacular depends upon a neoliberal ideology that accentuates the possibilities open to the individual who is both willing and able to make a name for themselves.[23]

---

20. *Late Night with Jimmy Fallon*, NBC, March 25, 2009, Television.
21. Ibid.
22. See Judith Halberstam, *Female Masculinity* (Durham, NC: Duke University Press, 1998).
23. The importance of ordinariness in constructing star texts that are accessible to the masses is discussed in Richard Dyer, *Heavenly Bodies*.

Maddow's professional trajectory relies upon the privileging of academic knowledge and the elite nature of the institutions where she received her education (Stanford, where she obtained a bachelor's degree in public policy, and Oxford, where she earned a doctorate in political science as a Rhodes Scholar). Her start as a media personality began when she entered a competition at a local radio station in Massachusetts and was hired that day. She moved to Air America, a now defunct progressive talk radio station, upon its launch in 2004 and gained her own show at MSNBC in 2008, due in part to the popularity of her guest hosting for lead anchor Keith Obermann. Throughout her media career she has been marked by her liberal sympathies, which have provided her with legibility in the world of political punditry, as well as her particular brand of reporting which, according to Alissa Quart in "The Sarcastic Times," "embodies the rise of [. . .] sarcasm news," which ties her to other parody new shows including *The Daily Show with Jon Stewart* and *The Colbert Report*.[24] Her success has been facilitated by her emergence at a time when expectations of political neutrality are nearly dead in a cable news landscape bifurcated by conservative and liberal news personalities. Her education, along with the fervor she displays for her subject matter, provides Maddow with the foundation upon which her expertise is built.

Orman spent seven years as a waitress in a bakery following a brief stint in college, a point that has been emphasized in any article or interview referencing her rise to fame. After a negative experience with a corrupt financial planner, she decided to educate herself about fiscal matters, eventually taking part in an internship program at Merrill Lynch where she gained the skills necessary to become a financial planner. Orman rose to the position of vice president of investments at Prudential Bache Securities, before starting her own firm, writing multiple best-selling books on DIY financial planning, and gaining her own television show. Her personal and professional experience, her "encyclopedic command of financial planning and her [ability to provide] advice [that] is always clear and generally unimpeachable," and the stamp of approval she received from Winfrey, provides her television show with credibility, persuading her viewers to trust her when dealing with personal finances.[25] Orman's authority is legitimized by her transformation from a working-class childhood to her current multi-millionaire status. She has set herself up as a role model whose actions should be mimicked in order to achieve financial stability and professional success. Orman invokes neoliberal principles which suggest that following the correct path to success for an individual can translate to mass success while failure to make good choices leads to each individual's rightful decline.

According to Jeffrey Louis Decker, "the Horatio Alger formula for success

---

24. Alissa Quart, "The Sarcastic Times: For Rachel Maddow and the Other Ironic Anchors, Absurdity is Serious Stuff," *Columbia Journalism Review* 47(6), (2009): 12.
25. Eric Schurenberg, "If You Knew Suze . . . " *Money*, July 2008, para. 1.

Figure 11.1 **Suze Orman (photo by Dimitrios Kambouris for *Life*).**

failed to survive its appropriation by women, blacks, and immigrants."[26] Yet, Orman relies upon a reimagined Horatio Alger mythology in the construction of her public image. Incorporating neoliberal rhetoric, which rejects social hierarchies that may hinder an individual's ability to achieve success based on group affiliation, Orman takes on a role that she may have previously been denied. Her reliance upon credos of individualism is evidenced in the conspicuous inclusion of her years of waitressing in discussions of her rise to fame. Given the emphasis upon her history as a waitress, it appears that her popularity is contingent upon the ability of her audiences to identify with her perceived struggle, while simultaneously acknowledging the experiences that lead to her current status. Orman's reliance upon neoliberal ideals is accentuated through the use of her personal history as the foundation upon which she builds a relationship with her audience.

Television's relationship to neoliberal ideology functions on multiple levels, not the least of which is its ability to provide public instruction concerning the "proper" way to live, and in the case of Suze Orman, spend. According to Laurie Ouellette and James Hay, "TV's instrumentality as citizenship training depends as much upon viewers learning the *responsibilities* of self-investment as upon enjoying what is *fun* — even sexy — about self-accounting and the world of personal finance."[27] The ethic of self-care, emphasized on *The Suze Orman Show*, provides the means through which the show's audience member/consumer is charged with personal responsibility for their own financial well-being. Ouellette and Hay assert that television provides pedagogical tools for the individual, in a benefit process that then translates to the family and radiates out to society as a whole.[28]

26. Jeffrey Louis Decker, *Made in America: Self-Styled Success from Horatio Alger to Oprah Winfrey* (Minneapolis, MN: University of Minnesota Press, 1997), 133.
27. Laurie Ouellette and James Hay (eds), *Better Living Through Reality TV: Television and Post-Welfare Citizenship* (Malden, MA: Blackwell, 2008), 149.
28. Ibid., 14–15.

Orman relies upon notions of individual responsibility and training for success. Yet she retains the role of expert giving advice to the uninformed, not only through her tutorials, but also through one-on-one interaction with members of her audience. By setting up this dynamic, Orman ensures that her judgment remains supreme. In a regular segment entitled "Can I Afford It?" Orman interacts with audience members who want to know if they can afford their "dream" items. The segment infantilizes the viewer, while Orman's authority is legitimated and reinforced. In these instances Orman moves from a neoliberal posture in which she urges her viewers to make the "best" choice for their own survival, to an ideology in which the viewer must rely upon Orman, rather than themselves, to make the proper decision. Orman often uses shaming language that questions either the sanity or intelligence of those unable to afford the desired item. In fact, "Have you lost your mind?!" is a recurring phrase uttered by Orman during this segment. Her statement of judgment can be based on either the object of desire or the clear inability of the individual to afford the item without endangering their financial security. The potential consequences of engaging in behavior that counters Orman's advice is implied through her neoliberal rhetoric that emphasizes the cost of individual failure in a marketplace with no social safety net. However, her demeanor, rather than being seen as off putting or abrasive, is read by numerous magazine articles and her audience as "no nonsense" and relatable. The display of aggressiveness, often associated with masculinity, may be read as a certain license granted to her because of her expert status and because her advice reinforces, rather than challenges, prevailing financial "wisdom." In her role as advisor Orman draws upon a history of female advice icons, ranging from Ann Landers to Judge Judy. In mirroring this authoritative position she is distinctive (specifically in her focus on finances), but not unprecedented.

The only time Orman is willing to "approve" a purchase which may prove financially questionable is if it falls within her system of financial prioritization. A recurring theme in the show is Orman's mantra, "People first, then money, then things." In one instance a pregnant woman (represented on screen as a disembodied pregnant belly) wants to invest in umbilical blood storage as a precautionary measure against future illness for her unborn fetus. Orman's rationale for approving this investment is not only her support for stem cell research, but also because it may prove beneficial for the fetus once it is born.[29] Significant to this examination of Orman's image is the fact that the viewer is a woman who seeks to purchase services for her unborn child. In "permitting" her access to the funds that would allow the purchase, Orman essentially positions the family as the highest priority. This exchange typifies Orman's enactment of postfeminist and neoliberal ideologies that emphasize the role of women as nurturers and consumers who

---

29. *The Suze Orman Show*, CNBC, May 25, 2008, Television.

must prioritize care for their family over other concerns. Martha Burk, writing for *Ms.* suggests that Orman is a "champion of women's independence when it comes to that most important of commodities: money."[30] However, Orman relies upon assumptions of feminine irresponsibility when it comes to financial concerns. Further, the advice given on her show counters her critique of women's relationship to money in her *New York Times* best seller *Women and Money* where she contends that women are willing to sacrifice their own fiscal health for the sake of their family, friends, and so forth, a tactic she discourages. Unlike the majority of the advice given on her show, in which Orman advocates being "selfish," in this instance maternal interest supersedes other financial concerns. Orman is able to fuse postfeminist constructions of womanhood that rely upon women's roles as maternal caregivers with neoliberal constructions of consumerism as a means of enacting individual power. By approving the woman's investment in umbilical blood storage, Orman encourages her to advocate for her child, while simultaneously advocating for the legalization of stem cell research through her power as consumer. Orman and Maddow's success, regardless of their group affiliations and their histories, reinforces the rightness of the marketplace, which is reemphasized by the fame and popularity garnered through their enactment of neoliberal principles.

Performing Lesbian Relationships

Whereas discussions of Maddow and Orman's roles as experts rely primarily upon neoliberal rhetoric, in depictions of their romantic partnerships, both Maddow and Orman employ homonormative, postfeminist, and neoliberal conventions that privilege dominant constructions of the ideal relationship. Their reliance upon homonormative ideologies can also be seen in both women's rhetoric in regard to their relationships with their romantic partners. Their focus upon the committed monogamous couple, foundational to homonormativity, also permits an incorporation of a modified neoliberal "family values" that integrates rather than contests the inclusion of affluent gay couples and families. Orman and Maddow each emphasize the longevity of their relationships and discuss their commitment as one of the most significant aspects of their private lives. Their focus on the normative aspects of their partnerships ensures that their relationships are constructed for the public as comparable to heterosexual relationships. The privileging of the status quo can be seen in the language used by Orman in the "revelation" of her lesbianism.

Orman began her television show five years before coming out to *The New York Times Magazine* in 2007.[31] Her venue of choice is significant for a

---

30. Martha Burk, "Suze Orman's Bottom Line," *Ms.*, October 1, 2008, para. 1.

31. Deborah Solomon, "She's So Money," *The New York Times Magazine*, February 25, 2007, 19.

number of reasons. First, it is significant that she chose this mainstream publication as the vehicle by which to convey this information to the public, rather than relying upon a traditionally gay medium such as *The Advocate*. In *"Ellen*, Television, and the Politics of Gay and Lesbian Visibility," Bonnie J. Dow states that because Ellen DeGeneres chose to talk to the "mainstream" media, her "coming out campaign was clearly geared toward gaining the approval of mainstream, heterosexual Americans."[32] Warner also critiques this tactic when he suggests that "the public face of the lesbian and gay movement is increasingly determined not in queer counterpublics [such as *The Advocate*] at all, but on the pages of *Newsweek* [or other mainstream media texts]."[33] Orman mirrors DeGeneres's focus on "mainstream" audiences in her "coming out" process. She had already established her celebrity and situated herself in heterosexual homes as a trusted advisor prior to the revelation of her lesbianism. Her maintenance of homonormativity permits her to rely upon a language of similarity, in which her sexuality has little bearing upon her relationship with her audience.

Orman's bid for heterosexual acceptance is seen in her performance of homonormativity when she focuses upon the monogamy and tenure of her relationship and the individuality of her partner choice. In the "coming out" interview Orman declares, "K.T. is my life partner. K.T. stands for Kathy Travis. We're going on seven years. I have never been with a man in my whole life. I'm still a 55-year-old virgin."[34] Her statement relies upon four assumptions which reinforce the homonormativity of her relationship with her partner. First, she privileges K.T., over the broader category of gender, suggesting that it is not the sex or gender she is attracted to, but rather the individual. Second, she does not use a label to describe the relationship she is in or to "identify" her sexuality. She prioritizes the relationship and does not claim a community or political consciousness associated with lesbianism. Third, she emphasizes the longevity of the relationship, implying a monogamy associated with "normative" sexuality. Orman suggests that she and her partner are "just like" heterosexual couples because they believe in monogamy. This is especially important in a capitalist system that depends upon and favors the secure couple and family as the primary unit of social and financial wealth. Her focus upon the longevity of the relationship also works to dismiss any claims that her sexuality may be a phase. Finally, she desexualizes the relationship between herself and K.T. In stating that she is a virgin she implies that the relationship that she has with K.T. does not involve "sex," giving precedence to heterosexual intercourse and the penetrative penis, ultimately suggesting that, whatever it is that lesbians do, it is not sex.

---

32. Bonnie J. Dow, *"Ellen*, Television, and the Politics of Gay and Lesbian Visibility," *Critical Studies in Mass Communication* 18(2), (2001): 128.
33. Warner, *The Trouble with Normal*, 68.
34. Solomon, "She's So Money," para. 9.

She can therefore retain her virginity regardless of her sexual activity, or lack thereof, with her female partner. Orman's claim falls in line with conventional demands for female sexual purity, while simultaneously enacting an unconventional sexuality based on the gender of her object of desire.

Maddow's public image has more prominently included her lesbian sexuality as she has scaled the ranks of celebrity, and in some ways is built upon her role as a pioneer as both the first openly gay Rhodes Scholar and the first lesbian political talk-show host, a feat she minimizes, labeling it "a very small glass ceiling I've broken."[35] In a style similar to Orman's, her discussion of her relationship with her partner marks it as "just like" that of heterosexuals. The longevity (ten years) of the relationship is often emphasized, and she is quoted as saying that her partnership

> is the thing about which I'm most proud and most protective. And if it made sense for my relationship with Susan [Mikula] that I needed to stop being on TV, and stop being on the radio, and go live full time in the Upper Peninsula in Michigan and raise chickens, we'd go live in the Upper Peninsula and raise chickens. It's the single clearest thing in my life.[36]

Maddow suggests that her main concern lies not in furthering her fame, but rather in caring for her partner and the relationship they have developed. Her account here is framed in accordance with the trope of retreatism, a characteristic Negra associates with dominant media constructions of successful women and their flight to familial homes.[37] Retreatism requires the rejection of hectic urban centers that distract from feminine priorities, in favor of idealized rural settings that encourage, not only a rediscovery of self, but a recommitment to the idealized family. Maddow's declaration privileges the domestic and the private over the civic and the public. Homonormativity and postfeminism thus play a strong part in constructing the dialogue used to characterize both Maddow and Orman's relationships with their significant others. Media representations of both women are complicit with and emphasize Orman's emphasis upon the asexuality of her relationship with K.T. and Maddow's prioritization of her relationship over her career. These tactics actively depoliticize their lesbian relationships and situate their sexualities in ways that contribute to normative readings mitigating potential homophobic backlash.

---

35. Jeffery, "The Maddow Knows," para. 25.
36. Baird, "When Left is Right," para. 16.
37. Negra, *What a Girl Wants?* 15–17.

Mainstreaming LGB Activism

Like the divergent construction of their gender presentation, the ways in which Maddow and Orman engage in activism, specifically as it relates to LGB concerns, varies, and can be tied to the ways in which they perform their lesbian identities. Whereas Orman advocates for same-sex marriage, as implied in the quote cited in the epigraph of this article, Maddow has been critiqued by voices within LGB communities for her early lack of involvement in actively making LGB issues visible to her mainstream audience. Although Maddow's ambiguous gender display and Orman's conservative arena of expertise may limit their ability to engage in more controversial aspects of LGB politics, both promulgate homonormative and neoliberal rhetoric which allows their activism on behalf of LGB communities to remain within the realm of the mainstream without wandering into a potentially "queer" space. Ultimately, the activism Maddow and Orman take part in reinforces homonormativity and neoliberalism by focusing upon individual rights (to legal and financial equality) while simultaneously refusing to mark LGB communities as "special" interest groups. In so doing, equality is defined via issues that reinforce race and class privilege, effectively making concerns about bodily safety and other forms of oppression invisible.

Orman's activism around same-sex marriage focuses upon financial equality relying upon an undermining of difference in favor of claims to sameness, simultaneously invoking neoliberal ideals which focus upon fiscal concerns and undermine governmental involvement in the marketplace. Although Orman has, both in publicity appearances and on her own television program, advocated for the legalization of same-sex marriage and the protection of assets within same-sex partnerships, her rhetoric continues to rely upon conservative demands for equal citizenship and rights under the law, while she remains silent on issues concerning basic safety and continuing discrimination in other areas. Orman has been vocal about the need for financial protection for same-sex partners, a topic that falls firmly within her area of expertise, protection that can only be achieved through the legal sanctioning of same-sex marriage. She has also been active in advocating institutional changes, as she did with the Federal Deposit Insurance Corporation, to provide services to same-sex couples that are equal to those offered to heterosexual married couples.[38] Orman's focus upon neoliberal mandates related to financial equality has been praised by both the Human Rights Campaign and GLAAD, two of the most mainstream and visible LGB activist organizations.

Early in her career at MSNBC Maddow was critiqued by vocal members of the LGB community for her silence around LGB concerns. Journalist and LGB activist Michelangelo Signorile and political blogger Pam Spaulding

---

38. Neal Boverman, "Smart Money," *The Advocate*, December 2, 2008, para. 5.

suggested that in her quest for a "broad" viewing audience, Maddow marginalized LGB issues. In his article "Whither Maddow?" in the February 2009 issue of *The Advocate*, Signorile writes, "she's lacking and, perhaps inadvertently, sometimes dismissive when it comes to focusing on the very big rights movement of our time, LGBT rights."[39] Signorile directly correlates the passing of California's Proposition 8, a measure in California defining marriage as existing only between a man and a woman, with Maddow's refusal to engage conservative politicians on their anti-gay beliefs. His critique points directly to Maddow's attempts to maintain a homonormative persona as a symptom of the continuing homophobia that, despite recent gains in gay rights, continues to exist within the broader culture.

As Maddow's tenure has progressed, she has increasingly addressed LGB concerns regarding the ban on out LGB military service, epitomized by the policy "Don't Ask, Don't Tell," and same-sex marriage. This implies a significant shift in the visibility of her involvement with LGB politics. Yet, both military service and marriage remain in the realm of neoliberalism when framed in the context of financial discrimination (via lost wages and tax breaks respectively) faced by LGB individuals unable to engage in these institutions. Framed as "Don't Ask, Don't Tell, Don't Work," Maddow's discussions of "Don't Ask, Don't Tell," like Orman's advocacy for same-sex marriage, focus upon the financial oppression of openly gay individuals who are denied occupational opportunities in the military. As shown throughout this essay LGB acceptance in mainstream society is often tied directly to the assumed race and class privilege of LGB individuals. In essence they are permitted to buy their citizenship via their economic prowess. In denying the financial benefits associated with military service, including funding for college, "Don't Ask, Don't Tell" diminishes the ability of many working-class LGB individuals and LGB of color to climb the socio-economic ladder and obtain the rights and freedoms associated with full citizenship. The

Figure 11.2 **Rachel Maddow (photo by Ali Goldstein for MSNBC).**

---

39. Michelangelo Signorile, "Whither Maddow?" *The Advocate*, February 10, 2009, para. 6.

neoliberalism of Maddow's rhetoric is taken a step further when, rather than focusing on effects of this policy on the LGB community, Maddow spotlights specific, often exceptional, individuals like Lt. Col. Victor Fehrenbach, an F-15 fighter pilot, and Lt. Daniel Choi, a graduate of West Point.[40] While this is, in some ways, a legitimate strategy that puts real faces and names to an otherwise amorphous cause, Maddow's focus on exceptional individuals highlights potential LGB contribution to the state, rather than the state's obligation to lessen the oppression of a stigmatized group.

Homonormative and neoliberal rhetoric is also seen in Maddow's discussion of same-sex marriage. Rather than focusing upon LGB activism for marriage rights, Maddow's coverage has centered upon undermining work done by anti-same-sex organizations like the National Organization for Marriage (NOM).[41] In September 2009, Maddow addressed the concern that same-sex marriage would undermine heterosexual marriage, a key argument made by groups opposing the legalization of this institution. Using government statistics, Maddow reported that divorce rates in Massachusetts, a state that has legalized gay marriage, had fallen to the lowest in the country. Reframing the argument of the opposition Maddow declared, "[I]t turns out gay marriage is a defense of marriage act."[42] Maddow does not openly advocate for what has already been acknowledged as a homonormative issue, gay marriage; she instead focuses upon undermining arguments against the LGB campaign for same-sex marriage. Unlike Orman, who engages in an editorial moment, cited in the epigraph, in which her support of gay marriage is inferred, Maddow's reports center, not on the reasons why same-sex marriage should be legalized, but rather on why those who contest it are wrong. Making this issue visible is a significant step in working to challenge arguments against gay marriage. However, by placing the opposition as the focus of her reports, Maddow concedes to mainstream pressures that demand the centering of heterosexist perspectives. In their quest to obtain mainstream acceptance Orman and Maddow's focus is only upon the most visible and financial of LGB concerns reflecting homonormative and neoliberal ideologies.

Summing It Up

Rachel Maddow and Suze Orman's invocation of homonormativity, postfeminism, and neoliberalism in constructions of their celebrity images allows for the mitigation of readings that may code them as "queer" or controversial and unmarketable to a mainstream audience. Their enactment of race and

---

40. Both Lt. Col. Fehrenbach and Lt. Choi, officers in the Air Force and Army respectively, are fighting discharges after revealing their homosexuality. *The Rachel Maddow Show*, MSNBC, May 19, 2009, and March 19, 2009, Television.
41. *The Rachel Maddow Show*, MSNBC, April 9, 2009, Television.
42. *The Rachel Maddow Show*, MSNBC, September 3, 2009, Television.

class privilege and conformity to other social norms has provided them with the opportunity to purchase mainstream success. The visibility of both Maddow and Orman as lesbians diversifies lesbian representations of professionalism and expertise, yet maintains neoliberal ideologies that prioritize the individual, focus on the power of the consumer, and present conformity as the only means by which mainstream success can be achieved. Their compliance with mainstream ideological strictures limits their contribution to LGB acceptance and narrows potential paths to mainstream success. Their examples make it okay to be gay, but not queer.

The celebrity trajectories of Maddow and Orman suggest that while there is room for (sexual) diversity in the representation of female celebrities, the price of this visible difference is the ultimate maintenance of the cultural status quo. The significance of Orman and Maddow's lesbianism is undermined by their willingness to maintain hegemonic norms of race and class privilege, simultaneously enacting ideological tenets that reaffirm the propriety of individualism, normative sexual practices, and capitalism. Ultimately, the threat to larger social power structures associated with the potential influence of lesbian celebrities must be destabilized as a condition for their mainstream success.

Bibliography

Baird, Julia. "When Left is Right; Rachel Maddow Always Thought of Herself as An Outsider. How Did she Become a Star?" *Newsweek*, December 1, 2008, 55.

Boverman, Neal. "Smart Money." *The Advocate*, December 2, 2008, 11.

Browne, Kath, Jason Lim, and Gavin Brown. *Geographies of Sexualities: Theory, Practices, and Politics*. Burlington, VT: Ashgate, 2007.

Burk, Martha. "Suze Orman's Bottom Line." *Ms.* October 1, (Fall 2008): 34–7.

Butler, Judith. *Gender Trouble: Feminism and the Subversion of Identity*. New York: Routledge, 1990.

Colon, Suzan. "The New American Classic." *The Advocate*, December 2, 2008, 34–9.

Decker, Jeffrey Louis. *Made in America: Self-Styled Success from Horatio Alger to Oprah Winfrey*. Minneapolis, MN: University of Minnesota Press, 1997.

Dow, Bonnie J. "*Ellen*, Television, and the Politics of Gay and Lesbian Visibility." *Critical Studies in Mass Communication* 18(2), (2001): 123–40.

Dyer, Richard. *Heavenly Bodies: Film Stars and Society*. New York: Routledge, 2004.

Ferguson, Roderick A. "Race-ing Homonormativity: Citizenship, Sociology and Gay Identity," in E. Patrick Johnson and Mae G. Henderson (eds), *Black Queer Studies: A Critical Anthology*. Durham, NC: Duke University Press, 2005.

Halberstam, Judith. *Female Masculinity*. Durham, NC: Duke University Press, 1998.

Jeffery, Clara. "The Maddow Knows." *Mother Jones* January 2009: 72–3.

Late Night with Jimmy Fallon. NBC. March 25, 2009. Television.

Miller, Toby. *Cultural Citizenship: Comopolitanism, Consumerism, and Television in a Neoliberal Age*. Philadelphia, PA: Temple University Press, 2007.

Negra, Diane. *What a Girl Wants? Fantasizing the Reclamation of Self in Postfeminism*. New York: Routledge, 2009.

Olson, Theodore B. "The Conservative Case for Gay Marriage: Why Same-Sex Marriage is an American Value." *Newsweek*, January 18, 2010, 48–54.

Ong, Aihwa. *Neoliberalism as Exception: Mutations in Citizenship and Sovereignty*. Durham, NC: Duke University Press, 2006.

Orman, Suze. *Women and Money: Owning the Power to Control Your Destiny*. New York: Spiegel & Grau, 2007.

Ouellette, Laurie and James Hay. *Better Living Through Reality TV: Television and Post-Welfare Citizenship*. Malden, MA: Blackwell, 2008.

Puar, Jasbir K. *Terrorist Assemblages: Homonationalism in Queer Times*. Durham, NC: Duke University Press, 2007.

Quart, Alissa. "The Sarcastic Times: For Rachel Maddow and the Other Ironic Anchors, Absurdity is Serious Stuff." *Columbia Journalism Review* 47(6), (2009): 12–14.

The Rachel Maddow Show. MSNBC. September 2008 – present. Television.

Schurenberg, Eric. "If You Knew Suze . . . " *Money*, July 2008: 106–7.

Signorile, Michelangelo. "Whither Maddow?" *The Advocate*, February 10, 2009, 70–1.

Solomon, Deborah. "She's So Money," *The New York Times Magazine*, February 25, 2007, 19.

"Suze Orman." *The Advocate*, January 13, 2009, 69.

The Suze Orman Show. CNBC. March 2002 — Present. Television.

Tan, Michelle. "MSNBC's Rachel Maddow: At Home & Unplugged." *People*, April 12, 2010, 105–6.

Tasker, Yvonne and Diane Negra. "Introduction: Feminist Politics and Postfeminist Culture," in Yvonne Tasker and Diane Negra (eds), *Interrogating Postfeminism: Gender and the Politics of Popular Culture*. Durham, NC: Duke University Press, 2007, 1–25.

Tracy, Ben. "Meet 'The Money Lady': Suze Orman Talks About Her Life, Her Philosophy and Financial Mistakes Everyone Makes," *CBS News*, February 17, 2008. Available at: http://www.cbsnews.com/stories/2008/02/17/sunday/main3841256.shtml (accessed January 6, 2010).

The View. ABC. March 5, 2009. Television.

Warner, Michael. *The Trouble with Normal: Sex, Politics, and the Ethics of Queer Life*. Cambridge, MA: Harvard University Press, 2000.

Widner, Jonanna. "The Rachel Papers: What a Hot, Smart, Lesbian Pundit Means For an Uneasy America." *Bitch: Feminist Response to Pop Culture* Spring 2009: 36–9.

12

Living *The Hills* Life
Lauren Conrad as Reality Star, Soap Opera Heroine, and Brand

ALICE LEPPERT AND JULIE WILSON

MULTIPLE ACCOUNTS OF REALITY TELEVISION discuss its ability to make a celebrity out of anybody, to pluck an ordinary person out of obscurity and thrust her or him into the limelight. For the most part though, the celebrity that reality television provides for its endless parade of "cast members" is fleeting at best. Most reality TV performers fit neatly into Chris Rojek's concept of the celetoid — a form of celebrity whose lifespan in the public eye is brief and whose fame is, in the first place, constructed by the media. However, Lauren Conrad, star of MTV's *Laguna Beach* and *The Hills*, has become not a celetoid, but a star.

Lauren's[1] life first hit the airwaves on September 28, 2004, when she starred in MTV's reality serial *Laguna Beach*, which chronicled the lives of teenagers in California's wealthy Orange County. Lauren narrated the show, and much of the plot focused on a love triangle between Lauren, her friend Stephen, and his on-and-off girlfriend, Kristin. *Laguna Beach* set up Lauren as the nice girl (perpetuated through her voiceover narration) and Kristin as the bitch. Season one of *Laguna Beach* proved to be a modest hit for MTV, and the second season saw it become the second most successful show on MTV, behind *The Real World*.[2] Lauren turned out to be so popular that MTV produced *The Hills* as a spin-off focusing solely on her. *The Hills* primarily follows Lauren as she lives, works, and parties in Los Angeles.

The Hills premiered on August 31, 2006, and quickly grew into a ratings success for MTV. The first season averaged 2.3 million viewers and the second season 2.5 million viewers.[3] During the third season, *The Hills* was the

---

1. Throughout this article we refer to Conrad as "Lauren" to reflect the manufactured intimacy with audiences that enlivens what we elaborate as her unique model of reality stardom.
2. James Hibberd, "Reality Star Gets New MTV Show," *Television Week*, November 14, 2005, 30.
3. Stephanie D. Smith, "Teen Beat," *WWD: Women's Wear Daily*, March 23, 2007, 10.

highest rated show for its time slot among viewers age 12–34[4] with the season premiere reaching approximately 3.7 million viewers: "[O]f that number, women under the age of 18 made up 17 percent, and women between the ages of 18 and 34 were 49 percent."[5] The season three finale reached an unprecedented 4.6 million viewers.[6]

Throughout her MTV tenure, Lauren's image and persona increasingly permeated multiple media markets as she graced the covers of *Us Weekly*, *Seventeen*, *CosmoGirl*, *Shape*, *Rolling Stone*, *Entertainment Weekly*, *Cosmopolitan*, and *Teen Vogue*.[7] In addition to all of this exposure, MTV's marketing machine worked overtime to push products related to Lauren and *The Hills*, including books, calendars, soundtracks, and the website seenonmtv. com, where viewers could purchase items featured on the program. When Lauren left *The Hills* in 2009, a ratings plummet to 2.1 million viewers was indicative of her star power.[8] Today, Lauren remains constant fodder for celebrity gossip magazines and popular gossip blogs like perezhilton.com and tmz.com. Meanwhile the first book in her HarperCollins teen book series, *L.A. Candy* topped the *New York Times* Best Seller list for several weeks in 2009.

In the context of this over-saturation of media coverage and product tie-ins, we seek to understand how and why Lauren has become such a popular soap opera heroine, star, and brand. Germane to industrial trends in post-network broadcasting, the workings of contemporary celebrity culture, and the post-Fordist historical moment, Lauren signals a new mode of US reality television stardom — a profoundly gendered solution to some of the economic limits of previous forms of reality television celebrity. Through its peculiar adherence to, and adaptation of, both cinematic aesthetics and soap opera conventions, MTV's *The Hills* has been able to adapt earlier modes of female stardom to reality programming. This melding of "high" and "low" cultural forms — of reality program and cinematic production value, of soap opera narrative and the glamorous life of Hollywood stars — engenders a paradoxical feminine form of celebrity. *The Hills* brings the power and value of traditional forms of female stardom into the aesthetically dismissed, "low" cultural landscape of reality television providing significant economic benefits for MTV and its advertisers, as well as a broader network of lifestyle and cultural industries. We argue that Lauren's stardom takes a particularly

---

4. "'The Hills' Phenomenon Continues On-air and Online." CNNMoney.com, December 12, 2007.

5. Khanh T. L. Tran, "MTV Partners With Conrad For Fashion," *WWD: Women's Wear Daily*, August 24, 2007, 4.

6. "'The Hills' Phenomenon," CNNMoney.com, December 12, 2007.

7. *Teen Vogue* saw a distinct increase in profits thanks to Lauren's diegetic employment with the magazine: "Since the MTV reality show 'The Hills,' based on Teen Vogue intern Lauren Conrad, returned in mid-January, newsstand sales for the Cond [*sic*] Nast teen title have increased by double digits over last year" (Smith, 10).

8. Alex Werpin, "Ratings: MTV's 'The City' Shines, 'The Hills' Slow." *Broadcasting & Cable*, September 30, 2009.

gendered form, one that brings together elements of the preeminent feminine genre, the soap opera, with the feminized gossip industry and consumer culture. This unique gendered articulation of reality TV celebrity allows MTV to capitalize on earlier forms of female stardom previously inaccessible within US reality TV.

Ordinary Girl/Extraordinary Life: Lauren's Reality Stardom

We argue that Lauren is perhaps the first US reality *star*, and as such, the contours of her stardom deserve critical attention. Stardom, as a historical and social phenomenon, is linked to key developments in the institution of cinema. According to Richard deCordova, the invention of the star worked to engage consumers in ongoing hermeneutic activity in regards to the "true" identity of the person behind and apart from the representations of characters, and thus constituted audiences as fans interested and invested in the "real" lives of screen actors. The star, as the object of ongoing audience speculation and investigation, helped cement the profitability and viability of cinema, enabling the institution to reach further into the everyday lives of consumers. Stardom then is an economically motivated discourse fueled by audience interest in the private and real lives of stars, and as Shelley Stamp shows, beginning in the 1910s, "the audience" was increasingly conceived as female.

In addition to contributing to the process of commodifying cinema, stardom, as a discourse focused on the ways stars live, came to perform important ideological work by, as Richard Dyer argues, allowing the exceptional and charismatic qualities of the star to evanesce while, at the same time, insisting on the normalcy and ordinariness of stars. Edgar Morin has theorized this co-mingling of the extraordinary and ordinary enabled by the star as a form of embourgeoisement: as a capitulation of the cinema to middle-class sensibilities and imagination in the wake of the Depression. As stars shifted from embodying an ideal to appearing more typical, they became points of identification for audiences rather than transcendent "gods and goddesses" and thus contributed to the solidification and expansion of Western, bourgeois norms and values.

Female stars in particular have historically proven especially important to the economic life of film and television institutions. According to Charles Eckert, as Hollywood sought out new means of profitability, female stars became highly effective vehicles for early forms of product placement and tie-ins, emerging as a potent economic force within the institution of cinema for their ability to promote particular products through their constructed stardom.[9] Lauren Conrad, as a reality television star, must be considered as

---

9. Eckert, Charles, "The Carole Lombard in Macy's Window," 30–9, in Christine Gledhill (ed.), *Stardom: Industry of Desire* (London: Routledge, 1991).

part of a long line of female stars whose value rests primarily on their ability to act as a relay between desired female audiences, a host of lifestyle industries, and particular arms of the culture industry itself. Indeed, the products Lauren endorses are the same "feminine" products her predecessors pushed: clothing (The Lauren Conrad Collection and LC Lauren Conrad Collection), accessories (a handbag line in conjunction with Linea Pelle), and cosmetics (Avon's Mark).

As John Langer and others have pointed out, television — as a more explicitly commercialized and domestic medium — has historically emphasized the "ordinariness" of its stars, capitalizing not on the cinematic distance encouraged by modes of theatrical spectatorship but on the intimacy and regularity of relationships fostered between television "personalities" and their home-based viewers. Embedded in the rhythms of everyday life and contingent on commercial sponsorship, television developed modes of female stardom that relied on less rigid distinctions between the ordinary/ extraordinary aspects of star images. While the film industry tried to hide the mechanisms behind the glamorous and illusory world of film stars, fearing that the appearance of mass commodification would upset the star image, the industrial structure and more commercialized "lowly" status of television both demanded and sanctioned more blatant forms of marketing through stars. As Susan Murray notes: "Television stars were explicitly connected to a variety of products both within their program text and outside of it, while film stars were most commonly used implicitly to sell clothes, makeup, and other products placed within their films without directly addressing spectators and engaging in overt salesmanship."[10]

Lauren Conrad, however, is not a film or television star, but a reality television star, firmly embedded within the industrial conditions that circumscribe US post-network television production and which have given rise to the era of reality TV. In this context, "quality" shows thrive alongside cheaper-to-produce reality programs. In its earlier incarnations (docusoaps, gamedocs, and talent competitions), US reality television had not been able to capitalize on its casts of ordinary contestants as stars, relying heavily on what Rojek describes as the celetoid form of celebrity. Turner has taken up this concept to understand the "accelerated life cycle" of reality TV celebrity made possible by an endless and more readily controllable pool of free labor provided by "ordinary" people desiring fame.[11] Reality TV took television's earlier decision to highlight the "ordinariness" of its stars to the extreme, evacuating "extraordinariness" from its representational landscape, and making a total and literal commitment to the ordinariness

---

10. Susan Murray, *Hitch Your Antenna to the Stars: Early Television and Broadcast Stardom* (New York: Routledge, 2005), 146.

11. Graeme Turner, "The Mass Production of Celebrity: 'Celetoids', Reality TV and the 'Demotic Turn,'" *International Journal of Cultural Studies* 9 (2006): 156.

of television personalities. Here celebrity is a de-gendered phenomenon, as men and women alike are invited to be exploited by the "mass production of celebrity." However, Lauren's rise and prominence on MTV is anything but mercurial, suggesting that the "accelerated life cycle" of reality TV and the "ordinary," "democratic," gender-neutral forms of celebrity it provides for are not a condition made necessary by the genre itself. With Lauren, MTV has pioneered a gendered mode of reality celebrity that harks back to earlier versions of both film and television female stardom, while simultaneously and paradoxically forwarding the commitment to ordinariness that has proven so important to reality television.

In her analysis of Sarah Jessica Parker (SJP), Deborah Jermyn suggests that there is an "increasingly complex relationship between television and stardom."[12] Jermyn is interested in how today's celebrity culture and television production system give rise to figures like SJP who have much in common with traditional film stars. SJP's construction in popular media texts, especially celebrity gossip magazines, mirrors that of earlier stars: audiences are urged to know not only Carrie Bradshaw (the stylish, single, shoe-obsessed, relationship-challenged heroine of HBO's *Sex and the City*) but also the real SJP (wife of Matthew Broderick, mother, and real life fashionista). What's more, SJP — a fashion icon and style guru — has been tapped to endorse a wide array of products through advertising campaigns that center on the fantasies her stardom underwrites. *Sex and the City*'s status as "quality" TV authorizes the meshing of film and television modes of female stardom embodied by SJP — a meshing that was fully realized with the first successful film version of *Sex and the City*.

Lauren's reality television stardom however suggests a more complicated story about the relationships between television and film stardom, as Lauren's celebrity status emerges on the opposite end of the US post-network television landscape, from within the sullied genre of reality TV. Like SJP Lauren serves as the voice-over narrator for a show that revolves around relationships between four females living glamorous working lives while struggling at love; Lauren is also ongoing fodder for celebrity magazines, and has her own fashion line. However, whereas SJP's stardom upholds and illustrates previous modes of film stardom that are contingent upon distinctions (albeit slippery) between a real person, the characters or roles performed, and a constructed star image, Lauren's reality television stardom is realized in the near total collapse of these distinctions. If stardom is "an image of the way stars live" that presents invested audiences with a "generalized lifestyle" through which to interpret the real identity of the star,[13] Lauren

---

12. Deborah Jermyn, "'Bringing Out the Star in You': SJP, Carrie Bradshaw and the Evolution of Television Stardom," in Su Holmes and Sean Redmond (eds), *Framing Celebrity* (London: Routledge, 2006), 70.

13. Richard Dyer, *Stars*, new ed. (London: British Film Institute, 1998), 35.

signals a more immanent structure of stardom, where the gap between the role performed by and the real life of the star is completely elided at the level of representation itself. Lauren plays herself; yet on *The Hills,* the representations of Lauren *are* the image of the way she lives. Within this structure of reality stardom, hermeneutic activity on the part of audiences and Lauren's fans is still facilitated and invited; however, this audience work feeds directly back into the show itself. Gossip magazines preview and anticipate Lauren's upcoming feuds, breakups, hookups, and other happenings to be aired later on the show, firmly circumscribing audience interest in the star within the context of *The Hills.*

While the elision of distinction between persona and real life realized by Lauren's reality stardom bears a homologous structure to the "ordinary" celebrity of other reality formats, *The Hills* leaves intact and thrives off Lauren's extraordinariness, a feat which we will show *The Hills* achieves through soap opera conventions, cinematic aesthetics, and fictional codes of realism derived from film and television. However, Lauren's extraordinary status is paradoxically produced by a representational insistence on her ordinariness, that is, by refusing to allude to Lauren's actual reality stardom within the discourse of *The Hills.* As Amanda Klein argues, *Hills*' producers work hard to ensure that the reality show remains about "ordinary," relatable young women and not about being stars; activities such as photo shoots for magazines, press interviews, and run-ins with paparazzi are not represented. Lauren's life on *The Hills* is presented as that of a "good girl" (as opposed to the "bitch") working hard to make it in the fashion industry, while struggling romantically and negotiating close friendships. Lauren's stardom depends on viewers' willingness to see Lauren first and foremost through the fictionalized "real" world constructed by *The Hills.* While gossip magazines often feature photos of Lauren on red carpets or at fashion shows alongside other Hollywood stars and celebrities, the majority of the coverage focuses on events unfolding on *The Hills.* Shot on location across Los Angeles, with the paparazzi just outside the frame, the reality format works as a built-in, though imperfect, policing mechanism, ensuring that the actual processes underwriting Lauren's reality stardom remain subservient to her working girl persona. While some revel in finding and publicizing evidence that *The Hills* is indeed scripted and fake (a practice not at all unique to *The Hills*), Lauren's "real" identity is rarely if ever in question. Unlike her cast mates, whose true motivations are continuously interrogated by the gossip industry and fans, Lauren's presence in and on *The Hills* is for the most part taken for granted and naturalized. While her cast mates are treated more like celetoids (ordinary people desiring celebrification), Lauren is represented as a unified self, whose intentions and commitments, both professionally and personally, remain transparent, sincere, and consistent. In this way Lauren's reality stardom works as an ideological justification for the exploitative celetoid-dominated system of reality TV — elevating her above this system, while eliding the very practices that make her elevation possible.

Mingling the extraordinary (Lauren's star quality and lifestyle) with the ordinary (her "real" entry level work in the fashion industry and the "feminized" melodrama represented on the show), Lauren's paradoxical reality stardom enables a kind of working girl's fantasy germane to the gendered cultural imaginary of post-Fordism. *The Hills* taps into the promises of pre-recession post-industrial work life and contemporary consumer culture, where labor in the creative, cultural, and lifestyle industries was presented as an increasingly viable and inviting option for young middle-class women. However, as Angela McRobbie has argued, the invitation of women into contemporary workplaces entails a postfeminist sexual contract, where women must leave feminism behind and instead agree to imagine their life possibilities in terms of highly individualized choices. In this postfeminist context, patriarchy is largely displaced by fashion, as women navigate more diffused and unnamed forms of hegemonic masculinity by cultivating appropriate "feminine" selves through dress and self-presentation that temper the threat of their growing economic capacity and presence in the workplace. While makeover shows like *What Not to Wear* provide technical and practical instruction to middle and working class women already in the workplace, *The Hills* works less directly, more as an orienting device for young women, presenting both the fashion world and work in the creative industries in fantasy form, thus signaling a distinctly post-Fordist, postfeminist form of embourgeoisement.

Imperatively, this fantasy hinges on Lauren's paradoxical female stardom that *The Hills* meticulously constructs through viewer identification with, and idealization of, Lauren as a soap opera heroine. Scholars of reality TV have long noted similarities between reality programs and soap opera, but the specific format of the docusoap has proven rather unsuccessful in the US context. MTV is unique in its development of the format, from *The Real World* to its most recent version of *Laguna Beach, Newport Harbor*; however, *The Hills* represents a significant and economically successful break with key aspects of the docusoap with its branding of Lauren Conrad as a reality star.

Figure 12.1 **Lauren works the Marc by Marc Jacobs Young Hollywood Fashion Show in "Young Hollywood."** ***The Hills: The Complete Third Season.***

In order to better understand the production of Lauren's paradoxical female stardom and the unprecedented success of *The Hills* which underwrites it, we ask: How specifically are the conventions of stardom articulated to reality TV by a docusoap that looks more like a film than a documentary, and feels more like a soap opera than reality?

Identifying with and Idealizing Lauren: Making a Soap Opera Heroine

In an attempt to begin to answer this question, it's important to understand the specific ways in which Lauren is produced as a star. The representational strategies adopted by *The Hills* engender Lauren's paradoxical female celebrity by fusing cinematic aesthetics and soap opera conventions into a reality format. Constructed as an ordinary girl in the context of an extraordinary "real" life, *The Hills* invites viewers to relate to Lauren as a soap opera heroine while simultaneously encouraging us to see her as exceptional, an image to be aspired to. Chronicling Lauren's emotional struggles against the backdrop of trendy clubs, alluring work settings, and stylized apartments, *The Hills* rearticulates the soap opera to the world of young Hollywood for a female prime-time audience imagined to be highly invested in both celebrity culture and the high-end products associated with the LA lifestyle.

The Hills uses soap opera conventions in order to achieve identification with Lauren; however, the resulting identification is quite different from the kind soaps foster. With its large cast and multiple storylines, which are dropped one day and picked up later in the week, the daytime soap opera relies on multiple identifications; in order to be invested in a daytime soap, the viewer must be able to align herself with more than a single axial character. Similarly, while the cast of the prime-time soap is much smaller than that of the daytime soap, most prime-time soaps have ensemble casts, where the viewer is not urged to identify with a single character.[14] With only three supporting characters — who appear to barely live lives outside of the way they affect and interact with Lauren — *The Hills* does not neatly fit into either the prime-time or daytime soap models. Instead it adapts key soap opera conventions to emotionally connect the viewer with Lauren's "real life" melodrama. Melding the spectacle of the Hollywood lifestyle connected with film stars with a deep investment in Lauren's struggles at love and work, *The Hills* constructs Lauren's reality stardom in large part through inviting intense forms of identification with Lauren.

Most *Hills* episodes revolve around one personal problem or set of related problems that Lauren discusses with several of her friends. As in soap operas, conversation is the crux of *The Hills*, but here conversation most always

---

14. While US daytime soaps are struggling to survive, prime-time soaps have successfully courted a teenage audience for the last two decades, from *Beverly Hills, 90210* to *Dawson's Creek* to *Gossip Girl.*

revolves to varying degrees around Lauren in the service of elaborating her point of view. As Tania Modleski notes, "on soap operas, action is less important than *re*action and *inter*action."[15] *The Hills* makes Lauren's reactions to difficult personal situations and her interactions with friends and rivals much more important than any narrative "event." In fact, the events in the show last a fraction of the time that Lauren spends reacting to them and discussing them with her friends. As Elana Levine points out, episodes of *The Hills* do not develop a plot, rather they obsess over relationship conflicts. In "You Have Chosen," an episode from the second season, Lauren discusses her deteriorating relationship with her best friend Heidi in all but one scene in which she appears, and in every scene in which she is absent, other people discuss her problems. The structure of the episode makes the conversations repetitive, yet also relays the common structure of gossip. While the variety of perspectives this structure offers might seem to allow for what Christine Geraghty refers to as decentered identification — that is, the diffusion of viewer identification with a variety of soap characters — Lauren is at once the main discussant (she talks to Heidi, Spencer, Whitney, Audrina, and Brody) and the main topic of discussion (Heidi, Spencer, and Brody discuss her). Furthermore, when others discuss Lauren, her views of them are overwhelmingly confirmed — Spencer indeed does want Heidi to cut Lauren out of her life, and we see firsthand that he has a roving eye. *The Hills* consistently legitimates Lauren's point of view, strongly urging viewers to identify with her and her alone.

 The Hills solidifies Lauren's narrative centrality by using voiceover to further align the viewer with Lauren, giving her access to Lauren's thoughts. Through her voiceovers, Lauren explicitly shapes the narrative and provides a frame through which the viewer is to understand conflicts and events. Lauren narrates *The Hills* through an introductory voiceover at the beginning of each episode, a technique that harks back to radio soap operas, though as Robert C. Allen points out, the radio narrators were all male. Describing the narrator's function, Allen argues, "He controlled the flow of the story; his voice described the world in which all characters appeared; he knew and related the thoughts of characters and conditioned the reader's reception of those thoughts."[16] Indeed, even when Lauren and Heidi are no longer on speaking terms, Lauren still tells the viewer exactly what is going on in Heidi's life and how Heidi feels about her work and her relationships. Although we do not see Heidi and Lauren spending any time together in season three (outside of a few contentious "coincidental" confrontations), through her voiceover Lauren appears omniscient. The limited number of

---

15. Tania Modleski, "The Rhythms of Reception: Daytime Television and Women's Work," in E. Ann Kaplan (ed.), *Regarding Television* (Los Angeles: AFI, 1983), 68.
16. Robert C. Allen, *Speaking of Soap Operas* (Chapel Hill: University of North Carolina Press, 1985), 161.

characters on *The Hills* combined with Lauren's enunciative control over the diegesis works to solidify identification — encouraging the viewer to align herself with Lauren's point of view. As Louise Spence argues, "part of the process of watching soap operas is making friends with characters. In fact, we may feel that we know a character in a soap opera better than we know some of our own friends or colleagues."[17] With extended access to Lauren over several years and via multiple media, coupled with her narrative centrality, viewers may indeed feel as though they know her very well. However, while *The Hills* goes to great lengths to nurture identification and intimacy with Lauren, it also insists on her exceptional status, which is central to her construction as a reality star.

The Hills moves away from the docusoap conventions exemplified by *The Real World* through eliminating the documentary codes which docusoaps use to connote the real and instead pursuing a more cinematic aesthetic. The program does away with handheld camerawork, harsh lighting, and direct address (or "confessional") moments, in favor of steady, even framing, flattering soft lighting, and a perfectly intact fourth wall.[18] While most reality television programs rely on a less polished look to maintain an air of immediacy and "reality," *The Hills* is less concerned with claims on the real than it is with producing a female star whose celebrity can be mobilized for the MTV *Hills* brand and its advertisers. The cinematic look of *The Hills* elevates Lauren and her lifestyle above reality TV celetoids, making her into the star of what often appears to be a fictionalized narrative of her own life.

While the cinematic aesthetic of *The Hills* spectacularizes Lauren's everyday life, the reliance on close-ups maintains a familiarity with her at the same time, thus sustaining audience identification. Close-ups provide the viewer with unmitigated access to Lauren's emotions and thoughts — as Tony DiSanto, executive producer of *The Hills* notes, Lauren has a particularly expressive face. In the season two episode "With Friends Like These . . ." Lauren has an emotional breakdown, rendered in a series of close-ups of her arguing with Heidi and getting progressively more upset. The close-ups display Lauren fighting tears then crying, her lip quivering, and a vein in her forehead protruding. Finally, Lauren turns her head and gazes offscreen, closes her eyes and just as a tear begins to fall, the camera cuts to an exterior shot of her apartment complex's swimming pool and the credits appear. While the close-ups bring us into Lauren's emotional world, we can only stay

17. Louise Spence, "'They Killed Off Marlena, But She's On Another Show Now': Fantasy, Reality, and Pleasure in Watching Daytime Soap Operas," in Robert C. Allen (ed.), *To Be Continued . . .: Soap Operas Around the World* (London: Routledge, 1995), 189.
18. Hisham Abed, director of photography for *The Hills*, details the technical decisions the production crew made in order to facilitate a cinematic look. In addition to using a wide-screen aspect ratio, producers selected cameras with attractive lighting in mind to create a more cinematic aesthetic distinct from the lighting of most reality shows ("Creating the Cinematic Look," 8).

Figure 12.2 **Lauren reacts to Heidi's betrayal in "With Friends Like These . . ."** *The Hills: The Complete Second Season.*

for so long before the camera pulls away, preserving a significant amount of mystery around Lauren. Every episode of *The Hills* ends in this manner — an emotional climax followed by a cut away to exterior or aerial shots. This convention contributes to a critical distance between the viewer and Lauren. *The Hills* does not allow the viewer to get too close to Lauren, thus maintaining the necessary distance to keep Lauren as an extraordinary figure. In order to produce Lauren as a star, *The Hills* cannot risk making her too familiar to the viewer, who must both aspire to be Lauren and recognize that she can never be Lauren. *The Hills* underscores this impossibility through attention to Lauren's flawless appearance, her wealth, and her early career success.

The temporality of *The Hills* in conjunction with celebrity gossip magazines and blogs furthers the emotional intensity of the viewer's involvement with Lauren, while simultaneously promoting her star status. Magazines and blogs detail Lauren's personal life weeks or months before we see the same events occur on the show; thus, the invested viewer has knowledge while watching *The Hills* that Lauren does not, and must watch Lauren suffer. As Lynne Joyrich claims, "it is this relative powerlessness that drives melodrama's viewers to tears; we cry from the lack of coincidence dramatized on the screen, a lack we are unable to change — the gap between our knowledge and that of the characters, between what should happen and what actually does, between the 'rightness' of a union and its delay."[19] For example, in the third season of *The Hills*, Lauren reconnects with her ex-boyfriend Jason over three episodes, airing on September 10, 17, and 24. However, gossip site tmz.com broke the news of Jason's engagement on August 28 and a story appeared in *Us Weekly*'s September 17 issue. Due to this temporal lag, the viewer watches Lauren become reinvested in Jason, knowing that she will be heartbroken in the end. In "Second Chances," Lauren tells the viewer in voiceover, "for once, my career and my personal life were under control. Why is it that just when you get things together, you hear from the one person who can pull it

---

19. Lynne Joyrich, *Re-Viewing Reception: Television, Gender, and Postmodern Culture* (Bloomington: Indiana University Press, 1996), 60–1.

all apart?" which leads into the beginning of the episode. Lauren arrives at work and immediately reveals this "person's" identity, telling Whitney that Jason called her the night before. The anticipation of Lauren's heartbreak intensifies the narrative pathos — the viewer watches Lauren agonize over her ambiguous relationship with Jason, yet the viewer is powerless to save Lauren any pain. This temporal gap between gossip reporting and broadcast is similar to that produced by soap opera spoilers that the soap opera press often report. John Fiske explains that the temporal gap allows the viewer to relish the characters' reactions — the viewer is not so much concerned with what will happen, but with how the character will handle it. Charlotte Brunsdon suggests that soap operas come close to "heroine television," where "It is the 'trying to cope' which is crucial."[20] However, *The Hills*'s high profile in celebrity gossip magazines also underscores Lauren's exceptional status, as the events of her "ordinary" life are positioned alongside those of other stars. Audience hermeneutic activity regarding Lauren corresponds to the modes of reception surrounding other Hollywood VIPs except here the pleasures associated with gossip and delving into the private lives of stars are channeled back into the narrative context and melodramatic structure of *The Hills*.

As in fictional soap operas, *The Hills* focuses primarily on Lauren's personal life and the way it permeates her work life — as Allen explains, most soap operas only feature occupations that allow for constant conversation about personal life. Work life figures centrally in the discourse of *The Hills*, both as an occasion for the extended "conversation" at the heart of the narrative and as a way to accentuate Lauren's exceptional qualities while paradoxically insisting on her ordinariness. When Lauren is at work, her work time mostly consists of telling her friend and co-worker Whitney all about her personal problems. Each of the four women on the first three seasons of *The Hills* works in the culture industries — Lauren and Whitney at *Teen Vogue* and fashion PR firm People's Revolution, Audrina first at Quixote Studios (a facility primarily used for photo shoots) then at Epic Records, and Heidi at Bolthouse Productions, an event planning firm. Their jobs allow for maximum conversation time — especially with Lauren and Whitney working out of the same tiny office at *Teen Vogue*. Although their tasks are often menial (answering phones, addressing invitations, steaming clothes, taking inventory), all of the women on *The Hills* hold jobs that the average viewer of the show could aspire to — and the jobs have a glamorous air about them. Lauren may be an (ostensibly) unpaid intern, but she flies to New York and Paris on assignments for *Teen Vogue*. Heidi may have to fetch lunch for her boss, but she is in charge of the guest lists for some of the most celebrity-filled

---

20. Charlotte Brunsdon, "The Role of Soap Opera in the Development of Feminist Television Scholarship," in Robert C. Allen (ed.), *To Be Continued . . .: Soap Operas Around the World* (London: Routledge, 1995), 54.

clubs in Los Angeles. Audrina may sit at a desk answering phones, but she works with popular recording artists like Sean Kingston. These women hold entry-level positions, making them relatable to the viewer; however, their jobs also revolve around living an enviable lifestyle. In this way the representations of work life not only buttress *The Hills'* soap opera narrative but also work to temper some of the paradoxes surrounding Lauren's reality stardom, resolving a bit of the tension between Lauren's ordinary working girl persona and her alluring Hollywood lifestyle. These representations of work life take on increasing significance in the post-Fordist context, glossing over the risks and insecurities associated with post-industrial labor in the creative industries and presenting the contemporary work situation in highly feminized fantasy form.

Constructing Lauren as the soap opera heroine of her spectacular "real life," *The Hills* begets a paradoxical mode of female celebrity that carefully holds in tension the ordinary and extraordinary aspects of earlier forms of film and television female stardom through a pioneering and tightly controlled reality format marketed towards young women. Through watching Lauren work, play, live, and love across LA, *The Hills* invites viewers to both identify with and idealize Lauren as the star of her own real life fairy tale. However, the tensions permeating the construction of Lauren's reality stardom signal more than a unique aesthetic achievement by the "lowly" genre of reality TV: through these tensions Lauren's life on *The Hills* becomes an immeasurable source of value not only for MTV, but also for a host of lifestyle and cultural industries associated with the program. As a female reality star, Lauren emerges as both a potent lifestyle brand and a new form of cultural intermediary.

Living The Hill$ Life: Branding Lauren's "Reality"

Noting, "L.A. is an expensive place when you have expensive taste," a mid-season three MTV promo asked "How much money do they spend to live in the Hills?" "Living the Hill$ Life" — a re-broadcast of early season three episodes this time with running pop-up commentary detailing the costs of clothes, accessories, and cars of *Hills* cast members — answered this question. Each re-broadcast episode begins by instructing viewers via a pop-up message to "Look out for price tags during the show to find out what it takes to live the Hill$ life." "Prada shirt $368." "Diesel denim vest $158.40." "Dolce Vita Mary Jane pumps $139.95." "Want Lauren's look? Head over to seenonmtv.com." With an implicit nod to the paradoxical nature of Lauren's reality stardom, the show also included some hints on how to get a specific look for less, featuring cheaper yet similar items available at mass market stores including Target, JC Penney, and Macy's.

It's easy to conceptualize "Living the Hill$ Life" as "advertainment" in its most unapologetic form. As June Deery notes, in response to new tensions placed on relationships between advertisers and broadcasters in the wake of media convergence and new technologies, producers are once again relying on "branded content" that conflates entertainment with advertising. With its flexible and mass customizable formats, coupled with a claim on the real, reality TV has emerged as a genre of television exceptionally well-suited for new experiments in product placement and corporate sponsorship.[21] However, seeing *The Hills* and its related texts as simply a form of reality television "advertainment" obfuscates the specific branding practices performed by the show, especially those that hinge on Lauren's status as a soap heroine and reality star in a converged media context. Lauren's paradoxical female celebrity and its unique purchase on its female audience authorize the blatant forms of commodification at work in "Living the Hill$ Life."

Lauren's reality stardom and the success of *The Hills* are situated in a new media, post-network landscape where the television program extends across multimedia platforms seeking to constitute a highly invested, interactive niche audience. According to Joseph Turow, what is commonly referred to as lifestyle branding arises from processes of increased market segmentation, where "the new portraits of society that advertisers and media personnel invoke involve the blending of income, generation, marital status, and gender into a soup of geo-graphical and psychological profiles they call 'lifestyles.'"[22] Lifestyle brands rely less on demographically imagined audiences — characterized by shared gender, race, or income — and are instead engendered to speak to the identities, experiences, and values of particular lifestyle groups. In 2007, MTV Networks (MTVN) (the parent company of MTV and a host of other cable networks owned by Viacom) altered its sales approach, adopting more explicit lifestyle branding strategies. In imagining its television programming in terms of distinct clusters of lifestyle brands, MTVN hoped to make itself a more attractive and profitable venue for advertisers whose products can be more readily and precisely articulated to particular lifestyle groups.

Lifestyle branding practices are made possible by developments in database and monitoring technologies that allow marketers to gather more specific data on consumer behavior. Mark Andrejevic provides a more nuanced vision of reality television's political economy than Deery, examining how the medium is able to pioneer new marketing strategies based on enhanced consumer observation in the converged media context. According to Andrejevic, reality TV is unique in its uncanny ability to convert the promise of interactivity and participation heralded by new media into what he calls "productive surveillance," or "the work of being watched." In the case of *The Hills*, the generation of "productive surveillance" requires new forms

---

21. June Deery, "Reality TV as advertisement," *Popular Communication* 2, (2004).
22. Joseph Turow, *Breaking Up America: Advertisers and the New Media World* (Chicago: University of Chicago Press, 1997), 3.

of interactivity, as voting rituals and participant surveillance, so key to talent competitions and gamedocs, are not as relevant to the particular format of the docusoap turned soap opera. In 2006 MTVN attempted to bolster its on-line presence by introducing virtual worlds based on MTV brands. The Virtual Hills invites fans of the show to participate in a virtual and simulated version of *The Hills* reality by creating an avatar who interacts with other fans, as well as *Hills* characters, in a sort of 3-D chat room. MTVN was the first to apply the avatar-based social networking model — pioneered by the likes of Sims Online, Second Life, and There.com — to a reality TV brand. Richard Siklos comments on the promise of MTV's virtual worlds:

> One of the appeals of virtual worlds for MTV is the possibility that advertising can spill over into the real one. Visitors might buy a digital outfit for parties using currency they earned watching an infomercial or checking out a new product for an MTV advertiser. Then, they might decide that they would like to buy the same outfit for their offline selves, and, with a few clicks of the mouse and some real dollars, have one shipped to their home.[23]

The Virtual Hills is a branding strategy and interactive interface that fits nicely with the MTV/VH1 cluster's target audiences of young adults and teens who are increasingly inventing, sharing, and promoting themselves on-line via social networking sites like MySpace and Facebook. Seenonmtv.com is another attempt on the part of MTVN at consumer monitoring and lifestyle branding. On this interactive website, *Hills* viewers can not only purchase the products featured on the show but also peruse an immense sea of clothes, accessories, music, and even cars catalogued by episode, character, and/or brand.

These interactive sites developed around *The Hills* take on heightened significance when considered in relationship to Lauren's reality stardom. Lauren's status as soap heroine and reality star potentially makes these life-style branding strategies more effective; for without the productive tension between viewer identification with Lauren and idealization of her lifestyle, the Virtual Hills or "Living the Hill$ Life" make less sense. These industrial strategies play off Lauren's paradoxical female celebrity and its currency with young female audiences, shrewdly merging the more overt historical forms of sales(wo)manship Murray elaborates in connection with Lucille Ball with processes of commodification associated with cinema through the synergistic and interactive capabilities of media convergence. As a "friend" who happens to be a fashion expert, Lauren becomes a highly accessible and attractive model consumer for her audiences who are navigating the post-industrial labor market and negotiating the postfeminist sexual contract. While some scholars such as Henry Jenkins have found democratic potential

23. Richard Siklos, "Not in the Real World Anymore," *New York Times*, September 18, 2006, C1.

for interactive fans in the "affective economics" practiced by contemporary media industries, *The Hills* signals a highly gendered, tightly controlled venture that channels carefully cultivated affective involvement with a female star into endless opportunities to participate in her further commodification while promoting the gendered rules of engagement germane to the post-Fordist workplace. In this way, the embourgeoisement signaled by *The Hills* is not only achieved at the level of representation and ideology but also by the interactive practices of media reception invited by the program and its construction of Lauren as reality star. Viewers may meet Lauren in The Virtual Hills or buy the headband she wore on her last coffee date with Jason, but they will never really live the Hill$ life as Lauren does.

The Virtual Hills and seenonmtv.com not only signal innovations in the lifestyle branding of reality television but also intimate how the show's unique reality format and construction of Lauren as star contribute to the branding of the Hollywood lifestyle itself. More specifically, we argue that Lauren's representation on *The Hills* enables an intensified form of lifestyle branding, where what is branded is not a particular service, product, corporation, program, or experience, but a more generalized lifestyle. Turow explains that for advertising industry professionals engaged in practices of lifestyle branding the "goal is to imagine the product in a social environment that reflects the intended audience and its values."[24] *The Hills* makes this relationship between product, social environment, and intended audience more immanent; it places products directly in a naturalized social environment (*The Hills*) while cementing an alignment of values between the product and target market (young women) through viewer identification with Lauren. *The Hills* then is not simply a lifestyle brand of reality television selling Prada bags alongside Pepsi products to young women aspiring to *The Hills* lifestyle; at the same time, *The Hills* represents a branded lifestyle. The products that populate *The Hills* featured on seenonmtv.com or in The Virtual Hills are not simply discreet entities articulated to or "placed" in a reality television platform to create "branded content;" they appear as firmly embedded within and already belonging to the generalized, glamorous lifestyle represented by the show.

This more general branded lifestyle is anchored by Lauren's paradoxical reality stardom, but achieved by the representational landscape and reality format of *The Hills*, which follows the entire cast through the young Hollywood scene. As noted, Lauren, Whitney, Audrina, and Heidi all work in cultural industries; they appear as part of the labor force that supports Hollywood, and their jobs often afford them access to exclusive events and parties usually not open to other reality TV celetoids. What's more, *The Hills* regularly features scenes in trendy clubs and restaurants. For example, throughout season three the cast frequented hotspots developed by the

---

24. Turow, 15.

Dolce Group (a company that owns night clubs and restaurants catering to "industry" people and supported by a slew of celebrity investors) among them Ketchup, Les Deux, and Bella. A sure bet for paparazzi as well as amateur star-chasers, these sites are also featured regularly in celebrity gossip magazines. There is a circuitous, synergistic relationship between *The Hills'* reality format and the gossip industry that enables this branding of lifestyle. Lauren then is at once a star, a brand, and a new form of cultural intermediary; her status as reality star of the branded *Hills* lifestyle with an affectively invested female audience uniquely positions her to help manage and mediate the increasingly risky relationship between consumption and production for an expansive set of media, cultural, and lifestyle industries that hope to profit via their association with the Hollywood lifestyle. In this way, *The Hills* is situated to generate forms of immaterial value that not only feed back into the coffers of specific corporations (most notably, MTVN and its advertisers) but also work to buttress a more loosely organized set of lifestyle and cultural industries that owe their survival and existence to Hollywood's celebrity culture which *The Hills* brands through Lauren's reality stardom.

As a female reality star, Lauren is never off the clock. *Teen Vogue* intern, MTV employee, perpetual fashion model, clothing designer, celebrity endorser, soap heroine of real life, girlfriend on *The Hills*, a virtual friend to thousands on-line — Lauren's life is rendered constantly productive of value not only for her own personal brand and MTV's *Hills* brand, but also for a wide variety of industries that are articulated to her world. Just as Lauren's reality stardom works to support this branded lifestyle, the branded lifestyle also functions to reinforce Lauren's reality stardom. While many scholars have offered more optimistic accounts of reality TV celebrity and the democratic potentials of the post-network television era, *The Hills* exposes some of the limits of these interpretations. Lauren's paradoxical reality stardom signals heightened forms of exploitation of both female stars and their audiences by media industries in the era of reality TV. Tapping into the pleasures of celebrity gossip and melodrama, the promises of post-industrial work life, anxieties about self-presentation in the postfeminist context, and the participatory dimensions of convergence culture, *The Hills* has pioneered a highly gendered and profoundly paradoxical form of celebrity, transcending the limits of the celetoid system and opening up new horizons for commodifying female stars and their fans.

Works Cited

Allen, Robert C. *Speaking of Soap Operas.* Chapel Hill: University of North Carolina Press, 1985.

Andrejevic, Mark. *Reality TV: The Work of Being Watched.* Lanham, MD: Rowman and Littlefield Publishers, 2004.

Beverly Hills, 90210. Fox. 1990–2000. Television series.

Brunsdon, Charlotte. "The Role of Soap Opera in the Development of Feminist Television

Scholarship," in Robert C. Allen (ed.), *To Be Continued . . .: Soap Operas Around the World.* London: Routledge, 1995, 49–65.

Conrad, Lauren. *L.A. Candy.* New York: HarperCollins, 2009.

——. *Sweet Little Lies.* New York: HarperCollins, 2010.

"Creating the Cinematic Look for The Hills," *Videography*, June 1, 2006.

Dawson's Creek. WB. 1998–2003. Television series.

DeCordova, Richard. *Picture Personalities: The Emergence of the Star System in America.* Urbana: University of Illinois Press, 1990.

Deery, June. "Reality TV as Advertainment," *Popular Communication* 2, (2004): 1–20.

Dyer, Richard. *Stars* (new edn). London: British Film Institute, 1998.

Eckert, Charles. "The Carole Lombard in Macy's Window," in Christine Gledhill (ed.), *Stardom: Industry of Desire.* London: Routledge, 1991, 30–9.

Fiske, John. *Television Culture.* London: Routledge, 1987.

"For Better or Worse." *The Hills: The Complete Third Season.* MTV. 2007. DVD. MTV Home Entertainment, 2008.

Geraghty, Christine. *Women and Soap Opera: A Study of Prime Time Soaps.* Cambridge: Polity Press, 1991.

Gossip Girl. CW Television Network. 2007 – present. Television series.

Guarente, Gabe. "Jason Wahler Engaged: How Love Saved Me," *Us Weekly*, September 17, 2007.

Hibberd, James. "Reality Star Gets New MTV show," *Television Week*, November 14, 2005.

"'The Hills' Phenomenon Continues On-air and Online." CNNMoney.com. December 12, 2007.

"Jason Wahler — Engaged!" tmz.com, August 28, 2007. Blog post. Available at: www.tmz. com/2007/08/28/jason-wahler-engaged (accessed 29 November 2010).

Jenkins, Henry. *Convergence Culture: Where Old and New Media Collide.* New York: New York University Press, 2006.

Jermyn, Deborah. "'Bringing Out the Star in You': SJP, Carrie Bradshaw and The Evolution of Television Stardom," in Su Holmes and Sean Redmond (eds), *Framing Celebrity.* London: Routledge, 2006, 67–85.

Joyrich, Lynne. *Re-Viewing Reception: Television, Gender, and Postmodern Culture.* Bloomington: Indiana University Press, 1996.

Klein, Amanda. "Postmodern Marketing, Generation Y and the Multiplatform Viewing Experience of MTV's *The Hills*," *Jump Cut* 51, (Spring 2009). Available at: http://www. ejumpcut.org/currentissue/HillsKlein/index.html (accessed 29 November 2010).

Laguna Beach: The Real Orange County. MTV, 2004–2006. Television series.

Langer, John. "Television's Personality System," in P. David Marshall (ed.), *The Celebrity Culture Reader.* New York: Routledge, 2006, 181–95.

Levine, Elana. "The New Soaps? *Laguna Beach, The Hills*, and the Gendered Politics of Reality 'Drama,'" *FlowTV* 4(10), (August 18, 2006). Available at: http://flowtv.org/?p=19 (accessed 29 November 2010).

McRobbie, Angela. "Top Girls? Young Women and the Post-feminist Sexual contract," *Cultural Studies* 21, (2007): 718–37.

Modleski, Tania. "The Rhythms of Reception: Daytime Television and Women's Work," in E. Ann Kaplan (ed.), *Regarding Television.* Los Angeles: AFI, 1983, 67–74.

Morin, Edgar. *The Stars.* Translated by Richard Howard. Minneapolis: University of Minnesota Press, 2005.

Murray, Susan. *Hitch Your Antenna to the Stars: Early Television and Broadcast Stardom.* New York: Routledge, 2005.

Newport Harbor: The Real Orange County. MTV, 2007–2008. Television series.

The Real World. MTV. 1992 – present. Television series.

Rojek, Chris. *Celebrity.* London: Reaktion, 2001.

"Second Chances." *The Hills: The Complete Third Season.* MTV, September 10, 2007. DVD. MTV Home Entertainment, 2008.

Sex and the City. HBO, 1998–2004. Television series.

Sex and the City. Directed by Michael Patrick King. New Line Cinema, 2008.

Siklos, Richard. "Not in the Real World Anymore," *New York Times*, September 18, 2006, C1.

Smith, Stephanie D. "Teen Beat," *WWD: Women's Wear Daily*, March 23, 2007, 10.

Spence, Louise. "'They Killed Off Marlena, But She's on Another Show Now': Fantasy,

Reality, and Pleasure in Watching Daytime Soap Operas," in Robert C. Allen (ed.), *To Be Continued . . .: Soap Operas Around the World.* London: Routledge, 1995, 182–98.

Stamp, Shelley. *Movie-Struck Girls: Women and Motion Picture Culture After the Nickelodeon.* Princeton, NJ: Princeton University Press, 2000.

"They Meet Again." *The Hills: The Complete Third Season.* MTV, September 17, 2007. DVD. MTV Home Entertainment, 2008.

Tran, Khanh T. L. "MTV Partners With Conrad For Fashion," *WWD: Women's Wear Daily,* August 24, 2007, 4.

Turner, Graeme. "The Mass Production of Celebrity: 'Celetoids', Reality TV and the 'Demotic Turn,'" *International Journal of Cultural Studies* 9 (2006): 153–65.

Turow, Joseph. *Breaking Up America: Advertisers and the New Media World.* Chicago: University of Chicago Press, 1997.

"An Unexpected Call." *The Hills: The Complete First Season.* MTV, June 14, 2006. DVD. MTV Home Entertainment, 2007.

Werpin, Alex. "Ratings: MTV's 'The City' Shines, 'The Hills' Slow." *Broadcasting & Cable,* September 30, 2009.

What Not to Wear. TLC. 2002 – present. Television series.

"With Friends Like These . . ." *The Hills: The Complete Second Season.* MTV, February 26, 2007. DVD. MTV Home Entertainment, 2007.

"You Have Chosen." *The Hills: The Complete Second Season.* MTV, February 19, 2007. DVD. MTV Home Entertainment, 2007.

"Young Hollywood." *The Hills: The Complete Third Season.* MTV, November 5, 2007. DVD. MTV Home Entertainment, 2008.

13

Immigration, Authorship, Censorship, and Terrorism

The Politics of M.I.A.'s US Crossover

CANDICE HADDAD

N 2007, ROLLING STONE MAGAZINE named M.I.A.'s sophomore effort *Kala*, as the best album of the year.[1] With the album's sales beating those of other highly acclaimed artists such as Bruce Springsteen, Jay-Z, Kanye West, and Arcade Fire, M.I.A. was on the scene and making her presence known. In claiming the number one spot on a world-renowned music magazine's top annual award, this dark-haired, dark-eyed, lanky woman with a British accent rapping "Pull up the people, pull up the poor" had knocked off some of the most powerful (male) artists and groups in the music industry. Born in Britain, but raised in Sri Lanka for the first half of her childhood, Mathangi Arulpragasam, better know as M.I.A., or Maya, spent the first years of her life amidst the turmoil of the Sri Lankan Civil War. As displaced subjects moving throughout Sri Lanka and India, M.I.A., her mother, and two siblings spent most of their time estranged from their father and husband Arul Pragasam, a Tamil activist and leadership figure in various Tamil independence movements.

In the mid-1980s, M.I.A. and her family moved back to London as refugees leaving her father behind in Sri Lanka. She graduated from London's Central Saint Martins College of Art and Design with a degree in fine arts, film, and video. However, M.I.A.'s love and talent for music were never far from the picture; it was in the syncretic refugee neighborhoods of West London where she began to cultivate her eclectic sound. In 2003, M.I.A. started to make a name for herself with her tape recordings created on a 4-track tape machine and a Roland MC-505. After receiving much attention from dance club disc jockeys and college radio stations, she was signed to XL records and released her first album, *Arular*, in 2004. Having set a new

---

1. Robert Christgau, et al. "The Top 50 Albums of 2007," *Rolling Stone*, December 27, 2007.

standard for contemporary, eclectic, hybrid music throughout the indie music scene, M.I.A.'s highly anticipated release of *Kala* set the stage for her to cross over into the mainstream US music industry.

The censorship of "Paper Planes" (the first single from *Kala*) during M.I.A.'s appearance[2] on the *Late Show with David Letterman* and the debut of a censored version of the music video on MTV's website[3] factor strongly in an investigation into the politics of her music, persona, and representation in mainstream Western media. Because of these early moments of controversy and censorship, M.I.A.'s crossover into the US mainstream plays out the politics of female, ethnic transnational identity.[4] In this regard, in reading M.I.A.'s star persona, it is crucial to consider how sex, gender, race, ethnicity, and citizenship status structure her discursive circulation. Moments of controversy surrounding her crossover transition exemplify the cultural norms and standards an ethnic, female, diasporic figure is held to exceed in terms of the "appropriateness" expected from a mainstream music artist. M.I.A.'s brown, female body combined with her political lyrics strike a particular rousing chord in US mainstream popular culture, and she has encountered a number of barriers in crossing over, including visa denials, censorship (as I have alluded to above), and slanderous rumors (see Figure 13.1). The crux of this article analyzes these controversies by examining the discourse surrounding the rise of M.I.A.'s career from the beginning of her crossover with the release of *Kala* in 2007 to her "retirement" and Grammy performance in early 2009. In doing so, this article explores M.I.A.'s star persona as the embodiment of particular values — some of which are deemed threatening to United States hegemony.

It is useful to examine how M.I.A.'s persona, as a non-white woman from outside the United States, is introduced and sustained (or not) in the US mediascape. In her book *Off-White Hollywood*, Diane Negra conducts a number of in-depth star studies looking at off-white women and the ways in which their ethnic femininity functions in Hollywood cinema and US popular culture. Negra determines, "The ethnic female star is a figure of great potential ideological disruption, for she threatens to expose the fragile construction of white, American patriarchy."[5] Granted, M.I.A. is a woman of color, "darker" than the European-associated stars Negra deems "off-white," but her persona works in a similar fashion through her explicit, unapologetic presentation of self. M.I.A. is certainly not the first disruptive, political female musician to enter the US mainstream. Sinead O'Connor,

---

2. On September 19, 2007.

3. The censored video was posted on MTV's website in December 2007.

4. This article operates from the understanding that race and ethnicity are arbitrary social constructs. Race is commonly viewed as a biological trait, whereas ethnicity works more through socialization and is understood to reflect cultural background.

5. Diane Negra, *Off-White Hollywood: American Culture and Ethnic Female Stardom* (London: Routledge, 2001), 8.

Figure 13.1   **M.I.A. commanding attention and calling for people around the world to "make a sound" in the video for "Bucky Done Gun," the third single off *Arular*.**

Courtney Love, and Madonna come to mind when identifying precursors to M.I.A. However, M.I.A.'s ethnic status as a displaced Tamil makes it difficult to read her as white, further complicating her potential to make a smooth transition into the mainstream. While M.I.A.'s displaced and diasporic status can work against her, it also allows her to become a figure of inspiration for masses of marginalized peoples both in and outside the US. This in a sense grants her a mobility other disruptive female musicians could not obtain. With mobility comes power, and with power comes a sense of urgency to silence the disruptor in order to sustain the status quo.

Further, M.I.A.'s Tamil identity, an ethnic identity known to many in the US as vaguely associated with "terrorism," separates her ethnic stardom from other non-white or off-white female music artists with mobility such as Shakira.[6] Overarching the entire schema of M.I.A.'s transition are the dominant ways in which multiculturalism functions in the United States. The version of multiculturalism I believe to be most prominent and accepted in the US is what Ella Shohat and Robert Stam call "liberal multiculturalism," or "a state or corporate-managed United-Colors-of-Benetton pluralism whereby established power promotes ethnic 'flavors of the month' for commercial or ideological purposes."[7] Implicit in this version of multiculturalism is the idea that different "flavors" do not contest their placement in the cultural hierarchy — representation and mere exposure in the mainstream media are accepted as sufficient evidence of equality. M.I.A.'s persona and political agenda do not abide by the unspoken terms of this dominant version of US multiculturalism.

Examining the ways in which M.I.A.'s ethnic femininity potentially functions as an ideological disruption through her transition into US mainstream

----

6. As a Colombian with a Lebanese father, Shakira's hybrid identity is not as explicitly threatening as M.I.A.'s. Further, Shakira's music itself follows more along the lines of mainstream pop standards, whereas M.I.A.'s sampling of gunshots and political lyrics do not.

7. Robert Stam and Ella Shohat, *Unthinking Eurocentrism* (London: Routledge, 1994), 48.

culture, the main points of discussion in this article concern M.I.A.'s US censorship and immigration. I believe M.I.A.'s inability to receive a visa, disputes over authorship of *Kala*, and moments of censorship exemplify "official" responses to her disruptive persona. In addition to these moments, other less controversial developments in her career and life since she crossed over into US media are also elements to be considered. Although highly publicized events such as retirement, pregnancy, marital engagements, and crossing into other forms of artistic promotion (i.e. the release of her clothing line) do not veer far from the dominant mode of cultivating celebrity, the ways in which they are discursively framed do indeed expose how M.I.A.'s ethnic femininity functions in the US and the disruptions it potentially poses.

Discursive Negotiations of US Immigration Policy

After the wide acclaim of her first album *Arular* (2005) in the US independent music scene, M.I.A.'s next project was to break into mainstream markets by working with top brand name producers in creating high-ranking Billboard chart singles.[8] The original plan for M.I.A. to travel to the United States to work with mainstream hip-hop and R&B producers and artists such as Timbaland, Three 6 Mafia, and Nelly Furtado was brought to a halt when she was denied a working visa to enter the US.[9] While the specific posting addressing this issue no longer exists on M.I.A.'s MySpace blog, internet archives and articles concerning the event reveal M.I.A.'s alleged disdain for the denial of her entry into the US. She wrote, "I was mennu [*sic*] work with timber startin' this week . . . I'm locked out! They wont let me in! Now I'm strictly making my album outside the borders!!!!"[10] Lacking a US visa, M.I.A. recorded in multiple, often makeshift studios around the world. While her persona and style of music was already recognized by critics as "worldly" and eclectic, the accounts of her recording process further promoted M.I.A.'s hybrid aesthetic and displaced identity. The genre of "world music" is in and of itself a problematic category that discursively constructs artists as inherently different and Other to normatively read Western music artists. Defining M.I.A., or any musician, as a "world music" artist discursively places them into the realm of "safe" internationalism, containing their perceived excessive and norm-challenging personae and sounds.[11] By homogenizing difference through the all-encompassing label of "world music," the strange is contained and constructed as non-threatening.

---

8. Ben Sisario, "An Itinerant Refugee in a Hip-Hop World." *The New York Times*, August 19, 2007. Spelling and grammar were not changed from the original text.
9. "MIA Denied Entry to the US: The Star Wants to Get On With Her New Album," *NME*, May 19, 2006.
10. Ibid.
11. See Susan Faludi, *The Terror Dream: Fear and Fantasy in Post 9/11 America* (New York: Metropolitan Books, 2007).

In deeming M.I.A. a threat, yet also a praiseworthy and unique musician, the US music press exemplifies the ways in which M.I.A.'s debut to a mainstream Western audience points up fissures in the discourse of ethnic female musical artistry.

M.I.A. began her crossover into the mainstream US music scene within the maelstrom of post-9/11 fears and US foreign policy tensions. The introduction of the US Patriot Act in 2001, which deregulated government surveillance of US citizens and increased discretionary elements of immigration laws, and the Homeland Security Act in 2002, which created the US Department of Homeland Security as the body to exercise the US Patriot Act, worked in an effort to not only respond to the events of 9/11 by arresting and detaining people perceived as threats to US security, but also to rebuild and restore the national myth of invincibility that had been shattered.[12] M.I.A.'s father's alleged status as a leader of a Tamil militant group, the Tamil Tigers, a nationalist organization that waged a number of offensive attacks against the Sri Lankan government and is on the official list of terrorist organizations considered threatening to the United States, United Kingdom, European Union, Canada, and India, in combination with her political agenda to contest stereotypes of women and non-white peoples and bring representation to marginalized voices inevitably resulted in clashes with US ideologies at this specific sociocultural moment.[13] As a result, much of the discourse concerning M.I.A.'s visa and immigration issues subscribes to a paradigm of preventative homeland security and, ultimately, works to promote sympathy and understanding for US measures in exercising racial profiling. For example, in the Associated Press article "M.I.A. Doesn't Need a Visa, Just Inspiration," the author explains the visa-denial situation: "Her political stance may have made her more exciting to the music world, but to the United States, officials apparently worried she could be inciting — so they denied her a visa to enter the country, despite her growing success here."[14] Seeking to make clear that success and recognition as a music artist do not necessarily grant you the ability to cross the literal borders of the United States, the article leaves unquestioned the validity of the reasons M.I.A. was denied entry.

Throughout most of the texts that address M.I.A.'s denied entry into the US, racial profiling — as a common technique of US homeland security policy — is not an explicit topic. However, M.I.A.'s interview with George

---

12. Ibid., 12–13.
13. M.I.A.'s first circulated compilation of songs, not released on a major label, is titled *Piracy Funds Terrorism Volume 1*. By giving her first collection of songs such a name, M.I.A. certainly seems to be inviting the projection of terrorism upon her persona. Undeniably, M.I.A. at times does not shy away from controversy and even seems to welcome it. Nonetheless, I believe her positionality as a diasporic woman of color from outside the US in combination with her explicit critiques of US institutions brings to the fore the latent racism inherent in the liberal multiculturalism permeating US society and culture.
14. "M.I.A. Doesn't Need a Visa, Just Inspiration," *Associated Press*, August 21, 2007.

Stroumboulopoulos on *The Hour*, a late-night Canadian talk show, brings up the singer's US visa denial and questions it as a moment when racial profiling was indeed exercised. After Stroumboulopoulos asks her if she knows why she was added to the US Homeland Security's watch list, M.I.A. replies, "They just said I matched an identity of a terrorist . . ." Responding to her statement, Stroumboulopoulos knowingly replies, "You were brown . . ." The explicit statement of her "brownness" as an issue is not found to be outrageous by M.I.A., Stroumboulopoulos, or seemingly the studio audience, but rather a logical explanation for her denial of entry to the United States. This moment clearly brings to the forefront the taboo subject of racial profiling by governmental agencies. What is important to point out is that this moment of explicit discussion of racial profiling takes place during an interview produced outside the US. Widely available for anyone to view, for it is accessible through both YouTube and M.I.A.'s MySpace page, the video is attainable to all English-speaking audiences and very much present in the discourse surrounding M.I.A.'s crossover into the US mainstream. These excerpts suggest some of the ways that M.I.A.'s persona and music confront the status quo of US racial politics and a liberal multiculturalist paradigm of how to speak about (or silence) questions of race and ethnicity.[15]

Much of the discourse surrounding M.I.A.'s denial of access into the US to record her second album inadvertently goes as far as to attribute US governmental policies for the success of the album. An article titled "Multiculti Ambassador: US Visa Delay proves to be the Catalyst that Shapes the Global Sound of M.I.A.'s Sophomore Disc, *Kala*" states:

> Let's give the reigning US government credit where a modicum of credit is due: it's inspired some decent music . . . we can also indirectly thank the United States Department of Homeland Security for sparing stylish, Brit-born electro-agitante M.I.A. and her bristling new album, *Kala*, from the dreaded "sophomore slump," and the double-edged honour of being saddled with omnipresent A-list producer Timbaland as the assumed architect behind what could become Mathangi "Maya" Arulpragasam's first proper mainstream incursion.[16]

In a similar tone, the author of "Mesmerizing Singer's Style is Perfectly Perplexing" states, "I'd like to personally thank our immigration department: the organic sounds M.I.A. was forced to find overseas helped her make

---

15. For more on this concept see Kimberle Williams Crenshaw, "Color-Blind Dreams and Racial Nightmares," in Toni Morrison and Claudia Brodsky Lacour (eds), *Birth of a Nation'hood* (New York: Pantheon, 1997).
16. Ben Rayner, "Multi-culti Ambassador: US Visa Delay Proves to be the Catalyst that Shapes the Global Sound of M.I.A.'s Sophomore Disc, *Kala*," *The Toronto Star*, September 6, 2007, V03.

one of the best albums of the year."[17] In addition to such characterizations, another strategy indirectly giving US institutions and dominant ideologies credit for the success of M.I.A.'s album is to describe her displacement as a blow to her creative ability. This rhetorical technique works in opposition to the portrayal of her displaced identity as an empowering aspect of persona. Throughout her core texts, music videos, interviews, album covers, etc., M.I.A.'s displacement is visually and lyrically represented as the key feature behind her supposed ability to be a voice for and leader of disenfranchised peoples. The same article states:

> Though she bought an apartment in Brooklyn, it remained empty as she kept reapplying to enter the country . . . In the meantime, M.I.A. had already decamped from London, so for the next two years, she was in essence, homeless, leaving her out of sorts and unsettled.[18]

Attributing the US as the force behind M.I.A.'s music style diverts any racist acts by governmental agencies away from the narrative of the making of *Kala.* Another common discursive strategy found in these articles is framing M.I.A.'s visa denial within discussions of her rumored relations to the Tamil Tigers. These articles never blatantly deem M.I.A. as a supporter of terrorism, but the use of this strategy certainly suggests it. Further, invoking M.I.A.'s potential relations to a Tamil militant group can have a censoring effect on her persona and music.

By neglecting M.I.A.'s first album *Arular* (2005), which also featured an array of sampling from music styles around the world and set the precedent for her eclectic, hybrid persona, this contextualization of her second album and, thus, her introduction into the US mainstream transfers the power of accomplishing the recording of *Kala* to US dominant social, cultural, and governmental state apparatuses. However, there is certainly a give-and-take relationship working within the discourses of M.I.A.'s persona. My use of the concept of discourse invokes the Foucauldian notion of it as a site of *negotiation.* Foucault's definition of power further elaborates the necessity in invoking this idea:

> Power must be understood in the first instance as the multiplicity of force relations immanent in the sphere in which they operate and which constitute their own organization; as the process which, through ceaseless struggles and confrontations, transforms, strengthens, or reverses them, as the support which these force relations find in one another, thus forming a chain or a system, on the contrary, the disjunctions and contradictions which isolate them from one another; and

---

17. Sean Daly, "Mesmerizing Singer's Style is Perfectly Perplexing," *St. Petersburg Times,* August 25, 2007, 1E.
18. Ibid.

lastly as the strategies in which they take effect, whose general design or institutional crystallization is embodied in the state apparatus, in the formulation of the law, in the various social hegemonies.[19]

These moments in which the success of *Kala* is indirectly attributed to rigid US homeland security policies reveal the discursive strategies working to place power in the hands of US government institutions. However, such strategies do not go uncontested by M.I.A. and others (as we have seen, for instance, in the interview with George Stroumboulopoulos).

In interviews, M.I.A. does indeed participate in the discourse of her crossover into the US music and popular culture market and, thus, negotiates the power dynamics of her representation. For instance, in an article about M.I.A. not being able to obtain a visa to enter the US to go on tour, she states, "Immigration offices are my second home . . . I'm just going through the standard procedures. There's a reason you don't have many Sri Lankans coming to sing [in the United States]."[20] Playing into her outspoken, political persona, M.I.A. confronts how she is spoken about in the media and in the crossing over of her music, stardom, aesthetic, and identity into the US. Such moments of contestation exemplify how the dispersal of power does not necessarily function in a purely top-down fashion, but rather in a circulatory negotiation.

In his book *Celebrity and Power: Fame in Contemporary Culture,* P. David Marshall discusses the significance of celebrity as a site of discourse stating:

> The celebrity offers a discursive focus for the discussion of realms that are considered outside the bounds of public debate in the most public fashion. The celebrity system is a way in which the sphere of the irrational, emotional, personal, and affective is contained and negotiated in contemporary culture.[21]

This example of the denial of M.I.A.'s US visa and the ways in which she confronts it exemplify Marshall's point about how celebrities bring to the forefront debates in contemporary culture. These moments particularly point to debates surrounding the policies of the United States government and how it does or does not participate in racial profiling and, thus, racist practices in the name of homeland security. I believe that it is not only the mere acts of challenging these policies that invoke discussions considered outside the boundaries of public debate, but also the fact that they are coming from both an immigrant and woman of color.

---

19. Michel Foucault, *The History of Sexuality,* vol. 1 (New York: Random House, 1980), 92.

20. Todd Martens, "XL Finds Hot Prospect in M.I.A.," *Billboard,* March 26, 2005, 11.

21. David P. Marshall, *Celebrity and Power: Fame in Contemporary Culture* (Minneapolis, MN: University of Minnesota Press, 1997), 72.

Issues of Authorship

Another element in need of interrogation in the discourse of M.I.A.'s transition into the US mainstream concerns the production and authorship of her albums. Undeniably, many creative forces come together to produce a music album. Collective action, culturally accepted tastes, and industry conventions play roles in the construction of art and a star's creative output, in this case music in the form of an album.[22] In the crossing over of M.I.A. into the US mainstream, a recurring narrative contextualizes the release of *Kala*. In the dominant narrative of her rise to stardom in the United States, the Philadelphia-based DJ, Diplo, is often cited as the man behind her projects. Her first, non-mainstream studio released LP titled, *Piracy Funds Terrorism Vol. 1*, credits Diplo and M.I.A. as the producers of the album — with the track list featuring 13 out of the 21 songs as "Diplo Mixes." Without a doubt a collaborative effort between Diplo and M.I.A. was certainly the guiding creative force behind *Piracy*. However, his presence as a force behind her eclectic style and success is disproportionately implied in the discourse concerning much of her career. M.I.A.'s first studio-backed album, *Arular*, lists a total of eight producers including Diplo.[23] Her most recent album (and the one said to *be the* album introducing her to a mainstream US audience), *Kala*, credits M.I.A., Diplo, and Timbaland. Despite his having produced only a couple of tracks on *Arular* and only one on *Kala*, dominant discourses consistently feature and credit Diplo for much of the album's success. Characterizations such as "Backed by Diplo, her D.J., she rode tracks new and old, bringing together old-fashioned electro and futuristic dancehall reggae, London grime and Atlanta crunk. Maybe that's why her music sounds somehow inevitable,"[24] "Diplo . . . the astute producer behind M.I.A.'s 'Paper Planes,'" "Her songs benefit greatly from Diplo's recent baile funk fetish," and "Diplo ironically saves M.I.A.'s best cuts for last"[25] and other strategies of contextualizing her albums by referring to Diplo and other producers (who are sometimes mentioned, but always alongside Diplo[26]) emphasize the hand that others — particularly Diplo — had in the making of M.I.A.'s music. While this can certainly be seen as merely straightforward creative attribution, I argue that it is significant that Diplo and the other producers of M.I.A.'s albums are all men, and that their presence in

---

22. See Howard S. Becker, "Art as Collective Action." *American Sociological Review* 39(6), (1974): 767–76.
23. Other producers credited include Switch, Paschal Byrne, KW Griff, Steve Mackey, Ross Orton, Anthony Whiting, and Richard X.
24. Kelefa Sanneh, "Give Them What They Want but Keep it Sort of Cool," *The New York Times*, February 7, 2005, E3.
25. Nick Sylvester, Album review of *M.I.A.: Piracy Funds Terrorism, Vol. 1* [mixed by Diplo], *Pitchfork*, November 22, 2004.
26. See Kitty Empire, "Flash-forward: M.I.A.'s Innovative Beats and Rhymes Are Distilled in London But Fed by Her Intriguing Past in Sri Lanka," *The Observer*, March 20, 2005, 28.

the discourse of her music career and transition into the mainstream US music scene is visible and very much a part of the dominant narrative of her crossover. In his discussion of DJs and authorship, Bill D. Herman states, "In a society that is demarcated by patriarchy, the author function is predictably constructed along highly gendered lines . . . Bestowing authorship on men and preventing its bestowal on women serves to perpetuate long-standing sexist oppression."[27] Contextualizing M.I.A.'s music and background in a way that highlights the men — particularly white men such as Diplo — behind the curtain works to contains the excess, threat, and perceived volatility of ethnic femininity by upholding US social hierarchies.

M.I.A. participates in the dialogue concerning the ways in which she is represented and addressed in the media by explicitly confronting media institutions that she feels are attributing her success to the wrong people. In one interview conducted and published by *Pitchfork Media*, a popular internet publication that focuses on independent and popular music, M.I.A. reveals her frustrations with the perceived authorship of her albums.[28] From the beginning, M.I.A. approaches the interviewer with hostility to make her point clear:

Pitchfork: How are you doing?

M.I.A.: How am I doing, or what am I doing?

Pitchfork: Well, both.

M.I.A.: I'm about to eat . . .

Pitchfork: So tell me a bit about *Kala*. I just heard it for the first time today, and—

M.I.A.: Diplo didn't make it.

Pitchfork: Uh, what?

M.I.A.: He never made *Arular*, but you guys keep writing it.

Pitchfork: "He" being Diplo?

M.I.A.: You're not listening to me at all, are you?

Pitchfork: I'm trying. It's a little hard to hear you.

---

27. Bill D. Herman, "Scratching Out Authorship: Representations of the Electronic Music DJ at the Turn of the 21st Century," *Popular Communication* 4(1), 2006: 24.
28. This interview is in transcript form.

M.I.A.: Forget what I said. [*Pauses*] What do you think I said?

Pitchfork: I heard you say something to the effect of "he didn't make *Arular* and he also didn't make this record." . . .

M.I.A.: Yesterday I read like five magazines in the airplane — it was a nine hour flight — and three out of five magazines said "Diplo: the mastermind behind M.I.A.'s politics!" And I was wondering, does that stem from [Pitchfork]? Because I find it really bonkers . . . If you read the credits, he sent me a loop for "Bucky Done Gun," and I made a song in London, and it became "Bucky Done Gun." But that was the only song he was actually involved in on *Arular*. So the whole time I've had immigration problems and not been able to get in the country, what I am or what I do has got a life of its own, and is becoming less and less to do with me. And I just find it a bit upsetting and kind of insulting that I can't have any ideas on my own because I'm a female or that people from undeveloped countries can't have ideas of their own unless it's backed up by someone who's blond-haired and blue-eyed. After the first time it's cool, the second time it's cool, but after like the third, fourth, fifth time, maybe it's an issue that we need to talk about, maybe that's something important . . .

Pitchfork: I think it's very important. I talked to Diplo about a month ago and he seemed to think he had a bit to do with both of these records . . .

M.I.A.: Well, I finished *Arular* and then I met Diplo, and when I went to make the mixtape [*Piracy Funds Terrorism, Vol. 1*], I gave him all the tracks, the acappellas, and instrumentals already done. On this album [*Kala*] I self-produced most of the album with Switch, and nobody's talking about that . . . I just wanted to set the record straight and make sure that credit goes to people, where it's due . . .[29]

One of M.I.A.'s more poignant statements, "And I just find it a bit upsetting and kind of insulting that I can't have any ideas on my own because I'm a female or that people from undeveloped countries can't have ideas of their own unless it's backed up by someone who's blond-haired and blue-eyed"[30], explicitly confronts the racial and gender barriers she sees herself as encountering. From the discourse examined earlier regarding the framing of Diplo around the production of her albums, it is apparent that Diplo's presence is determined by both explicit and implicit discursive strategies.

An intertextual reading of this interview would bring into consideration M.I.A. and Diplo's personal relationship. In multiple accounts, M.I.A. speaks about her intimate relationship with Diplo and how the two were a

29. Maya Arulpragasam, "M.I.A. Confronts the Haters," interview with Paul Thompson, *Pitchfork*, August 3, 2007.
30. Ibid.

couple during the recording of *Piracy*. Therefore, one could read her prickly reaction to the *Pitchfork* interviewer as a combination of remnants from a relationship gone sour and her desire to contest the way the authorship of her albums has been represented. However, her statements concerning the hegemonic racial and gender barriers in the music industry and the cultural industries at large show how her frustrations challenge not only micro-personal issues, but also macro social and cultural issues. Further into the interview, M.I.A. expounds upon these ideas:

> **Pitchfork:** . . . It seems strange that people would portray you as being a puppet. Still, I've definitely read things about you that suggest a lot of the work was done by someone else.

> **M.I.A.:** Yeah! In America, that's such a norm, for women to be puppets. Me, I go searching for answers. And the people around me and the people that really help me to work hard on this project . . . undermined by something like it's some fucking fad . . . Even things like Pitchfork writing that thing about my MySpace, that was a clear sign of where it was coming from. I didn't think it was Pitchfork who's conjuring up the thing about me being something that's masterminded and I'm a puppet for some blond-haired, blue-eyed person to pull a string on. It's just that, on the one hand, those kind of things cannot be generated. And I think it's really sort of dangerous to laugh in the realness of that, in order for me not being able to talk about Liberia and stuff like that on my blog because it's not cool by your standards.[31]

> **Pitchfork:** I see what you're saying. I can't speak for that particular news item — I didn't write it — but I think it was meant to touch on statements you made about both your work in Liberia and your personal life.

> **M.I.A.:** At the time, it was really like "I think I'll talk about Liberia and stuff like that" and it didn't really mean much to me, but it means much to me now when I hear it being juxtaposed with the fact that, oh, this guy is allowed to come in and bring issues forward about whatever, but the person from Africa can't bring us issues . . . And that's what this album is about. It's filling in the bridge and the gap so that somebody in Liberia can articulate exactly what they want to say without having this middle-man person who has to be from the first world. It's like, guess what? I came from the fucking mud hut. And I got here. And I'm here, and I did it in 15 fucking years flat. It's not a three-generation experience like people in America.[32]

---

31. The *Pitchfork* article M.I.A. is referring to is a piece called "M.I.A. Goes Crazy On MySpace" that talks about her MySpace blog posting talking about her ex-boyfriend (presumably Diplo) and her trip to Liberia to visit families and build a school. See Kati Llewellyn, "M.I.A. Goes Crazy on MySpace," *Pitchfork*, December 13, 2006.
32. Arulpragasam, "M.I.A. Confronts the Haters."

Not only does M.I.A. challenge conventional gender and race representations in the US, but she also contests the manner in which mainstream US media represent non-Western countries. These moments of negotiation in the discourse concerning M.I.A. and the authorship of her music and stardom bring to the forefront the hegemonic conventions of US media outlets.

In a similar vein, it is imperative to acknowledge that in these instances of M.I.A. confronting dominant discourses surrounding her music and persona, the media, through which her interviews are released, are participating in acts of self-regulation that implicitly uphold social hierarchies. In order for a media outlet to be deemed mainstream, certain standards and modes of production must be adhered to. *Pitchfork* covers "indie" music and is published solely online, but its influence stretches across independent and mainstream music categories.[33] The *Pitchfork* interview heavily excerpted in this analysis is a case in point example of such self-regulation. For even an interview that takes on the topic of the hegemonic constructions of women and racialized subjects in the US media ends in a return to subscription to social and cultural norms:

> **Pitchfork:** They're going to cut us off, but I've gotta ask another question. I'm just curious what your plan is for the immediate future . . .
>
> **M.I.A.:** I'm just going to tour because I haven't toured for a long, long, long time, and I think this time I'm just going to have more fun with it . . . Until they kick me out of the country again I'll be here.
>
> **Pitchfork:** . . . Does it seem like you'll actually be able to live here?
>
> **M.I.A.:** I'm only here on a year visa, so if you could just advertise, I'm looking for a husband.
>
> **Pitchfork:** I'll make sure everyone knows . . .[34]

While not completely eradicating all of her statements, ending on a note about how M.I.A. is looking for a husband to stay in the US and, thus, acquiescing to policies and cultural norms that she only moments before denounced, certainly marks what might have been considered a strong

---

33. *Pitchfork*'s status as an independent, non-conglomerate, non-corporate organization does not by default make it subversive to dominant ideologies; on the contrary, I believe the tastes the site promotes operate under an elitist, albeit independent, criterion that privileges patriarchal and heteronormative ideologies. Therefore, the argument that *Pitchfork* does not fit into the scope of media outlets studied falls flat, for it operates within tangentially similar ideologies as US mainstream media. This is not to say moments of subversion are not possible even in the mainstream media.

34. Arulpragasam, "M.I.A. Confronts the Haters."

contestation as a rather ambiguous message. This quieting down of M.I.A.'s position on race, gender, and authorship tempers her rebellious persona. These struggles in the discourse around her agency to present herself as she chooses and to give a voice to those less represented exemplifies the ambiguous politics of the female, ethnic crossover star.

Censorship and Discourses of Terrorism

The first instances of censorship of M.I.A. and her music by a mainstream media outlet occurred in 2005. The music video for the song "Sunshowers" off M.I.A.'s first album *Arular* was banned on MTV because of its lyrics "you wanna go? you wanna win a war? Like PLO, I don't surrendo."[35] The reference to the Palestinian Liberation Organization (PLO), the official representative organization of the Palestinian people, apparently struck a chord for the MTV broadcast standards department. This moment of censorship foreshadows and sets the precedent for the ways in which mainstream media approached M.I.A.'s debut in the US with the release of *Kala*. One of the most prominent topics of discussion in the discourse of M.I.A.'s crossover into mainstream US culture is censorship. Two of the most significant events in her debut to mainstream audiences were subjected to acts of censorship by Viacom via MTV's *Total Request Live* and Westinghouse via CBS's *Late Show with David Letterman*. The significance of these two moments serves for me as two case studies in analyzing the censorship and, thus, controversy M.I.A. encountered in the early stages of her mainstream US career. Stemming from the analysis of these two moments, M.I.A.'s reaction via her MySpace blog is taken into consideration to acknowledge the ways she explicitly confronts the censorship of her work. Lastly, this section analyzes the rise of M.I.A.'s career immediately following the success of the "Paper Planes" single and ends with the event of her Grammy performance in early 2009. Through this analysis, we see a subtle, yet telling, shift occur in M.I.A.'s persona.

On September 13, 2007, M.I.A. performed "Paper Planes" on the *Late Show with David Letterman* and encountered censorship of the chorus's gunshot sounds.[36] It is apparent that during her performance on the *Late Show* neither M.I.A. nor her back-up dancer were expecting the gunshot sounds to be removed. M.I.A.'s look of confusion towards her DJ as soon as she realized the gunshot sounds were replaced, marks this moment as a deliberate act of policing by Westinghouse/CBS.[37] During this same time period, the debut of

35. Richard Harrington, "M.I.A., No Loss for Words," *The Washington Post*, September 16, 2005.
36. You can see the *Late Show* performance here: http://youtube.com/watch?v=XaxIELjpDxc
37. An interesting connection this event gestures to is Sinead O'Connor's October 1992 live performance on *Saturday Night Live* when she tore up a picture of Pope John Paul II. O'Connor's performance is basically the exact opposite of M.I.A.'s; rather than O'Connor being censored without her acknowledgment during her live performance, she publicly

the "Paper Planes" music video was set to air on MTV's weekday, afternoon show *TRL* (more formally known as *Total Request Live*). Prior to airing on the show, the music video was released by MTV on its website. Instead of airing the original version that samples gunshot sounds in the chorus, MTV presented a version that replaced these noises with ambiguous popping sounds, and took out what was considered offensive language.[38] The "Paper Planes" song and its music video present image and audio signifiers that can be understood to connote a critique of dominant conservative United States ideologies such as the American Dream, assimilation, capitalism, and xenophobia. In the version of "Paper Planes" that aired on MTV, the shots of M.I.A. pumping her arm in the air with her hand in the shape of a gun, the lyrics "weed and bongs," and the abrupt gunshot sounds featured in the chorus are edited out. Airing this video on MTV and performing the song on the *Late Show with David Letterman* untouched would have brought ideas of immigrant rebellion into many US homes. This is not to say that media companies never attempt to push the envelope; both the *Late Show with David Letterman* and *Total Request Live* think of themselves as relatively hip and progressive. What these moments suggest, however, is a discomfort in broadcasting such sounds and images in association with a figure such as M.I.A. An exotized, female Other preaching against assimilation into US capitalistic culture was obviously deemed by producers as too disruptive a spectacle to be sending out to *Late Show* and *TRL* audiences.

The discourse that ensued from these moments of censorship opens up another instance of public contestation from M.I.A. on how the US perceives her. However, these moments of contestation are met with another layer of censoring (perhaps self-censoring) and present an interesting example of the struggles over media representation in the United States, and particularly the politics of crossover, ethnic female representation. Immediately following the debut of the "Paper Planes" video by MTV, M.I.A.'s MySpace blog had a new posting openly protesting both of these acts of censorship. However, the present iteration of her blog does not show these postings from December 2007. Speculatively, we can assume they were deleted for public relations reasons. While I am hesitant to say that this is definitely the missing posting, a number of different articles use the same excerpt claiming it is the text that was posted to M.I.A.'s blog in December 2007 after the *TRL* and *Late Show* incidents.[39] The section of her blog post addressing the *Late Show* and MTV reads:

---

contested the Roman Catholic Church to the surprise of producers who had seen her employ a different photo in rehearsal.

38. You can see the edited version at: http://youtube.com/watch?v=x-B03-rtob0.

39. Examples of articles mentioning this infamous blog post can be found here: "New M.I.A. Video – 'Paper Planes,'" Stereogum, December 17, 2007. Available at: http://stereogum.com/archives/video/new-mia-video-paper-planes_007509.html#more.

WHEN LETTERMAN CENSORD ME IT WAS WAC OF COURSE!!!!!!, AND
YES I FELT SOOOOOO BAD FOR WHAT THEY DID TO MY SOUND. I WAS
ABEL TO SOUND CHECK FOR THAT SHOW AND THEY LET ME SOUND
CHECK FINE, THEN ON THE ACTUAL TAPING MY SOUND WAS SOOO
DIFFERENT FROM WHAT ID AGREED, AS SOON AS I OPENED MY MOUTH
THE DIFFERENCE BLEW ME AWAY, I FELT I WAS GETTING BULLIED ON
NATIONAL TELEVISON, AND I COULDNT EVEN REACH OUT TO MY
LABELS OR MY MANAGEMENT TO HELP, SINCE THEY ARE NEW TO WHAT
HAPPENS TO AN ARTIST LIKE ME IN MAINSTEAM AMERICAN CULTURE.

SO THEY TRIED TO SHUT ME DOWN AGAIN. I MADE THE PAPER PLANES
VIDEO. I MADE IT HOW THEY WANTED. NO VIOLENCE. AMBIGUOUS.
MTV — FRIENDLY. NOW TODAY, I CHECK YOUTUBE AND SEE THE LEAKED
MTV PAPER PLANES VIDEO UP FOR THE FIRST TIME. I CLICKED ON
IT AND OUT COMES THIS FUCKED UP MESS WITH DOUBLE-TRACKED
BULLSHIT MESS

WHO THE THE FUCK IS DOING THIS TO ME?????

THE VIDEO WAS SABOTAGED FOR WHATEVER REASON AND IM
DISAPPOINTED THAT MTV HAS HAD SUCH A MAJOR ROLE IN THIS . . .
BECAUSE PUTTING MEANINGS IN YOUR VIDEOS, IN MY OPINION IS A
DYING ART . . . .

TO ALL MY FANS . . . IM LEARNING THINGS ABOUT THIS WORLD
WITH YOU . . . I WANT YOU TO SEE HOW PEOPLE WILL SIT AND SPEND
ALL SUNDAY TEARIN ME DOWN FOR SOMETHING I DIDNT EVEN MAKE
OR PUT OUT, SO PEOPLE WELCOME TO MODERN DAY PROPAGANDA
MESSAGE MANGLING . . . MY MESSAGES AND IDEAS AND MEANING WILL
ALWAYS BE BROUGHT TO YOU WITH SLIGHTLY TAINTED CHANNELS. IF
YOU SUPPORT ME BE SMART, AND KNOW THAT . . ."[40]

The fact that this posting is no longer available on her blog sparks questions
over the politics regarding M.I.A.'s (and/or her publicist's) decision to self-
regulate and tone down her aggressive statements towards US institutions
and dominant ideologies. Through the trajectory of M.I.A.'s career, I believe
a significant, gradual quieting of M.I.A.'s opinions about the US and its
policies and ideologies takes place.

As "Paper Planes" took off in 2008 and M.I.A. became popular among
music fans — indie and mainstream — in the US, public instances of contestation from M.I.A. that gained publicity become more sparse. Granted,
her performances during her "People vs. Money Tour," that took place in
the US during the first half of 2008 immediately following her *Kala* tour,
still packed a political punch by presenting a live show littered with political

---

40. "M.I.A. Angry with MTV and Letterman over 'Paper Planes,'" *Hypeful*. Blog post.
December 17, 2007. The capitalization of the text has been left untouched to convey
original emphasis (and disgruntlement).

images, loud, multiple instances of gunfire, and moments of direct address to the audience to talk about assimilation, US immigration laws, and representation of women in the media.[41] But in general M.I.A. has slowly retracted her political views from the public eye.[42] During her performance at the Bonnaroo Music Festival on June 13, 2008, M.I.A. announced to the crowd that that performance would be her last, for she was retiring.[43] While personal reasons were given for her decision to retire (only a few months later M.I.A. announced her engagement and pregnancy), it is possible to argue that discourses of terrorism played a large part in her decision to retire from performing in order to suppress these rumors and allow her to more easily transition into the US mainstream by diluting her aggressive image. During M.I.A.'s transition into the mainstream mediascape, the discourse around these instances of censorship, and the release of her single "Paper Planes," were very much marked by an association with "terrorism."[44] Her family history is of particular importance in this discourse; it is well known that her father was, and perhaps still is, a highly regarded member of the Tamil Tigers. Despite her disassociation with the Tamil Tigers by being a long-term exile from Sri Lanka, her father's past and present connections with the group undoubtedly inform the ways in which M.I.A.'s star persona is read.

Numerous viral videos and articles circulating on the internet accuse M.I.A. of being a terrorist. One particularly striking video is by a rapper of Sri Lankan descent named DeLon. By rewriting the lyrics to "Paper Planes" and layering these new lyrics over images of the Sri Lankan Civil War, DeLon explicitly and powerfully accuses M.I.A. of being a member and supporter of the Tamil Tigers. He raps: "Yo! This is for all you people who really think M.I.A. is a freedom fighter. For all of you who dress like her and shit. All she want to do is [gunfire shots] . . . Straight to my head! First off let me gets some facts straight . . . M.I.A. you represent terrorism in the worst way . . ." DeLon continues rapping over the "Paper Planes" beat making claims about

---

41. For an example of a description of a concert from M.I.A.'s People vs. Money Tour see Chad Jones, "Concert Review: Holy F*ck/M.I.A. at Palladium Ballroom (May 2)," *Pegasus*, May 3, 2008.

42. Using the space of the live performance as a platform for contestation is quite different than using a mainstream television network. This differentiation is important when taking into consideration the spaces in which M.I.A. takes an overtly political stance on the status of minority people and women in the US and the impact they have on her persona and the reach of her message. The audience attending her live performances is narrow in terms of demographics and size in comparison to a major television network's audience. Recognizing this differentiation between live performance and mainstream television is essential in analyzing when and where M.I.A.'s political message is conveyed and censored.

43. Matthew Solarski, "Was Bonnaroo Really M.I.A.'s 'Last Gig Ever'?" *Pitchfork*, June 16, 2008.

44. Undeniably, the use of the word "terrorism" in the US context carries with it connotations associated with the 9/11 events. With the Bush administration's ubiquitous use of the word terrorism to describe the "other" as the ones against whom the United States is fighting, it is understood here that it certainly connotes acts of racial profiling in the name of national security.

the imagery in M.I.A.'s album covers and videos. Adding to the dramatization of his accusations are gruesome pictures presumably of violence in Sri Lanka. Decapitated heads and dead bodies add a shock value to the video (so shocking YouTube banned it). In a reaction statement to the video and other accusations, M.I.A. maintained: "I don't support terrorism and never have. As a Sri Lankan that fled war and bombings, my music is the voice of the civilian refugee. Frankly, I am not trying to start dialogue with someone who is really just seeking self-promotion."[45] While proclaiming herself as a voice for the voiceless, M.I.A. denounces these accusations in a moderate tone. Her summer 2008 retirement and public declaration of her alignment with the innocent detach M.I.A. from her antagonistic statements from years prior. These events set the stage for M.I.A. to further propel herself into the mainstream.

Since her announcement of retirement, M.I.A. has launched into a different role as a music artist. Just as she put down the microphone, her status as a US star took off. Undeniably, the song that put M.I.A. on the map in US popular culture is "Paper Planes." Propelling her career and the heavy rotation of this song was the use of the single during the promotional trailer of the Judd Apatow film *Pineapple Express*, which was released August 6, 2008.[46] By the end of the summer, "Paper Planes" peaked on Billboard's Hot 100 list at number 4 and was in heavy rotation on mainstream pop, hip-hop, and R&B radio stations across the country.[47] Later in the year, a remix of "Paper Planes" was featured on the soundtrack for the ten-time Oscar-nominated film *Slumdog Millionaire* and nominated for Record of the Year at the 51st Grammy Awards — further propelling M.I.A. into mainstream celebrity status. It is important to note that the remix of "Paper Planes" in *Slumdog Millionaire* does not have the loud gunshot sounds in the chorus, thus diminishing its threatening character and rendering it acceptable to accompany an Oscar-winning drama.[48] At this point in the history of "Paper Planes" as a single in the United States, the song is now coming (much like *Slumdog Millionaire* itself) to be associated with "safe" internationalism and a palatable foreignness. In addition to "Paper Planes," M.I.A. collaborated

---

45. "MIA Denies Supporting Terrorism: Rapper Speaks out after DeLon Issues Video Accusation," *NME*, August 11, 2008.
46. In the *Pineapple Express* trailer, "Paper Planes" becomes the non-diegetic background music introducing audiences to the story of two marijuana users who witness a murder and are on the run from the group of people associated with the killing. The gunshots in the song are edited to images of violent scenes in the movie. However, the bouncy, poppy beats of the song combined with the antics of the two friends on the run set a comedic tone for the film.
47. "M.I.A.: Chart History," *Billboard*.
48. It is important to take note of the traditionalist gender representations in both Judd Apatow's and Danny Boyle's films. Apatow's comedy presents a "hipness" (a stand in for progressive politics) that belies a deep devotion to traditionalist patriarchal norms. Boyle's film is similarly traditionalist in its placement of the lead female character as a passive love object for the male protagonist.

with the composer of the soundtrack of *Slumdog Millionaire,* A. R. Rahman, to produce the Oscar-nominated "Best Original Song," "O . . . Saya." Ejecting herself out of the performing arena into the more backstage roles of producer, wife, and mother and developing her most popular single into a representation of "safe" internationalism dilutes her once explicitly loud, political persona.

The trajectory of M.I.A.'s crossover and career in the US is heavily influenced by the discourses of terrorism surrounding her persona. Because she initially stepped onto the US scene with an agenda to contest conservative US ideologies, the discursive strategy of aligning herself with terrorism in a cultural context that uses this term to describe "evil-doers"[49] works as a way to contain the threat of her agenda and image — the image of a non-white woman with an opinion.[50] Whether the allegations of her affiliation with an organization deemed terrorist by the United States are factual or not, the provenance of such discourse in M.I.A.'s crossover transition presents an example of how social and cultural hierarchies under threat are negotiated by making contestations in a more implicit way. In this case, the negotiations settled seem to be in favor of a capitalist, post-feminist, post-race ideology.

M.I.A. continues to insert counter-hegemonic moments into her repertoire of images. It should be noted that although dominant, patriarchal ideologies in the United States might situate motherhood and pregnancy as signs of weakness indicative of a succumbing to gender ideals, the figure of a very pregnant woman continuing to contest and confront the US media's regime of representation, albeit through a new presentation of self, can certainly be read as subversive. An example of M.I.A. presenting a potentially counter-hegemonic moment is her performance to fans' delight at the 2008 Grammy Awards. The details of her performance were undisclosed and created quite a stir — for the due date of her baby and the date of the Grammy Awards show fell on the same day. The circumstances under which she performed present an interesting example of the ways in which M.I.A. continues to moderately subvert dominant representations of women and women of color in popular US culture, while attempts to contain her excessive female ethnicity simultaneously occur. Donning a black mesh, see-through, full-body suit with black and white polka-dotted pieces of cloth covering her breasts and belly, M.I.A. walked onto the stage at the Grammy's to the beginning beats of "Paper Planes." Moving with enthusiasm and purpose, M.I.A. and her huge, pregnant stomach provocatively took center stage in front of a loud and enthusiastic crowd. Less than thirty seconds into her performance, the stage's curtains open and the tempo of the song shifts.

---

49. For an example of the rhetoric surrounding terrorism and the "War on Terror," see Manuel Perez-Rivas, "Bush Vows to Rid the World of 'Evil-Doers,'" CNN.com, September 16, 2001.
50. For more on the use of "terrorism" as a discursive strategy to silence contesting viewpoints see Susan Faludi, *The Terror Dream.*

The "Paper Planes" hook "No one on the corner has swagga like us, swagga, swagga like us" begins to repeat itself, and rappers Kanye West, Jay-Z, Lil' Wayne, and T.I. enter the stage to sing their Grammy-award-winning song (for Best Rap Performance by a Group) "Swagga Like Us," which samples the hook from M.I.A.'s "Paper Planes" over and over again. This performance is a case in point example of the negotiations being made over the representation of M.I.A. While the very pregnant, exposed body of a woman of color commanding attention on a worldwide stage presents a moment in which a blatant act of subversion was performed, the quick return to domination of the stage and performance by the elite "Boys' Club" of the mainstream hip-hop community is, I believe, indicative of the anxiety and fear of M.I.A.'s body and persona confronting dominant patriarchal ideologies. While this performance in its entirety (and M.I.A.'s lack of being credited whatsoever for her role in creating the song "Swagga Like Us") could be read as an overt example of her marginalization on a worldwide stage, I want to acknowledge this performance as a formative moment when M.I.A.'s image presents an instance of negotiated subversion.

Conclusion

A number of issues arise when looking at the discourse of the M.I.A. star text. We first delved into the initial stages of M.I.A.'s crossover into US popular culture by looking at the ways in which her denials of a visa are framed in the US media. What emerged through this analysis was a reoccurring discursive strategy that revealed the underpinning anxieties of immigration and racial profiling working within hegemonic US ideologies. By framing the United States in a way that credited US governmental institutions and the fuzzy policies of the Homeland Security Act for her eclectic sound and style, the controversies of racist profiling of non-white people were deferred and, instead, covered up by the success of M.I.A.'s album. While some articles present her visa denials in a rather tongue-in-cheek manner, the use of comedic or satirical tones does not weaken the message; rather these strategies of delivery actually expose more explicitly the ways that racist practices of US institutions have become ingrained in a dangerous post-race, liberal multiculturalist ideology.

In this age of late capitalism, there is a basic, collective understanding that production practices in the mainstream music industry are collaborative. That said, dominant discourse regarding the practices of the popular music industry that produce the images and sounds for factory-styled pop stars do include a trend of framing these puppet-on-strings pop stars being pulled by often faceless, behind-the-scenes producers and DJs. This common trope of how the music industry is portrayed can be found in the discourse surrounding the authorship and debut of M.I.A. The man who is more often than not credited as the mastermind behind her work is her former beau and

US-based artist and producer DJ Diplo. M.I.A. explicitly confronts the ways in which her entrance into the US is framed by overtly calling out both racist and sexist discursive and representational practices she sees at work in the media, bringing to the forefront how they have shaped her image. However, in these moments of contestation, other strategies — such as displaying her participation in and subscription to heteronormativity — are implemented to weaken her contestations in an effort to restore the status quo of representation and contain her excessive ethnic femininity. It should also be noted that the status of M.I.A.'s fiancé Ben Brewer, son of billionaire Edgar Bronfman Jr., CEO of Warner Music Group, and a member of one of the most wealthy and powerful families in Canada (and with a strong presence in New York City) also contributes to the shift in her positionality as a voice for those discriminated against by the US government and her ability to be seen as an authentic contester of capitalistic culture and its associated ideologies. In the late spring of 2010, a *New York Times* article by Lynn Hirschberg confronted, possibly unethically,[51] the authenticity of M.I.A.'s positionality and ability to stand as a leader for marginalized peoples. After the article was published M.I.A. confronted Hirschberg about how she framed the piece and alleged that she took words and sentences out of context. An ensuing series of exchanges between M.I.A. and Hirschberg included the singer sending out the writer's personal phone number via microblogging website Twitter and various interviews of the two women by third party sources. These latest, highly publicized debates and confrontations between M.I.A. *and The New York Times* reveal how negotiations and questions of authenticity continue to be ongoing.

Finally, I have examined discourses of censorship in conjunction with associations to terrorism by exploring how they shape the trajectory of M.I.A.'s career and its potential in US popular culture. After experiencing a number of censorship events, M.I.A. explicitly contested and lashed out against these attempts at silencing her agenda of being a leader for marginalized people. While these moments of contestation were well documented at the time of their occurrence, they slowly but surely become less recurrent and even begin disappearing. Granted M.I.A. continues to voice her concern for civilian refugees around the world, but the ways in which these concerns are framed present M.I.A. in a less domineering, more compliant manner. Since her "retirement" announcement in June 2008, M.I.A. has been anything but erased from the mainstream. Instead, she has propelled her stardom and career to a new level. With a clothing line debut during New York City's Fashion Week, an Academy Award nomination, and a Grammy Award nomination, this civilian refugee is now most certainly considered A-list material. The timing of her retirement and retraction from

---

51. An editor's note was later added to the article stating that the order in which some of M.I.A.'s sentences were presented in the original article was inaccurate.

live performance, the platform for her most aggressive proclamation of her politics, allowed her to be projected to mainstream status.[52] Unmistakably, these events coincided with the release of the mainstream film *Pineapple Express* — thus, setting the stage for M.I.A. to be part of the promotion for the highly acclaimed, multiple Academy Award-winning film *Slumdog Millionaire*. Through this transition, M.I.A. reformed the manner in which she speaks out against US ideologies. The underlying message this signals is that M.I.A. does indeed present ironic, complicated, and sometimes hypocritical images of contestation against dominant US ideologies. The ambiguous mode in which her representation of ethnic femininity is currently operating certainly leaves us with a stagnant sense of progress. However, her image and persona as a strong, non-white female working in US popular music and fashion should not be disregarded.

Bibliography

Arulpragasam, Maya. "M.I.A. Confronts the Haters," Interview with Paul Thompson, *Pitchfork*, August 3, 2007. Available at: http://www.pitchforkmedia.com/article/news/44529-mia-confronts-the-haters (accessed January 30, 2009).

Becker, Howard S. "Art as Collective Action," *American Sociological Review* 39(6), (1974): 767–76.

Christgau, Robert, et al. "The Top 50 Albums of 2007," *Rolling Stone*, December 27, 2007. Available at: http://www.rollingstone.com/news/story/17601851/the_top_50_albums_of_2007. (accessed May 1, 2008).

Crenshaw, Kimberle Williams. "Color-Blind Dreams and Racial Nightmares: Reconfiguring Racism in the Post-Civil Rights Era," in Toni Morrison and Claudia Brodsky Lacour (eds), *Birth of a Nation'hood*. New York: Pantheon, 1997, 97–168.

Daly, Sean. "Mesmerizing Singer's Style is Perfectly Perplexing," *St. Petersburg Times*, August 25, 2007, 1E.

Empire, Kitty. "Flash-Forward: M.I.A.'s Innovative Beats and Rhymes are Distilled in London but Fed by her Intriguing Past in Sri Lanka," *The Observer*, March 20, 2005, 28.

Faludi, Susan. *The Terror Dream: Fear and Fantasy in Post 9/11 America*. New York: Metropolitan Books, 2007.

Foucault, Michel. *The History of Sexuality*, vol. 1. New York: Random House, 1980.

Harrington, Richard. "M.I.A., No Loss for Words," *The Washington Post*, September 16, 2005. Available at: http://www.washingtonpost.com/wp-dyn/content/article/2005/09/15/AR2005091500697_pf.html (accessed February 2, 2009).

Herman, Bill D. "Scratching Out Authorship: Representations of the Electronic Music DJ at the Turn of the 21st Century," *Popular Communication* 4(1), 2006: 24, 21–38.

Jones, Chad. "Concert Review: Holy F*ck/M.I.A. at Palladium Ballroom (May 2)," *Pegasus*, May 3, 2008. Available at: http://www.pegasusnews.com/news/2008/may/03/concert-review-mi-holy-fck (accessed February 2, 2009).

Llewellyn, Kati. "M.I.A. Goes Crazy on MySpace," *Pitchfork*, December 13, 2006. Available at: http://www.pitchfork.com/article/news/40161-mia-goes-crazy-on-myspace (accessed January 30, 2009).

---

52. During the summer of 2010, M.I.A. had scheduled a few live shows outside of the US for her summer tour. The only shows she had scheduled for the summer in the US were in Los Angeles and New York City. Keeping her provocative performances mostly outside the US and only within the confines of L.A. and New York, the two main hubs for entertainment in the US, M.I.A. restricted her most explicit political proclamations to a carefully delimited audience.

Marshall, P. David. *Celebrity and Power: Fame in Contemporary Culture.* Minneapolis, MN: University of Minnesota Press, 1997.

Martens, Todd. "XL Finds Hot Prospect in M.I.A.," *Billboard,* March 26, 2005, 11.

"M.I.A. angry with MTV and Letterman over 'Paper Planes,'" *Hypeful.* Blog post. December 17, 2007. Available at: http://www.hypeful.com/2007/12/17/mia-angry-with-mtv-and-letterman-over-paper-planes/(accessed February 2, 2009).

"M.I.A.: Chart History," *Billboard.* Available at: http://m.billboard.com/artist/m-i-a/chart-history/629381#/artist/m-i-a/chart-history/629381 (accessed February 2, 2009).

"MIA Denied Entry to the US: The Star Wants to Get on With Her New Album," *NME,* May 19, 2006. Available at: http://www.nme.com/news/mia/23110 (accessed January 26, 2009).

"MIA Denies Supporting Terrorism: Rapper Speaks out after DeLon Issues Video Accusation," *NME,* August 11, 2008. Available at: http://www.nme.com/news/mia/38789 (accessed 2 February 2009).

"M.I.A. Doesn't Need a Visa, Just Inspiration," *Associated Press,* August 21, 2007. Available at: http://www.msnbc.msn.com/id/20379484/(accessed January 26, 2009).

Negra, Diane. *Off-White Hollywood: American Culture and Ethnic Female Stardom.* London: Routledge, 2001.

"New M.I.A. Video – 'Paper Planes,'" Stereogum, December 17, 2007. Available at: http://stereogum.com/archives/video/new-mia-video-paper-planes_007509.html#more (accessed November 18, 2010).

Perez-Rivas, Manuel. "Bush Vows to Rid the World of 'Evil-Doers,'" CNN.com, September 16, 2001. Available at: http://archives.cnn.com/2001/US/09/16/gen.bush.terrorism/ (accessed February 2, 2009).

Rayner, Ben. "Multi-culti Ambassador; US Visa Delay Proves to be the Catalyst that Shapes the Global Sound of M.I.A.'s Sophomore Disc, *Kala,*" *The Toronto Star,* September 6, 2007, V03.

Sanneh, Kelefa. "Give Them What They Want But Keep It Sort of Cool," *The New York Times,* February 7, 2005, E3.

Sisario, Ben. "An Itinerant Refugee in a Hip-Hop World," *New York Times,* August 19, 2007. Available at: http://www.nytimes.com/2007/08/19/arts/music/19sisa.html (accessed December 8, 2008).

Solarski, Matthew. "Was Bonnaroo Really M.I.A.'s 'Last Gig Ever'?" *Pitchfork,* June 16, 2008. Available at: http://www.pitchforkmedia.com/article/news/51333-was-bonnaroo-really-mias-last-gig-ever (accessed February 2, 2009).

Stam, Robert and Ella Shohat. *Unthinking Eurocentrism.* London: Routledge, 1994.

Sylvester, Nick. Album review of *M.I.A.: Piracy Funds Terrorism, Vol. 1* [mixed by Diplo], *Pitchfork,* November 22, 2004. Available at: http://www.pitchforkmedia.com/article/record_review/20217-piracy-funds-terrorism-vol-1-mixed-by-diplo (accessed January 29, 2009).

Van Buskirk , Eliot. "M.I.A. Blasts MTV for Censoring 'Paper Planes' Video," *Wired,* December 18, 2007. Available at: http://blog.wired.com/music/2007/12/mia-blasts-mtv.html (accessed November 18, 2010).

"Was MTV Right to Edit M.I.A.'s 'Paper Planes' Video?" PopWatch, December 18, 2007. Available at: http://popwatch.ew.com/popwatch/2007/12/mia-paper-plane.html (accessed November 18, 2010).

14

We Love This Trainwreck!
Sacrificing Britney to Save America

ANNA WATKINS FISHER

Honestly, I think we should just trust our president in every decision that he makes, and we should just support that, you know, and be faithful in what happens.

— BRITNEY SPEARS IN AN INTERVIEW FEATURED IN FAHRENHEIT 9/11[1]

We know for a fact that there are weapons there.

— WHITE HOUSE SPOKESMAN ARI FLEISCHER, JANUARY 9, 2003[2]

And so we go to war.

— AVITAL RONELL, STUPIDITY[3]

Introduction

Britney Spears' cameo in *Fahrenheit 9/11*, Michael Moore's scathing 2004 documentary on the War in Iraq, follows a brutal sequence of images: shots of dead and mutilated Iraqi civilians and an extended scene featuring a distraught older Iraqi woman just after the US bombing of her home. The woman's cries are translated in subtitles, "They have slaughtered us! They have destroyed our houses! . . . We're all civilians . . . We've had five funerals because of the bombings . . . Where are you, God?" The next shot is an abrupt cut to Spears, shown during an interview with CNN wearing a blonde wig and chewing gum. "Do you trust the president?" the off-camera interviewer asks her. "Yes, I do," she responds sweetly.

---

1. *Fahrenheit 9/11.* Directed by Michael Moore [2004]. Weinstein Company, 2007. DVD.
2. Agence France-Presse, "US Keeps up Hunt for Smoking Gun in Iraq," *Global Policy Forum,* January 10, 2003.
3. Avital Ronell, *Stupidity* (Champaign, IL: University of Illinois Press, 2002), 15.

That Spears' image would be conjured at the most difficult and graphic moment of the film would seem a highly calculated editing decision on the part of Moore. Why is it that Spears, of all people, is made to "answer to" the extreme violence and destruction brought about by the US occupation of Iraq? In a film loaded with jabs at the Bush administration for failing to produce reasonable justification for a costly and ill-conceived war,[4] why is it *Spears' poor judgment* that gets called into question at this juncture? By featuring her in the film, and at this precise moment, Moore implies that Spears *has something to do with the Iraq war* — that she is, in some way, to blame.

Everything about Spears' saccharine presence in the interview — the banal naïveté of her politics, the insulation suggested by her surroundings, the polite impassivity of her affect — is marshaled in that moment to jolt the spectator into feelings of disgust and alienation for the American cultural present as represented by the female celebrity, a response heightened by the sharp contrast of Spears' apparent privilege and isolation to the desperation and pathos in the streets of Baghdad. Juxtaposed with the desperation of the Iraqi situation, the profanity of her female celebrity — signified in close-ups by her made-up face, low-cut shirt, and gaudy jewelry — is called upon to throw into relief the sanctity of the destruction and lost life in Iraq. Moore re-contextualizes this archival footage of Spears, originally from a network news interview, to produce a formal, and emotional, disjuncture between the scenes in Iraq and the clip of Spears. It appears that Moore's point about the sacredness of human life depends on his portrayal of Spears as a token of abject American imperialism — an association of a once top-of-her-game pop star to an unsteady US superpower — yoking celebrity femininity to American patriotism as logics conceptually bound by the rubric of failure. He figures the celebrity woman as sign for excess and ignorance in order to sound a warning about what he believes America has become — a nation he implies is as indulgent and uninformed as the celebrities it is obsessed with.

Significantly, Moore's agenda also depends on the spectator *identifying* with Spears. Asked for her response to the War in Iraq, Spears is figured, however surreally, as the *typical American* whose unswerving patriotism indexes an American public's initially uncritical support of the war that emboldened

---

4. As has been widely reported, the Bush administration's stated motive for going to war was to disarm Iraq of weapons of mass destruction (WMDs), yet intensive searching failed to turn up any weapons and the main US inspection team was ultimately withdrawn. After failing to find evidence of WMDs, the Bush administration shifted its emphasis to Saddam Hussein's regime's brutality, systematic oppression, and repeated flouting of UN resolutions, an argument that security expert Paul Rogers has described as "difficult to sustain . . . given that Saddam Hussein was on several occasions closely allied to the United States, even at a time when his regime was engaging in systematic repression . . ." Describing the views of many, Rogers continues, "A suspicion across the region has long been that the Iraq war was essentially about the control of oil and the need to decrease dependence on Saudia Arabia." Notably, Moore makes the same argument in *Fahrenheit 9/11*. Paul Rogers. "Aftermath," in *A War Too Far* (London: Pluto Press, 2006), 49.

the Bush administration's drastic actions in its post-9/11 governance. As a result, the spectator, who is always understood as the uninformed American citizen by the film's address (and who, like Spears, is portrayed as lacking knowledge about what is "really happening"), is sent back an image that is both caricature and mirror reflection. The film offers a complex bifurcation of Spears as female celebrity and uninformed American citizen. How, we might ask, does a female celebrity like Spears come to be held as symbolically responsible for a war? How is it that Spears' so-called ignorance comes to seem more reprehensible than Bush's "failed intelligence?"

Who is allowed to fail in America and how? To answer this question, this essay will interrogate the curious relationship between the War in Iraq and the War on Britney, two contemporaneous global media "events" that have powerfully drawn together questions of excess and failure in the public sphere over the last decade. Both media sagas have constituted states of "national crisis" that have played out over the last decade and been remarkable for indexing the increasingly fractured identification between the spectator and media event. This essay attempts the ambitious work of trying to think about how these seemingly unrelated media dramas might be understood as co-constitutive in the shaping of public opinion. I argue that within the temporal arc of the war — beginning around the March 2003 invasion of Iraq and reaching its crescendo with the tabloid-fueled vitriol of George W. Bush's final years in office — Britney Spears came under such increasing and persistent attack that by 2007, her very personhood had come to represent a state of deep-seated and deeply displaced cultural conflict. I want to suggest that, as an effigy for everything the US has reviled about its own excess, Spears came to represent the country's "supersized" libidinal and commercial investment in the realm of the "too much," following what was widely perceived to be the abysmal failure of her supposed comeback performance at the 2007 Annual MTV Video Music Awards. In contradistinction to the unyielding harassment Spears faced for her personal and professional setbacks, President Bush, despite low approval ratings, left office in January 2009 to retire comfortably in Crawford, Texas, largely unscathed in the aftermath of having driven the country to a violent and costly war while refusing all along the way to stop and "ask for directions."

During the two terms that Bush held US office, spanning 2001–2009, the American public found itself more and more deeply entrenched in a war of which many did not approve. Beginning in 2003, the public faced nightly televised reminders of its entrenchment with news of unrelenting violence from suicide bombings and roadside attacks and weary talk of troop resurgence and partisan exhaustion. By the time Britney Spears took the *VMA* stage in September 2007, the civilian death toll in Iraq had surged upwards of 85,000[5] and US military deaths approached 4,000.[6] It seems that somewhere between the search for "WMDs" and Spears' subsequent hospitalization for a mental breakdown in early 2008, excess and failure had become cultural watchwords for the United States' increasingly entrenched status as a superpower in crisis. As the losses continued to mount and their justifications called into question, Americans appeared to take the path of least resistance, changing the channel, and reflexively absorbing in haste a heady mix of glamour and detritus.

With the cozy multimedia merger of "news-to-amuse" with so-called "real news," the media-consuming public has become increasingly confronted by the two-part harmony of entertainment news, with its preference for stumbling young starlets, and the far-less-entertaining news that the world is going up in flames from global terror and global warming that has come to be referred to as "infotainment." We devoured news of Lindsay Lohan's latest nightclub bust, Paris Hilton's vomitous victories in late capitalism, and the "news" that, alas, a newly bald Britney Spears was no longer the American darling, sex-kitten-next-door she once was. In this essay, I want to think through this historical moment to ask how Spears might represent a revealing case study for charting the unraveling of democracy during the Bush era, despite the fact that celebrity culture is often seen as divorced from "real" politics. I am not interested in arguments that would work to maintain a strict separation between the so-called "high" and "low" or promote any kind of essentialist logic though I do recognize that my argument walks a critical tightrope, at times touching on concepts that flirt with essentialism while actively working to avoid any essentializing influence. Instead, I want to take seriously the historical coextension of the rise in infotainment and the War in Iraq to think about how media representations of female celebrity, so often treated as apolitical "filler" slotted in between "real news" stories, come to do profoundly important political work under the guise of seeming triviality. While a scholarly argument claiming a connection between Britney Spears and George W. Bush might appear to some a work of provocation or idiosyncrasy, I would argue that such a knee-jerk response serves only as further evidence of the importance of pursuing such an analysis and the power of hegemonic discourses to cordon off certain media objects from other ones in an effort to foreclose lines of interrogation that might breach unspoken rules about what counts as important and what does not. The point of this essay is to ask exactly this: why does it seem at first so unthinkable that Britney Spears and George W. Bush might have a direct connection? How is it that these figures are constructed in the public sphere

---

5. The Iraq Body Count Project (IBC) reports between 78,213 and 85,221 civilians have been killed in the Iraq War and Occupation. "Documented Civilian Deaths from Violence," Iraq Body Count, December 14, 2007.
6. "US Military Deaths at 3,895," *The New York Times*, December 16, 2007.

in such a way that makes thinking through their relationship to each other in the cultural field seem so difficult?

This essay will offer a study of Spears' treatment by the mainstream media during the height of her personal and professional setbacks. It will examine the intensity and substance of the attacks against her — slander about her postpartum weight gain, criticism of her lackluster singing and dancing, and public questioning of her abilities as a single mother — in order to suggest a critical framework as a means of thinking through the gender politics behind the widespread vitriol directed at her and for comparing the relatively low cost ultimately paid by Bush for far more consequential breaches of decorum. If entertainment news can be understood as functioning as a kind of cultural release valve for the political, as René Girard's important theorization of the surrogate victim might suggest, how has the media's unprecedented scapegoating of Spears functioned to relieve Bush of political pressure he might otherwise have faced for the Iraq war? As one blogger asks, "What is this shit? Ragging on Britney Spears is the new Bush joke."[7]

In sorting through the train wreckage of this important historical and cultural moment, this essay pays particular attention to the role of TV convergence, or the synergistic blurring of commercial lines between television and digital media outlets (online news sites and blogs). I will also consider the role of digital media in producing instantaneous, uninterrupted, immediate, and anonymous platforms for disciplining Spears for her professional and personal setbacks, while in contrast, relatively little of the public anger over the Iraq war seemed to find a place to stick to Bush.[8] As the rise of digital technologies make possible the endless capture and archiving of visual evidence of mistakes made, comments flubbed and dance steps stumbled, it often seems that the work of the mainstream press, and underlying multimedia conglomerates, has become not merely to capture but to *produce* these failures.[9]

Increasingly, a right to privacy, or the right *not to be surveilled* (made all the more tenuous by the Bush administration's introduction of The USA Patriot Act on October 26, 2001), has become a luxury afforded to only the truly powerful, a fact that has exposed the ironic disempowerment of celebrity in tabloid culture. Whereas Spears appears unable to have a

---

7. Here I am quoting a message board post by "Klixy" from September 10, 2007, "I Cry Watching the Days: Britney Spears Performs at MTV's Video Music Awards," Gawker.com, September 10, 2007.

8. A CNN poll on November 8, 2007, just two months after Spears' failed comeback performance, found opposition to the War in Iraq higher than it had ever been in the United States at 68 percent. "Poll: Opposition to Iraq War at High," United Press International (UPI), November 8, 2007.

9. The role of the media in shaping public perception has long been discussed, assuming the name *the CNN effect* in recent years. Thomas Keenan, "Publicity and Indifference: Media, Surveillance, 'Humanitarian Intervention,'" in Thomas Y. Levin, Ursula Frohne, and Peter Weibel (eds), *CTRL [SPACE]* (Cambridge, MA: The MIT Press, 2002), 544–61.

moment go undocumented and the very fact of her celebrity forces her into public exposure, as Head of State, Bush holds executive power over the public record and retains the high level of protection afforded by his office (though many criticized Bush for overextending this entitlement). Indeed, this essay finds itself faced with a revealing imbalance of documentation representing the failures of Spears versus Bush: she is overexposed while he would seem to be underexposed. So perhaps this essay is not about who gets to fail in America, but rather, who *gets away* with failing and who is not allowed to forget it.

Infotaining America

The influential rise of "infotainment" over the last ten years (particularly apparent in the American television and digital news coverage of 24-hour-news providers like CNN, Fox News, and MSNBC) has provided a dangerous smokescreen for the accountability of US politicians to citizens. In her book blasting the rise of the corporate news network for lowering journalistic standards, Bonnie Anderson describes infotainment as "the intrusion of entertainment into news" brought about by demands for news networks to entice more viewers and to hit higher profit margins.[10] "How did television journalism get to a place where showing a singer's digitalized breast for the umpteenth time is considered more important than informing Americans that the US Capitol was closed due to a toxin emergency . . .?" she asks.[11] Anderson is, of course, referring to Janet Jackson's infamous "wardrobe malfunction," also referred to as "Nipplegate," a telling episode in the age of infotainment that has been characterized as the partial replacement of "real news" with something used to entice wider audiences (goodbye "Watergate," hello "Nipplegate"). Anderson points to the contemporary media landscape of mega-mergers as producing multimedia conglomerates that promote and thrive on a culture of cross pollination, described as "an attempt to save money while getting cross promotion by having the separate entities within the corporation work together on projects,"[12] that produces commercial juxtapositions that move back and forth between "entertainment" and "news."

The mainstreaming of tabloid culture has been aided in part by the influence of media convergence. A formal extension of the cross pollination of content Anderson describes, convergence makes content available across diverse media platforms, from TV news shows to entertainment news sites to personal blogs. Convergence culture produces interactions between

---

10. Bonnie Anderson, "The Rise of the Corporate News Networks," in *News Flash* (San Francisco, CA: Jossey-Bass, 2004), 15.

11. Ibid., 3.

12. Ibid., 13.

previously distinct media forms, leading to a proliferation of devices for users to interact with and participate in the circulation of mass media content. According to media scholar Henry Jenkins, convergence culture also has the effect of producing what he calls a "collective intelligence," that links individuals into collectivities networked by their shared habits of consumption.[13] The implications of this kind of *"intelligence,"* the promises and perils of good and bad intelligences, serves as an important theoretical touchstone for this essay. The phenomenon of media convergence over the past decade has put into place the conditions of possibility for failure to become an inevitable byproduct of discursive proliferation, to use another term that echoes Bush's primary justification for going to war in Iraq in 2003, despite the fact that no evidence of weapons was found. Convergence culture, effectively the mapping of globalization onto the state of modern media, has the effect of confusing how one processes, and prioritizes information by putting everything everywhere, making an otherwise banal story about Britney's latest haircut the topic of national debate.

While Anderson writes from the perspective of the former journalist for whom entertainment appears as a kind of parasite "intruding on" serious journalism, I am interested not in whether infotainment is a "good" or "bad" thing but rather the conditions of its emergence and what it has created in the larger cultural landscape. Under the banner of infotainment, so-called "soft news," as a "feminized" or "degraded" form indexing stories perceived to be overtly sentimental in content (entertainment, lifestyle, human interest, celebrity news), comes into direct contact with so-called "hard news," or "masculinized" news forms committed to topics whose "seriousness" would appear bequeathed by an uncontested commitment to the absolute value of preserving human life in the face of legal, environmental, and cultural threats to it (politics, economics, crime, war, and disasters). I argue that infotainment's purported drawing together of what is said to be otherwise two different types of information, entertainment news as soft news and "real news" as hard news, falsely treats them as entities that are diametrically opposed to each other while on the other hand, actively and contradictorily conjoining them as equals in a word like *infotainment.*

In other words, there is a double discourse at work in infotainment. Interposing entertainment news with so-called "real news" effectively presents the two as gendered foils of each other (the supposed yin and yang of a well-balanced daily news diet). This comingling emerges in a moment of TV convergence, linking television and new media across any number of platforms, so as to suggest that giving the infantilized news-watching public its "dessert" might mean they will more willingly eat their "vegetables." As Jean Baudrillard compellingly argued about Disneyland in relation to the

---

13. Henry Jenkins. "Introduction," in *Convergence Culture* (New York: New York University Press, 2006), 2.

rest of the United States ("Disneyland is a perfect model of all the entangled orders of simulacra"),[14] this rise in the prevalence of entertainment news that stands *beside* and *next to* "real news" stories of White House sound bites and political punditry would seem to suggest that there is somehow such a thing as real news in the first place. By playfully indulging viewers in the overblown hyperbole of "fake" or "unbelievable" stories, they suggest that the other stories are both real and wholly credible. Placing the news of Britney Spears' over-the-top nightclub antics *up against* and *adjacent to* clips of Bush's public statements arguing a rationale for war based on the presence of weapons of mass destruction implies that they are somehow comparable or equal in the scale of their importance and impact in the realm of public debate. Moreover, their discursive proximity indicates not only the important ways in which soft and hard news mutually structure audience reception but also the extent to which their co-constitutive relationship is constantly under denial, as the thing that is so public that it cannot easily be seen. By presenting moralistic narratives that attack celebrities like Spears for being unfit, unreliable, and uncontrolled, politicians like Bush are seen as being more real, trustworthy, and mastered in their actions, lulling us into a false dichotomy and, against her will, making Britney into Bush's alibi.

Sacrificing Spears

In the spring of 2008, stickers with the words "BRITNEY SPEARS" in black-and-white block text began to cover the East Village of New York City. Slapped across fire hydrants, metro seats, and on the walls of bathroom stalls, they seemed to come out of nowhere, as if a part of a guerrilla street protest. Ultimately claimed by a writer as a part of a targeted marketing campaign

Figure 14.1   **In Spring 2008, stickers with Spears' name mysteriously appeared throughout New York City's East Village neighborhood. (Photo credit: Alex Pittman.)**

---

14. Jean Baudrillard, "The Precession of Simulacra," in Sheila Glaser trans., *Simulacra and Simulation* (Ann Arbor, MI: University of Michigan Press, 1994), 12.

to sell his new book,[15] the sticker's enigmatic strangeness and utter ubiquity seemed nonetheless to index something urgent and presumably instantly communicable to the public. While an exploitative commodification of the pop star was nothing new, this time "Britney Spears," set against the stark white background, seemed to stand in for some kind of political provocation, as if the very presence of her name had come to replace a radical act of protest.

The uncanny sense one had during this period that Britney Spears had become a cultural placeholder, an ever-present spectral figure standing in for *something else* happening (or significantly, *not happening*) in American culture is the central concern of this essay. For what exactly had Britney Spears come to stand, *stand in for*, and be held accountable? Is it merely by coincidence that the American fascination for celebrity "trainwrecks" (Michael Jackson, Courtney Love, Anna Nicole Smith, and most recently, Tiger Woods, to name but a few) has reached its zenith at a cultural moment so marked by political turmoil, civic impotence, and environmental disillusionment? If the promotion of a culture of celebrity bashing can be taken as a democratizing gesture, a form of "speaking truth to power," that seeks to level the playing field of American citizenship, has celebrity bashing become a dominant form of political engagement in America? And if so, what is it about Britney, *in particular*, that has produced a rage louder and more powerful than all the rest?

In the wake of the *2007 MTV Video Music Awards*, the once-adored Spears — at the time, a recent divorcee and young mother of two — found herself a target of public bitterness most consistently aimed at her post-partum corporeality and identity as a struggling mother.[16] Spears became a timely and convenient target for the American public's growing resentment of the Bush administration's devastating incompetence. The spectacularization of Spears' personal turmoil constituted a chain of repeated, uninterrupted blows in the form of taunting headlines, bad photos, and intrusive speculation that only stopped when in 2008 Spears yielded legal and professional

---

15. Jen Carlson, "Tao Lin Brings Britney to NYC," *Gothamist*, May 22, 2008.
16. Public backlash over Spears' performance of motherhood comes at a cultural moment dominated by obsessive celebrity coverage emphasizing the glorification of motherhood in general and the magically disappearing effects of pregnancy on the post-partum celebrity body. In *What a Girl Wants?* Diane Negra describes the fetishization and eroticization of pregnancy across an array of contemporary media forms noting that pregnancy has emerged as a hyped state of transcendent femininity. Negra references Spears' pregnancy to make her point, a contribution that throws into relief the short-lived duration of this fantasy in the case of Spears. Negra writes, "The re-classification of the pregnant body as natural, normal, and healthy has transitioned in recent years to a new physical and ideological exhibitionism that is facilitated by fashion trends such as the belly-baring t-shirt . . . [for example] pop star Britney Spears' first pregnancy in which the star was photographed wearing a t-shirt that read 'I've Got the Golden Ticket' with a downward arrow pointing to her stomach . . ." Diane Negra, *What a Girl Wants?: Fantasizing the Reclamation of Self in Postfeminism* (London: Routledge, 2009), 63.

control to her father, Jamie Spears, and re-engaged the rhetoric of self-help through physical fitness and personal salvation securing hard work and family values.[17]

By what mechanisms did there come to be such a profound breakdown in the way that the public processes and compartmentalizes important distinctions between trivial and critical public knowledge? René Girard's theorization of sacrifice provides this article with its major theoretical grounding. Girard writes,

> Violence is frequently called irrational. It has its reasons, however, and can marshal some rather convincing ones when the need arises. Yet these reasons cannot be taken seriously, no matter how valid they may appear. Violence itself will discard them if the initial object remains persistently out of reach and continues to provoke hostility. When unappeased, *violence seeks and always finds a surrogate victim.* The creature that excited its fury is abruptly replaced by another, chosen only because it is vulnerable and close at hand.[18]

Girard's theory of the surrogate victim suggests the mimetic correspondence between the War on Britney and the War in Iraq as organized by a logic of sacrifice as that which works to sustain the dominant order at the expense of a more vulnerable position. His theory suggests the function of comparison for understanding the application of one representational paradigm of violence for another (". . . nothing resembles an angry cat or man so much as another angry cat or man").[19] I argue that Spears' personal failure was such an attractive sacrificial substitute[20] for Bush's diplomatic failure for the less immediately striking resonances that her personal narrative shared with his, Spears as the Louisiana "country bumpkin" and Bush the Texas "good ole boy."[21] The two have in common a selective

---

17. Spears' father assuming control of her estate underscores the realignment of the cultural order in the narrative of Spears' breakdown and the cultural desire for restored patriarchy authority. Her return to "health" (represented in the media as a return to exercise) would seem to reinforce what Shelley Cobb has called "the role of father-savior in the narrative of her downfall." Cobb writes, "Jamie Spears was hardly seen as an element in his daughter Britney's life until January of 2008 when he became conservator of his mentally ill daughter's life and estate . . ." As Cobb argues, Spears' father was treated as the hero of the story while Spears' mom, Lynne Spears, was vilified in the press for her bad parenting, accusations that reached their zenith in December 2007, when Spears' younger sister, Jamie Lynne, announced that she was pregnant at the age of 16. Shelley Cobb, "Mother of the Year," *Genders OnLine* 48 (2008).

18. René Girard, *Violence and the Sacred* (London: Continuum, 2005), 2.

19. Ibid.

20. This idea that Spears has become a sacrificial lamb is one that has been expressed in popular culture. The animation comedy show *South Park* dedicated an episode, "Britney's New Look," on March 19, 2008, to a storyline that saw the South Park community band together with the paparazzi to offer Britney Spears up for ritual human sacrifice, by photographing her to death, in order to ensure a good corn harvest.

21. For further discussion of the South's central role in the national imagination, see Tara

activation of their "Southernness" in the national imagination: Spears as the white-trash pageant queen and Bush as the blue-blooded cowboy. In this sense, Spears' white trash mythology depends on Bush. Set against his family money and political connections, Spears' rise to fame from a low-income background is precisely what makes her "white trash."[22]

Spears and Bush have in common a rise to meteoric heights of global recognition on the strength of an anti-intellectual backlash in American culture and politics in the late 1990s and early 2000s. Both have walked the line between a fame based on the desire to see the everyman succeed and the desire to watch the everyman fail utterly. They have both acted the part of the "idiot savant" in the "American sitcom," with high jinks ensuing as their inevitable failure to assimilate to their respective statures plays out. These sagas unfold via daily news clips, compositing a patchy "reality TV" plotline. They are rendered all the more compelling by the appearance of "darker forces" behind their ostensibly naïve achievements. Indeed, Karl Rove, Bush's Senior Advisor and Deputy Chief of Staff, was widely characterized as the mastermind behind Bush's presidency, as was Vice President Dick Cheney. For Britney, however, the menacing shadows of bad managers, loser husbands, and creepy boyfriends raised many more eyebrows than the white-collar intrigue of the Bush administration.[23]

It is, however, the ways in which Spears and Bush are *not comparable* that is most revealing of the inequity of their treatment. Indeed, the public treatment of Spears and Bush during this period suggests a profound gender inequity at work in the affective economies of the mainstream press, increasingly characterized by a feverish moralizing discourse bestowing Manichean portraits of guilt, empathy, and cruelty in the commodity form of gossipy video bites played out in the endless loop of a news cycle that requires the camera remains "always on" its celebrity object. The high-profile stakes of good personal and professional management — who and what gets to be well managed, what a national figure can look like under bad managerial light, and when the demands of celebrity become altogether too unmanageable — came into view during this time period, as did the epic failure of FEMA under the Bush Administration during Hurricane Katrina. In reading the treatment of Spears in contrast to Bush in the 2000s, the complex dynamics of class call out for finer distinctions to be made in public discourse between

---

McPherson's book *Reconstructing Dixie: Race, Gender, and Nostalgia in the Imagined South* (Durham, NC: Duke University Press, 2003).

22. Cobb, 4.
23. On April 8, 2009, *The Guardian* online blog *Lost In Showbiz* posted a story on Spears' former boyfriend, paparazzo Adnan Ghalib, for whom a restraining order had been issued after a judge found him to be injurious to her well-being. The post suggested that if Ghalib violated the conditions of the order, he might be deported back to his native Afghanistan: "Should he indeed break his bond, the Britney Spears story will officially collapse into the War on Terror . . ." Marina Hyde, "Save Britney — Deport her Ex to a War Zone!" *The Guardian*, April 3, 2009.

"new money" and "old money," as well as these categories' relationship to race and geography, as shades of white supremacy get read differently in the respective narratives of Spears and Bush.

We Love It, We Live For It, and We're Burning In Hell For It

I imagine most retain a mental picture of Britney Spears as she first emerged — the sublime virgin/whore, child/woman, goddess/mortal whose siren songs sang out with perfect contradiction. In her school uniform she called out, "Hit me baby one more time" and later "I'm not a girl, not yet a woman." Spears' success was founded not on her vocal or dancing abilities but rather her seamless embodiment of a constant state of flux, or the erotic possibilities of a youth that is always already in bloom. Spears also seemed to embody the very impossibility of such an interstitial fantasy space — where one can almost touch a fresh-faced child-angel with the body of a busty red-leather-clad dominatrix (as we see Spears in the video for her single "Oops, I Did It Again!"). Spears appeared effortlessly to glide down and in between poles of ethereality and reality, the naiveté and naughtiness, adolescence and maturity. Her pop princess persona not only operated within conventional discourses of race, class, beauty, desire, and embodiment but *thrived* on them and, in turn, she was adored for it.

One almost cannot talk about the birth of Britney into the American consciousness, without talking about MTV. The network was Spears' performative playground, hosting her at its *2000 Video Music Awards* where she gave what, as one TV critic writes, "*everyone* remembers as her big bow."[24] Spears celebrated a new millennium with her own panting version of the Rolling Stones' "(I Can't Get No) Satisfaction" — performed in black suit and matching fedora — before tearing away her clothes to her lip-synced hit "Oops! . . . I Did It Again," to reveal a sparsely sequined, flesh-colored bodysuit. Her striptease announced to the world that Britney was no longer the schoolgirl-next-door of the ". . . Baby One More Time" video, but rather a sexually superlative, adult woman. At the performance's end, *VMA* co-host Marlon Wayans proclaimed, "Girl done went from 'The Mickey Mouse Club' to the strip club!"[25] The performance earned Spears a standing ovation.

Seven years, one annulled marriage, one divorce, two children, and what seemed like a lifetime's worth of scandal and intrigue later, MTV became the talk of the country when it invited Spears to perform again at its *2007 Video Music Awards*. After more than a year of a paparazzi-chronicled personal downward spiral that included a scalp-shearing breakdown, multiple trips

---

24. James Montgomery, "Britney Spears' Greatest VMA Hits: Barely There Costumes, Giant Snakes and a Scandalous Lip-lock," *VH1*, September 6, 2007.
25. Ibid.

to rehab, ongoing visits from the department of child welfare, and a befuddling amount of tabloid genital exposure, this performance was expected to serve as Spears' big comeback and became a topic of widespread speculation and national anticipation. If the national position on the War in Iraq was ever divided, the position on Spears' "comeback performance" of her latest single "Gimme More" was most definitely not. Entertainment critic Rebecca Traister pretty much sums up the rest:

> Spears' performance was execrable. Dressed in an unflattering sparkly bikini, Spears stumbled, wobbled, looked disoriented and confused; she barely moved through much of the routine, stepping tentatively around the stage while the dancers around her flipped and twirled. She couldn't remember the words to the song to which she was lip-syncing and eventually stopped trying to even pretend to recognize them.[26]

A review posted the night of the show on CNN.com carried a similarly strong message, "One woman dressed in a low-plunging floral gown did manage to eke out a few words. They were not nice. 'Britney looks like a hot, sweaty mess,' she declared, 'Look at her. She's barely moving.'"[27] The *New York Times* review was more restrained: ". . . no one was prepared for Sunday night's fiasco, in which a listless Ms. Spears teetered through her dance steps and mouthed only occasional words in a wan attempt to lip-synch her new single . . ."[28] Spliced into the live performance, MTV's cameras panned to *VMA* guests staring in disbelief. Afterwards, the show's host comedian Sarah Silverman took the stage to deliver a very low blow, identifying Spears as a 25-year-old who has "already accomplished everything she's going to accomplish in her life," calling her two young sons "the most adorable mistakes you will ever see," and imitating what Spears' much-photographed "hairless vagina" looks like by pulling her lips together sideways. Traister goes on,

> It was spectacularly painful, mostly because it violated one of the rules of dirty mean comedy: You don't sharpen your talons on the weak. Imagine Spears having come off a stage where she had been invited to humiliate herself only to hear a crowd roar in whooping, derisive appreciation for the woman narrating her breakdown. But then, imagine Spears accepting the invitation to her latest public self-immolation and then obligingly lighting the match.[29]

26. Rebecca Traister, "Hit Her, Baby, One More Time," *Salon Magazine*, September 12, 2007.
27. Lola Ogunnaike, "Behind the VMAs: Britney Ripped Mercilessly," CNN, September 10, 2007.
28. Jeff Leeds, "Spears's Awards Fiasco Stirs Speculation about her Future," *The New York Times*, September 13, 2007.
29. Traister.

The utter failure of Spears' performance — "evidenced" by her glazed and listless countenance, protruding stomach, and tentative choreography — may have been most terrifying because it effectively collapsed all of the smoke and mirrors previously in place around her artfully crafted, formerly young and sculpted self. Her glazed and disinterested expression exposed the feigning of youthful euphoria, a requirement of the kind of celebrity Spears had attained. Spears' forte had always been the quality of her package, as the "packaged-ness" of her musical product had long been accepted, even celebrated, as such. Those previous news-making appearances that had received so much praise were suddenly thrown into stark relief against a far less-carefully executed and meticulously planned spectacle.

Maybe the fallout following Spears' performance would not have been so shaming if the digital age did not boast such seductive anonymity and instantaneous gratification for lacerating the ever-deserving Other. Following the genealogy elaborated by Michel Foucault in *Discipline and Punish,* it comes as no surprise that the body that was once a direct instrument or intermediary of punishment comes under a more indirect, semiotic kind of torture in the digital age — public exhibition, pillory, flogging, branding — that is no less extreme for its virtual proximity to the sovereign.[30] It should also come as no surprise that baiting Britney has become a profitable online industry. With an increasing smack of "sado-entertainment," online posts convulse with pure pleasure: one person writes, "I love this trainwreck!"[31] and another, "We LOVE this mess!!!"[32]

The self-described "Queen of All Media" Perez Hilton of the eponymous perezhilton.com has sought fame in his own right promoting "Celebrity juice, not from concentrate" on his "hilarious" blog. Hilton's blog would seem exemplary for the way that new media markets continue to produce new and diverse channels for celebrity consumption by perverting paradigms of fan culture. One recalls Bonnie Anderson's allusion to entertainment news as a form of parasite "intruding on" serious news. Rather than refute someone like Anderson, Hilton and countless other bloggers capitalize on the association of entertainment with unseemliness or bad taste to cash in on an industry of tabloid bottom-feeding. Hilton's treatment of Spears' *VMA* meltdown was, of course, thoroughly documented on his site — replete with wallpaper advertising his latest success at the time — a new TV show on VH1 called "What Perez Sez" with the tagline "We love it. We live for it.

30. Michel Foucault, *Discipline and Punish: The Birth of the Prison* (New York: Random House, 1975), 33.

31. Here I am quoting a message board post by "PWHEAT" from September 10, 2007, at 10:30 p.m. "I Cry Watching the Days: Britney Spears Performs at MTV's Video Music Awards," Gawker.com, September 10, 2007.

32. Perez Hilton, "Nothing Gets Between Brit Brit & her Frappuccino!" perezhilton.com, December 14, 2007.

We're burning in hell." Bloggers like Hilton posit a "no holds barred" take on celebrity culture that has found a lucrative commercial formula in lashing out at celebrities, spectacularizing the reversal of the treatment of the star as beyond the realm of the mere mortal to popularize an Industry of Mean. His blog archives the pleasure he visibly takes in recasting celebrity in a negative relation instead of a positive, privileging the bad over the good, the minor car accident over the academy award, the Sunday afternoon fashion misstep over the red carpet entrance.

Perez's post-VMA page, filed under "Icky Icky Poo > Britney Spears . . . In Case You Missed It . . ." is an "Open letter to Britney Spears" (see Figure 14.2). Following a pair of photographs of bikini-clad Spears during her *VMA* performance with the words "You Suck" scratched across in a childlike doodle, the letter reads:

Dear Britney,

Fuck you! FUCK YOU!!!!!!! We are insulted, offended and disgusted by your "performance" at the VMAs. Are you fucking serious??? What you did was disrespectful to your few remaining fans. And it was disrespectful to MTV! You didn't even try!!!!! You should have just cancelled, bitch. Your performance was beyond pathetic. The old Britney Spears, who was at one point (a long time ago) truly great, would be embarrassed by your lack of professionalism and utterly shiteous appearance at the VMAs…You seemed dead onstage. You have lost that spark and shine that used to ooze out of you! We all know you lipsynch, but you couldn't even do that well at the VMAs! And you barely danced! You couldn't even get good hair extensions?????? You have no one to blame for your failure but YOU! There was no way you were going to be good. You were out partying every night before the VMAs for three days in a row until almost sunrise! You were probably still drunk or high during your performance!!! You almost tripped a few times, you fucking mess!!!!!!! No bullshit excuse that you or your camp will come up with can make up for how pathetic your performance was. You heard Sarah Silverman was going to make fun of your kids and it upset you? Deal with it! Rise above it! Or don't go on! A true professional will DELIVER - no matter what!!!! Let's repeat that. It's worth repeating. A true professional will deliver - NO MATTER WHAT!!!!!!!!!!!! What you did was inexcusable!…You should apologize to everyone, Britney!!!! You are pathetic! FUCK YOU!

xoxo

Perez

P.S. Your beer belly looked hot!

Figure 14.2 **Perez Hilton's "Open letter to Britney Spears," posted on perezhilton.com on September 10, 2007.**

This open letter — accompanied by a sidebar advertising "T-shirts Worth Dying/Killing For" emblazoned with a caricature of a bald Britney Spears over the word "TRAINWRECK" — was a gross example of exactly how much malicious satisfaction Americans seemed to take in Spears' disgrace. In a dramatic display of the energetic participation of the postfeminist "gay guru" in the rigorous policing of normative femininity, Hilton licked his lips with sadistic satisfaction at her expense, mocking Spears' "beer belly" and repeatedly screaming "FUCK YOU!!" But lest we forget, Hilton, whose real name is Mario Armando Lavandeira, was *also performing* his own marketable brand of disturbed queer hysteria and lapping up the voyeuristic returns on his ecstatic, misogynist output. Sites like perezhilton.com appear to try to upstage, even as they claim moral superiority over, the *excessiveness* of the celebrity antics they hunt for profit. Harvey Levin, managing editor of tmz.com has said that when it comes to online traffic, "Britney is Old Faithful."[33] Levin added that page views spike when an item about Spears appeared on the site, which heaped daily ridicule on the comings and goings of Spears, mimicking her accent, parenting abilities, and wardrobe choices. As more ridicule produces more interest, excessive negative attention paid to Spears became a self-perpetuating cycle normalized and condoned by commercial logics of supply-and-demand. Digital media offer the privileged conduit for these sites, not simply in terms of speed of access but also in facilitating an archive of failure that offers *limitless* permutations in production and manipulation of content.

What ideological work does the Industry of Mean do? How might a website like Hilton's be read as emblematic of how a sense of "anti-establishment" or "queer" community gets leveraged around mainstream moral codes of conduct and social mores to do a dangerous kind of work? How do potential political alliances between gay men and straight women get wrenched apart and re-fitted to support the policing of patriarchal norms? How might sites like Hilton's, that appear to promise a certain kind of liberation from the false consciousness of Hollywood worship, be read as, in fact, *profoundly conservative* — serving to discipline not so much the stars they claim to attack but rather a readership that absorbs the moralistic lessons of good taste and good citizenship offered up by the mocking of a few choice targets? What should we make of the "professional amateur" blogger who performs his manic public critique in the name of codes of proper self-comportment, professionalism, and respect? What are we to make of the political resonance of Hilton's dogmatism with the violence of the Bush doctrine, as rhetorical systems that operate by representing themselves as divined by their exclusive access to a higher plane of principle irregardless of the feelings or beliefs of others? The entitlement of the masculine exceptionalism that underwrites the agendas of both Hilton and Bush draws a straight line connecting the

---

33. Mireya Navarro. "Britney's Loss, Their Gain," *The New York Times*, October 7, 2007.

logics of highly influential media sources like perezhilton.com to those of Fox News and other channels widely cited for the mainstreaming of conservative rhetoric.

A regular presence on reality programs on channels like VH1 and entertainment news programs like *Extra,* Hilton is also a frequent guest on talk shows like the *The View.* Far from being an outsider to the mainstream media, Perez Hilton is a well-connected and well-rewarded representative of a greater network of financial success that depends on commodifying the failure of Spears and celebrities like her. By claiming the transgressive position of outsider gay Latino blogger engaging in target practice with Hollywood celebrities who are "fair game," Perez Hilton, in fact, activates his own insider access to the very spheres he would seem to call out for being corrupt, fashioning his own name after Paris Hilton as more of an act of homage than parody. Hilton gives us anti-endorsements that nevertheless function as endorsements, engaging us in the activity of consuming the latest Hollywood product.

Fall of an Empire: The State of Becoming Unfit

The very real influence of Perez Hilton's hysterical cultural performance becomes apparent as one peruses MTV's 2007 VMA website, where the unbridled rage projected at Britney Spears in post after message board post begins to subsume all notions of conventional sanity and plain good sense. The ubiquity of Hilton-derived rhetoric (in tone and style) is stunning, as anonymous viewers of MTV adeptly, if unconsciously, impersonate Hilton, and I argue, not the other way around. "Dancing_freak31" writes, "BRITNEY SUX!!! WHEN I WAS LITTLE I USED TO LOVE BRITNEY BUT NOW SHE'S SUCH A WHORE."[34] "JazzyPha22" echoes this sentiment writing, "Britney SUCKS, WHAT HAPPENED TO THE OLD BRIT, SHE'S JUST SOOOO DIRTY!"[35] While these are the kinds of contributions to discourse that often get left aside by intellectual debate, and for good reason, I would argue that what makes these kinds of posts most compelling is that they could have been written by anyone, thus making them the voice of *everyone.* What is also fascinating about these posts, demonstrating as they do a nasty *other* side to fan culture, is their mutually drawn conclusion that Britney not only "sucks" but "sucks" because she was been found to be a degraded woman in the duration of her onstage performance, deemed a "whore" who is "just so dirty." Having reached this conclusion, both "Dancing_freak31" and "JazzyPha22" gesture toward their melancholic desire to return to a past

---

34. Here I am quoting a message board post by "dancing_freak31" from December 12, 2007, at 22:08. "Gimme More (Live)," MTV, December 12, 2007.

35. Here I am quoting a message board by post by "JazzyPha22" from December 11, 2007, at 0:00. "Gimme More (Live)," MTV, December 12, 2007.

moment, a moment that is profoundly and traumatically lost where Britney was, to them, someone else entirely. "Dancing_freak31" writes "When I was little I used to love Britney." And yet, "now she's such a whore."

I am struck by the semantic strangeness of the insistence of "whore" here. What is it about Britney's lackadaisical dancing and tentative lip-syncing that renders her somehow unanimously legible as a "whore"? Has the contemporary use of the word become a banner to cover *any* feminine "sin"? Was it merely her costuming that earned it — ill-fitting bra and underwear, fishnets, and high-heeled boots? Yet, if so, how was this costume any different than the even more scanty attire the American public has witnessed on (or perhaps off) Spears in the past? Why would her libidinal performance have suddenly leapt into the realm of sex work? Of course, there was no actual sex act performed on stage. In fact, there was far less indication of sex than in performances past in which Spears had ripped off her clothes, groped and gyrated with reckless abandon, and made out with her mentor Madonna.[36] Lest we forget Britney was most heavily criticized for sexually *underperforming*, under-delivering (dazed appearance and lethargic dancing) on expectations of the sexual spectacle she became famous for, and not for her "overactivity," as claims of literal promiscuity in "whore" would seem to denote.

Perhaps it was the very recognition of her glazed-over appearance that pricked the puritanical American subconscious with the flickering association of the prostitute imagined as oversexed and yet barely present enough to register her own blasphemous indecency. However, I postulate something else entirely. Britney Spears was called a "dirty whore" not because of her lack of clothing, her disinvested expression, her sexual over-activity or inactivity, but rather because to be a whore is to be a *failed woman*. "Whore" has become such a far-reaching epithet for women read as excessive or failing because the term equates a certain attitude toward sexualized female bodies deemed less than desirable, even as they reach and register complex and nuanced forms of desire hidden under layers of repulsion and pity. The whore is also the "working girl" who is not quite professional. In other words, the whore registers as the amateur — she is the less-than-talented actress who must audition on the casting couch, the woman who cannot find remunerated, respectable work and is thus relegated to its margins. The whore lacks any distinction between her sexual and professional life and wears that lack on her body as excess. Britney's excess spills out of her once-sleek costume and is worn on her undisciplined, post-prime, post-partum frame.

"What happened to the old Brit . . ." "JazzyPha22" wants to know. What happened to the Britney whose superhuman physical discipline marked her highly sexualized performances with the consummate professionalism of a

---

36. At the *2003 Video Music Awards*, Britney Spears made waves opening the show in a performance with Madonna that culminated in a kiss between the two women (the performance also featured Christina Aguilera, who is often elided in accounts of it).

seasoned performer? At this juncture, it seems the notion of a "real Britney" is less compelling than that of *many and interchangeable Britneys* — ones we love, ones we hate, new ones, old ones, classic ones, and *disposable ones*. The revolving door of Britneys cycle in and out of our collective mind's eye, day in and day out — spectacularized by a rainbow of wigs and hair extensions, a chronicle of weight gain and weight loss, and the frantic and fluctuating wardrobe of *Us Weekly's* Worst Dressed Celebrity two years running. The effect is one of a *cartooning* of a human being and is what makes possible the destruction of the stakes of her material embodiment.

In June 2006 — more than a year prior to her notorious *VMA* performance — Britney Spears gave a rare and candid interview to *Today Show* personality Matt Lauer on *Dateline NBC*. In the interview she discusses the state of her (soon-to-end) marriage to Kevin Federline, whom she describes as "awesome" adding, "He helps me. He has to. I'm (an) emotional wreck right now." Lauer asks Spears why she is choosing to speak out. She responds that the tabloids have "gone too far" and are intruding on her private moments by taking photographs of her on her private property. Spears says, "They've crossed the line a little bit . . . they like to have the person they pick on, I feel like I'm a target." Spears responds to questions about her portrayal by the media as a negligent mother, from an incident where she was photographed driving with her son, Sean Preston, on her lap to a series of images that show Spears nearly dropping the boy after stumbling in a New York City street (a spectacle made all the more desperate by reports of Spears crying alone in a fast food restaurant later that day). Spears says, "I can't go anywhere without someone judging me . . . I did it with my dad. I'd sit on his lap and I drive. We're country[folk]." Significantly, Spears' abjection comes to be deeply intertwined with class politics — the puncturing of her public persona as glamorous and disciplined producing sharp critiques of her ability to parent, as poor or working-class women are often targeted as bad mothers. As Shelley Cobb has noted, in being called a bad mother (much in the way that her mother, Lynne Spears, has) it was as if Spears "couldn't achieve the balance that middle-class motherhood prizes."[37] When asked if she was upset by the headlines that ensued, questioning her parental judgment, Spears defends herself: "I know I'm a good mom."[38]

This interview quickly became a hot topic for bloggers and satirists alike. A foreboding precursor to her *VMA* fall-out, once again the question became — "What is she thinking?!" *The Washington Post* ran a particularly vicious editorial in its "Fashion" pages. A caption under an unflattering photo of Spears during the interview reads, "In her *Dateline* interview last week, the

---

37. Cobb, 4.
38. *Dateline*. Television program. New York: NBC, June 15, 2006.

ill-clad Britney Spears was merely a shadow of her former hotness."[39] In the article that follows, writer Robin Givhan eviscerates Spears for her low class, bad taste, and shameful sense of style in an article entitled "Oops Again and Again: Britney Dresses for a Backyard Pity Party":

> Pregnancy cleavage can be a beautiful development, but serving up one's bosom like melons at a picnic is aggressively self-indulgent, enormously distracting and, unless you're auditioning for a spread in *Penthouse*, unnecessarily vulgar.
>
> Spears fidgeted, blathered and wept through the interview last week and one couldn't help but gape in amazement at her astonishing aesthetic meltdown. It's hard to recall the last time someone as famous as Spears — without any accompanying substance-abuse rumors — appeared so startlingly, slovenly wretched. The pop singer's golden glow of stardom had been dimming, but this was the moment when it dropped below the horizon.[40]

Interested in the meltdown as an aesthetic rather than emotional event, the article blasts Spears' personhood at the level of her wardrobe — enumerating her "poor choices" and pointing to her "miniskirt and sheer babydoll top" to suggest, in fact insist, that Spears ultimately is "getting what she deserves" for looking like a teenager or "like a stereotypical hick — and wretchedly vulnerable." Of course, Spears had worn such outfits before without criticism, as it was her image that changed, not her taste. Givhan writes with moralizing zeal, "They were not the sexy clothes of a confident woman defending herself or standing up for her man. They weren't the teasingly body-conscious attire favored by pregnant women who proudly show off their bellies."[41] Givhan mobilizes an empty feminist rhetoric in order to secure a soapbox from which to make declarations about what she believes constitutes "dignified female comportment" that discipline Spears based on her style squeamishness. Givhan is profoundly, and meanly, moved by Spears' failure to wear her motherhood correctly — to choose and wear the appropriate archetypical costuming of the supportive, doting wife or the virginal young mother. Givhan's criticism of Spears' aesthetic confuses "the sexy clothes of a confident woman" with the glamorous costuming of a woman who has people working for her to create an upper-class illusion of postfeminist autonomy.

Givhan's point seems to be that were Spears to *just try a little harder*, to have *just a little more "self respect,"* to present herself with more discipline and sophistication, she might not be as "wretchedly" pathetic; she might deserve a little public dignity. It is Spears' own failure to *get her act together*

---

39. Robyn Givhan, "Oops Again and Again: Britney Dresses for a Backyard Pity Party," *The Washington Post*, June 23, 2006.
40. Ibid.
41. Ibid.

that is the justification given for her continued public flogging. This "victim-blaming" logic is reminiscent of a certain discourse around a "merit-based" occupation of Iraq that emerged in mid-2007 when Republican senators submitted a proposal for US troop withdrawal based on the performance of the Iraqi government that was ultimately rejected by a Senate vote of 67–29. One *New York Times* article reported, "That second proposal, by Senator John Warner, Republican of Virginia, would require Mr. Bush to report to Congress in mid-July and mid-September on how well the Iraqi government was performing against a set of benchmarks. Foreign aid could be *withheld for lack of progress* . . ."[42]

I bracket this connection to gesture to an American cultural logic that would simultaneously hold Iraq accountable for the violence and chaos resulting from the 2003 US invasion and subsequent occupation, and hold Britney Spears accountable for her failure to rebound from a constant barrage of ridicule from the American public. What is significant here is how the obsession with "evidence" of good taste or the ability to make "good choices" comes to be linked to how the American public alternately confers and withholds empathy. In declaring Spears' "aesthetic meltdown," Givhan's not-so-subtle suggestion is that if you dress like "you're auditioning for a spread in *Penthouse*," then you must be auditioning for a spread in *Penthouse*, and thus you must be an unfit mother.[43] While Spears' interview with Lauer was ostensibly intended or designed to defend her skills as a parent, her goal was made all the more retrospectively desperate by her subsequent loss of custody of her children to Federline in late 2007, following the aftermath of her *VMA* blow-up.[44] This sobering blow was reported on Gawker.com, a popular New York-based entertainment blog in a post filed under "Gossip Roundup." The post teases: "What Has Britney Spears Done Wrong?" then goes on to deadpan, "Revealed! Britney Spears lost her kids by being an incredibly terrible parent. Also, not signing some papers."[45] *OK! Magazine* carried the story on its cover with a headline reading "Goodbye Mommy." According to its representatives, the magazine expected another best-selling issue after a summer cover announcing "Britney's Meltdown" sold 1.2 million

---

42. Carl Hulse and Jeff Zeleny, "Senate Rejects Iraq Troop Withdrawal," *The New York Times*, May 17, 2007.

43. Givhan's argument relies on a faulty mimetic logic that suggests that resemblance renders equivalence: if you look like a whore, then you are a whore. Pierre Macherey offers a way of thinking around this problem to understand how things may be similar without being the same, ". . . the relationship between the mirror and what it reflects . . . is partial: the mirror selects, it does not reflect everything. The selection itself is not fortuitous, it is symptomatic . . ." In other words, I would suggest that while Spears' attire might be argued to *suggest or be symptomatic* of her degradation, it cannot be treated as the direct reproduction or very source of her degradation, as Givhan suggests. Pierre Macherey, "Lenin, Critic of Tolstoy," in *A Theory of Literary Production* (London: Routledge Classics, 2006), 135.

44. "Spears Will Lose Custody of Children," CNN, October 2, 2007.

45. "Gossip Roundup: What Has Britney Spears Done Wrong?" Gawker.com, October 3, 2007.

copies (compared to average sales of around 930,000).[46]

In her essay "Moms Don't Rock: The Popular Demonization of Courtney Love," Norma Coates writes of a 1995 interview Barbara Walters conducted with Love, presenting an astounding moment of cultural déjà vu with respect to Lauer's interview with Spears:

> In her interview . . . Love looked like the "trainwreck" that Walters described. Although clad in beige Armani, with her normally disheveled hair put up in a fairly neat bun, Love presented a vision of disorder and chaos. Her trademark slut-red lipstick looking like a smear across the lower section of her face, Love cried, smoked, managed to make Barbara Walters say "suck," and otherwise acted like a woman out of control. The climax of the interview came when Walters asked the question that everyone was waiting for: "Are you a good mother?" Love answered, "Yes, yes, yes."[47]

Like Love, Spears is represented as the "trainwreck" mother whose tragic relationships, substance abuse and/or psychological issues must be surveilled by a suspicious American viewing public. This phenomenon has the effect of aligning the cultural regime of family values with tabloid commercial interests. Coates writes of Love, "The question of her fitness to mother lurks just beneath the surface, when it does not emerge openly, in mainstream representations of Love; it is the source of the media's fascination with her."[48] The mainstream media's panoptic relationship to Spears suggests an even deeper fascination with the way in which her motherhood (her maternal "fit-ness") has been worn and continues to wear on her face and body (her sexual "fitness"). Britney Spears' public image is once again, but differently this time, caught between two poles of impossibility. Far from stuck in the provocative and profitable purgatory of her girlishness, Spears is caught between her role as a young divorcee and mother of two toddlers and her role as the once-and-just-maybe-once-again American sexpot. She embodies the fierce and frustrated impossibility of two roles believed by the American public to be *fundamentally incompatible* and yet she continues to receive intense pressure, on both ends, to surmount their impossibility. Her unthinkable desire to be both sexual and maternal is constantly being policed by her continued public demonization in arguments by so-called "family values" proponents, pseudo-feminists, and a combination of the two. One online post reads:

> Tell me she can't feel that her ASS is hanging out. *She is a mother. What a slut.* Even

---

46. Navarro.
47. Norma Coates, "Moms Don't Rock: The Popular Demonization of Courtney Love," *'Bad' Mothers: The Politics of Blame in Twentieth Century America* (New York: New York University Press, 1998), 319.
48. Ibid., 320.

when I was in my early 20's and a single mom, I would never have dressed like
that. I liked to go out with friends and even get drunk sometimes but, come on
lady. What are your kids gonna think of you when their [sic] older. What a skank!

— Message posted by "Melissa"[49]

The inevitability of her maternal failures and public meltdowns can be
attributed to what has become a national compulsion to force Spears to live
up to America's expectations *of itself*. If the consummate performer cannot
perform the expectations set forth by the American value system, then something would have to be wrong.[50] The American public was fairly unfazed by
Spears' decision to marry and start a family until this came to mean that she
had reneged on her implicit contract with the American public to maintain
the public persona the country had come to expect from her. By 2007, it had
become clear that Spears was no longer able to turn America on with her
abs-of-steel performances *and* be the consummate mother. The American
response seemed to be that if Britney wants our empathy, she must earn it
by showing us she can be not only the *perfect mother figure* but also the *mother
with the perfect figure*. It becomes a win/win for the American public: If she
succeeds (which she cannot) then she reaffirms our value system and if she
fails (*when* she fails), it will make for one hell of a good show.

Love's incarnation of the unrefined celebrity mother pilloried by the
public illustrates that Spears' dilemma is not unique. Unlike Love, however,
who was always the bad girl, motherhood for Spears appeared a state that
violently confounded the virgin/whore dichotomy that her younger self
became famous for holding in place. The question is: what does motherhood
really represent? Motherhood, for Spears, would seem a two-headed cultural
monster inciting attacks on her for *being too sexy to be a mother* and suggesting, on the other hand, that for *being a mother, she can never be sexy*. Is such
profound hostility toward so-called failing mothers really about a public fear
that a child will be put in danger? Is the American public really so up-in-arms
because we are worried that Britney's son, Sean Preston, will fall on his head
or will suffer an untimely death in a car accident? Is it emotional pathos
that drives an identification with a child whose mother may not "love him

---

49. Here I am quoting a message board post by "Melissa" from 11 December, 2007. "Lonely
in Pink," perezhilton.com, December 11, 2007.
50. In his November 2007 public debate with Alain Badiou entitled "Democracy and
Disappointment: On the Politics," the philosopher Simon Critchley prefaces his remarks
with a moment of comic relief in which he makes brief mention of Britney Spears' "tragic"
performance at the *VMAs* in order to highlight an introductory point about the ineluct-
able failure of the emblematic liberal figure facing its own limitations. Notably, Spears is
invoked at the margins of Critchley's philosophical remarks, treated as pre-critical fodder
rather than as a serious case study for his ultimate argument about the status of political
meaning in a present moment he characterizes as one of "military neo-liberalism," using
the term to deisgnate a faith in neoliberal economic policy combined with a metaphysical
belief in freedom and human rights that is backed up by military force. "Democracy and
Disappointment: On the Politics of Resistance," Slought Foundation, 15 November, 2007.

enough" the way a "good mother" would? "Mom-ism," a critique of women that first emerged in post-war America, singles out the mother figure as the cause of many of America's ills. The trope of motherhood comes to be seen as what somehow "softens or weakens" sons in particular, and American values more broadly.[51] Perhaps Spears' and Bush's cultural narratives represent, above all, different sides of the cultural imperative demanding the *protection of the son* at all cost.[52]

Failed Intelligence

Placing Spears in relation to Bush renders visible the systemic incongruities of power when mere money and fame are not enough to buy a certain kind of protection, as the grounds by which public/private distinctions get fundamentally redrawn by gender. Nancy Fraser has usefully articulated the political stakes of the public/private binary, writing that it "enclave(s) certain matters in specialized discursive arenas so as to shield them from general debate . . . This usually works to the advantage of dominant groups and individuals and to the disadvantage of their subordinates."[53] Fraser's reading suggests that the dividing line between what gets articulated as public information versus private information is one ordered by the logic of dominance, suggesting an important distinction to be made between the mere stardom of Spears and the sovereignty of Bush.

Around the same time period that those rather curious stickers I discussed earlier began appearing in the spring of 2008, posters advertising *VH1*'s *I Love the New Millennium* TV show also began appearing around New York City (see Figure 14.3). "Oops! There Goes the Decade" the posters teased, depicting the now-famous image of Spears nearly dropping her young son with George W. Bush's pouting face superimposed over the baby's. The poster renders *literal* what is at stake in a misstep — the protection of the

---

51. In *The Mommy Myth*, Susan J. Douglas and Meredith W. Michaels have more recently revisited the concept of "Momism" that was initially coined by the journalist Philip Wylie in his 1942 book *Generation of Vipers*. The derogatory term was first used by Wylie to attack women for "being so smothering, overprotective, and invested in their kids, especially their sons, that they turned them into dysfunctional, sniveling weaklings, maternal slaves chained to the apron strings, unable to fight for their country or even stand on their own two feet." Douglas and Michaels seek to reclaim the term to describe (in "New Momism") an ideology of motherhood that has snowballed since the 1980s: "a highly romanticized and yet demanding view of motherhood in which the standards for success are impossible to meet." Susan J. Douglas and Meredith W. Michaels, *The Mommy Myth: The Idealization of Motherhood and How It Has Undermined Women* (New York: Free Press, 2004), 4.

52. This son is, of course, always a very particular son. Comparative disinterest in thousands of young soldiers and young Iraqi civilians killed or maimed during war suggest the representational logics by which white middle- and upper-middle-class male bodies are protected to the endangerment of working-class persons of color. Moore's *Fahrenheit 9/11* makes this same point.

53. Nancy Fraser, "Rethinking the Public Sphere," in *The Phantom Public Sphere*, ed. Bruce Robbins (Minneapolis, MN: University of Minnesota Press, 1993), 22.

Bibliography

Agamben, Giorgio. *State of Exception*, trans. Kevin Attell. Chicago: The University of Chicago Press, 2005.

Agence France-Presse, "US Keeps Up Hunt for Smoking Gun in Iraq," *Global Policy Forum*, January 10, 2003. Available at: http://www.globalpolicy.org/component/content/ article/168/37572.html (accessed April 20, 2010).

Anderson, Bonnie. "The Rise of the Corporate News Networks," in *News Flash: Journalism, Infotainment, and the Bottom-Line Business of Broadcast News*. San Francisco, CA: Jossey-Bass, 2004, 1–24.

Badiou, Alain and Simon Critchley. "Democracy and Disappointment: On the Politics of Resistance," Slought Foundation online, November 15, 2007. Available at: http://slought. org/content/11385/ (accessed June 26, 2010).

Baudrillard, Jean. "The Precession of Simulacra," in Sheila Glaser trans., *Simulacra and Simulation*. Ann Arbor, MI: University of Michigan Press, 1994, 1–42.

"Britney Spears: Speaking Out," television program, New York: NBC, June 15, 2006.

"Bush Defends Iraq War, Economic Record," CNN, February 9, 2004. Available at: http:// edition.cnn.com/2004/ALLPOLITICS/02/08/elec04.prez.bush (accessed April 20, 2010).

Carlson, Jen. "Tao Lin Brings Britney to NYC," *Gothamist*, May 22, 2008. Available at: http:// gothamist.com/2008/05/22/tao.php (accessed March 11, 2010).

Coates, Norma. "Moms Don't Rock: The Popular Demonization of Courtney Love," in Molly Ladd-Taylor and Lauri Umansky (eds), *"Bad" Mothers: The Politics of Blame in Twentieth-Century America*. New York: New York University Press, 1998, 319–33.

Cobb, Shelley. "Mother of the Year: Kathy Hilton, Lynne Spears, Dina Lohan and Bad Celebrity Motherhood," *Genders OnLine* 48 (2008). Available at: http://www.genders.org/ g48/g48_cobb.html (accessed March 11, 2010).

Decker, Jeffrey Louis. *Made in America: Self-Styled Success from Horatio Alger to Oprah Winfrey*. Minneapolis, MN: University of Minnesota Press, 1997.

Douglas, Susan J. and Meredith W. Michaels. *The Mommy Myth: The Idealization of Motherhood and How It Has Undermined Women*. New York: Free Press, 2004.

Fahrenheit 9/11. Directed by Michael Moore. Weinstein Company, 2007 [2004]. DVD.

Foucault, Michel. *Discipline and Punish: The Birth of the Prison*. New York: Random House, 1975.

Fraser, Nancy. "Rethinking the Public Sphere," in Bruce Robbins (ed.), *The Phantom Public Sphere*. Minneapolis: University of Minnesota Press, 1993, 1–32.

"Gimme More (Live)" [Britney Spears], MTV, December 12, 2007. Music video. Available at: http://www.mtv.com/overdrive/?id=1568788&vid=173440.

Girard, René. *Violence and the Sacred*. London: Continuum, 2005.

Givhan, Robyn. "Oops Again and Again: Britney Dresses for a Backyard Pity Party," *The Washington Post*, June 23, 2006, Style section. Available at: http://www.washingtonpost. com/wp-dyn/content/article/2006/06/22/AR2006062201870.html (accessed December 14, 2007).

"Gossip Roundup: What Has Britney Spears Done Wrong?" Gawker.com, October 3, 2007.

Hilton, Perez. "An Open Letter to Britney Spears," perezhilton.com, September 10, 2007. Blog post. Available at: http://perezhilton.com/?p=5263 (accessed December 17, 2007).

Hilton, Perez. "Lonely in Pink," perezhilton.com, December 11, 2007. Blog post. Available at: http://perezhilton.com/?p=10285#respond (accessed December 17, 2007).

Hilton, Perez. "Nothing Gets Between Brit Brit & her Frappuccino!" perezhilton.com, December 14, 2007, Blog post. Available at: http://perezhilton.com/?cat=74 (accessed December 17, 2007).

Hulse, Carl and Jeff Zeleny. "Senate Rejects Iraq Troop Withdrawal," *The New York Times*, May 17, 2007. Available at: http://www.nytimes.com/2007/05/17/washington/17cong. html?_r=1&oref=slogin (accessed December 17, 2007).

Hyde, Marina. "Save Britney — Deport her Ex to a War Zone!" *The Guardian*, April 3, 2009. Available at: http://www.guardian.co.uk/lifeandstyle/lostinshowbiz/2009/apr/03/ marina-hyde-britney-spears (accessed April 4, 2010).

"I Cry Watching the Days: Britney Spears Performs at MTV's Video Music Awards," Gawker.com, September 10, 2007. Available at: http://gawker.com/

news/i-cry-watching-the-days/britney-spears-performs-at-mtvs-video-music-awards-298070.
php?cpage=2 (accessed December 14, 2007).

Iraq Body Count (IBC), "Documented Civilian Deaths from Violence," December 14, 2007.
Available at: http://www.iraqbodycount.org/database/ (accessed December 14, 2007).

Jenkins, Henry. "Introduction: 'Worship at the Altar of Convergence': A New Paradigm for
Understanding Media Change," in *Convergence Culture: Where New and Old Media Collide.*
New York: New York University Press, 2006, 1–24.

Keenan, Thomas. "Publicity and Indifference: Media, Surveillance, 'Humanitarian
Intervention,'" in Thomas Y. Levin, Ursula Frohne, and Peter Weibel (eds), *CTRL
[SPACE]: Rhetorics of Surveillance from Bentham to Big Brother.* Cambridge, MA: The MIT
Press, 2002, 545–61.

Leeds, Jeff. "Spears's Awards Fiasco Stirs Speculation about Her Future," *The New York
Times,* September 13, 2007. Available at: http://www.nytimes.com/2007/09/13/arts/
music/13brit.html (accessed December 13, 2007).

Macherey, Pierre. "Lenin, Critic of Tolstoy," in *A Theory of Literary Production.* London:
Routledge Classics, 2006, 117–51.

McPherson, Tara. *Reconstructing Dixie: Race, Gender, and Nostalgia in the Imagined South.*
Durham, NC: Duke University Press, 2003.

Montgomery, James. "Britney Spears' Greatest VMA Hits: Barely There Costumes, Giant
Snakes and a Scandalous Lip-lock," *VH1,* September 9, 2007. Available at: http://www.
vh1.com/news/articles/1568995/20070906/spears_britney.jhtml (accessed December 14,
2007).

Navarro, Mireya. "Britney's Loss, Their Gain," *The New York Times,* October 7, 2007.
Available at: http://www.nytimes.com/2007/10/07/fashion/07britney.html (accessed
December 14, 2007).

Negra, Diane. *What a Girl Wants?: Fantasizing the Reclamation of Self in Postfeminism.* London:
Routledge, 2009.

Ogunnaike, Lola. "Behind the VMAs: Britney Ripped Mercilessly," CNN, September 10, 2007.
Available at: http://www.cnn.com/2007/SHOWBIZ/TV/09/10/behind.vmas/index.html
(accessed December 13, 2007).

Parker, Trey. "Britney's New Look," *South Park,* season 12, episode 2 (originally aired
March 19, 2008). Television program.

"Poll: Opposition to Iraq War at High," United Press International (UPI), November 8, 2007.
Available at: http://www.upi.com/NewsTrack/Top_News/2007/11/08/poll_opposition_
to_iraq_war_at_high/8796/ (accessed December 18, 2007).

Rogers, Paul. "Aftermath," in *A War Too Far: Iraq, Iran, and the New American Century.* London:
Pluto Press, 2006, 30-49.

Ronell, Avital. *Stupidity.* Champaign, IL: University of Illinois Press, 2002.

"Spears Will Lose Custody of Children," CNN, October 2, 2007. Available at: http://edition.
cnn.com/2007/SHOWBIZ/Music/10/01/spears.federline/ (accessed December 14,
2007).

Stolberg, Sheryl Gay. "Mistakes, I've Made a Few, Bush Tells Reporters," *The New York Times,*
January 13, 2009. Available at: http://www.nytimes.com/2009/01/13/us/politics/13bush.
html (accessed January 1, 2010).

Thussu, Daya. *News as Entertainment: The Rise of Global Infotainment.* London: Sage, 2008.

Traister, Rebecca. "Hit Her, Baby, One More Time," *Salon Magazine,* September 12, 2007.
Available at: http://www.salon.com/mwt/feature/2007/09/12/britney_vma/ (accessed
December 13, 2007).

"US Military Deaths at 3,895," *The New York Times,* December 16, 2007. Available at: http://
www.nytimes.com/aponline/us/AP-Iraq-US-Deaths.html?_r=2&oref=slogin&oref=slogin
(accessed December 18, 2007).

"What Has Britney Spears Done Wrong?" Gawker.com, October 3, 2007. Available at: http://
gawker.com/306470/what-has-britney-spears-done-wrong (accessed December 14, 2007).

Index